Fiction, Invention and Hyper-reality

The twentieth century was a period of rapid change for religion. Secularisation resulted in a dramatic fall in church attendance in the West, and the 1950s and 1960s saw the introduction of new religions including the International Society for Krishna Consciousness (ISKCON), the Church of Scientology, and the Children of God. New religions were regarded with suspicion by society in general and Religious Studies scholars alike until the 1990s, when the emergence of a second generation of 'new new' religions – based on popular cultural forms including films, novels, computer games and comic books – and highly individualistic spiritualities confirmed the utter transformation of the religio-spiritual landscape. Indeed, Scientology and ISKCON appeared almost traditional and conservative when compared to the radically de-institutionalised, eclectic, parodic, fun-loving and experimental fiction-based, invented and hyper-real religions.

In this book, scholarly treatments of cutting-edge religious and spiritual trends are brought into conversation with contributions by representatives of Dudeism, the Church of All Worlds, the Temple of the Jedi Order and Tolkien spirituality groups. This book will simultaneously entertain, shock, challenge and delight scholars of religious studies, as well as those with a wider interest in new religious movements.

Carole M. Cusack is Professor of Religious Studies at the University of Sydney, Australia. She trained as a medievalist and her PhD was published as *Conversion among the Germanic Peoples* (1998). She now specialises in contemporary religious trends (pilgrimage and tourism, modern Pagan religions, NRMs, and religion and popular culture). Her books include *Invented Religions: Imagination, Fiction and Faith* (2010), *The Sacred Tree: Ancient and Medieval Manifestations* (2011) and (with Katharine Buljan) *Anime, Religion, and Spirituality: Profane and Sacred Worlds in Contemporary Japan* (2015). She has published widely in edited volumes and journals, and is the editor (with Christopher Hartney) of *Religion and Retributive Logic: Essays in Honour of Garry W. Trompf* (2010) and (with Alex Norman) of *Handbook of New Religions and Cultural Production* (2012).

Pavol Kosnáč is an independent scholar based in Bratislava, Slovakia. He has studied Religious Studies at Comenius University, where he obtained his BA and MA, and political philosophy, jurisprudence and European culture at the Collegium of Anton Neuwirt (both in Bratislava). Afterwards he moved to England to continue his studies at the University of Oxford, completing an MSt in Study of Religion. He held a six-month placement at INFORM in London, then travelled extensively working as a freelance analyst for British, Slovak and Asian think-tanks. He plans to start a PhD next year. His academic background is mostly in sociology of religion, history of Christianity and Islam, and the study of new religious movements. He is interested especially in new and alternative religiosity, non-religiosity, the contemporary religious situation in Europe, and overlaps between religion, violence and war.

Routledge Inform Series on Minority Religions and Spiritual Movements
Series Editor: Eileen Barker
London School of Economics (UK)

Inform is an independent charity that collects and disseminates accurate, balanced and up-to-date information about minority religious and spiritual movements.

The *Routledge Inform Series* addresses themes related to new religions, many of which have been the topics of Inform seminars. The series editorial board consists of internationally renowned scholars in the field.

Books in the series will attract both an academic and interested general readership, particularly in the areas of Religious Studies, and the Sociology of Religion and Theology.

For a full list of titles in this series, please visit www.routledge.com/religion/series/AINFORM

Visioning New and Minority Religious
Projecting the future
Edited by Eugene V. Gallagher

'Cult Wars' in Historical Perspective
New and minority religions
Edited by Eugene V. Gallagher

New Religious Movements and Counselling
Academic, professional and personal perspectives
Edited by Hamish Cameron and Sarah Harvey

Minority Religions and Uncertainty
Edited by Kim Knott and Matthew Francis

Minority Religions in Europe and the Middle East
Mapping and monitoring
Edited by George D. Chryssides

Fiction, Invention and Hyper-reality
From popular culture to religion
Edited by Carole M. Cusack and Pavol Kosnáč

Fiction, Invention and Hyper-reality

From popular culture to religion

Edited by Carole M. Cusack and
Pavol Kosnáč

LONDON AND NEW YORK

First published 2017
by Routledge
2 Park Square, Milton Park, Abingdon, Oxon OX14 4RN

and by Routledge
711 Third Avenue, New York, NY 10017

Routledge is an imprint of the Taylor & Francis Group, an informa business

© 2017 selection and editorial matter, Carole M. Cusack and Pavol Kosnáč; individual chapters, the contributors

The right of Carole M. Cusack and Pavol Kosnáč to be identified as the authors of the editorial material, and of the authors for their individual chapters, has been asserted in accordance with sections 77 and 78 of the Copyright, Designs and Patents Act 1988.

All rights reserved. No part of this book may be reprinted or reproduced or utilised in any form or by any electronic, mechanical, or other means, now known or hereafter invented, including photocopying and recording, or in any information storage or retrieval system, without permission in writing from the publishers.

Trademark notice: Product or corporate names may be trademarks or registered trademarks, and are used only for identification and explanation without intent to infringe.

British Library Cataloguing in Publication Data
A catalogue record for this book is available from the British Library

Library of Congress Cataloging in Publication Data
Names: Cusack, Carole M., 1962- editor. | Kosnáč, Pavol editor.
Title: Fiction, invention, and hyper-reality : from popular culture to religion / edited by Carole M. Cusack and Pavol Kosnáč.
Description: New York : Routledge, 2016. | Series: Inform series on minority religions and spiritual movements | Includes bibliographical references and index.
Identifiers: LCCN 2016025031 | ISBN 9781472463029 (hardback : alk. paper)
Subjects: LCSH: Religion and culture. | Popular culture. | Religion in literature. | Cults.
Classification: LCC BL65.C8 F53 2016 | DDC 201/.7—dc23
LC record available at https://lccn.loc.gov/2016025031

ISBN: 978-1-4724-6302-9 (hbk)
ISBN: 978-1-315-58228-3 (ebk)

Typeset in Sabon
by Swales & Willis, Exeter, Devon, UK

Contents

Notes on contributors	viii
Introduction: fiction, invention and hyper-reality in new religions and spiritualities CAROLE M. CUSACK AND PAVOL KOSNÁČ	1

PART I
Tolkien's Legendarium, the Elven lineage and the Internet 13

1 The Elven Path and the Silver Ship of the Valar: two spiritual groups based on J. R. R. Tolkien's Legendarium MARKUS ALTENA DAVIDSEN	15
Appendix 1.1 Tië eldaliéva REVEREND MICHAELE ALYRAS DE CYGNE AND CALANTIRNIEL	31
Appendix 1.2 Ilsaluntë Valion GWINETH	34
2 Spirituality and self-realisation as 'other-than-human': the Otherkin and Therianthropy communities CAROLE M. CUSACK	40
3 Salvation and animation: religion, fandom and identity in the romantic narratives of mystics and Soulbonders VENETIA LAURA DELANO ROBERTSON	58
4 The development of spirituality in the Brony community PAVOL KOSNÁČ	79

vi *Contents*

PART II
Film and television as sacred texts   99

5 Spirituality-struck: anime and religio-spiritual
   devotional practices   101
   KATHARINE BULJAN

6 Jediism and the Temple of the Jedi Order   119
   ASH WILLIAMS, BENJAMIN-ALEXANDRE MILLER AND
   MICHAEL KITCHEN

7 Virtual knights and synthetic worlds: Jediism in
   Second Life   134
   HELEN FARLEY

8 A brief history of Dudeism   148
   OLIVER BENJAMIN

9 Diego Maradona and the psychodynamics of football
   fandom in international cinema   158
   MARCUS FREE

PART III
Online mediation of invented, fiction-based and
hyper-real religions   179

10 "Discordians stick apart": the institutional turn within
    contemporary Discordianism   181
    J. CHRISTIAN GREER

11 SubGenius vs The Conspiracy: playfulness and sincerity
    in invented religions   198
    DAVID G. ROBERTSON

12 Kopimism and media devotion: piracy, activism, art and
    critique as religious practice   213
    DANIELLE L. KIRBY AND ELISHA H. MCINTYRE

13 Beyond belief: revival in virtual worlds   226
    WILLIAM SIMS BAINBRIDGE

Contents   vii

PART IV
Countercultural personal spiritualities and religions   **241**

14 African-American ufology in the music and
    mythos of Sun Ra   243
    JOHANNA J. M. PETSCHE

15 The Church of All Worlds   261
    OBERON ZELL

16 An implicit hyper-real religion: real-life superheroes   272
    ADAM POSSAMAI AND VLADISLAV IOUCHKOV

    Index   291

Contributors

William Sims Bainbridge earned a doctorate in sociology from Harvard University in 1975, came to the National Science Foundation in 1992 to run the Sociology Program, and in 2000 moved to NSF's Directorate for Computer and Information Science and Engineering. He has written nine books in the sociology of religion, and about an equal number focused on computer or spaceflight technology. At NSF he has been a leader in the Converging Technologies movement, helping to organise conferences and edit books on the unification of all fields of science and engineering. His 2013 solo-authored book, *Personality Capture and Emulation*, outlines methods to give information systems the memories and personality characteristics of specific human beings, and he co-edited the 2013 book *Convergence of Knowledge, Technology and Society*. A new book currently in press analyses in great depth the public opinion poll data about space exploration.

Oliver Benjamin, the current 'Dudely Lama' of Dudeism, founded the Church of the Latter-Day Dude in 2005. The Church has ordained over 350,000 Dudeist Priests as of 2016, and continues to grow in popularity all over the world, albeit at a leisurely pace. Benjamin has been featured in major international publications, several radio shows, as well as television programmes such as ABC Nightline (US) and the French/German network ARTE. He was raised and educated in Los Angeles, but lives in Chiang Mai, Thailand.

Katharine Buljan is a visual artist/animator and lecturer at JMC Academy in Sydney. She was awarded a PhD in Studies in Religion from the University of Sydney (2007), a Master of Animation from the University of Technology, Sydney (2008) and a Master of Arts (Hons) from the University of Western Sydney, Nepean (1998). Katharine has been a sessional/guest lecturer at the universities in Sydney and at the Australian Film, Television and Radio School. She has published in the area of animation and visual arts. Katharine Buljan is the author (with Carole M. Cusack) of *Anime, Religion and Spirituality: Profane and Sacred Worlds in Contemporary Japan* (2015). She has exhibited her work in various countries and has received a number of art prizes. Katharine was an Artist in Residence at the University of Tasmania in 2015.

Calantirniel (San Diego, CA, USA) is published in nearly two dozen Llewellyn annuals since 2007 and also in three anthologies published in the UK. She has practiced many forms of natural spirituality for over two decades. She is a professional timing expert as well as an astrologer, herbalist, tarot card reader, dowser, energy healer, ULC reverend and flower essence creator/practitioner. She is also a co-founder of Tië eldaliéva (the Elven Path), a spiritual practice based upon the Elves' viewpoint in J. R. R. Tolkien's Middle-Earth stories, particularly *The Silmarillion* (1977). Websites: ElvenSpirituality.com and IntuitiveTiming.com

Carole M. Cusack is Professor of Religious Studies at the University of Sydney, Australia. She trained as a medievalist and her doctorate was published as *Conversion Among the Germanic Peoples* (1998). She now researches contemporary religious trends (pilgrimage and tourism, modern Pagan religions, NRMs, and religion and popular culture). Her books include *Invented Religions: Imagination, Fiction and Faith* (2010) and *The Sacred Tree: Ancient and Medieval Manifestations* (2011). She has published widely in edited volumes and journals, and is the editor of (with Christopher Hartney) *Religion and Retributive Logic: Essays in Honour of Garry W. Trompf* (2010) and (with Alex Norman) *Handbook of New Religions and Cultural Production* (2012). She is Editor of *Literature & Aesthetics* (the journal of the Sydney Society of Literature and Aesthetics) and (with Rachelle Scott, University of Tennessee, Knoxville) she is Co-Editor of *Fieldwork in Religion*.

Markus Altena Davidsen holds an MA in the Study of Religion from the University of Aarhus, Denmark, and a PhD in the Study of Religion (*cum laude*) from the University of Leiden, the Netherlands. He was awarded the Arenberg-Coimbra Group Prize for Erasmus Students for his MA thesis on Jediism, and the Gerardus van der Leeuw PhD Dissertation Award from the Dutch Association for the Study of Religion for his doctorate, *The Spiritual Tolkien Milieu: A Study of Fiction-based Religion* (2014). Dr Davidsen has published articles on method and theory in the study of fiction-based religion and other forms of contemporary religion in *Religion, Method and Theory in the Study of Religion, Culture and Religion* and *Implicit Religion*. He is currently preparing a monograph based on his dissertation for publication with De Gruyter. Markus Altena Davidsen is employed as an Assistant Professor in the Sociology of Religion at the University of Leiden.

Helen Farley is a Senior Research Fellow within the School of History, Philosophy, Religion and Classics at the University of Queensland, Australia. Her research interests include manifestations of religion in

x   *Contributors*

virtual worlds, the history and practice of divination and the history of esotericism. She has taught across a range of topics including world religions, meditation and mysticism, Hinduism, the history of divination and the history of secret societies. Helen Farley has published widely. Her book, *A Cultural History of Tarot: From Entertainment to Esotericism*, was published in 2009.

Marcus Free is a lecturer in Media and Communication Studies at Mary Immaculate College, University of Limerick, Ireland. He has previously taught at the Universities of Sunderland and Wolverhampton, UK. His current research interests are mainly in the fields of sport as lived culture, the cultural politics of the representation of sport in film and popular media, and the psychodynamics of fans' emotional and cultural investment in sport. He is co-author (with John Hughson and David Inglis) of *The Uses of Sport: A critical study* (2005). He has published many international journal articles and book chapters on constructions of gender, race and national identity in sport, sport fandom and sport media. He also published work on Irish migration, gender and national identity in contemporary film and television drama.

J. Christian Greer is working on his doctorate in the History of Hermetic Philosophy and Related Currents from the University of Amsterdam, the Netherlands. His dissertation focuses on psychedelic religions, such as Discordianism and the Church of the SubGenius, as well as the underground media in which they flourish. He holds an MA from the University of Amsterdam, the Netherlands, and a Masters of Divinity from Harvard Divinity School, USA.

Gwineth is a computer programmer, visual artist and animator from the Netherlands with degrees in physics and visual arts. Coming from a progressive Catholic family, she identified as agnostic humanist and rationalist skeptic since her teens, though she has also always felt an impulse to find a more fitting spiritual framework. This eventually happened when she was contacted by a member from *Ilsaluntë Valion* while studying Tolkien's elvish languages. She joined the forum soon thereafter and considers hearing Dr Stephan Hoeller's lectures (of http://gnosis.org), together with experiences during 'active imagination' meditations, to be her gnostic *epinoia*. This considerable change in perspective was of course personally significant in the spiritual sense, but it also sparked a strong creative impulse that she hopes might eventually help others (re) discover their mythical imaginative talents.

Vladislav Iouchkov is a PhD candidate within the School of Social Sciences and Psychology at Western Sydney University, Australia. His research interests lie in the sociology of religion and spirituality, criminology, risk and a focus on the impact of popular culture on individual life trajectories. His current research is in examining the forms of personal and spiritual development that members of the Real-Life Superhero Movement undergo in reshaping their lives with self-created superhero identities, and how this translates into community action.

Danielle L. Kirby is an independent researcher in the fields of religion, popular culture and media, with particular emphasis upon digital manifestations of alternative religion. In particular, she explores topics such as the construction of metaphysics from popular texts, remix and art within occultural spiritualities, and the relation of religious practitioners to consumption and late modernity. Her most recent publications include the monograph *Fantasy and Belief: Alternative Religions, Popular Narratives, and Digital Cultures* (2014) and co-editing (with Carole M. Cusack) the multi-volume *Sects, Cults, and New Religions* (2014). Danielle Kirby graduated with a PhD in the Study of Religion from the University of Queensland, Australia (2010). She held a lectureship in communication at RMIT University, Melbourne, Australia (2011–2016).

Pavol Kosnáč is an independent scholar based in Bratislava, Slovakia. He has studied Religious Studies at Comenius University, where he obtained his BA and MA, and political philosophy, jurisprudence and European culture at the Collegium of Anton Neuwirt (both in Bratislava). Afterwards he moved to England to continue his studies at the University of Oxford, completing an MSt in Religion. He held a six-month placement at INFORM in London, then travelled extensively, working as a freelance analyst for British, Slovak and Asian think-tanks. He plans to start a PhD next year. His academic background is mostly in sociology of religion, history of Christianity and Islam and the study of new religious movements. He is interested especially in new and alternative religiosity, non-religiosity, the contemporary religious situation in Europe and overlaps between religion, violence and war.

Elisha H. McIntyre holds a PhD in Studies in Religion from the University of Sydney, Australia. Her research interests come under the broad umbrellas of religion and popular culture and New Religious Movements. She has published articles on Hillsong Church, religious kitsch, Christian and Mormon film, Pastafarianism and Kopimism, and has guest co-edited the journal *Literature & Aesthetics*. She has lectured and tutored for the Department of Studies in Religion and the US Studies Centre at the University of Sydney. Her recent research focuses on religion and humour as expressed in popular religious entertainment and material culture. Currently she is focusing her research on The Church of Jesus Christ of Latter Day Saints (Mormons) and working on a book about religious humour.

Johanna J. M. Petsche graduated with a PhD in Studies in Religion from the University of Sydney, Australia, in 2013. Her dissertation, entitled *Music For Remembering: The Gurdjieff/de Hartmann Piano Music and*

xii *Contributors*

its Esoteric Significance, centred on Greek-Armenian spiritual teacher George Ivanovitch Gurdjieff (*c*.1866–1949) and the diverse body of music he produced in collaboration with a pupil, Thomas Alexandrovich de Hartmann (1885–1956). This was published as part of Brill's prestigious *Aries Book Series* as *Gurdjieff and Music* (2015). Johanna is currently working as a lecturer and tutor at the Australian Catholic University. She has published on Gurdjieff, H. P. Blavatsky, E. J. Gold, Scientology, Discordianism and musicians Keith Jarrett and Sun Ra. She also teaches clarinet, performs in the chamber music group, *Ensemble Spiritoso*, and studies the Gurdjieff Movements.

Adam Possamai is Professor of Sociology at Western Sydney University, Australia, Director of Research and Higher Degree Research in the School of Social Sciences and Psychology, and the past President of the International Sociological Association's Committee 22 on the Sociology of Religion. Some of his latest books are: (edited with James L. Cox) *Religion and Non-Religion among Australian Aboriginal Peoples* (2016); (edited with James T. Richards and Bryan Turner) *The Sociology of Shari'a: Case Studies from Around the World* (2015); (edited with Helena Onnudottir and Bryan Turner) *Religious Change and Indigenous Peoples: the Making of Religious Identities* (2013); and *Handbook of Hyper-Real Religions* (2012). He is the Series Editor of the *Popular Culture, Religion and Contemporary Society: a Social-Scientific Approach* book series.

David G. Robertson is co-founder of the Religious Studies Project, and co-editor of the journal *Implicit Religion*. His work applies critical theory to the study of alternative and emerging religions and 'conspiracy theory' narratives, and the history of contemporary alternative religions. He is the author of *UFOs, the New Age and Conspiracy Theories: Millennial Conspiracism* (2016) and co-editor of *After 'World Religions': Reconstructing Religious Studies* (2016). He blogs at: davidgrobertson. wordpress.com

Venetia Laura Delano Robertson is a tutor, lecturer and PhD candidate in the Studies in Religion department at the University of Sydney, Australia. She has written articles for *Literature & Aesthetics*, *Nova Religio*, *International Journal of Cultural Studies*, *Journal for the Academic Study of Religion* and *The Pomegranate*. She has given papers at a number of international and multi-disciplinary conferences on the intersecting themes of her PhD thesis: identity, human-animal studies, alternative spirituality, popular oc/culture and digital media. Venetia Robertson is a member of the Contemporary Esotericism Research Network (ContERN) and the Human Animal Research Network (HARN) at the University of Sydney.

Ash Williams, Benjamin-Alexandre Miller and Michael Kitchen (contributing authors) are members of The Temple of the Jed Order (TOTJO), which is not a community of *Star Wars* roleplayers, but a church of a genuine religion, Jediism. The Jedi at this site are not the same as those portrayed within the *Star Wars* franchise. *Star Wars* Jedi are fictional characters that exist within a literary and cinematic universe. The Jedi of TOTJO are real people within this world that live or lived their lives according to the principles of Jediism, the real Jedi religion. Jedi followers, ministers and leaders embrace Jediism as a real living, breathing religion and sincerely believe in its teachings. Jediism does not base its focus on myth and fiction but on the real life issues and philosophies that are at the source of myth. We believe in Peace, Justice, Love, Learning and Benevolence: it is unlikely that the Jedi way conflicts with other beliefs and traditions.

Oberon Zell (b. 1942) is Primate of the Church of All Worlds (CAW), the Pagan religion he founded in 1962 with his closest friend Lance Christie, while they were both students at Westminster College, Fulton Missouri. Zell and Christie were deeply influenced by their psychology professor, Gale Fuller, and devised two parallel organisations, the religious CAW (which Zell led) and the secular ecological 'water brotherhood' ATL (Association for the Tree of Life) (which Christie led). In the late 1960s Zell became aware of the mystical philosophy of Frederick McLaren Adams, of Feraferia, and registered CAW formally as a Pagan religion in Missouri. In 1973 he met his soul-mate Morning Glory (1948-2014), and they married in 1974. In the 1970s CAW developed a distinctive thealogy of the Earth as Gaea, the living Goddess, as a result of Zell's 'TheaGenesis' vision, received in 1970. The Zells moved to the country, raised unicorns, sailed the world seeking mermaids and other magical creatures, founded the Holy Order of Mother Earth (HOME), and pursued polyamory as a mode of fulfilled life. In the twenty-first century, Zell is founder and Headmaster of the Grey School of Wizardry, an online magical school, and provides inspiration to the worldwide Pagan community as a philosopher and leader. Zell's first water-brother and co-founder Lance Christie died in 2010, and his beloved Morning Glory died in May 2014.

Introduction

Fiction, invention and hyper-reality in new religions and spiritualities

Carole M. Cusack and Pavol Kosnáč

An emergent subject area

The academic field encompassed in *Fiction, Invention and Hyper-reality: From popular culture to religion* is that of contested contemporary religions that are based on fictional texts (films, novels, *manga* and so on) or include fictional texts in their canon of scriptures or inspirational phenomena. Scholarly investigation of these religions formally commenced in the early 2000s, but is still a small (though rapidly expanding) subfield. In their studies, scholars include both self-identified religious groups and non-self-identified, non-institutionalised religious and spiritual practices that are pursued by unorganised movements or by individuals under the rubrics 'fictional', 'invented' or 'hyper-real' religions. Various methodological lenses have been applied to the study of such phenomena, the most common being sociological and psychological approaches to questions arising about the claims to legitimacy of these religious groups and practices, such as how can they be distinguished from mock or parody religions (Chidester 2005) or from fandoms and fan communities; that is, groups of enthusiasts for certain film and music stars, and cult or popular film, television and literary phenomena (Jindra 1994). Issues which follow on from such preliminary definitional questions include further questions concerning the motives of the movements' originators (if there are known founders) in creating religions based on obviously human-generated stories or characters, when there are many other religions from which to choose (Lewis 2003). This question is particularly important as traditional religions claim to be authentically transcendent, ancient and true. Many of the religions included in this volume sidestep or repudiate the usual legitimating claims that underpin the reputation of most existing religious groups. Within Religious Studies the closest subfield to that of 'fictional', 'invented' or 'hyper-real' religions is the study of new religious movements (NRMs). Research into NRMs is multi-disciplinary and encompasses perspectives from sociology of religion, history of religion, cultural history, behavioural psychology, sociology, theology, ethics, art and aesthetics, and a range of other disciplines including biology, health, law and environmental studies.

2   Carole M. Cusack and Pavol Kosnáč

The field is controversial for a number of reasons. First, as with much social scientific research into the sensitive subject of religion, it has the potential to be misunderstood by traditionally religious people who may be offended by the deconstruction of what are understood as typical features of religion, and by the sometimes intimate and taboo nature of the topics under investigation. Second, even amongst scholars, religion and spirituality are viewed and defined in many different ways, be it for academic or practical reasons. The social constructionist approach advocated by scholars from Peter Berger and Thomas Luckmann in the 1960s to Adam Possamai in the 2000s may thus be rejected by some. Third, religion and popular culture are typically treated as opposites; the first being the "sacred" reality, and latter a site of profanity (Demerath 2000). The claim that this view is false, and that scholars like Sean McCloud, who insist that the "project of the self", while important, is not religious and thus, fandoms and veneration of pop culture figures, are not wrong either, may be controversial as well (McCloud 2003: 187).

The study of popular culture-based religions using social scientific methods

The term 'new religious movements' is also a somewhat problematic concept, but there are occasions when it fits perfectly. Popular culture-based religions are both new in the sense of being contemporary, as well as being equally new in all parts of the globalised world. Considering those facts, they could be considered the NRMs *par excellence*. Invented, fiction-based and hyper-real religions began appearing in the second half of twentieth century and continue to do so to the present day. They are normally based on some type of pop culture phenomenon (usually a book, film or character, fictional or real). These three designators are derived from the scholarship of Carole M. Cusack, Markus Altena Davidsen and Adam Possamai respectively. Possamai debuted the notion of "hyper-real religions" in his *Religion and Popular Culture: A Hyper-real Testament* (Possamai 2005). This term was derived from Jean Baudrillard's notion of the hyper-real, in which "a new reality logic based upon simulation rather than representation constitutes the dominant organizing principle" (Luke 1991: 349). Objections have been raised to Possamai's use of this term, chief of which is that Baudrillard regarded all religions as hyper-real (they are all simulations, as there is no supernatural realm for them to represent in the first place). Cusack proposed the term "invented religions" in her monograph *Invented Religions: Imagination, Fiction and Faith* (2010). While she acknowledged that in some sense all religions are 'invented', this designator was used specifically to delimit a class of religions that are "explicitly invented, fictional religions, which refused the strategies of legitimation that were customarily employed by new religions" (Cusack 2010: 141). In 2012, Markus Altena Davidsen argued that "fiction-based" was the most accurate description of these popular culture derived religions (Davidsen 2012: 185–204; 2013). This volume

Introduction 3

will introduce readers to several invented, fiction-based and hyper-real religions, from those that are quite well known, like Jediism, to the less known ones, like Dudeism or Tolkien-based spirituality groups.

The principal reason to study the phenomena of fiction-based, invented or hyper-real religions is the challenge that such study presents to the classical understanding of what religion is and what 'holiness' and 'religiosity' look like. Hyper-real religions challenge notions of divine legitimacy and ancient authenticity through the selection of a piece of modern popular culture as an inspiration, and often as a basis, for their teachings and practices. The study of hyper-real religions may well be the study of religious forms of the future, when the 'religious (or spiritual) supermarket' is extended to include all manner of hitherto unimagined products for the consumption and satisfaction of the spiritual "seeker" (Campbell 1972). As mentioned above, the topic of NRMs, and especially the subgroup of hyper-real religions, is a controversial one. Studying such a subject area by applying social scientific tools, rather than engaging in methodology-light polemics against (or quasi-theological affirmations of) these religions will assist in the rationalisation of this potentially heated issue.

The chapters included in this volume are very diverse, ranging across religions and spiritualities based on television productions, through sports and popular music, to underground subcultures and cyberspace. The scholarship included is relevant because all chapters have two features in common: first, the beliefs and practices examined are of a kind that can be described as religious or spiritual, and are based on some kind of popular cultural phenomena; and second, these phenomena actually affect the individual or the group in real life. By 'affect' we mean that the described hyper-real religious practice has a discernible influence on their ethics, decision making, ritual life and so on. This is crucial, because it would otherwise be impossible to differentiate between a hyper-real religion and, for example, a role-playing experience, which may be emotional as well, yet in the end is perceived as only a game that has no profound influence on the player's everyday life.

The volume includes chapters from members of fiction-based, invented and hyper-real religious movements, who present their point of view and introduce their particular groups (the Church of All Worlds, Dudeism, the Temple of the Jedi Order and two Tolkien-based religious groups). There is also a chapter from the distinguished sociologist of religion, William Sims Bainbridge, which will help readers to understand the reasons and motivations of founders and/or members of these groups, enabling a deeper understanding of the topic, which is enriched by the emic approach. "Insider" chapters may be briefer and more personal, but fulfil academic standards in that they seek to inform readers about little-known groups and do not engage in either preaching or special pleading.

One final point worth noting is that it is particularly important to distinguish the religions discussed in this volume from examples of what James R. Lewis has termed "religious forgery", that is situations where documents

4   *Carole M. Cusack and Pavol Kosnáč*

have been created that are expressly "motivated by the desire to legitimate the authority of certain opinions, systems of religious ideas, and/or the revealer" (Lewis 2014: 202). Lewis explicitly treats religious documents devised "simply for the 'fun of it'", which would encompass texts such as *Principia Discordia*, the scripture authored by Malaclypse the Younger (Greg Hill) and Omar Khayyam Ravenhurst (Kerry Thornley) and the various Church of the SubGenius publications, as a separate phenomenon from forgeries that seek to legitimate certain positions. He offers support for the methodological project of classifying religions based on fictions by arguing that even overt forgers often "produce documents expressing ideas in which they really do believe and which they hope to promote by their fabrications" (Lewis 2014: 202).

Part I: Tolkien's Legendarium, the Elven lineage and the Internet

The first section opens with Markus Altena Davidsen's chapter, 'The Elven Path and the Silver Ship of the Valar: two spiritual groups based on J. R. R. Tolkien's Legendarium', which profiles two contemporary groups, Tië eldaliéva (the Elven Path) and Ilsaluntë Valion (the Silver Ship of the Valar), but traces their lineage back to the earliest Elven groups in the late 1960s and early 1970s. The paperback edition of Tolkien's *Lord of the Rings* (1965–1966) brought this epic fantasy trilogy to a vastly expanded audience, and from the hippies and seekers of the counterculture, there emerged groups that integrated the beings of Tolkien's fictions (in particular, his Elves) into their spiritual identity and practices. These included the Elf Queen's Daughters and the Silver Elves, who are in the twenty-first century the elders and chroniclers of the Elven movement. Davidsen's research is supported by two insider documents: statements about Elven spirituality from both Tië eldaliéva and Ilsaluntë Valion, which provide readers with an idea of what the practice of this new religious path might involve.

The second contribution is Carole M. Cusack's 'Spirituality and self-realisation as "other-than-human": the Otherkin and Therianthropy Communities', which is a broad overview of the emergence of these two (largely online) groups that have their historical origin in the Elven movement. Otherkin are a diverse group that identify as partly human and partly 'other-than-human', and their non-human identities include dragons, angels, vampires, aliens and unicorns, that is, creatures from beyond the natural world. Therianthropy is a similar movement that has concepts and practices in common with Otherkin, but in which the 'other-than-human' element, referred to as the 'therioside' is derived from the animal realm of the natural world (Robertson 2013). In the twenty-first century, the range of fictions and popular cultural forms that are drawn upon by Otherkin and Therians is broad and deep and includes mythology, legends, folktales and fairy tales, as well as manga and anime, film, television, comics and computer games.

The third chapter in this section is Venetia Robertson's 'Salvation and animation: Religion, fandom, and identity in the romantic narratives of mystics and Soulbonders', which is an original attempt to understand the seemingly extreme narratives of two 'Soulbonders', Mrs Sephiroth and Sephirothslave, who developed complex relationships with Sephiroth, the villain of the *Final Fantasy* videogame. Robertson follows Kirby (2006) in classifying Soulbonders as a subgroup of Otherkin, perhaps better described as Mediakin, due to the beings that are the focus of the devotion being from the mass media, rather than from myths or folktales. Robertson examines the passionate relationships with the Christian saviour, Jesus Christ, that a number of female mystics of the Middle Ages experienced, and relates these seemingly very different phenomena to the passionate and devoted 'fangirls' of the modern era, who are similarly marginalised by the masculinist 'geek' culture, as mystics such as Julian of Norwich and Margery Kempe were by the masculinist culture of the Catholic Church.

The final chapter in this section, 'The development of spirituality in the Brony Community' by Pavol Kosnáč, examines a recent phenomenon that began as fandom but has developed spiritual qualities over time. Bronies originated at the start of the second decade of the twenty-first century, and are fans of the animated television series *My Little Pony: Friendship is Magic* (2010–2014). What is interesting about this group from the viewpoint of the sociology of religion is that they have generated an internal spiritual movement that may be called Brony 'spiritualists' (a term that distinguishes those who embrace this particular spirituality from other members of the fan group, borrowed from the Furry subculture, a fandom that to a certain extent overlaps with Bronies). The spiritual movement within this group is very diverse, drawing inspiration from mainstream religions, different New Age phenomena, and a rich Eastern and Western esoteric milieu, including shamanism, Taoism and other religio-spiritual sources. There is an obvious overlapping relationship between these new spiritual communities and the Otherkin and Soulbonders. Both traditional religious and popular cultural sources are woven together and reinterpreted through the lens of love for anthropomorphised animal art and magical ponies.

Part II: film and television as sacred texts

Katharine Buljan's contribution 'Spirituality struck: Anime and religio-spiritual devotional practices', details the emergence of anime fandom in the West from the 1960s and the growth of specific fan activities, often facilitated via conventions and other large public gatherings where anime films and television series were screened (Buljan and Cusack 2015: 163–208). Fans have developed complex devotional practices, including dressing and posing as their favourite anime characters (cosplay ritual); visiting places they saw in anime (anime pilgrimage); and creating fiction-based religions from anime, such as Haruhiism, based on the series *The Melancholy of Haruhi Suzumiya*

(2006). This chapter includes primary data gathered through questionnaires and interviews with anime fans and employs a mixed methodology of 'lived religion' combined with media and cultural studies approaches to anime and new media.

The sixth chapter, 'Jediism and the Temple of the Jedi Order', written by three members of the Temple of the Jedi Order, Ash Williams, Benjamin-Alexandre Miller and Michael Kitchen, is the first of several chapters written from an insider viewpoint and provides an insight into the lives and practices of living Jedi. The chapter covers some of the fundamental features and practices of the Jedi of the Temple of the Jedi Order (TotJO). The chapter describes the religion in terms of the six dimensions of religion proposed by Ninian Smart, with additional explanations for some of the original inspiration of the movement sourced from works by such scholars and religious commentators as Joseph Campbell, Alan Watts and Jiddu Krishnamurti (Campbell and Moyers 1991 [1989]; Krishnamurti 1975 [1969]; Smart 1996; Watts 1989 [1966]). A brief history of the TotJO is outlined, which includes information on how certain practices have changed over time. This work is very much the product of members of one particular church of Jediism and thus does not represent the entirety of the Jedi movement, though there are many similarities between different groups.

The next chapter, Helen Farley's 'Virtual knights and synthetic realms: Jediism in Second Life', explores one specific online presence of a fiction-based religion. Farley considers the expression of a hyper-real religion, Jediism, through role-play in Second Life. There are a number of role-playing groups that draw their inspiration from Jediism in the virtual world, including Jedi of the Republic and Jedi of Second Life. Most require strict adherence to a code of behaviour, context-appropriate costume that reasonably might appear in *Star Wars* and which must be worn at all times, and a requirement to remain in character while role-playing. This chapter conducts an etic investigation into the motivations behind role-playing in Second Life and whether or not role-play acts as a form of religious expression in this environment by using Johan Huizinga's concept of the "Magic Circle", a walled-off but temporary location within the real world dedicated to the performance of an act alone (Huizinga 1971[1949]: 10–11). Rather than thinking of the spaces within virtual worlds as being totally sealed, Farley follows Edward Castronova, considering them to be porous, leaking through into the real world and vice versa. Hyper-real religion in Second Life is considered in light of this theoretical lens.

The eighth contribution is 'A short history of Dudeism' by the Dudely Lama, Oliver Benjamin, the founder of this new religion based on Joel and Ethan Coen's film *The Big Lebowski* (1998). Benjamin explains the new religion of Dudeism, focusing on three themes. These are, first, the origins of Dudeism when he inaugurated the Church in 2005; second, the pre-Dudeist cult reception of *The Big Lebowski* from 1998 to 2005; and third, the contention that Dudeism has existed since the beginning of civilisation, usually as an antidote to the excesses and difficulties that arose contemporaneously with modern pluralistic and superorganic civilisation. Benjamin also gives an account of the current structure and operations of the Church, covering its ongoing projects as well as future plans for expansion. He acknowledges that as a new religion, Dudeism faces challenges in avoiding the problems that have plagued traditiomal religions, as well as difficulties in achieving recognition, particularly outside the United States, which is arguably unique in its tolerance of and openness to 'alternative' religions.

The final piece in this section, Marcus Free's 'Diego Maradona and the psychodynamics of football fandom in international cinema', is the only reprinted article in the volume. Free adopts a psychoanalytic approach and compares how three films, the British documentary *In the Hands of the Gods* (2007), the Argentine road movie *El Camino de San Diego* (2006) and Emir Kusturica's *Maradona by Kusturica* (2008), explore the psychodynamic processes of fan investment in Argentine former football star Diego Maradona. These films illustrate how his meaning as an international cultural icon is refracted by specific fan experiences and fantasies, and are variously informed by, and critically explore, the myths of virtual death, resurrection, redemption and geopolitical opposition to global capitalism associated with Maradona. This chapter may, at first glance, be deemed irrelevant as Free's focus is the phenomenon of Maradona fandom in three films, rather than an examination of the Iglesia Maradoniana, the Church that worships Maradona as a god. Yet it is included for three reaasons: first, sport is a prime site for the development of popular cultural religions, and Iglesia Maradoniana is the foremost example to date; second, there is nothing written about Iglesia Maradoniana from a Religious Studies perspective, and third, Free has clearly identified the necessary (though not sufficient) preconditions to enable fandom to morph into religion. The films in question are directly relevant and the majority of the discussion turns on the nature of the idol/icon (Diego Maradona) and the shared alternative reality (or mass delusion) of the fandom that aimed to deify him (out of which Iglesia Maradoniana was founded).

Part III: online mediation of invented, fiction-based and hyper-real religions

J. Christian Greer's chapter, '"Discordians stick apart": the institutional turn in contemporary Discordianism', contends that scholars have focused on a 'golden age' of Discordianism from 1958 to 1975, when the rise of internet culture from the mid-1990s resulted in exponential growth in Discordianism. Greer focuses on three examples of contemporary Discordianism. First is the organisation of the 'Discordian archives' from 2009 by Adam Gorightly and his utilisation of particular legitimisation strategies in the 'official' history of Discordianism that Gorightly presents in his books and blog, *Historia Discordia*. Second is the Maybe Logic Academy, created in 2004 as a way

8   *Carole M. Cusack and Pavol Kosnáč*

for the prominent Discordian writer, Robert Anton Wilson (1932–2007), to disseminate his ideas on the Internet. Third is the 'Chasing Eris' project, which was undertaken in 2012 by the intrepid young Discordian 'Placid Dingo' (b. Brenton Clutterbuck). A 'crowd sourced' venture based on documenting the lived religious experience of Discordians worldwide, this project has afforded Clutterbuck the opportunity to conduct participant observation within Discordian groups in over a dozen countries. Greer notes that the three projects are not the totality of contemporary Discordianism, but their prominence provides scholars with an opportunity to assess contemporary Discordianism as a lived religion.

The next contribution is David G. Robertson's 'SubGenius vs the Conspiracy: playfulness and sincerity in invented religions', which examines the ambiguous nature of 'the Conspiracy' in the writings of the Church of the SubGenius (CoSG), which is often regarded as a Discordian offshoot. Robertson interrogates the tension between two contradictory constructions. The CoSG position on religion is explicitly satirical and intended to destabilise traditional ways of thinking (as with many other invented religions), and thus a satirical view of conspiracism's positing of hidden agencies and teleological, Manichaean cosmologies would be in keeping. On the other hand, CoSG theology frequently seems to reproduce conspiracy theory narratives without irony; 'the Conspiracy' is posited as the enemy of the CoSG, seeking to suppress 'true slack'. Conspiracy theories challenge both hegemonic power structures and historical narratives, which are also targets of the CoSG. Robertson highlights an ambiguity in the CoSG and in 'invented religions' more broadly: do such religions challenge institutional and epistemic norms primarily a) in an attempt to relativise all belief systems, or b) in order to replace them with an alternative system?

Danielle Kirby and Elisha McIntyre's chapter 'Kopimism and media devotion: piracy, activism, art, and critique as religious practice', examines the very new religion of Kopimism, founded in 2010 by Isak Gerson. The late twentieth and early twenty-first centuries have seen a rise in religions that are heavily entwined with media. Indeed, the adoption of media logics into the realms of the religious is staggering in its variety, ranging from the performative spectacles of African Pentecostal megachurches through to the personal internalisation of fictional characters. Kopimism makes this integration of media even more explicit in its belief that copying and disseminating information is ethically right, and that remixing is a sacred act. Kopimism has branches in many countries and is a recognised religious community by the Swedish government. Like a number of newly born alternative religions, Kopimism sits somewhat ambiguously between sincerity and satire. Claiming piracy as a sacred duty, Kopimists unequivocally constitute a critical voice against traditional copyright law and its particular application in digital contexts on an international scale. Yet public critique is not their only goal. This chapter explores the entwined influences of political activism, the critique of traditional religiosity and digital arts practice as they manifest under the rubric of Kopimism.

Introduction 9

This section concludes with William Sims Bainbridge's 'Beyond belief: revival in virtual worlds', a chapter which employs psychodrama, a method developed by Jacob L. Moreno, whose career blended social science and religion, to study the most modern artistic expression of quasi-religious culture, massively multi-player online role-playing games (MMORPGs). Specifically, the chapter is Bainbridge's own observational data, gathered by running for hundreds of hours an *avatar* based on the author's sister who was religious and died nearly half a century ago, in two very different MMOs. One, *Pirates of the Burning Sea*, is a somewhat realistic historical virtual world, set in 1720 in the Caribbean, in which many of the missions involve local clergy or members of radical cults. The other, *Neverwinter*, is a highly fantastic ghoul-oriented MMO, based on the influential *Dungeons and Dragons* tradition, in which players create elaborate missions for each other, often involving supernatural powers and radical religious movements. The perspective is etic, yet empathic and reflexive. The research methodology is a new form of participant observation ethnography, and the chapter is an 'insider' meditation on the spiritual meaning that Bainbridge family members have derived from online memorialisation of their dead kinswoman, Constance.

Part IV: countercultural personal spiritualities and religions

The fourteenth chapter is Johanna J. M. Petsche's 'African-American ufology in the music and mythos of Sun Ra'. Sun Ra (1914–1993), a jazz virtuoso, changed his name to Sony'r Ra in 1952, and from that point claimed to be from the planet Saturn. His band, the Sun Ra Arkestra, drew inspiration from electronica and contemporary *avant-garde* classical music. The Arkestra recorded the anthems 'Interplanetary Music' and 'Space is the Place', and Sun Ra wrote poems and prose on 'Afrofuturist' themes. Petsche argues that Sun Ra's unique and eccentric vision is congruent with other, possibly more mainstream, manifestations of African-American ufology, such as the Nation of Islam, founded by Wallace Fard Muhammad (which teaches that UFOs will destroy White infidels), the Moorish Science Temple, founded by Noble Drew Ali (which notes UFOs in passing), and the Nuwaubian Nation, which was founded by Dwight York, also a musician and devoted to the Afrocentric vision of Ancient Egypt (whose teachings incorporate multiple alien races, his own extraterrestrial origin on the planet Rizq and a developed apocalyptic scenario in which Whites are destroyed). It is argued that ufology is an invented tradition or fiction, upon which both Black and White new spiritualities have drawn. For Blacks, the promise of space and life beyond planet Earth was linked to the end of White oppression and the utopian possibilities of freedom and dignity in new worlds. Sun Ra's assertion that 'space is the place' and his dedicated preaching of a utopian interplanetary vision through inspired jazz music (many music critics have likened the Arkestra's ecstatic performances to religious rituals

10   *Carole M. Cusack and Pavol Kosnáč*

and spiritual experiences) is a distinctive and under-researched contribution to the subfield of African-American ufology, itself a component part of one of the largest (arguably second in size and influence only to modern Paganism) 'invented' religions of the twentieth century, UFO and alien-based religions.

The next chapter is an 'insider' view by Oberon Zell, 'The Church of All Worlds'. The origins of the Church of All Worlds (CAW) lay in Robert A. Henlein's science fiction novel *Stranger in a Strange Land* (1961), which inspired college students Tim (now Oberon) Zell and Lance Christie to share water and found a new religion in 1962. During the 1960s, further inspiration was found in Abraham Maslow's self-actualisation psychology and the Human Potential Movement, and the broader NeoPagan movement (incidentally, Zell was the first to explicitly use the term Pagan for nature- and goddess-based religions in 1967) whose tenets include immanent divinity, worship of goddesses as well as gods, honouring nature as sacred and holy, celebration of the eight seasonal holidays, and a return to certain progressive values of organic living, sexual freedom and high ethical standards. Yet, even within the Pagan community, with its reclaiming of the appellations 'witch' and 'witchcraft', and other ancient or medieval rural and alchemical traditions, CAW stands out as robustly contemporary, forward-thinking and creatively innovative. Further, it has heart-opening rites of passage, deep neo-tribal community and an orientation towards the future, and it publishes the pioneering Pagan journal *Green Egg*. With its nine-circle programme of development leading to ministerial investiture and the Pagan priesthood, CAW is a (r)evolutionary church with implications for transforming the individual, society and the world. This chapter traces the history of CAW from the 1960s through back-to-the-land hippies and spiritual new agers such as David Spangler, to Ray and Anderson's Cultural Creatives and postmodern progressives, emphasising ecospirituality as the overarching cultural meme in which modern Paganism and CAW emerged. In this way, the beliefs, praxis and worldview of the Church are given a cultural and sociological framework of interpretation.

The final chapter, Adam Possamai and Vladislav Iouchkov's 'An implicit hyper-real religion: real life superheroes', explores the importance of fictional superheroes, found in Marvel comics and Hollywood films, to people (mostly men) who seek to have a transformative impact on society. The real life superheroes movement is used as a case-study of both an implicit religion and a hyper-real religion. Possamai and Iouchkov first detail the movement as found online (for example, in chat rooms, on blogs and via YouTube clips), and then offer an account of people who dress up as superheroes and walk the streets of contemporary metropolises to curb violence and crime. Recent theories of implicit religion, hyper-real religion and consumer culture are harnessed to explain, first, how comics first secularised and commercialised mythic gods and figures into superheroes, and, second, how consumer culture provided a platform for people to bring works of popular fiction into their reality-construction.

Conclusion

Eventually, all chapters will touch upon the problem of authenticity and legitimacy, since those are the first and pivotal questions that come to mind when contemplating hyper-real religions, or must be answered if someone plans to be part of one. Each author and group has his/her own 'take' on this problem, but one follower of Jediism captured the essence of it:

> Who are you to tell me what to do, what to believe, how to dress or who to sleep with, in what position and when? How to live my life? Why should I listen to [the] pope, a rabbi, a minister or whoever runs Islam? Yes, Christianity, Jews, Islam, they are all big and old religions with a lot of very wise guys working for them throughout the ages, especially their founders, I admire and respect that, but why should I obey them? They were [a] bunch of guys who wanted the same things we want as well – understand the world and how to live our lives well. So they sat down and wrote a book about it, or went on a road-trip and talked about it with others they met, addressing the issues that were important in their times. Some of those issues are similar today, some are completely different. Well, I can do, today, the same thing they did then. I don't know why should I mirror them and do what they thought was a good idea to do in the Middle Ages or the Bronze Age. I can do it myself.[1]

The perception regarding who may speak with authority over belief, lifestyle or ethics is shifting. This book captures and explores different ways in how it manifests in our place and time. It is hoped that readers will be entertained and informed in equal proportions.

Note

1 Personal communication to Pavol Kosnáč with a self-identified Jediist calling himself Master Jinn, November 2013.

References

Buljan, Katharine and Carole M. Cusack. 2015. *Anime, Religion, and Spirituality: Profane and Sacred Worlds in Contemporary Japan*. Sheffield, UK and Oakville, CT: Equinox.

Campbell, Colin. 1972. 'The Cult, the Cultic Milieu, and Secularisation'. *A Sociological Yearbook of Religion in Britain* 5: 119–136.

Campbell, Joseph and Bill Moyers. 1991 [1989]. *The Power of Myth*. New York: Anchor Edition.

Chidester, David. 2005. *Authentic Fakes: Religion and American Popular Culture*. Berkeley, CA and London: University of California Press.

Cusack, Carole M. 2010. *Invented Religions: Imagination, Fiction, and Faith*. Farnham, UK and Burlington, VT: Ashgate.

Davidsen, Markus Altena. 2012. 'The Spiritual Milieu Based on J.R.R. Tolkien's Literary Mythology'. In Adam Possamai (ed.), *Handbook of Hyper-real Religions*. Leiden, The Netherlands and Boston, MA: Brill, pp. 185–204.

Davidsen, Markus Altena. 2013. 'Fiction-based Religion: Conceptualizing a New Category Against History-Based Religion and Fandom'. *Culture and Religion* 14(4): 378–395.

Demerath, N. Jay III. 2000. 'The Varieties of Sacred Experience: Finding the Sacred in a Secular Grove'. *Journal for the Scientific Study of Religion* 39(1): 1–11.

Huizinga, Johan. 1971 [1949]. *Homo Ludens: A Study of the Play Element in Culture*. London: Paladin.

Jindra, Michael. 1994. '*Star Trek* Fandom as a Religious Phenomenon'. *Sociology of Religion* 55(1): 27–51.

Kirby, Danielle. 2006. 'Alternative Worlds: Metaphysical Questing and Virtual Community Among the Otherkin'. In Frances di Lauro (ed.), *Through a Glass Darkly: Reflections on the Sacred*. Sydney: University of Sydney Press, pp. 275–287.

Krishnamurti, Jiddu. 1975 [1969]. *Freedom From the Known*, Mary Lutyens (ed.). San Francisco, CA: Harper SanFrancisco.

Lewis, James R. 2003. *Legitimating New Religions*. New Brunswick, NJ: Rutgers University Press.

Lewis, James R. 2014. 'Using the "F" Word in Religious Studies: Towards a General Model of Sacred Forgeries'. *Alternative Spirituality and Religion Review* 5(2): 188–204.

Luke, Timothy W. 1991. 'Power and Politics in Hyperreality: The Critical Project of Jean Baudrillard'. *The Social Science Journal* 28(3): 347–367.

McCloud, Sean. 2003. 'Popular Culture Fandoms, the Boundaries of Religious Studies, and the Project of the Self'. *Culture and Religion* 4(2): 187–206.

Possamai, Adam. 2005. *Religion and Popular Culture: A Hyperreal Testament*. Oxford, UK: Peter Lang.

Possamai, Adam. 2012. *Handbook of Hyper-Real Religions*. Leiden, The Netherlands and Boston, MA: Brill.

Robertson, Venetia Laura Delano. 2013. 'The Beast Within: Anthrozoomorphic Identity and Alternative Spirituality in the Online Therianthropy Movement'. *Nova Religio: The Journal of Alternative and Emergent Religions* 15(3): 7–30.

Smart, Ninian. 1996. *The Religious Experience of Mankind*. Upper Saddle River, NJ: Prentice Hall.

Watts, Alan. 1989 [1966]. *The Book: On the Taboo of Knowing Who You Are*. New York: Vintage Books.

Part I

Tolkien's Legendarium, the Elven lineage and the Internet

1 The Elven Path and the Silver Ship of the Valar

Two spiritual groups based on J. R. R. Tolkien's Legendarium

Markus Altena Davidsen

An unexpected email

On 7 May 2009 I received an unexpected email. I had just begun a PhD project, intending to focus on *Star Wars*-inspired Jediism, but now Gwineth wrote this: "I thought that maybe you might be interested to know – though maybe you already do – that there is a small number of people who are trying to build a 'spiritual path' on the mythical history of Prof. J.R.R. Tolkien. I am one of them".[1] I had never heard of any such Tolkien-based spiritual groups, but eagerly replied and was soon introduced to the other members of Gwineth's online-based group. These members approached Tolkien's stories about Middle-earth, his so-called Legendarium, in a variety of ways, but they all agreed that the Legendarium was an effective means of transportation to the Faery Otherworld or "Imaginal Realm". Several members were also well versed in Tolkien's Elvish languages and had named the group Ilsaluntë Valion, which means the Silver Ship of the Valar in Qenya.[2] The Valar referred to in the group name are the angelic beings or lower gods of Tolkien's cosmology; the Silver Ship is a poetic reference to the Moon.

Gwineth's email became the start of a co-operative adventure. For the next six years, I had regular contact with Gwineth and other members of Ilsaluntë Valion, especially Nathan Elwin and Eruannlass, and I was introduced to the group's history and ritual practices.[3] I followed the forum's discussions on topics ranging from the true nature of the Valar to the 're-discovery of Limpë', the Elves' favourite beverage which the group took to be saffronated mead. I witnessed the coming and going of dozens of peripheral members while about six individuals formed a stable and active core group.

Ilsaluntë Valion had existed for less than two years when Gwineth introduced me to the group, but some of the members had been practising Tolkien spirituality for several years. They were also in contact with likeminded individuals and other Tolkien-based spiritual groups, some of which were much older than their own. Gwineth immediately put me in touch with members of Tië eldaliéva (Quenya: The Elven Path; founded 2005), a group from which Ilsaluntë Valion had broken off in 2007, but with which it continued

16 *Markus Altena Davidsen*

to cooperate very closely.[4] Calantirniel of Tië eldaliéva, in turn, helped me uncover an entire network of Tolkien spirituality that had existed since the late 1960s.

The spiritual Tolkien milieu proved so fascinating and complex that I decided to devote my entire dissertation to the topic (Davidsen 2014; also 2012, 2013), leaving Jediism aside for a future project. In this chapter, I present a small selection of some of the most interesting material. Following a brief overview of the history of Tolkien spirituality, I zoom in on Tië eldaliéva and Ilsaluntë Valion. These groups are interesting because they have gone the furthest in creating an exclusively Tolkien-based spiritual tradition. In cooperation with other members of their groups, Michaele Alyras de Cygne and Calantirniel (Tië eldaliéva) and Gwineth (Ilsaluntë Valion) have authored two short pieces that outline the practice of their respective groups from the members' own perspective. These two pieces are included as appendices to this chapter. We think that this combination of insider and outsider perspectives constitutes the richest and most fair way to represent of the material. In addition to the three pieces on Tolkien spirituality published in this volume, readers might be interested in studying also the Enderi ritual, an exemplary Tië eldaliéva ritual that has been published, together with a glossary and an overview of Tië eldaliéva's ritual calendar, on the group's homepage.[5]

Tolkien spirituality: a brief history

The Lord of the Rings (*LR*) had been published in three hardback volumes in 1954–55, but it was the paperback edition of 1965–66 that took the general audience by storm. In the United States, *LR* outsold the Bible in 1967 and 1968 (Helms 1978: 105), and it became "the absolute favorite book of every hippie" (Hinckle 1967: 25). Hippies married each other in ceremonies based on the book[6] and read passages from *LR* during LSD-trips to amplify the spiritual experience (Ratliff and Flinn 1968: 144; Clifton 1987).[7] Some readers wondered whether *LR* was in fact a parable about Faery and joined the emerging Neo-Pagan movement to explore the Celtic and Germanic mythologies from which Tolkien had drawn much of his inspiration. Pagan scholar, Graham Harvey, has observed that even today Pagans typically mention "Tolkien's *Lord of the Rings* and other Fantasy writings" rather than "how to do it" manuals when asked to name the sources that have most significantly influenced their Pagan world-view (Harvey 2007: 176).

We have evidence of one 1960s-group that read *LR* as ancient history and hoped to excavate Minas Tirith in the Mojave Desert (Ellwood 2002: 133), but typically hippies and Pagans considered Tolkien's books to be inspiring fiction rather than revelation or historiography. For them, Tolkien's narratives did not refer directly to real supernatural beings and powers, but provided, in Harvey's words, the "metaphorical binoculars through which the realm of Faery became visible again" (2000). Following Harvey, I suggest using the designation 'binocular mode' to refer to the approach to a narrative corpus, such as the Neo-Pagan approach to *LR*, that does not ascribe metaphysical reference to the texts themselves, but stresses instead the texts' sacred intertextuality.

Tolkien died in 1973, but in 1977 his son Christopher published an edited collection of his father's mythological backstories entitled *The Silmarillion (S)*. *S* narrates the history of the world according to the lore of the Elves and begins OT-style with the creation of the world *ex nihilo* by the over-god Eru (the One) or Ilúvatar (All-Father). The Ainur (Holy Ones), a group of angelic beings, reside with Eru outside Eä (the World), but some of them choose to incarnate and help shape the world and instruct Ilúvatar's Children, the Quendi (Elves) and the humans. The 14 most powerful demiurges are referred to as the Valar (Powers); the less powerful are the Maiar (the Beautiful). We learn that the Wizard Gandalf, a major character in *LR*, belongs to the class of Maiar, and that Elbereth, the chief deity of the Elven religion in *LR*, is Queen of the Valar.

The publication of *S* led to the emergence of enduring groups that went beyond the binocular approach to Tolkien's literary mythology. These groups build elements from Tolkien's cosmology into their regular ritual practice and typically approach Tolkien's narratives in what I call the 'mytho-cosmological mode'. That is, they consider the storyline to be fictitious, but believe that at least some of the supernatural entities, such as the Valar, exist in the actual world and can be communicated with in ritual. A minority go even further and approach the Legendarium in the 'mytho-historical mode', considering some or all of the actions of the supernatural beings in Tolkien's narratives to refer to real interventions of these beings in the actual world.

The largest of the *S*-based groups is the Tribunal of the Sidhe, a Neo-Pagan organisation founded in 1984 on the American West Coast. The Tribunal of the Sidhe synthesises Tolkien's literary mythology with Celtic mythology, Wicca, and Robert Graves-inspired goddess worship – and some of the group's rituals are directed at the Valar, including the fertility Valië Yavanna.[8] Members of the Tribunal also claim to be Changelings, that is Elves (or similar beings) from an astral world who have been incarnated in human bodies by mistake. They say that "magickal research" has established that Tolkien was a Changeling himself and that *LR* and *S* tell the history of the Changelings in mythic form. Today, the Tribunal boasts a total of 150 members, many of whom are second generation.[9]

Already prior to the publication of *S*, a movement of self-identified Elves had emerged when a Ouija board spirit allegedly instructed a group of American magicians to name themselves the Elf Queen's Daughters sometime around 1970. The original members of the Elf Queen's Daughters told Margot Adler (1986: 319) that their identification as Elves was tongue-in-cheek, but they inspired other people to self-identify as Elves, and these people went on to speculate about possessing Elven genes or Elven souls. The publication of *S* in

1977 consolidated the Elven movement's foundation on Tolkien and inspired members to experiment with Valar-directed rituals. This did not last, however, and from the 1990s onwards, most self-identified Elves have distanced themselves from Tolkien's fiction and emphasised their dependence on sources they consider more legitimate, especially as pre-Christian mythology and folklore. They did so under the influence of the broader Otherkin movement (cf. Laycock 2012), which has itself been eager to deny its fiction-based character. Zardoa Love and Silver Flame, together known as the Silver Elves, are the Elven movement's most important intellectuals, and their regular Magical Elven Love Letters have provided coherence and direction for a growing Elven community from the early 1980s.[10]

In 2001, 2002 and 2003 Peter Jackson's successful movie adaptation of *LR* premiered in three instalments, and, in the years that followed, a large number of Tolkien-inspired groups emerged online, especially on Yahoo! Groups and ProBoards. Most of these groups were devoted to two new types of Tolkien spirituality: Middle-earth Paganism and Legendarium Reconstructionism. Middle-earth Pagans drew most of their inspiration from Jackson's movies, which they considered as canonical as Tolkien's books. Since the Valar do not play any role in the movies, Middle-earth Pagans directed their ritual communication at the characters of the movies – especially Gandalf and Galadriel, but also Arwen and Aragorn, and even Frodo and Éowyn. The aim of these groups was not to develop a fully fledged tradition, but to construct a Middle-earth 'path' that Pagans could use in combination with other paths.

Tië eldaliéva and Ilsaluntë Valion are examples of Legendarium Reconstructionism, a form of Tolkien spirituality which stands in stark contrast to Middle-earth Paganism. Legendarium Reconstructionists do not consider Jackson's movies to have any spiritual significance, but draw instead on a whole range of textual sources. They prefer *S* to *LR*, and, in addition to this, they familiarise themselves with Tolkien's letters (Tolkien 1981) and Christopher Tolkien's 12 edited volumes of *History of Middle-earth* (*HoMe*) (Tolkien 1983–1996). *HoMe* includes the earliest drafts of the stories that were to become *LR* and *S*, non-narrative material about the Elves and the Valar, and two aborted 'time-travel' stories in which Tolkien stages Middle-earth as our world in prehistory. The firm textual foundation of Legendarium Reconstructionism has made possible a second key characteristic of this type of Tolkien spirituality: Legendarium Reconstructionists attribute a centrality to Tolkien's texts not found in any other type of Tolkien-inspired spirituality. Whereas Middle-earth Pagans, the Tribunal of the Sidhe and all other groups discussed above integrate Tolkien material into some broader (typically Neo-Pagan) framework, Tië eldaliéva and Ilsaluntë Valion aim to base their spiritual practice exclusively on Tolkien's Legendarium. The ambition has been to construct a fully fledged and independent tradition by systematising the scattered information on the Valar and the Quendi (the Elves) in Tolkien's texts and by adding 'Tolkien-true'

Elven Path and Silver Ship of the Valar   19

inventions to fill the gaps where needed. I refer to this form of Tolkien spirituality as Legendarium Reconstructionism, because it mirrors the approach of Pagan Reconstructionists.

The emergence of Legendarium Reconstructionism

Tië eldaliéva was founded in August 2005 on the initiative of two Americans, Nathan Elwin and Calantirniel (Lisa M. Allen MH). At this time, Elwin had spent almost three decades searching for likeminded people. He had often encountered people who integrated Tolkien's mythology into a broader Neo-Pagan framework, but felt more affinity with individuals who asserted that Tolkien's works convey esoteric knowledge or 'gnosis'. A lecture by Stephen Hoeller, entitled "J.R.R. Tolkien's gnosis for our day", had made a particularly strong impression. In this lecture, the long-time leader of the Ecclesia Gnostica in Los Angeles explained that Tolkien had visited the Imaginal Realm and that his narratives reflected the gnosis which he had so received.[11] After listening to this lecture, Elwin decided to found a group devoted to the gnostic exploration of the Legendarium, and in February 2005 he launched the newsgroup UTolk (short for United Tolkienists) on Yahoo Groups![12]

One of those attracted to UTolk was Calantirniel. A Neo-Pagan and an astrologer, Calantirniel had been fascinated with the Star Queen deity in various mythologies, and she had thoroughly enjoyed Jackson's *LR* movies. When she finally read *S* in 2005, she discovered that the name of the main deity of the Elves – Elbereth in Sindarin and Varda in Quenya – means 'Star Queen', and she instantly knew that she wanted to join or found a tradition based on the spirituality of Tolkien's Elves. After a few weeks of hectic online networking, she found Elwin and UTolk, and took the Elvish name, Calantirniel, meaning (Lady) Guardian of the Gift of Light in Sindarin.

In early 2005, a group of UTolk members, including Elwin and Calantirniel, decided to construct a Tolkien-based tradition and name it Tië eldaliéva (The Elven Path). The new tradition was officially launched with a 'birthing ritual' held via phone on 23 August 2005, and on 23 January 2006, a discussion forum was launched on the bulletin board hosting site Freebb. com. The forum remained active until Freebb.com closed its services on 30 August 2007, at which time it had 59 registered members, out of which 27 were active posters. All significant contributions, however, came from a smaller core group that besides Elwin and Calantirniel counted Lomion, a Wiccan who helped create the birthing ritual; Llefyn Mallwen, a Canadian Pagan; Niennildi, Elwin's wife and a metaphysical Christian; Lomelindo, who had a background in Heathen Reconstructionism; and Ellenar, who claimed to have been communicating with fairies and elementals since childhood. In early August 2007, the core group launched a homepage stating that Tië eldaliéva aimed to "re-create, as closely as possible the original spirituality and way of the Elves, and in particular of the 'Quendi' . . . described in

20   *Markus Altena Davidsen*

JRR Tolkien's . . . writings".[13] Members believed it possible for humans to possess a partly Quendian soul and/or some portion of Quendian genes, but the emphasis of the group was on the *wisdom* of the Elves. As Calantirniel put it, the guiding question – on both spiritual and quotidian matters – was 'What would the Elves do?'

Legendarium Reconstructionist rituals

The Elves in Tolkien's narratives worship Eru and venerate the Valar, but Tolkien's texts provide few clues to *how* the Elves went about doing this. This is because Tolkien, himself a devout Catholic, was afraid that explicit descriptions of Pagan cult would make his novels look too blasphemous. Individuals engaging in Tolkien-based spirituality are therefore required to construct their own rituals. The Tië eldaliéva core group did this by adapting the form and content of Wiccan and ceremonial magical rituals to the Legendarium.[14] Furthermore, Elwin constructed a ritual year calendar with 13 lunar and 8 solar observances, based on scattered references in the Legendarium.

From August 2006 onwards, rituals following the new format and calendar were carried out by about four to seven people over the phone and later on Skype. After the hive-off in late 2007, Ilsaluntë Valion members modified the format, and members continued to do rituals collectively throughout 2008 – over Skype in Tië eldaliéva and over the phone in Ilsaluntë Valion. From 2009, it became normal practice in both groups to perform rituals individually, though ideally still according to the shared format. The transition to individual rituals had to do partly with the disadvantages of the media, as the phone/Skype-mediated rituals were experienced as hectic and counterproductive to inducing a meditative state of mind. Other reasons were that post-schism Tië eldaliéva had become too small to muster enough members for collective rituals, while Ilsaluntë Valion had attracted new core members from Europe for whom it was impractical to perform rituals simultaneously with the original North American members. Despite these practical problems, members hope to revive the practice of collective, mediated rituals and to perform them with members of Tië eldaliéva and Ilsaluntë Valion together. Table 1.1 below gives a synoptic overview of the phases of a typical Tië eldaliéva ritual, compared to the standard Wiccan circle casting ritual and to the rituals of Ilsaluntë Valion as they were developed after the schism.

Tië eldaliéva rituals

Tië eldaliéva constructed a new ritual format according to the logic of ritual innovation which Ivan Marcus (1996) has termed "inward acculturation". Coined in a study of Jewish ritual innovation in a dominating Christian context, inward acculturation refers to the integration of ritual content and forms from a larger tradition (Marcus: Christianity; here: Wicca and

Table 1.1 Structure of Legendarium Reconstructionist rituals

	Wiccan Circle casting	Tië eldaliéva (2007–)	Ilsaluntë Valion (2009–)
Separation phase	1 Preparation of food 2 Drawing the circle 3 Grounding; centring 4 Calling the Quarters	1 Song of the Starflower 2 Draw septagram in the air to seal energy (see Figure 1.1) 3 Acknowledgement of the directions and evocation of the Valar 4 Reading from Tolkien's literary mythology 5 Drinking starflower-infused water 6 Visualisation of Oneness with Arda	1 Preparation of altar and food 2 Blessing Circle Dance (or Song of the Starflower) 3 Awareness of Arda as Sacred Sphere 4 Reading from Tolkien's literary mythology 5 Intonation of Valarin name 6 Communication with Lunar Radiance
Liminal phase	5 Communication with deities; other magical work	7 Individual Otherworld experience, including direct communication with one or more of the Valar, initiated by reading	7 Individual Otherworld experience, initiated by reading 8 The flower of Telperion is thanked
Reintegration phase	6 Opening the circle 7 Cakes and wine ceremony	8 Returning awareness to physical space 9 Opening the circle	9 Returning awareness to physical space 10 The blessed food is eaten

Figure 1.1 Figure of the Septagram.

ceremonial magic) into one's own, typically smaller, local or dependent tradition (Marcus: Judaism; here: Legendarium Reconstructionism). The effect of inward acculturation is to construct and maintain an independent tradition and identity, while at the same time adapting and naturalising foreign elements.

Most fundamentally, Tië eldaliéva's rituals adopted the general structure of Wiccan circle casting and ceremonial magical rituals, with (a) a separation phase in which a sacred space is created and the participants prepare themselves, (b) a liminal phase in which contact with the deities (here: Valar, Maiar and Quendi) is established and experienced, and (c) a reintegration phase in which the deities are thanked and dismissed, and the circle is opened. Also, the individual separation rites were crafted by adapting existing Wiccan/magical rites to Tolkien's mythology. First, the lesser pentagram ritual, which ceremonial magicians use to prepare a space for magical work, was developed into a septagram ritual called Lindë Elenlótë (Quenya: Song of the Starflower), as members felt seven to be the sacred number in Tolkien's literary mythology. Second, the Wiccan Calling of the Quarters was transformed into a seven-phased evocation of the Valar in pairs of two. This entailed adding two directions, Above and Below, to the five ordinary directions, East, South, West, North and Within.[15] Gestures and intonations in Quenya were crafted for all directions, and a short greeting was written for each Valar pair. Third, following the drinking of water infused by starflower essence,[16] a Tolkien-based visualisation sequence was constructed as a variation of the Middle Pillar exercise (cf. Regardie 1998: 85–100, 218–219). At this stage, participants visualise themselves circulating the light from Telperion and Laurelin (the two primordial trees and the first sources of light in Tolkien's world) through their chakras, then visualise themselves being one with Arda (the Earth).

At the end of the visualisation sequence, participants visualise themselves being within the Blessed Realm, the home of the Elves and the Valar in Tolkien's cosmology, and a short text, which is different in every ritual, is read aloud, describing a particular scene and perhaps introducing one of the Valar as a guide. Then follows the liminal climax of the ritual, 5–20 minutes of silent meditation in which the vision is allowed to unfold. Typically, the guide conveys some information of relevance for the personal lives of the participants, but some members have experienced receiving messages about the Valar or other aspects of Tolkien's cosmology as well. After the meditation, participants gradually return to the physical world, detach themselves from the Oneness with Arda and slow down the circulation of light/energy from the Two Trees. A bit of the "healing energy" from the Two Trees is brought back and the participants visualise carrying it in their pockets, ready for use when needed. To get an idea of the feeling of a Tië eldaliéva ritual, consider the climax of the visualisation ritual for Enderi, the Elven mid-year festival, falling around 25 September. This particular ritual is focused on the Vala Oromë.

> [Stage 6] Close your eyes and notice you are standing on Corollairë, the Green Mound of the Two Trees. . . . Circulate this silver light [of Telperion] to your Ajna or third eye chakra, as well as your sacral (orange) chakra, about 3 inches below your belly button. . . . Next, feel your tree roots pushing deeper and deeper into Arda, our Earth, and allow Arda to nurture and nourish you. . . . You are feeling VERY supported by Arda now, and in fact, you ARE Arda. . . . You may also connect with the Valar and/or your Maiar or Elven guides at this point. . . . You may be more fully re-awakening your Elven DNA and ancestral memory. . . .

> [Stage 7] Then, visualise yourself with the protective, hunting Vala Oromë on his white horse with his horn, and he may have hounds with him. . . . Allow all the time you need for this to occur . . . [Individual meditation].

> [Stage 8] Now, your meditation can come to a close when the time is right. Thank the Valar, especially Oromë, and your Maiar or Elven Guides for their assistance, and slowly come back to the physical world, remembering what transpired!

As mentioned in the introduction, the complete Enderi ritual, together with a glossary and an overview of Tië eldaliéva's ritual calendar, can be found on the group's homepage.[17]

Ritual practice is important for Legendarium Reconstructionists as it expresses their identity as both decidedly Tolkien-centred and markedly different from more mere fans. Perhaps for this reason, differences in ritual taste proved a source of tension and were one of the drivers behind the schism in 2007. The schismatic founders of Ilsaluntë Valion considered Tië eldaliéva "too Pagan" and championed a more purist take on Legendarium Reconstructionism. They modified the ritual format accordingly.

24 *Markus Altena Davidsen*

Ilsaluntë Valion rituals

In Ilsaluntë Valion's rituals, most references to Legendarium-foreign concepts (*mudras*, *chakras*) and rites (pentagram ritual, Middle Pillar) were purged and new ritual elements were developed as substitutions. To raise energy, for example, most Ilsaluntë Valion members use the gestures and intonations of the Blessed Circle Dance rather than the Song of the Starflower, because the former is not based directly on the pentagram ritual. Similarly, the visualisation sequence of Ilsaluntë Valion no longer includes a circulation of energy via the chakras, but has become richer in references to Tolkien's cosmology – for example to the three Airs (Vilna, Ilwë and Vaitya) and the Great Sea (Vai). Another new element, which substitutes the evocation of the 14 Valar in the Tië eldaliéva ritual, is the intonation of the name of the Vala or Maia to which the ritual is dedicated. The name is intoned in Valarin, the language of the Valar themselves, and several of the Valarin names used in this phase have supposedly been discovered by one of the members in trance.

Whereas the Ilsaluntë Valion ritual compresses the ceremonial separation rites to a bare minimum, it expands the liminal phase by doubling the ritual structure of separation-liminality-reintegration *within* the liminal phase itself. This has been done to create a feeling of actively journeying to the Blessed Realm via the Moon (in the case of a lunar observation) or via the Sun (in the case of a solar observation). As illustration, consider the climax of the Isilnarquelië (Moon of the Fiery Fading) ritual, a moon ritual focused on Oromë. This version of the ritual is from 8 October 2011.

> [Stage 6] Close your eyes and envision the full moon, aloft within the starry heavens, filling the Earth with slender lights and deep quick-moving shadows; sending radiant dreams that go with cool wings about the world. . . . Behold the last flower of Telperion, floating in a shimmering, water-like substance. . . . *Feel it, breathe it. Slowly.* Then, when you feel that you are ready to proceed, exhale – still very slowly – and while you do, the Moon-vessel recedes into the distance.
>
> [Stage 7] From afar you hear the rolling echo of the Master's horn Valaróma. Its majesty shakes the hills and the shadows of night flee at its music. You answer the call of Lord Aldaron as he circles his people and cattle on the shining white Nahar. . . . [Individual meditation] When your journey is complete, thank Oromë and any others who assisted you or offered teaching and retrace your steps to where you arrived.

Members explain that one can travel to the Blessed Realm via the Moon or the Sun because these heavenly bodies exist both in the physical world and in the Blessed Realm. It is done by first visualising the Moon/Sun as it looks in the physical world ("aloft within the starry heavens") and thereafter visualising it as it is described in Tolkien's mythology (holding the flower of Telperion as its light source). The core of the ritual has remained the silent meditation in which participants experience the Blessed Realm, but Ilsaluntë Valion has transformed the ritual frame around this climax from a ceremonial magical evocation of the Valar into something more reminiscent of a shamanic journey. The new format did not put an end to the debates about how to properly approach Tolkien's cosmology in ritual, however, and while all members of Ilsaluntë Valion make visualisation journeys to the Blessed Realm, some members prefer to use modified or simplified versions of the official liturgy. As members of Ilsaluntë Valion put it themselves, the ritualistic approach is only one of three ways of spiritually appreciating Tolkien's Legendarium. The other two are the (sub-)creative and the mytho-historic approaches. The (sub-creative) approach takes Tolkien as an artistic-cum-spiritual role model and seeks to connect to the Faery Otherworld, such as Tolkien is believed to have done, in order to draw from the same inspirational font as he did. The mytho-historical approach is more intellectual and aims to systematise the historical and religious lore in the Legendarium and to relate it to the historical record and the mythologies of the actual world. Most members combine several approaches, but tend to emphasise one in particular. A group of members emphasising the (sub-)creative approach have established a forum, Anima Mundi, in which they discuss their own experiences and those of Tolkien in the light of C.G. Jung's ideas.

Cosmology and theology in Legendarium Reconstructionism

I have emphasised that the rituals of Tië eldaliéva and Ilsaluntë Valion have been a cause of debate and division, but that is only half the story. Just as importantly, the groups' ritual formats result from collaboration and express two 'first-order beliefs' that all members share. These beliefs are (1) that Tolkien's literary mythology refers to real supernatural beings, namely the Valar, the Maiar and the Quendi, and (2) that these beings dwell in a world that is different from the physical world, but which can be accessed in ritual. On top of these core beliefs, Legendarium Reconstructionism has a superstructure of more detailed and reflective 'second-order beliefs' concerning Tolkien's world and its supernatural denizens.

All members of Tië eldaliéva and Ilsaluntë Valion agree that Tolkien's narratives refer to an independent, non-material reality, and, inspired by Henry Corbin (1972), they refer to this reality as "the Imaginal Realm". With references to Islamic esotericism, Corbin claimed that the Imagination (which he always capitalises) constitutes both a valid source of knowledge and a realm or mode of being, the *Mundus Imaginalis* or the Imaginal Realm. He coined the term "Imaginal" to emphasise the reality of the Imaginal as opposed to the non-reality of the merely "imaginary". The notion of the Imaginal Realm entered the vocabulary of Legendarium Reconstructionism through Stephan Hoeller who argues, in the lecture on Tolkien and gnosis already mentioned, that Tolkien had accessed the

26   *Markus Altena Davidsen*

Imaginal Realm and that his narratives are based on Imaginal experiences. Tolkien himself never spoke of the Imaginal Realm, but in his short-story *Smith of Wootton Major* he makes a comparable distinction between World and Faery.[18] The Legendarium Reconstructionists follow Hoeller in considering Tolkien's distinction between World and Faery synonymous with Corbin's distinction between the material world and the Imaginal Realm. They differ in opinion, however, on how to relate the distinction between the material world and the Imaginal Realm/Faery to another of Tolkien's cosmological distinctions, that between Middle-earth and the Blessed Realm. Those who approach Tolkien's narratives in the mytho-historical mode, and hence consider the Legendarium to refer in some way to historical events in the actual world, equate Middle-earth with our physical world, and consider the Blessed Realm synonymous with the Imaginal Realm/Faery. This makes good sense, for even though the Blessed Realm is part of the created world within Tolkien's cosmology, it is no longer physically connected to Middle-earth at the time of the narrator of *LR*.[19] By contrast, those members who approach Tolkien's literary mythology in the mytho-cosmological mode consider both the Blessed Realm *and* Middle-earth to be situated within the Imaginal Realm/Faery, or at least believe that Tolkien's descriptions of the Blessed Realm and Middle-earth reflect genuine experiences of Faery. For both groups, the notion of the Imaginal Realm serves to explain how the Valar and the Blessed Realm can be real, although they do not exist in our physical world. Table 1.2 below gives an overview of the mytho-historical and mytho-cosmological rationalisations of Tolkien's narrative cosmology.

Members of Tië eldaliéva and Ilsaluntë Valion largely agree on the nature of Eru/Ilúvatar and the Valar. Most fundamentally, they agree that Eru and the Valar exist and follow Tolkien's description of the relationship between them: Eru is the supreme deity and the Valar are created beings and subordinated Eru. Therefore, while members focus their ritual work on the Valar, they stress that they do not worship these beings. Those members in particular who have a Christian rather than a Neo-Pagan background, point out that the Valar are not gods, but are rather on a par with (arch)angelic

Table 1.2 Rationalisations of Tolkien's narrative cosmology

Corbin's esoteric cosmology	*The cosmology in Smith*	*Tolkien's cosmology in the Middle-earth text corpus*	
		The mytho-historical fit	*The mytho-cosmological fit*
The Imaginal Realm	Faery	The Blessed Realm	The Blessed Realm; Middle-earth
The Material World	World	Middle-earth	–

beings. In fact, all members de-emphasise the ontological difference between themselves and the Valar and approach them as teachers and role models, or even as friends with whom they "hang out", as Calantirniel put it when I participated with her and Llefyn.

In Tolkien's tales, Eru Ilúvatar is depicted as a male, theistic being residing in distant sovereignty outside the created World, but this image conflicts with the inclination of both Pagan and Christian members to conceive of the divine in holistic, pantheistic terms. Therefore, in the Tië eldaliéva ritual discussed above, Ilúvatar is not addressed directly as a personal power, but participants several times acknowledge their oneness with him in a way that is quite foreign to Tolkien's own theology. Elwin has attempted to solve the tension between Tolkien's patriarchal dualism and the member's holistic inclinations by declaring first Tië eldaliéva and later Ilsaluntë Valion to be *panentheistic* traditions. To the acclaim of the other members, Elwin explained that Eru Ilúvatar is both *outside* Eä (the World), such as Tolkien says, and Eä *itself*, such as the holistic world-view of the members dictates. Elwin supported this view with a reference to Tolkien's own texts, pointing out that Eru creates the world by sending his creative power, the Secret Fire or Flame Imperishable, into the Void (cf. Tolkien 1977: 9, 15). Even so, Tolkien himself never referred to this theology as panentheism and would probably rather have seen it as a reflection of Christian omnipresentism.

In ritual, Legendarium Reconstructionists treat the Valar as discrete, spiritual beings. In theological discussions outside ritual, the Valar are often referred to as "energies", "archetypes", or even "archetypal energies", but such references are not meant to reduce them to non-personal powers or cosmic principles. The Valar, and humans for that matter, are energies and persons at the same time. That the Valar embody *archetypal* energy means that their energy is of a subtler type than that of humans. It also indicates that the Valar stand in some relation to the deities of other pantheons. Members disagree, however, whether the Valarian pantheon constitutes just one manifestation among others of a set of cosmic archetypes that make themselves known also in other mythologies, or whether the Valar *are* these archetypes. According to the latter and bolder view, the Valar (and Maiar) have revealed themselves, in various guises, in the many mythologies and religions around the world, but only Tolkien describes them as they really are.

Why can Tolkien's fantasy function as authoritative texts for religion?

The existence of Tolkien spirituality prompts the question why Tolkien's fantasy can function as authoritative texts for religion, when this is not the case for all fantasy fiction. Why, for example, has no religion emerged from *Harry Potter*, while Tolkien's narratives have given us all kinds of Tolkien spirituality, and George Lucas' *Star Wars* has given rise to Jediism?

28   *Markus Altena Davidsen*

(On Jediism see Davidsen 2016, and the contribution by *The Temple of the Jedi Order* in this volume.) In short: what does it take for a piece of fantasy fiction to be a possible foundational text for a new religion? A comparative study is needed to answer this question properly, but let me risk some tentative conclusions.

First, for a fantasy text to work as a foundational text for a new religion it must include 'narrative religion', i.e. descriptions of religious teachings and institutions, and rituals engaged in by the characters of the story. Tolkien's literary mythology includes some such narrative religion. *LR* includes several Elven hymns to the Valië Elbereth, and an Elven ritual calendar is given in one of the appendices. *S*, and especially *HoMe*, convey much additional information on the theology, eschatology and ritual life of both Elves and humans. For example, *S* tells of the names, abodes and functions of the Valar and in various texts in *HoMe*, makes it clear that humans expect an afterlife with Eru, while the Elves believe in reincarnation. All in all, the narrative religion of Tolkien's literary mythology provides sufficient building-blocks for a religious tradition in the actual world to be based upon it. By comparison, *Star Wars* also includes a narrative religion that lends itself to emulation in the actual world, namely the Force religion of the Jedi Knights, but the *Harry Potter* books do not. This explains the lack of a *Harry Potter*-based religion.

Several additional textual traits can enhance the religious potential of a fantasy narrative. First, it helps if the narrative offers a strong, positive and slightly superhuman identity that people can adopt. In the case of Tolkien spirituality and Jediism, the attractive identities offered are those as Elves and Jedi Knights. Second, the nature of the narrative religion matters. It adds to the religious potential of a fantasy text if its narrative religion is at the forefront of the story, and the narrative religion should ideally present a set of teachings that is appealing to a contemporary audience while at the same time offering a new and distinct religious vocabulary. This is all the case with *Star Wars*. All the main characters are Jedi Knights, and the notion of the Force is immediately recognisable, yet distinctly its own. This may well account for the great success of Jediism, compared to Tolkien spirituality and other fiction-based religions. Third, it enhances the religious potential of a fantasy text if it thematises its own veracity. Tolkien's narratives do this to a remarkable extent, as do some of Tolkien's writings about his narratives. For example, the first edition of *The Fellowship of the Ring* included a preface in which Tolkien thanked both family and friends *and* those Hobbits who had allegedly helped him draw an accurate map of the Shire. Tolkien here mixed up the roles as author and narrator and hence anchored his narrative in the actual world. His preface could be read – and was read – as if he seriously believed in the existence of Hobbits. Tolkien later regretted this, and the second edition from 1965 included both a preface – in which Tolkien as *author* thanks family and friends – and a longer prologue in which a narrator, who is human and close to Tolkien in time and space, yet clearly different from the author, informs the reader of the customs of the Hobbits. *S* has no such frame narrative, but here Tolkien plays with historical anchorage in a different manner. For example, he tells us that Númenor, a continent which is destroyed by Eru after its inhabitants rebel against the Valar, is called Atalantë in the human language. 'Atalantë' is strikingly similar to 'Atlantis', and even if it was really Tolkien who borrowed from Plato, several practitioners of Tolkien spirituality argue that it is the other way around: Plato and Tolkien refer to the same historical event, but Tolkien's account is more accurate. In his letters, Tolkien goes even further, frequently suggesting that he received (divine) inspiration. In one letter he states, "I have long ceased to *invent* . . . I wait till I seem to know what really happened. Or till it writes itself" (Tolkien 1981: 231; original emphasis). In another, he plays with the thought of being a "chosen instrument" (1981: 413). In sum, it is the combination of narrative religion and thematisation of textual veracity that makes Tolkien's literary mythology usable as an authoritative text corpus for real world spirituality.

The persistence of Legendarium Reconstructionist online communities

I mentioned earlier that the success of Peter Jackson's film adaptation of *LR* led to the emergence of two new forms of Tolkien spirituality. Middle-earth Pagans focused on ritual interaction with *LR* characters (especially Gandalf and Galadriel) and offered an expansion pack, so to speak, to Pagans wanting to try out a new pantheon. Legendarium Reconstructionists, as we have seen, base themselves on Tolkien's written works, tolerate little blending of Tolkien's literary mythology with other religious frameworks, and focus on the exploration of Tolkien's cosmology in meditation.

Middle-earth Paganism and Legendarium Reconstructionism have differed remarkably in their ability to produce stable and enduring online communities. All Middle-earth Pagan online groups collapsed after just a few years, while the Legendarium Reconstructionist groups have survived, despite tensions and divergent opinions. I think that three factors can explain the relative success of Legendarium Reconstructionism. First, the Legendarium Reconstructionist online forums have been much better moderated. This has given members a feeling of contributing to a collaborative project and counteracted the "strain to variety" (cf. Campbell 1972: 128) that often causes cults to loose focus and dissolve. By contrast, the more loosely moderated forums and newsgroups of Middle-earth Pagans, Children of the Valar, the Eldalondë Society and many similar groups soon hosted more discussions of Vampirism, reiki healing, sunken Egyptian cities and guardian angels than on Tolkien spirituality. In these groups, total collapse followed quickly after the Tolkien focus was lost.[20]

30   *Markus Altena Davidsen*

A second reason for the success of Tië eldaliéva and Ilsaluntë Valion has to do with their membership. Already when joining, the core members had a substantial knowledge about Tolkien's literary mythology, and most had already experimented with Tolkien-based rituals. They were intelligent and highly educated individuals in their forties, thirties or late twenties, with plenty of knowledge and experience to share. This stands in contrast to the members of the Middle-earth Pagan groups who were mostly young people who were fascinated by Elves and Jackson's films, but were in no position to contribute substantially in terms of spiritual knowledge.

The third reason for the Legendarium Reconstructionists' successful community formation is that they from the beginning aimed to construct an independent tradition. This sometimes caused disagreement and tension, but it also led to the formulation of certain core ideas and a sense of shared identity. Most significantly, rituals were developed and carried out together. Even though most members eventually found it unsatisfying to perform rituals via Skype or over the phone, all members continued to believe that Tolkien's narratives describe a real world in some way, and that the various ritual techniques used by the members constitute a repertoire of legitimate ways of communicating with this otherworld and achieving gnosis about it. This again stands in contrast to the modest Middle-earth Pagan aim of developing an optional Tolkienesque add-on for eclectic Wiccans. Moreover, Legendarium Reconstructionism has had the advantage of being based on a larger authoritative text corpus. *S* and the many other texts by Tolkien simply demand more time and effort to discuss and digest than do the *LR* movies, and that provides for long-lived groups. The *LR* movies, by contrast, provided too little textual substance for tradition-building (they include no substantial narrative religion, and do not thematise their own veracity). After trying out some movie-based rituals, most Middle-earth Pagans went back to being 'normal' Pagans, while a few went on to read *S*, began working with the Valar and hence turned into Legendarium Reconstructionists.

It must be admitted that the relative stability of the Legendarium Reconstructionist online cults as social units says little about the attractiveness of Legendarium Reconstructionism relative to Middle-earth Paganism as a religious expression. The Legendarium Reconstructionist groups are stable, but they are tiny and hardly grow. Working occasional rituals with Gandalf and Galadriel has proved to be no basis for tradition-forming and institutionalisation, but it has been attractive for many Pagans to try out all the same. From a numerical perspective, Middle-earth Paganism, rather than Legendarium Reconstructionism, has been the most successful expression of Tolkien spirituality in the twenty-first century. But, if there were a prize for the most elaborate fiction-based religious tradition, it would probably go to the spiritual entrepreneurs of Tië eldaliéva and Ilsaluntë Valion.

Appendix 1.1 Tië eldaliéva

*Reverend Michaele Alyras de Cygne
and Calantirniel*[21]

Origins of the Elven Path

"Tië eldaliéva" (The Elven Path) began in May of 2005 when, seeking others who were like-minded regarding the sense of J.R.R. Tolkien's writings being more than fiction, Nathan Elwin (pseudonym) and Calantirniel (Lisa M. Allen MH) met online as kindred spirits. Quickly, they discovered they had great parity relative to their perspectives on Tolkien's work, and they began to lay the foundation for what is now known as the sacred tradition of "The Elven Path". By August of 2005, what began with Calantirniel and Elwin grew to involve others, from different spiritual backgrounds, and Tië eldaliéva (T-e) was formally established as an organization, centrally focused on advancing the awareness and formal practice of Elven spirituality, with a respectably wide diversity of spiritual backgrounds among its members. In November 2007, T-e evolved into two separate expressions of the Path, the other being led by Elwin and named "Ilsaluntë Valion, the Silver Ship of the Valar". Valuing the development of the Path in such a way that increasing numbers of Eldalië and Elendili (Elves and friends of Elves, respectively) would be able to be served by it, the group established its Inner Circle to be a core, guiding (rather than governing) body. Presently, T-e is based online at www.ElvenSpirituality.com, serving members worldwide.

Beliefs and practices

The principles of T-e's practices arise from their core beliefs which are, in turn, derived from the Legendarium, as well as innate talents and understood relationships. The core beliefs and practices of T-e enable its members to explore, apply and practice the Elven Path individually and together; differently and alike.

Beliefs. Embraced as a sacred text, T-e believes that all insight, wisdom and inspiration relative to the Path may be found in the Legendarium, without reference to any other text. Nonetheless, they all recognize that Truth is not confined to the Elven Path, nor, therefore to the Legendarium; hence, they are able to appreciate many principles of other sacred traditions, as

32   *Markus Altena Davidsen*

such traditions may be analogous to those of the Path and, at their discretion, to apply them in their individual practices. T-e members believe the Valar (reasonably analogous to Archangels) are literal entities, as Tolkien described them, who are the Powers underlying and sustaining all life on Earth, or "Arda". They believe the Valar deeply love and are profoundly interested in both Elves and humanity, and that they (the Valar) are willing to befriend, teach, nurture and even nourish human beings, no differently than Elves, in order progress the evolution of planetary Consciousness towards a collective transformation of Earth into a perfected expression of Arda, as it exists within the Mind of Eru (God). Consequently, T-e members believe that developing personal relationship with the Valar leads to insight, wisdom and a right perspective on how to live as spiritual beings in the context of the Elven Path; hence, the nature of their practices.

Practices. The practices of T-e are rooted ritual and meditation, and are primarily relative to developing the personal relationship between the individual and the Valar. To that end, monthly, circa the Full Moon, the group engages in a formal ritual focused on interacting with one or more of the Valar. As the year progresses, there are also several Tolkien-designated holidays, or Holy Days, upon which ritual is also performed that is also relative to the Valar, the Ainur (the siblings and offspring of the Valar, collectively), and/or the Maiar (servants of the Valar). T-e members practice their rituals individually, generally communicating their relative experiences, lessons and consequent insights with each other, privately, online.

One of the most important practices of T-e is education, i.e. providing the public, and particularly the Eldalië and Elendili, with educational materials (from their website and social media outlets) enabling them to become more familiar with the underpinnings of the Elven Path. At the time of this writing, the Inner Circle is preparing to expand that offering with materials providing a deeper understanding of principles and processes facilitating integration of the Path into the adherent's ritual and meditation practices, and into practical, daily life.

Practising differently, alike

Although the members of T-e's Inner Circle (Calantirniel, Llefyn, Earendil and Alyras) are united in their perspectives on the Legendarium, the Valar and the importance of maintaining the integrity of the Elven Path, the way they practically apply the Path in their lives remarkably differs, one from another. These practical differences primarily come from the varying spiritual backgrounds of each member prior to joining T-e; Alyras coming from a mostly Christian, mystical viewpoint, and the other three arriving from more earth-based, pre-Christian viewpoints. Earendil's primary practice is not through formal ritual at all, but, instead, he implements his healing skills through creating a lively, bustling, professional holistic herbology practice. In the context of what is effectively his own "Rivendell", he also created

Elven Path and Silver Ship of the Valar 33

and lives in an organic, vegan and eco-sustainable permaculture homestead. Llefyn explores the Path primarily in the context of the astral plane, engaging the Powers on subtle and dynamic levels more than the others. Calantirniel's practice is similar to Earendil's, insofar as she is a herbalist. However, her professional astrology and divination background provide a more esoteric, yet solid method of solitary ritual practice that easily scales to a group setting. (Calantirniel wrote much of the group's initial rituals.) Just as a composer has an intuitive relationship with Music, Alyras, (as the musician of the Circle), is primarily focused on developing and learning what's necessary to teach others how to have an intuitive, constant, in-the-moment camaraderie-like communication with the Valar – as a student, as a sibling and as a friend – with and without the ritual process facilitating such communion. With the lunar and other periodic rituals, and meditations as the lattice binding their practices, Tië eldaliéva's Inner Circle is a snapshot of the general demographic comprising its members, with respect to the organization's beliefs, principles and practices.

To give interested readers an idea of our ritual practice, we have published an exemplary ritual on the Tië eldaliéva homepage. We have chosen the Enderi ritual which takes place in late September and is dedicated to the Vala Oromë. The ritual is published together with a glossary of Tolkienesque terms and an overview of the solar and lunar observances of our ritual calendar. The ritual can be found here: http://www.tieeldalieva.org/docs/ritual/enderi.pdf.

Appendix 1.2 Ilsalunë Valion

Gwineth

Ilsalunë Valion is a small online community of individuals who have in common that they find the mythos as described by J.R.R Tolkien in his books meaningful and relevant to their own lives and the world at large beyond the level of mere amusement. However, there are significant differences among the members regarding how they exactly view the material, how it is integrated into their world-view and what they do with it. The word "gnosis" is used inside Ilsalunë Valion to refer to the individual and experiential nature of spiritual practices based upon Tolkien's mythology; but it also refers to the manner in which Tolkien dealt with his own creative experiences (as is shown by Stephan Hoeller and Lance Owens of gnosis.org).

I feel I should stress that there is no such thing as 'a Tolkien religion', as some newspaper journalists eagerly wrote following the publication of Markus Altena Davidsen's thesis, ostensibly misunderstanding this point and, in one case, even denying ever having received the explanation that I wrote and sent to them. Having said that, we can distinguish three basic approaches in how Ilsalunë Valion members deal with the subject matter. A common concept shared by all is "Faerie", which is the term that Tolkien used to denote the particular imaginative realm or 'creative space' that he explored and through which the raw material for his books came to him. Note the term "explore" here, as opposed to "making up", a distinction that he often stressed in his letters and elsewhere. "Faerie" seems to be equivalent to what C.G. Jung calls "the Collective Unconscious" (Jung 1990 [1959]), or Henry Corbin "the Imaginal" (Corbin 1964). We also have in common that accessing this realm is one of the basic elements of what we do in the context of Ilsalunë Valion.

The first approach could be described as ritualistic. It is loosely inspired by the (Neo-)Pagan tradition, and it tries to construct a consistent framework based on the mythos (especially the Elvish calendar), tied to a meaningful harmony with the nature and the Moon cycles. It can be combined with meditations on a key element identified for the occasion, readings of certain texts from the mythology and possibly other ritualistic or creative elements.

Next to the shared attraction we all feel to Tolkien's mythos, people can be motivated to take this approach in order to improve balance and (spiritual) well-being.

The (sub-)creative approach is different in that it is not motivated by explicitly seeking balance or spiritual growth, but by a deeply felt urge to create things: drawings, writings, music, whatever. You could say that this is similar to what drove Tolkien himself (and many other artists). Meditations using the active imagination technique can be very helpful; and vice versa, the creative act tends to enhance the awareness of Faerie so that, ideally, this becomes a self-amplifying process. Apart from the creative act itself, there is often the urge to "bring back some of the Faerie Gold": to do something with the result, no matter how small.

Then there is an approach that could labelled as mytho-historic. The overall goal of this approach is to gain a deeper understanding of Mytho-History: how the Imaginal and factual worlds interweave and interrelate. This approach can involve elements from other traditions that seem compatible with gnosis, such as animism. Entheogens can also be useful, if applied wisely and carefully. In contrast to the sub-creative approach described above, individuals with this motivation might want to share their experiences and findings as well – albeit in different form (e.g. rather a document than a painting).

Of course, this is just one possible categorisation. In reality, these categories overlap even in this very small population. The ritualistic approach can be a powerful tool in the creative process, even if you are not interested in following the integral Elvish calendar which, in turn, has been assembled using the mytho-historic approach. Inversely, creative results have proved very helpful in meditative trance-inducing formats. There are as many paths as there are persons, each one based on the individual's needs and talents.

The most striking feature of the whole business remains almost indescribable: the Imaginal experience itself and its profound, life-changing effects, and how it relates to the observable, factual world outside. Any factual description can only relate what it looks like from the outside, plus whatever people report about it. I have often found it a somewhat alienating experience to read Markus' descriptions; it was as if he were writing about something entirely different because the most important feature is missing altogether. But that can not be helped: a thesis is a scientific paper, dealing with observable facts only. However, the news articles following Markus' defence lacked his genuine interest and care, aiming straight for "look what these crazy people believe in!"

Still, I understand this reaction very well. Because of my background in physics, I have a well-developed rational side; at times I can almost feel that part of me shrugging. I have never been able to make sense of all this from that vantage point, even when it feels completely natural and homely as seen from the Imaginal position. These two worlds seem to be essentially orthogonal to one another: the Imaginal cannot be understood or described in factual terms, as many greater minds have concluded before me. Lacking this acknowledgement, you get religions claiming factual evidence, materialistic New-Age balderdash and other such distorted hybrid constructs; and from the other side, atheists who reject every religious notion because they think religion is about "unfalsifiable weirdo hypotheses". The reason is the notion that "the Imaginal" is nothing but a fanciful falsehood. If there is anything that I have learned from my experience in Ilsaluntë Valion, it is that this is wrong – but that, too, has been said before by many, such as Albert Einstein. If only people would listen.

Notes

1 Personal communication, 7 May 2009. Gwineth is a pseudonym.
2 Qenya is an early form of Quenya or 'Elf-Latin', one of Tolkien's two main Elvish languages. Sindarin, the other main Elven tongue, was the Elven vernacular in Middle-earth at the time of *The Lord of the Rings*. The homepage of Ilsaluntë Valion can be visited at westofwest.org. Accessed 15 April 2015.
3 Nathan Elwin is a pseudonym.
4 Tië eldaliéva's homepage is located at elvenspirituality.wordpress.com. Accessed 15 April 2015.
5 http://www.tieeldalieva.org/docs/ritual/enderi.pdf. Accessed 1 September 2016.
6 According to Tolkien's biographer, Humphrey Carpenter, in the documentary *J.R.R. Tolkien: Creator of Middle-earth* (2002).
7 On Tolkien and the hippies, see also Walmsley (1984).
8 Valië is the designation for a female Vala.
9 The Tribunal of the Sidhe consists of a number of local circles. For my PhD project, I interviewed Lady Danu who leads the Circle of the Coyote. The circle's Facebook page can be visited here: www.facebook.com/pages/The-Circle-of-Coyote/11524865848728O. Accessed 15 April 2015.
10 The homepage of the Silver Elves can be visited at silverelves.angelfire.com/. Accessed 15 April 2015. The Silver Elves have self-published more than 20 books on Elven spirituality, including 3 volumes with their letters.
11 Hoeller's lecture was given on 2 October 1998 and has been online since late 1998. It is available on YouTube at www.youtube.com/watch?v=xbuYlasPA7E. Accessed 15 April 2015. The website of the Ecclesia Gnostica can be found at www.gnosis.org/eghome.htm. Accessed 15 April 2015.
12 A Legendarium Reconstructionist forerunner for UTolk was Middle-earth Reunion: The Alternative Tolkien Society, which published *Reunion: The Journal of Middle-earth Studies* from 1996 to 2005. The society's homepage is still online and can be visited at alt-tolkien.com. Accessed 15 April 2015. Several articles from *Reunion* are available through the homepage.
13 Tië eldaliéva's original homepage was situated at www.thehiddenrealm.com, but is no longer online.
14 Another source of inspiration for Tië eldaliéva's rituals was the 'High Elvish Working Based Upon J.R.R. Tolkien's Mythic World', developed in 1993 by the Fifth Way Mystery School. This ritual can be accessed through the Internet Wayback Machine. Visit web.archive.org/web/20130430174512/http://www.fifth waymysteryschool.org/valar.html. Accessed 15 April 2015.
15 The correspondences between individual Valar and particular cardinal points are part of a much more elaborate system of correspondences which group members

(especially Elwin) have created based on Tolkien exegesis and trancework. Within this system, each Valar is also associated with certain 'key words' (for example, Mind, Clear Sight, Authority, Poetry, and Truth for Manwë, the King of the Valar) and with one of the Cirth and one of the Tengwar, the characters used for writing Sindarin and Quenya.

16 Starflower essence is used because it is believed to be connected to the Elves, who, in their own tongue (Quenya), refer to themselves as the People of the Stars (Eldar).

17 See http://www.tieeldalieva.org/docs/ritual/enderi.pdf. Accessed 1 September 2016.

18 See Flieger (2005) for a critical edition of *Smith*. Verlyn Flieger, the *grand dame* of Tolkien Studies, sees in *Smith* evidence that Tolkien may himself have believed in Faery – that he took "what was for a man of the rational twentieth century the far riskier position [riskier than seeing Faery as an altered state of consciousness] that Faërie is or could be an actuality" (Flieger 2006: 183).

19 Within Tolkien's narrative world, the Blessed Realm used to exist on the same plane as Middle-earth, but gradually became separated from this material plane, first through the Hiding of Valinor following a war against the Satan-figure Melkor, then through the Rounding of the World following the destruction of Númenor, and finally through the separation of the worlds after the retreat of the Elves from Middle-earth.

20 The Ilsaluntë Valion forum continues to be an important information centre, also for Tië eldaliéva members, and the Tië eldaliéva forum was important until it closed in 2007. Even so, the forums have never been the primary communication channels for Tië eldaliéva and Ilsaluntë Valion members. The most significant discussions take place bilaterally, over chat, phone or email, and new ideas are often generated and tested in this way before being introduced on the forum. Not only do core members communicate in this way, but new members typically also have much contact with the captain/moderator or another mentor figure via email for some time before becoming active posters on the forum.

21 The authors wish to thank Llefyn and Earendil for commenting on a draft of this article.

References

Written Sources

Adler, Margot. 1986. *Drawing Down the Moon: Witches, Druids, Goddess-Worshippers, and Other Pagans in America Today*, revised edition. London: Penguin.

Campbell, Colin. 1972. 'The Cult, the Cultic Milieu and Secularization'. *A Sociological Yearbook of Religion in Britain* 5: 119–136.

Clifton, Michael. 1987. 'Jewels of Wonder, Instruments of Delight: Science Fiction, Fantasy, and Science Fantasy as Vision-Inducing Works'. In George E. Slusser and Eric S. Rabkin (eds), *Intersections Fantasy and Science Fiction*, 97–106. Carbondale and Edwardsville, IL: Southern Illinois University Press.

Corbin, Henry. 1964. 'Mundus imaginalis ou l'imaginaire et l'imaginal'. *Cahiers Internationaux de Symbolisme* 6: 3–26.

Corbin, Henry. 1972. 'Mundus Imaginalis, or, the Imaginary and the Imaginal'. *Spring*: 1–19.

Davidsen, Markus Altena. 2012. 'The Spiritual Milieu Based on J.R.R. Tolkien's Literary Mythology'. In Adam Possamai (ed.), *Handbook of Hyper-real Religions*, 185–204. Leiden, The Netherlands and Boston, MA: Brill.

Davidsen, Markus Altena. 2013. 'Fiction-based Religion: Conceptualising a New Category against History-Based Religion and Fandom'. *Religion and Culture: An Interdisciplinary Journal* 14(4): 378–395.

Davidsen, Markus Altena. 2014. *The Spiritual Tolkien Milieu: A Study of Fiction-based Religion*, doctoral dissertation, Leiden University. A monograph based on the dissertation is currently being prepared for publication with De Gruyter under the title *Tolkien Spirituality: Constructing Belief and Tradition in Fiction-based Religion.*

Davidsen, Markus Altena. 2016. 'From *Star Wars* to Jediism: The Emergence of Fiction-based Religion'. In Ernst van den Hemel and Asja Szafraniec (eds), *Words: Religious Language Matter*, 376–389, 571–575. New York: Fordham University Press.

Ellwood, Robert S. 2002. *Frodo's Quest: Living the Myth in The Lord of the Rings.* Wheaton, IL: Quest Books.

Flieger, Verlyn, ed. 2005. *Smith of Wootton Major: Extended Edition.* London: HarperCollins Publishers.

Flieger, Verlyn. 2006. 'Faërie'. In Michael D.C. Drout (ed.), *J.R.R. Tolkien Encyclopedia: Scholarship and Critical Assessment*, 183–185. London: Routledge.

Harvey, Graham. 2000. 'Fantasy in the Study of Religions: Paganism as Observed and Enhanced by Terry Pratchett'. *Diskus* 6. At: basr.ac.uk/diskus_old/diskus1–6/harvey-6.txt. Accessed 15 April 2015.

Harvey, Graham. 2007. *Listening People, Speaking Earth: Contemporary Paganism*, second edition. London: Hurst and Co.

Helms, Philip W. 1978. 'The Evolution of Tolkien Fandom'. In Alida Becker (ed.), *A Tolkien Treasury*, 104–109. New York: Grosset and Dunlap. Originally published in *Appendix T* (May 1977).

Hinckle, Warren. 1967. 'The Social History of the Hippies'. *Ramparts* 5(9): 5–26.

Jung, Carl G. 1990 [1959]. *The Archetypes and the Collective Unconscious*, trans. R.F.C. Hull. Princeton, NJ: Princeton University Press.

Laycock, Joseph. 2012. '"We Are Spirits of Another Sort": Ontological Rebellion and Religious Dimensions of the Otherkin Community'. *Nova Religio: The Journal of Alternative and Emergent Religions* 15(3): 65–90.

Marcus, Ivan G. 1996. *Rituals of Childhood: Jewish Acculturation in Medieval Europe.* New Haven, CT and London: Yale University Press.

Ratliff, William E. and Charles G. Flinn. 1968. 'The Hobbit and the Hippie'. *Modern Age* 12 (Spring): 142–146. At: www.mmisi.org/ma/12_02/ratliff.pdf. Accessed 15 April 2015.

Regardie, Israel. 1998. *The Middle Pillar: The Balance Between Mind and Magic*, third edition, edited and annotated with new material by Chic Cicero and Sandra Tabatha Cicero, Woodbury, MN: Llewellyn Publications. First edition 1945. Second edition 1970.

Tolkien, John Ronald Reuel. 1954–1955. *The Lord of the Rings.* London: George Allen and Unwin. Comprising *The Fellowship of the Ring* (1954), second edition 1965 by Ballantine Books; *The Two Towers* (1954), second edition 1965 by Ballantine Books; and *The Return of the King* (1955), second edition 1965 by Ballantine Books.

Tolkien, John Ronald Reuel. 1977. *The Silmarillion*, Christopher Tolkien (ed.). London: George Allen & Unwin.

Tolkien, John Ronald Reuel. 1981. *The Letters of J.R.R. Tolkien*, Humphrey Carpenter (ed.). London: George Allen & Unwin.

Tolkien, John Ronald Reuel. 1983–1996. *The History of Middle-earth*, 12 volumes, Christopher Tolkien (ed.). London: George Allen & Unwin.

Walmsley, Nigel. 1984. 'Tolkien and the '60s'. In Robert Giddings (ed.), *J.R.R. Tolkien, This Far Land*, 73–85. London: Vision and Totowa, NJ: Barnes and Noble.

Motion pictures

J.R.R. Tolkien: Creator of Middle-earth (Documentary). 2002. Director: Michael Pellerin. Production: Kurtti-Pellerin. 22 min. Included in the bonus material of the extended edition of *The Lord of the Rings: The Fellowship of the Ring*.

Websites

Ecclesia Gnostica: www.gnosis.org/eghome.htm

'Enderi Enderi, the Middle Days: A Tië eldaliéva ritual': http://www.tieeldalieva.org/docs/ritual/enderi.pdf

'High Elvish working based upon J.R.R. Tolkien's mythic world': web.archive.org/web/20130430174512/http://www.fifthwaymysteryschool.org/valar.html

Ilsaluntë Valion: westofwest.org

'J.R.R. Tolkien's gnosis for our day': www.youtube.com/watch?v=xbuYlasPA7E

Middle-earth Reunion: The Alternative Tolkien Society: alt-tolkien.com

Silver Elves: silverelves.angelfire.com

Tië eldaliéva: elvenspirituality.wordpress.com

Tribunal of the Sidhe: www.facebook.com/pages/The-Circle-of-Coyote/115248658487280.

2 Spirituality and self-realisation as 'other-than-human'

The Otherkin and Therianthropy communities

Carole M. Cusack[1]

Introduction

In the twenty-first century West, the role of institutional religion is in retreat and the rise of personal spiritualities is clearly observable (Partridge 2004–2005). The oppositional cultural trends of the eighteenth century, the Enlightenment (which promoted rationality and scientific experiment) and Romanticism (which championed emotion and experientialism), are visible in both the public acceptance of secularism, science and technology, and the private emergence of a plethora of new self-concepts that embrace the contemporary narrative of the self as central, the creator of reality, and of self-actualisation as the fundamental spiritual quest and ultimate goal of life (Cusack 2015: 181–182; Lyon 2002 [2000]: 73–96). An important strand of contemporary Romanticism is magical thinking. Since the publication of Lupa's *A Field Guide to the Otherkin* (2007), scholarly interest in Otherkin (people who believe and live as if they are partly other-than-human, for example, part-dragon, unicorn, vampire, angel, fae or other mythological or supernatural creature) and Therianthropy (a term derived from the Greek for 'beast-man' and applied to a group generally distinguished from Otherkin by the 'otherness' of their selves being animal, such as wolf, horse, eagle, ram and so on) has emerged (Robertson 2015a, 2015b). This is partly due to the facilitative nature of the Internet, which has enabled hitherto separate individuals to form communities (Shane 2014: 263), and partly due to academic coverage of such crafted identities and niche spiritual communities, which has grown steadily since the Australian scholar, Danielle Kirby, published her pioneering book chapter, 'Alternative worlds: Metaphysical questing and virtual community among the Otherkin' (2006).

This chapter considers the internal logics of Otherkin and Therianthropy discourses and considers discursive strategies that locate the ancestry of these contemporary, chiefly online, communities in: a) religious and spiritual phenomena of the past, including shamanism, the hybrid animal-human gods of ancient world pantheons, and medieval and early modern literary monsters; and b) in popular cultural texts, such as fantasy fiction, anime and film (Kirby 2009a). The former functions more as a traditional legitimation

Otherkin and Therianthropy communities   41

strategy that seeks to identify resemblances between new religions and spiritualities and older, more established traditions, whereas the latter positions
the Otherkin and Therianthropy as "invented" religions or spiritualities
(Cusack 2010). These groups do not explicitly seek to legitimate themselves
via appeals to the past, but rather advertise their origins in fiction and proclaim that this recent (and in some cases transparently copied and pasted
online), ancestry is sufficient and credible (Singler 2014).

The third lens through which the Otherkin and Therianthropy is viewed
is that of scholarly engagement. The principal method used to research
Otherkin and Therianthropy is online ethnography, which is a contested
issue for researchers. Scholars researching these phenomena are, in the main,
not members of either community, and thus they are likely to 'lurk' (spend
time on websites and forums without registering or otherwise making their
presence known). In recent years, attempts have been made to classify information as either Private or Public, and Sensitive or Non-Sensitive. Within
this schema, it is argued that Public, Non-Sensitive information does not
require the standard human ethics clearances (McKee and Porter 2009:
20–21). There are clear issues with this position – most obviously that scholars using public information still need, under the conditions imposed by the
generic human ethics clearance, to inform those whose material they use, of
the purposes and ends of their research projects, something which happens
rarely in online ethnography – but to date, it is the generally accepted stance
regarding the use, for research purposes by the academy, of information
posted publicly on the Internet (Bernauer 2012). This chapter gives a historical overview of scholarly engagement with Otherkin and Therianthropy
that follows on from Markus Altena Davidsen's chapter.

Locating Otherkin and Therianthropy in historical sources

While the online communities of spiritual Therianthropy and the Otherkin
are recent phenomena, the historical antecedents of beings that were part-
human but also possessed features of the animal world or of mythological
and legendary creatures go back many centuries. The Ancient Egyptian
pantheon included deities such as Thoth, a human male with the head of a
falcon, and Sekhmet, a human female with the head of a lion (Armour 2001
[1986]: 126–132, 104). During the Christian Middle Ages, monsters, that
is, those that violated the God-given model of nature, both human and animal, were generally understood negatively. Yet, as Albrecht Classen notes,
"monstrous otherness serves far-reaching functions, both epistemologi-
cally and religiously, with respect to self-identity and the determination of
one's own position here on earth within society and in nature" (Classen
2013: 539). The most interesting point is that medieval texts involving,
for example, lycanthropy (humans transforming into wolf-form, that
is, werewolves), like the Old French *Bisclavet* and *Melion*, "associate

42   *Carole M. Cusack*

ethics and narrative with alterity and hybridity . . . they draw attention to the polymorphic, unfinalizable nature of individuals, circumstances, and events and to the inadequacies of a systematic . . . morality" (Guynn 2013: 181). This is similar to contemporary Otherkin and Therianthropy personal testimonies, which emphasise the fluidity and unfinalisability of personal identity, and draw attention to the limitations of conventional binary categories like animal/human, male/female, normal/abnormal and mainstream/fringe.

Divers cultures have folkloric traditions regarding special relationships between humans and particular animals, including shape-shifting ability, totemism and animals as 'familiars' or companions of witches and shamans. The prehistoric cave painting at Les Trois-Frères (Ariège), known as the 'Dancing Sorcerer', an apparent humanoid reindeer or human wearing reindeer skin and antlers, has been claimed as a Therianthropic image (Robertson 2013a: 8). The Dancing Sorcerer has long been regarded as a shaman, and shamans are often connected with animals. For example, in Japan, the most common animals associated with shamans are the snake and a dog- or fox-like beast (Blacker 1975: 32). Emiko Ohnuki-Tierney notes that pre-modern Japanese folklore contains 42 tales of human-into-animal transformation and 92 of animal-into-human transformation, with monkeys, foxes, herons, snakes, cats and dogs featuring (Ohnuki-Tierney 1987: 33). Tales such as these assist in the creation of a lineage for Therianthropy, as animals that occur in nature are featured, while a subset of such folklore features apparent animal-human and human-animal transformation, though the beings in question are from the spirit world and may be benevolent or demonic. These include the Japanese story of the love between Lady Bai (a snake demon) and the pharmacist Xu (Buljan and Cusack 2015: 93–94), and the Old Norse poem about Völundr the smith and his two brothers, who married swan maidens. The wives later reassumed their swan form and flew away (Burson 1983). Such creatures, which are definitely not human and may have a 'true' nature that is not animal either, perhaps fit better into the Otherkin lineage.

In Early Modern Europe, members of both the Protestant Reformation and the Catholic Counter-Reformation had an interest in the boundaries between the living and the dead, and between the human and the non-human. Intellectuals, including Catholic Giuseppe Davanzati (1665–1755) and Evangelical Michael Ranft (1700–1774), speculated about revenants, which are undead beings like corporeal vampires, zombies and incorporeal ghosts (De Ceglia 2011: 498–499). David Keyworth has surveyed theological explanations regarding undead corpses, showing that medieval Catholics tended to believe that the Devil could reanimate a corpse and that undead corpses might be associated with excommunicated individuals. In contrast, early modern Protestants regarded the undead "as an absurdity and the product of deranged minds, fuelled by popish superstition, and denied that the Devil had the power or even the authority to resurrect a corpse" (Keyworth 2010: 161). Yet Catholic devotional practices, such as displaying the incorrupt bodies of saints in glass cases in churches, may have influenced the eighteenth century vampire image, who appeared much as in life, though pallid and ageless. He argues that there are aesthetic similarities between the two phenomena, though these are outweighed by the differences. For example, "the liquid blood that still flowed in the veins of deceased saints originated with the corpse itself, while vampires were bloated with the supposed blood of their victims" (Keyworth 2010: 165).

In the eighteenth century, another important shift in thinking about revenants took place; folk beliefs in such beings declined dramatically, and in the nineteenth century they became the subject matter of sensational fictions including Sheridan Le Fanu's *Carmilla* (1872) and Bram Stoker's *Dracula* (1897). The early fictional prototypes Count Dracula and Carmilla exemplify two trends still evident in contemporary popular culture; the vampire as monster who must be destroyed, and the vampire as ambivalent, beautiful, melancholy and doomed 'other', by whom victims are fascinated or with whom they fall in love (Saler and Ziegler 2005: 221–222). The rise of fictional literary forms, in particular the novel, parallels the decline of Christian literature (such as sermons) as reading entertainment (Cusack 2010: 12). The development of film technology in the late nineteenth century led to a rapid transformation of leisure activities in the developed world, with films and television able to evoke other worlds in visual and sensual forms. Whereas the reader's imagination created visual forms for characters and settings in novels, the tangible nature of film and television's presentation of aliens, vampires and ghost (to name but a few of many other non-empirical beings) made it easy for viewers to affirm the reality of, and belief in, these beings and the other worlds they inhabit. The emergence of the Internet has intensified this cultural tendency, making contemporary Westerners individuals who often seek to 'make real' in the world fictions that they find meaningful for their lives and personal identity (Cusack 2010: 4). Danielle Kirby has termed this "narrative religion"; she uses this to refer to "a way of grouping a set of beliefs that directly addresses, and in various ways sacralises, narratives sourced from mediated popular culture" (Kirby 2012: 122). Examples of such popular culture-based religions and spiritualities are Jediism, Matrixism, Therianthropy and Otherkin (Kirby 2009b). Research by American scholar Lynn Schofield Clark indicates that young people are more engaged with alternative religious and spiritual trends, and that friendship was the strongest indicator as to whether certain fringe or esoteric beliefs and practices might be adopted (Clark 2003: 7).

Locating Otherkin and Therianthropy in popular culture

The development of film and television technologies, inexpensive printed novels and comic-books, and leisure activities such as role-playing and board games, made available a vast array of cultural information on which modern individuals could draw in order to craft a personal identity.

44   *Carole M. Cusack*

This explosion of information was accelerated by the development of the Internet, which speeded up cultural trends and fashion, and facilitated connections between geographically isolated people with common interests. In the 1990s, the influence of popular culture was most strongly manifested in the 'teen witch' phenomenon, in which teenage girls adopted Wicca (or more generic forms of Pagan witchcraft) after viewing films like "The Craft" (1996), or television series including "Buffy the Vampire Slayer" (1997–2003) and "Charmed" (1998–2006). Jediism emerged as a fiction-based religion as a result of the "Jedi Census Phenomenon" of 2001, in which an email campaign urged citizens of Australia, New Zealand, Canada and the United Kingdom to put "Jedi" as their religion when filling out the census (Cusack 2010: 124–126). This campaign would have been well-nigh impossible just ten years earlier, and the chapter in this book authored by members the Temple of the Jedi Order (TotJO) is evidence of how far Jedi religion and spirituality has developed in a short time. Jediism is a largely internet-mediated religion and community, as are a majority of the 'new new' religions featured in this volume. The misconception that online communities are less important than 'meat world' communities must be dispelled; the Internet is one of, if not the, most powerful culture machines in the contemporary world, and the imbrication of these new spiritualities with the Internet is a strength, not a disadvantage.

Specific fictions that influence contemporary Otherkin and Therianthropy range from mythology and folklore, through superhero comics and cartoons, films and television series, manga and anime, and (less often) poetry and the visual arts. The power of certain fictional texts and the passionate fandoms they inspire is undeniable. These include *Star Trek* and the 'Trekkie/Trekker' phenomenon, and the influence of J. R. R. Tolkien's *Lord of the Rings* trilogy of novels (particularly the cheap paperback edition issued in 1965) and the Peter Jackson film adaptations. Davidsen's chapter in this volume is relevant to the location of the Otherkin in popular culture, as the emergence of the Elven community in the late 1960s to early 1970s is the earliest recorded case of Tolkien-based spirituality and also of groups claiming to be other-than-human in a supernatural fashion. The Silver Elves, a couple known as Zardoa Silverstar and Silver Flame (or Michael J. and Martha C. Love), are still active and have taken on the role of historians and intellectuals of the Elven movement (Davidsen 2014: 240). They named Arwen and Elenor (also known as Suzie Creamcheese and Mary Sunshine, or "the Tookes") of the Elf Queen's Daughters as the first Elven group, and dated the formation of that organisation to 1972, though this date is disputed (Scribner 2012). The Elven movement is the parent of the Otherkin and is clearly linked to popular culture, most notably Tolkien's fictions (Silver Elves 2013, 2014).

The vagueness of the categories 'Otherkin' and 'Therians' is apparent when sub-groups like Furries and Soulbonders are analysed. Furries, "people who celebrate their interest in anthropomorphic animals, such as characters from comics, cartoons and Disney movies . . . sometimes donning

Otherkin and Therianthropy communities   45

full-body 'fursuits' . . . many engage in fandom to express their 'fursona', their true anthrozoomorphic self" (Robertson 2013a: 13) are often viewed a fandom. Yet Furries may identify as 'Mediakin', a subcategory into which Soulbonders might also fit. Kirby notes that Soulbonders form "full-blown interpersonal relationship(s)" with 'other-than-human' entities, who may be fictional. Venetia Robertson's chapter in this book on Mrs Sephiroth and Sephirothslave, two women who were the avowed lovers of Sephiroth, a character from the videogame *Final Fantasy*, and Zoe Alderton's research into the phenomenon of 'Snapists' (or SnapeWives), three women (Rose, Conchita and Tonya) who believed themselves to be in intimate sexual relationships with Severus Snape from the *Harry Potter* novels and films, are the only academic treatments of two intriguing phenomena that now seem to have ended (Robertson in this volume; Alderton 2014).

Other related fandoms and cultural phenomena include Bronies, who are primarily young male fans of the children's television series *My Little Pony: Friendship is Magic* (Crome 2014; Robertson 2014; Kosnáč in this volume), and people who Venetia Robertson terms 'Mermaiders', who are primarily women that costume themselves as mermaids and who may take part in "sites of mermaid performance . . . [such as] the famous Weeki Wachee theme-park in Florida, the Coney Island Mermaid Parade of New York, and the burgeoning global mermaiding subculture", which includes events like MerCon and MerPalooza (Robertson 2013b: 309, 313). Interest in the mermaid culture is nourished by magazines including *Tail Flip* and *Mermaids and Mythology*, and films like *Miranda* (1948), *Splash* (1984) and *The Little Mermaid* (1989). Mermaiders do not manifest spiritual or religious dimensions very often, but Robertson argues that, "the existence of subcultures like mermaiding is testament to the effectiveness of harnessing an other-than-human identity as an ontological project" (Robertson 2013b: 317).

The formation of identity has become the principal spiritual project of modern individuals, and the emergence of new spiritual communities and identities as a result of popular culture is unsurprising, as the demands of institutional religion, family obligations and traditional sources of the self have retreated since the mid-twentieth century (Cusack 2015). Joseph Laycock argues that Otherkin sacralise material from popular culture: "the writings of C. S. Lewis and Neil Gaiman, and the comic book *Elfquest*. Fantasy films such as *Labyrinth* (1986), *The Dark Crystal* (1982) are included, as are role-playing games such as *Dungeons and Dragons* and *Changeling: The Dreaming*" (Laycock 2012a: 76). Such material is used in three ways, as:

> [a] "personal mythology", an approach that views material from the fantasy milieu as personally meaningful in a metaphorical sense . . . [as] cosmological and metaphysical beliefs that are shared by, but not necessarily drawn from fictional fantasy narratives . . . there is a minority of Otherkin who argue that fictional narratives have a literal corresponding reality.
> (Laycock 2012a: 76)

46   *Carole M. Cusack*

Laycock's third group is the one that most closely fits the model of invented, fiction-based or hyper-real religion, though the project of identity construction confers upon his first and second groups a 'spiritual' dimension.

Locating Otherkin and Therianthropy online

When the Elven movement coalesced in the early 1970s, the Internet was in the early stages of development and was used primarily by the military. Finding people with common interests in 'other-than-human' identities depended on personal contact and random chance. A second source of information was 'zines and newsletters, and in the emergent United States Pagan community *Green Egg*, the periodical started by Tim Zell, co-founder of the Church of All Worlds (which itself was based on Robert A. Heinlein's 1961 science fiction novel *Stranger in a Strange Land*) led the way, both as a paper publication and, later, as a digitised online archive of Pagan history, theology, teaching and practice (Zell-Ravenheart 2009). The Elf Queen's Daughters issued letters, and in March 1975, one of these, which is the earliest attested primary source from the group, was published in *Green Egg* (Scribner 2012). As the Internet developed beyond niche military and technological uses, and in particular after the World Wide Web was launched in 1991, it became possible to connect with like-minded people in cyberspace.

Otherkin have long-standing and online presences. The six most prominent groups are: "Otherkin.net (founded 2000), the 'Otherkin' community on LiveJournal (founded 2001), and the four ProBoard-based sites, Embracing a Mystery (founded 2001), Otherkin Alliance (2005), Otherkin Phenomena (founded 2008), and Otherkin Community (founded 2009)" (Davidsen 2014: 251). For Therianthropy, "in 1992 a Usenet newsgroup alt. horror.werewolves, or AHWW, was founded for those interested in discussing the werewolf in popular culture" (Robertson 2013a: 9). In a year, the emphasis had changed to tales of human-animal and animal-human shifts and to questions of actual physical transformation compared to metaphysical transformation. The Frequently Asked Questions (FAQ) for AHWW "maintained that Therianthropy was very serious and real, 'for some of us it's tantamount to discussing a religion'" (Robertson 2013a: 16). There are many different ways the other-than-human identity might be imagined and explained. Robertson lists the following for Therians:

> [t]he presence or reincarnation of an animal spirit in a human body, or the memories lodged within a soul of a non-human past life. Some Therians believe that their spirit is an immutable blend of human and animal, while others contend they possess multiple souls.
>
> (Robertson 2013a: 17)

For both Therianthropes and Otherkin, the 'awakening' to the other-than-human identity is a crucial rite of passage, possessing a similar value to the conversion experience in the traditional 'world religions'. The affinities between Otherkin, Therianthropy and modern Paganism (itself partially inspired by fictions by Tolkien, Heinlein and others) mean that the awakening experience is expressed in analogous terms to self-realisation as a Pagan, which is explicitly distinguished from 'conversion' by Pagans, especially scholar-practitioners. Thus Graham Harvey speaks of "coming home and coming out", a return or disclosure, rather than a change (Harvey 1999: 233–246). Eyovah's lengthy account of 'awakening' reinforces the importance of popular culture in providing the backdrop for the quest, the vital importance of gatherings in making certain experiences possible, and of comrades in the same spiritual journey to reinforce the nascent 'other-than-human' self and assist in the crafting of a more developed identity. As a child, Eyovah loved dragons and collected dragon figures. Later, he and his brothers played *Dungeons and Dragons*. At Rialian's Otherkin Gathering, held at Four Quarters Farm in Pennsylvania in 1998 he had a transformative experience:

> A friend of Rialian, Leon, set up this reiki matrix thing he created. Babylon matrix he called it. Had a Labrodorite stone center. Covers a small area like a reiki grid does, but more portable and powerful. With that center stone it supposedly made it easier to see your Otherkin form, if you had one. I saw it having some affects with Rialian and others to see their etheric/energetic shapes. I saw Rialian become more elf like, pointed ears, cheekbones and all. Figured I'd give a try and see what it feels like.

> I stepped in the matrix. And felt the energy all around. It was pretty cool. Next thing I know, Rialian and Chaos-Magician saw me changing shape with a sound of surprise. I found myself playing with the energy. I felt bigger, and a feeling of wings . . . large wings. Didn't have a tail that I could sense. I felt like I was exploring sensations of a new body. Rialian and Chaos-Magician told me they saw me as a kind of dragon shape, but didn't know the real name for it. Somewhere between Dragon and Angel. Draconian is a good term. If you take the classic dragon look, take off the tail, stand it up like a humanoid, that would basically be it. I think I am multi-colored normally. Orange/Gold belly, Blueish under the wings, Grey/Silver on the outside wings and back and head. I go blinding white light in fight mode as far as I can tell. Tail can be morphed in and out at will, usually off. Hands/claws can be morphed into smaller more human hands. Possible full body morphing. Color can be changed as well. Breath weapons are varied (Eyovah 1999).

Eyovah was intrigued by this experience, which he followed up by leaving a job in computers to become a massage therapist and to teach reiki, and studying magic, meditation, crystals and astral travelling. In company with

48 *Carole M. Cusack*

key friends, Leon, Rialian and Chaos-Magician, he explored his dragon identity, perceiving shifts when under 'psychic attack', and receiving information about the dragon homeland from a guide, who also revealed his dragon name: "Before going to kinvention, I saw one of my guides above me in Dragon form. Talked to him for a while. He told me my dragon name, translated to an English speakable word is Eyovah" (Eyovah 1999). Eyovah's dragon identity was strengthened by each new piece of information he received, and the reinforcement of like-minded people who reassured him as he gradually accepted his draconian Otherkin nature.

Eyovah and his friends knew each other in the 'real world', but the same sorts of community structures can be seen on the Internet. Robertson has analysed the ways that online Therianthropy websites educate members in the process of awakening to their 'therioside', crafting an individual animal-human identity, and also to be enculturated into the community. While an early FAQ for the burgeoning Therian community insisted that, "There is no leader of the pack, no alpha", the fact that veteran Therians are honoured with the title "grey muzzles", and that a special vocabulary has been developed to describe the Therian experience, particularly "awakening", "realising" and "shifting", suggests that there is a hierarchy of longevity and experience as other-than-human in the online communities and also that esoteric religious and spiritual currents have influenced the idea of the awakened therioside and the liminal Therian identity that results (Robertson 2012: 265).

Apart from online communities and archives, there are a number of key print publications from popular authors or from within the other-than-human communities that publicised these subcultures to mainstream audiences. An early example was Christine Wicker's *Not In Kansas Anymore: Dark Arts, Sex Spells, Money Magic, and Other Things Your Neighbours Aren't Telling You* (2005), which chronicles journalist Wicker's encounters with what she calls "magical people", groups that include the Silver Elves, an Otherkin convention, and 'real' vampires (Wicker 2005). Two influential 'insider' texts are *The Psychic Vampire Codex* by psychic vampire Michelle Belanger (2004) and *A Field Guide to the Otherkin* (2007) by Lupa, who identified as a wolf Therian until 2013, when she revealed that she had withdrawn the book from circulation because:

> I no longer identify as a therianthrope, and I haven't for quite some time . . . There's still a piece of me that I feel resonates more with wolf than human, but at this point I don't think it's anything more than a bit of creative personal narrative, part of the ongoing myth I tell about myself . . . I am a human animal, 100%, just with a particular connection to the idea of "wolfness" . . . Don't get me wrong; I don't regret exploring myself in the Otherkin framework.
>
> (Lupa 2013)

Otherkin and Therianthropy communities 49

Lupa's book contains important insider information, and its withdrawal leaves a gap in the (print) literature, though online Therianthopy and Otherkin sites provide a rich stream of personal testimonies of awakening to 'other-than-humanness', spiritual development and community contributions.

One of the tests of new religious phenomena tends to be the lived reality that the members of the group experience and how praxis creates community. It is clear that certain beliefs are common to self-identified Otherkin and Therians, but it is not possible to give a *definitive* account of the activities of Otherkin and Therians that resonate with religion or spirituality. The first, obvious, shared religious act that they participate in is posting online. Sites abound in accounts of awakenings. So, Miaren Crow's Daughter, in "So . . . You're Awake?" discusses three models of awakening:

> The first is the "gradual or independent Awakening", in which the sleeper feels a certain distance from others, possibly proceeding through religious experimentation, until hopefully they find a supporting circle. These people may or may not be fae themselves, and the Sleeper may in fact not fully think of themselves as "fae". The second is the "alarm clock Awakening". This occurs when the Sleeper is exposed to a group of Awakened fae and their own nature surges to the front. This can take the form of recognizing a shared memory or even recognizing a person they've never met before. The third type is the "snooze alarm Awakening". In this form the Sleeper has seen evidence of their nature, but is choosing – consciously or unconsciously – to ignore it.
>
> (cited in Kirby 2013: 55)

Also, sites abound in wise advice to facilitate smooth relations online (which is difficult, given that the extra bodily dimension of face-to-face communication is absence). These 'rules' also assist in enculturating new members into the 'norms' of the group. Kirby cites examples:

> Avoid nit-picking another's interpretation of the same myth. If someone mistakenly calls themselves an (anime) Sylph when in fact everything they describe is Pixie-derived then contact them privately . . . Don't forget that what you're arguing about cannot be proved . . . in the physical realm. This also applies to stuff made up that is paralleled by myth.
>
> (cited in Kirby 2013: 47)

Another core practice, which is shared with the Pagan community, is attending conventions. These large-scale gatherings emerged in the 1960s to meet the need of fan groups of various popular cultural phenomena. Tim Zell, co-founder of the Church of All Worlds, loved science fiction and won a prize in "the Costume Ball of the World Science Fiction Convention in Los Angeles" in 1972, and won another costume prize with his wife Morning Glory (whom

50   *Carole M. Cusack*

he met at the Gnostic Aquarian Convention in 1973) at Discon in Washington in 1974 (Cusack 2010: 66–67). *Star Trek* fans have learned Klingon, which has been developed by linguists as a functional language, re-enacted scenes from episodes and filmed them, and attend conventions as costumed characters. DragonCon, advertised as the world's largest fantasy and science fiction gathering, was founded in 1987 and is held annually in Atlanta, Georgia. Anime conventions emerged in the Anglophone world around 1990, and cosplay (costume play), in which fans dress up as characters, has taken on ritual dimensions (Buljan and Cusack 2015: 181–187). Invented religions including the Church of the SubGenius also have events (Devivals and X-Day celebrations) that resemble fandom conventions (Cusack 2015).[2] Laycock reports on survey data collected at a furry convention (Laycock 2012a: 82), Orion Scribner's "Otherkin Timeline" includes Kinvention North in Canada in 2001 and MerCon in Las Vegas in 2011, and Robertson notes the participation of Bronies in anime conventions (Robertson 2014: 28), and in 2011 a specific BronyCon was founded in New York. These gatherings are important for the strengthening and maintenance of community.

Locating Otherkin and Therianthropy in scholarly discourses

The academic study of the Otherkin and Therianthropy communities is still in its infancy. The two most important scholars to date are Australians, Danielle Kirby and Venetia Robertson. Kirby's doctorate has been available from the University of Queensland's electronic thesis repository site since 2009 and, for a time, was the principal resource for any student interested in Otherkin, Therianthropy, Soulbonders and other related phenomena (the book resulting from her thesis was published in 2013). Kirby has also published articles and book chapters that extend her methodological approach to these online, popular cultural spiritual groups. She is interested in: their relative lack of hierarchy and diffuse authority structures; the fact that they are online communities; their use of bricolage and occultural motifs; and, particularly, in the way these groups function as reading communities producing religious and spiritual identities from narrative fictions (Kirby 2012). Kirby's "narrative religion" is close to Carole M. Cusack's "invented religion", but whereas Cusack emphasised the consumption of new products and experiences (including fictions) as the principal facilitator of invented religions (while still acknowledging that founders and participants in such endeavours were creative), Kirby emphasised the productive activity inherent in the creation and maintenance of new spiritualities (Kirby 2012: 123).

Kirby and Cusack draw on the work of English sociologist, Colin Campbell, as both use his notion of the "cultic milieu" and the "seeker" (Campbell 1972). Kirby also employs his idea of consumers as "postmodern identity seekers" and "craft consumers" to view Otherkin, though she concludes that neither of these models is quite right, as:

> [h]aving a specific mythological or textual precedent to the fantasy creature, while often considered positive, is not actually necessary for these beliefs . . . Rarely, at least in public community forums, do the popular sources for these fantasy creatures get discussed . . . individual engagement with the non-human entity is generally not mediated through a text, but rather is relocated. This relocation might be to other planes of existence or levels of reality, internal worlds, and so forth.
>
> (Kirby 2012: 129)

The creativity and evolving nature of fiction-based online identity movements or new spiritualities is also evident in the work of Venetia Robertson, which in the main addresses Therianthropy and related animal-focused groups. Robertson's focus emphasises methodological notions such as liminality and the monstrous, hybridity, embodiment and queering, in her investigations of the development of 'other-than-human' identities among Mermaiders, Therians and other groups engaged "in embodied identity play with fictional or mythological constructs" and the re-envisioning of "one's ontology to incorporate the nonhuman into the human self, [as] a source of personal re-enchantment" (Robertson 2013b: 315). Themes of sacredness and identity-formation underpin Robertson's analysis of initiation within online spiritual Therianthropy. Interestingly, although the field of religious studies has of late evidenced greater interest in 'lived religion' and a move away from analysis of 'beliefs', the beliefs of Otherkin and Therians are central to all academic studies of these groups, no doubt because the 'other-than-human' element of their selves is generally not manifested physically. Robertson notes that Therian:

> [i]dentity manifests in what is often called a "therioside", an animal aspect that the human may "shift" into mentally or spiritually through psychological or paranormal means, that is, temporarily taking on animal mindset, or a bestial subtle body or etheric form. Alternatively, the . . . Therian . . . may feel immutably blended with his or her animal side at all times.
>
> (Robertson 2012: 257)

The inner, psychological nature of identification and transformation among Otherkin and Therians necessitates that the scholar take an interest in beliefs, metaphysics and the ways that fictions are integrated into the personal worldviews of individuals. Similarly, online ethnography as a research method requires scholars to notice textual, discursive interactions, and to accord weight to expressed ideas and feelings, rather than to look for 'real-world' activities.

Several other academic commentators have made contributions to this new field. Markus Altena Davidsen's work on the "spiritual Tolkien milieu",

52 Carole M. Cusack

which has close ties with the Elven movement has been mentioned (Davidsen 2013, 2014). The vampire scholar, Joseph Laycock, published an important article on the Otherkin that was an explicit response to Kirby's work, though he used only two book chapters, "Alternative worlds" (Kirby 2006) and "From pulp fiction to revealed text: A study of the role of the text in the Otherkin community" (Kirby 2009b). His argument that it was incorrect to treat "Otherkinism" as a religion could only be made if he neglected to consult her doctoral dissertation and misrepresented Kirby's argument significantly, but the strength of Laycock's contribution was that he surveyed Otherkin and attended events, an approach that characterizes his research into "real vampires" (Laycock 2012a: 66, 2012b). Zoe Alderton's "'Snapewives' and 'Snapeism': A fiction-based religion within the Harry Potter fandom" (2014) merits attention if only for its exhaustive treatment of a (very nearly) singular phenomenon. Alderton synthesised a very large amount of primary textual materials from sundry online sites, and, using methodology drawn from Cusack, Davidsen and Kirby, she crafts a sympathetic understanding of a very emotional phenomenon that drew unwarranted and cruel censure from all quarters, perhaps simply because "the idea that middle-aged women have 'hobbies' with a sexualised dimension to them is just too much to bear" (Alderton 2014: 228).

It is perhaps important to note how many of the scholars who have attained some prominence via studying these groups are from Australia. Kirby's chapter appeared in 2006, the same year that her doctoral supervisor at the University of Queensland, Lynne Hume, also published a chapter on vampires, "Liminal beings and the undead", in a book she co-edited (Hume 2006: 3–16). Another of Hume's doctoral students, David Keyworth, has written on vampires, primarily from historical and theological viewpoints (Keyworth 2007, 2010). Of the three methodological approaches to emergent religions based on or incorporating fictions used in this volume, two are also Australian. Belgian born Possamai developed his notion of 'hyper-real religions' while living in Australia and working at the University of Western Sydney, and Cusack, the originator of the 'invented religions' model is also Australian (Cusack 2010; Possamai 2005). Additionally, Cusack's colleague, Jay Johnston, has published two short chapters that deal in part with Otherkin. These are only briefly noted here, chiefly because Johnston does not engage with the scholarly trajectory traced in this chapter. In "On having a furry soul: Transspecies identity and ontological indeterminacy in Otherkin subcultures" (Johnston 2013), Johnston relies on Lupa for information about Otherkin and makes no reference to Kirby's research. In "Vampirism, lycanthropy, and Otherkin" (Johnston 2015), one Kirby chapter is listed in the bibliography, but despite the fact that Tië eldaliéva is mentioned, Davidsen is not referenced, neither is Robertson. As there is no fresh ethnographic research and her approach is chiefly derived from French theory, Johnston's work is not examined in detail here.

Conclusion

It is important to note that the claim popular cultural phenomena have religious and spiritual dimensions and may in fact function as religion for an increasing number of people in the contemporary developed world, is still controversial in some parts of the academy. Sean McCloud's "Popular culture fandoms, the boundaries of religious studies, and the project of the self" (2003) employs Samuel Sandmel's term "parallelomania" to argue that although:

> [s]ome popular cultural communities, especially those surrounding dead celebrities, share many substantive and functional parallels to religious movements . . . fandoms are better understood as late modern "projects of the self", affiliational choices that act to establish self- identity and community during a time when these things are not given, but reflexively made and remade.
>
> (McCloud 2003: 188)

He is insistent that the "project of the self" is not religious (McCloud 2003: 199). In contrast, the scholars featured in this volume understand the project of the self to be a core religio-spiritual activity in the twenty-first century and regard the narratives that are co-opted, shared and developed by groups as taking on the role and function of scripture, for emergent religious communities.

The phenomenon of fiction-based, hyper-real or invented religions has been part of the spiritual and religious landscape of the West since the late 1950s. There was a particular spike in these phenomena around the year 2000, when Matrixism, Jediism and the Church of the Flying Spaghetti Monster emerged (Cusack 2010: 113–140). Since then Otherkin, Therianthropy, Kopimism (Kirby and McIntyre in this volume) and other similar phenomena have emerged and flourished, primarily online. Yet it is difficult to know if these phenomena will survive and flourish in the future. Two particular examples of soulbonding, the Snape Wives, focused on Severus Snape of the *Harry Potter* franchise, and Mrs Sephiroth and Sephirothslave, focused on Sephiroth of the *Final Fantasy* videogame, came to an end (in terms of there being no fresh posts online) in 2011 and 2012 respectively. Danielle Kirby reported a significant decrease in the members of Otherkin.net:

> From 2005 to 2011, these numbers have fluctuated between approximately 700 (2005) up to 2,500 (2010), with current numbers at 348 (October, 2011). This latest figure reflects a recent updating of the list, which I understand involved removing inactive members from the listing.
>
> (Kirby 2012: 127)

54   Carole M. Cusack

It may be that too much import has been placed on Lupa's repudiation of her 'wolf Therian' identity in 2013: members of older, traditional religions apostasise regularly, a phenomenon that does not affect the status of the faith. Lupa, a prominent member of a small, fringe spirituality (who authored the key primary text on Otherkin) doing likewise, appears more significant, due to both the newness and the smallness of the community in question, as well as its 'fringe' nature.

In a chapter from *Educational, Psychological, and Behavioral Considerations in Niche Online Communities*, the focus of which is far from the subject of religion and spirituality in Otherkin and Therianthropy, Margaret Shane conducted a SWOT (strengths, weaknesses, opportunities and threats) analysis of the online Otherkin community. She argued that the strengths included the freedom and creativity that the online environment afforded and that "online connectivity defeats real-world limits of social convention, propriety, and fear of censure that limit real-world expressions of the unorthodox, risky, and subversive" (Shane 2014: 264). Yet these strengths are also weaknesses: "online activity is not enough in itself to nurture and protect the subjectivity . . . real-world connections, though less frequent, offer an intensity that real-time or asynchronous online connectivity cannot match" (Shane 2014: 265–266). The opportunities she notes include the way that embracing the non-human frees Otherkin from the history of catastrophes that humans have caused, and also "being *kin to the other* does not supplant one's humanity . . . [but] insists that the otherside and the human-side must learn to accommodate and indwell each within the other" (Shane 2014: 266). Finally, she identifies as threats to Otherkin and similar movements commercialisation and branding, as "engaging with online identity construction means producing subjectivities ripe for capture, coding, and . . . commodification. Who will be the first to own an *Otherkin* lunchbox?" (Shane 2014: 267). These meditations from a scholar outside religious studies are timely in that some of the power has been sapped from the idea that the re-enchantment of the world is occurring through the romantic 'project of the self' and the enabling force of technology. This edited volume is a snapshot of a grouping of religio-spiritual expressions in 2015; what they may be in the future is as yet unknown.

Notes

1 My thanks are due to my colleague, Venetia Robertson, who worked as a research assistant on the initial library searches and note-taking for this chapter, and whose knowledge of Otherkin and Therianthropy far outstrips mine. Her advice on an earlier draft of this chapter is also appreciated. I am also grateful to Donald Barrett, whose tireless encouragement has contributed in no small way to my research over the years.
2 That SubGenii may be classified as Otherkin (as they have both human and Yeti genes) is a fact that has, to date, not been researched and is beyond the scope of this chapter.

References

Alderton, Zoe. 2014. '"Snapewives" and "Snapeism": A fiction-based religion within the Harry Potter fandom'. *Religions* 5: 219–267.

Armour, Robert A. 2001 [1986]. *Gods and Myths of Ancient Egypt*. Cairo and New York: The American University in Cairo Press.

Belanger, Michelle. 2004. *The Psychic Vampire Codex: A Manual of Magick and Energy Work*. York Beach, ME: Red Wheel/Weiser LLC.

Bernauer, Lauren. 2012. 'Ethics on the Internet: Public Versus Private, Is It That Simple?' At: www.religiousstudiesproject.com/2012/10/03/ethics-on-the-internet-public-versus-private-is-it-that-simple-by-lauren-bernauer/. Accessed 26 June 2015.

Blacker, Carmen. 1975. *The Catalpa Bow: A Study of Shamanistic Practices in Japan*. London: Allen and Unwin.

Buljan, Katharine and Carole M. Cusack. 2015. *Anime, Religion and Spirituality: Profane and Sacred Worlds in Contemporary Japan*. Sheffield, UK and Bristol, CT: Equinox.

Burson, Ann C. 1983. 'Swan Maidens and Smiths: A structural study of the *Volundarkvida*'. *Scandinavian Studies* 55: 1–19.

Campbell, Colin. 1972. 'The Cult, the Cultic Milieu and Secularization'. *A Sociological Yearbook of Religion in Britain* 5: 119–136.

Clark, Lynn Schofield. 2003. *From Angels to Aliens: Teenagers, the Media, and the Supernatural*. Oxford, UK: Oxford University Press.

Classen, Albrecht. 2013. 'The Monster Outside and Within: Medieval Literary Reflections on Ethical Epistemology. From *Beowulf* to Marie de France, the *Nibelungenlied*, and Thüring von Ringoltingen's *Melusine*'. *Neohelicon* 40(2): 521–542.

Crome, Andrew. 2014. 'Reconsidering Religion and Fandom: Christian Fan Works in *My Little Pony* Fandom'. *Culture and Religion: An Interdisciplinary Journal* 15(4): 399–418.

Cusack, Carole M. 2010. *Invented Religions: Imagination, Fiction and Faith*. Farnham, UK and Burlington, VT: Ashgate.

Cusack, Carole M. 2015. 'Lab Rats and Tissue Samples: The Human in a Contemporary Invented Religion'. In Kennet Granholm, Marcus Moberg, and Sofia Sjoo (eds), *Religion, Media and Social Change*, 175–188. London and New York: Routledge.

Davidsen, Markus Altena. 2013. 'Fiction-based Religion: Conceptualising a New Category Against History-Based Religion and Fandom.' *Culture and Religion: An Interdisciplinary Journal* 14(4): 378–395.

Davidsen, Markus Altena. 2014. *The Spiritual Tolkien Milieu: A Study of Fiction-Based Religion*. PhD, University of Leiden.

De Ceglia, Francesco Paolo. 2011. 'The Archbishop's Vampires: Giuseppe Davanzati's *Dissertation* and the Reaction of "Scientific" Italian Catholicism to the "Moravian Events"'. *Archives Internationales d'Histoire des Sciences* 61(166–167): 487–510.

Eyovah. 1999. 'The Awakening of a Dragon'. *Eyovah's Dragon Den*. At www.rialian.com/eyovah1/dragonawakepublic2.html. Accessed 25 October 2015.

Guynn, Noah D. 2013. 'Hybridity, Ethics, and Gender in Two Old French Werewolf Tales'. In E. Jane Burns and Peggy McCracken (eds), *From Beasts to Souls: Gender and Embodiment in Medieval Europe*, 157–184. Notre Dame, IN: University of Notre Dame Press.

56 Carole M. Cusack

Harvey, Graham. 1999. 'Coming Home and Coming Out (But Not Converting)'. In Christopher Lamb and M. Darrol Bryant (eds), *Religious Conversion: Contemporary Practices and Controversies*, 233–246. New York: Cassell.

Hume, Lynne. 2006. 'Liminal Beings and the Undead in the 21st Century'. In Lynne Hume and Kathleen McPhillips (eds), *Popular Spiritualities: The Politics of Contemporary Enchantment*, 3–16. Aldershot, UK and Burlington, VT: Ashgate.

Johnston, Jay. 2013. 'On Having a Furry Soul: Transspecies Identity and Ontological Indeterminacy in Otherkin Subcultures'. In Jay Johnston and Fiona Probyn-Rapsey (eds), *Animal Death*, 293–305. Sydney: Sydney University Press.

Johnston, Jay. 2015. 'Vampirism, Lycanthropy, and Otherkin'. In Christopher Partridge (ed.), *The Occult World*, 412–423. London and New York: Routledge.

Keyworth, David. 2007. *Troublesome Corpses: Vampires and Revenants from Antiquity to the Present*. Southend-on-Sea, UK: Desert Island Books.

Keyworth, David. 2010. 'The Aetiology of Vampires and Revenants: Theological Debate and Popular Beliefs'. *Journal of Religious History* 34(2): 158–173.

Kirby, Danielle. 2006. 'Alternative Worlds: Metaphysical Questing and Virtual Community Among the Otherkin'. In Frances di Lauro (ed.), *Through a Glass Darkly: Reflections on the Sacred*, 275–287. Sydney: University of Sydney Press.

Kirby, Danielle. 2009a. *Fantasy and Belief: Fiction and Media as Conjunct Locales for Metaphysical Questing and Spiritual Understanding*. PhD, University of Queensland.

Kirby, Danielle. 2009b. 'From Pulp Fiction to Revealed Text: A Study of the Role of the Text in the Otherkin Community'. In Christopher Deacy and Elisabeth Arweck (eds), *Exploring Religion and the Sacred in a Media Age*, 141–154. Farnham, UK and Burlington, VT: Ashgate.

Kirby, Danielle. 2012. 'Readers, Believers, Consumers, and Audiences: Complicating the Relationship between Consumption and Contemporary Narrative Spiritualities'. *Australian Journal of Communication* 39(1): 121–134.

Kirby, Danielle. 2013. *Fantasy and Belief: Alternative Religions, Popular Narratives, and Digital Cultures*. Durham, UK: Acumen.

Laycock, Joseph. 2012a. '"We are Spirits of Another Sort": Ontological Rebellion and Religious Dimensions of the Otherkin Community'. *Nova Religio: The Journal of Alternative and Emergent Religions* 16(3): 65–90.

Laycock, Joseph. 2012b. 'Real Vampires as an Identity Group: Analysing Causes and Effects of an Introspective Survey by the Vampire Community'. In Adam Possamai (ed.), *Handbook of Hyper-real Religions*, 142–163. Leiden, The Netherlands and Boston, MA: Brill.

Lupa. 2007. *A Field Guide to the Otherkin*. Stafford, UK: Megalithica Books.

Lupa. 2013. 'Letting Go Of Therianthropy For Good', 2 April. At: therioshamanism. com/2013/04/02/letting-go-of-therianthropy-for-good/. Accessed 26 June 2015.

Lyon, David. 2002 [2000]. *Jesus in Disneyland: Religion in Postmodern Times*. Oxford, UK: Polity.

McCloud, Sean. 2003. 'Popular Culture Fandoms, the Boundaries of Religious Studies, and the Project of the Self'. *Culture and Religion* 4(2): 187–206.

McKee, Heidi A. and James E. Porter. 2009. *The Ethics of Internet Research: A Rhetorical, Case-Based Approach*. New York: Peter Lang.

Ohnuki-Tierney, Emiko. 1987. *The Monkey as Mirror: Symbolic Transformations in Japanese History and Ritual*. Princeton, NJ: Princeton University Press.

Partridge, Christopher. 2004–2005. *The Reenchantment of the West: Alternative Spiritualities, Sacralization, Popular Culture and Occulture*, Volumes 1 and 2. London and New York: T. & T. Clark International.

Possamai, Adam. 2005. *Religion and Popular Culture: A Hyper-real Testament*. Brussels: Peter Lang.

Robertson, Venetia Laura Delano. 2012. 'The Law of the Jungle: Self and Community in the Online Therianthropy Movement'. *The Pomegranate* 14(2): 256–280.

Robertson, Venetia Laura Delano. 2013a. 'The Beast Within: Anthrozoomorphic Identity and Alternative Spirituality in the Online Therianthropy Movement'. *Nova Religio: The Journal of Alternative and Emergent Religions* 15(3): 7–30.

Robertson, Venetia Laura Delano. 2013b. 'Where Skin Meets Fin: The Mermaid as Myth, Monster, and Other-Than-Human Identity'. *Journal for the Academic Study of Religion* 26(3): 303–323.

Robertson, Venetia Laura Delano. 2014. 'Of Ponies and Men. *My Little Pony: Friendship is Magic* and the Brony Fandom'. *International Journal of Cultural Studies* 17(1): 21–37.

Robertson, Venetia Laura Delano. 2015a. 'Otherkin'. *World Religions and Spirituality Project* (WRSP). At: www.wrs.vcu.edu/profiles/Otherkin.htm. Accessed 26 September 2015.

Robertson, Venetia Laura Delano. 2015b. 'Therianthropy'. *World Religions and Spirituality Project* (WRSP). At: www.wrs.vcu.edu/profiles/Therianthropy.htm. Accessed 26 September 2015.

Saler, Benson and Charles A. Ziegler. 2005. 'Dracula and Carmilla: Monsters and the Mind'. *Philosophy and Literature* 29(1): 218–227.

Scribner, Orion. 2012. 'Otherkin Timeline: The Recent History of Elfin, Fae, and Animal People'. *The Art and Writings of O. Scribner*. At: orion.kitsunet.net/nonfic.html. Accessed 26 June 2015.

Shane, Margaret. 2014. 'Some People Aren't People on the Inside: Online Connectivity and Otherkin Subjectivities'. In Vivek Venkatesh (ed.), *Educational, Psychological, and Behavioral Considerations in Niche Online Communities*, 260–271. Hershey, PA: Information Science Reference.

Silver Elves. 2013. *The Elven Way: The Magical Path of the Shining Ones*. North Charleston, SC: CreateSpace.

Silver Elves. 2014. *Elf Magic Mail: Book 1. The Original Letters of the Elf Queen's Daughters with Commentary by the Silver Elves*. North Charleston, SC: CreateSpace.

Singler, Beth. 2014. '"SEE MOM IT IS REAL": The UK Census, Jediism and Social Media'. *Journal of Religion in Europe* 7(2): 150–168.

Wicker, Christine. 2005. *Not in Kansas Anymore: Dark Arts, Sex Spells, Money Magic, and Other Things Your Neighbours Aren't Telling You*. New York: Harper Collins.

Zell-Ravenheart, Oberon (ed.). 2009. *Green Egg Omelette: An Anthology of Art and Articles from the Legendary Pagan Journal*. Franklin Lakes, NJ: New Page Books.

3 Salvation and animation

Religion, fandom and identity in the romantic narratives of mystics and Soulbonders

Venetia Laura Delano Robertson

Introduction

The threads of religion and popular culture have been woven together by a number of scholars drawing on the role of ritual, belief and the sacred as present within fandoms. The correspondences between the two phenomena are so frequently pointed out that Sean McCloud has called it a case of "parallelomania", and has suggested a focus on identity formation rather than religiosity as a more fruitful endeavour (McCloud 2003: 188). Indeed, Adam Possamai, discussing the creation of "hyper-real religions" through the infusion of cultural products with religious meaning, emphasises that we should concentrate on "why and how some social actors find a spiritual/religious meaning in a popular piece of work and what they do with it" (Possamai 2007: 22). This chapter aims to add one more thread to this rich tapestry by investigating how the personal spiritual narratives of certain women have been formed through their descriptions of metaphysical yet sensual encounters with their supernatural idols. Case studies will be drawn from two distinct contexts – medieval Christendom and modern fandom – both in vastly different circumstances, yet with some striking similarities. How women from each have confronted the patriarchal norms of the male-dominated arenas of Christian theology and the geek subculture respectively, and articulated through confessional, autobiographical writing (historically, a man's technology) a sense of sacred selfhood, is the focus of this discussion. The effectiveness, even perhaps the necessity, of creative engagements with cultural products, from Jesus mythology to videogame worlds, for marginalised figures like women to craft a meaningful ontological and theological understanding of the world and their place in it will be demonstrated.[1]

Within the mainstream realms of Christendom in England's Middle Ages, and fandom and digital culture in the West of the contemporary period, the female subjects of this chapter find themselves on the fringes due to their unorthodox belief that they have unique mystical relationships to their gods. In the first scenario are two of history's most famous female mystics, Julian of Norwich (*c*.1342–1416) and Margery Kempe (*c*.1373–1438), who wrote of their visitations by Jesus Christ, the revelations he delivered and the romantic and esoteric nature of their connection to him. In the second are two women who belong to a far less-established phenomenon called 'Soulbonding' that shares many characteristics with centuries-old Christian experiences of theophany. Soulbonding is a term that describes an intimate relationship between an individual, in this case a fan, and a fictional character from a novel, television show, film or videogame, in short: "to form and/or experience a robust mental or empathic connection with one or more fictional characters" (*Soul Bonding* 2004–2015). The character, the 'Soulbond', is believed to be a sentient and often magical entity, autonomous from their fictitious setting and capable of interacting with the 'Soulbonder', a human who discovers a profound affinity (or 'bond') with this being.

This study looks at two young women, calling themselves Mrs Sephiroth and Sephirothslave, whose complicated Soulbond with the villain of the *Final Fantasy* videogame saga, Sephiroth, was detailed online between 2004–2012 via journals like Sephirothslave's (aka Julia) *Blurty*, blogs like Mrs Sephiroth's (as Summoner Yuna) *Dreaming of Sephiroth*, and discussions on 'fanatical' websites like the page for *Sephyism* or Sephirothslave's *DeviantArt* account. While belief in the divinity of Christ and his ability to commune with chosen people was, and remains, relatively normal in Christian society, and likewise within fandoms using the Internet to disseminate extra-canonical and imaginative expansions on fictional worlds, stories and characters is accepted, the narratives woven by Julian, Margery, Mrs Sephiroth and Sephirothslave provided such controversial and radical challenges to normative and traditional notions of authority and authenticity, disrupting the bounds of their gender, social status and identity as a believer/fan, and even their humanity, their work invited distrust, denigration and even derision by others.

Individually and collectively, these cases may be seen as examples of various phenomena. They resemble, but are not the same as the channelling experiences of female mediums with male spirit guides, for example, Helena Petrovna Blavatsky and her ascended masters; Hester Dowden and historical celebrities such as William Shakespeare and Oscar Wilde; Rosemary Isabel Brown and famous composers like Franz Liszt and Frédéric Chopin; and in more recent years, Jane Roberts and Seth, and JZ Knight and Ramtha. They are also not the same as the practice of tulpamancy or entity-creation, famously written about by Alexandra Davis-Neel who conjured a thought-form in the shape of portly Tibetan monk and which is having a recent resurgence in online communities (Laycock and Mikles 2015). Furthermore, in more mundane terms, they are not the same as having intentionally generated imaginary friends or pathologically induced multiple personalities, an explanation often levelled at people who hear the voice of God (Luhrmann 2012: 72–84, 227–266). Such paranormal epistemologies provide some context for the belief in otherworldly personas known only to a few special individuals. Other more recent developments in the alternative religion milieu, such as the postmodern blurring of fantasy with fact and the sacralisation of fiction, provide additional examples of the expansive metaphysical landscape of the contemporary West. Demonstrations can be found in the organised "invented religions" inspired by texts like Jediism and *Star Wars* (Cusack 2010; Possamai 2007). They can also be found in the personal mythologies forged by those who "poach" (Jenkins 1992) from the texts of popular culture as the Otherkin do, meeting consumption with craft and customisation (Kirby 2012). Finally, they can be found in the belief that characters from fiction can live independently of their texts and creators, as Soulbonders and other avid fans such as Snapeists or Snapewives, devotees of the antihero Professor Snape of the *Harry Potter* series, allege (Alderton 2014).

This volume extrapolates upon many components of this complicated web of re-enchantment, and so the following analysis will avoid repetition by focusing specifically on the context of the Soulbonding phenomena, the 'geek subculture' – allied as it is with the Internet, technology and fandom in general terms – and how female participation is trivialised. Though this subculture is receiving increasing interest from the academy, it still requires unpacking as a relatively new and dynamic arena. Comparisons in the theology and ontology of the selected mystics and Soulbonders will then shed light on the depth of the continuities between these women's spiritual identity narratives, separated by centuries, yet reflecting shared needs, desires, obstacles and solutions. This exploration of parallels serves as a demonstration of the perennial purposes of personal religion devised from extra or non-canonical readings of texts and seeks to show the productive outcomes of challenging traditional notions of authority, worth and authenticity in light of the ontological, epistemological and spiritual experiences of those who dwell in the margins.

The hermit and the lunatic: the medieval mysticism of Julian of Norwich and Margery Kempe

There are many insightful readings of Margery Kempe and Julian of Norwich available today (for example, McAvoy 2004), so only a brief sketch will be provided. Their works, *The Book of Margery Kempe* (c.1440) and Julian's *Revelations of Divine Love* or *Shewings* (c.1395), are commonly regarded as important sources for medieval European mysticism and also as two of the earliest, possibly the first, autobiographies, indeed books, written in English by women (Jelinek 1986: 14–16). Just how much autonomy a woman in this period could exert is debatable. In patriarchal Christendom, women – in mind, body and soul – were seen as deficient, impure and generally dismissed as 'a necessary evil'. Further to their social, religious and political limitations, not many women could write and read, in the liturgical language of

Latin particularly, and so their capacity to use language for self-expression was restricted. Yet, because writing was a masculine domain, medieval women's literature is a subversive category (Chance 2007), remaining so even when she was not penning the text herself. For example, Margery Kempe was traditionally believed to have been illiterate; she seemed to indicate as much in her text and dictated her *Book* to a scribe. This assertion has been challenged by several historians, like Jacqueline Jenkins who posits that Margery pleaded ignorance of such things in order to display conformity to expectations of her gender and class, to counter accusations of heresy such as Lollardy and to emphasise her pitifulness (Jenkins 2004: 113–128). She nonetheless exhibits control over her narrative throughout, disrupting the very expectations her hyper-feminine character consciously performs by using the 'masculine technology' of text to tell her woman's tale. Julian, writing from within her anchoress' cell, was literally sealed off from the rest of the world, and while her work became more influential than Margery's, it was passive enough in voice and sympathetic enough to the church to escape scrutiny in her lifetime, which may have been intentional on the author's part to avoid controversy (Maskulak 2011: 73–74).

As contemporaries, the two met once in 1414 (Margery, chapter 18), but few details are known regarding their personal lives. Especially little is known of Julian of Norwich, including her birth name. She began writing *Revelations* after enduring a long sickness and later finished it as anchoress at St Julian's in Norwich, which would become her namesake. Margery tells us herself that she was the daughter of a merchant and politician in Lynn, married John Kempe around the age of 20 and bore him several children. She too began to experience her visions after a period of illness (possibly post-natal depression), but was instructed by Jesus to wait a number of years before recording her *Book*. Both opted out of traditional female roles: Julian lived as a recluse in her anchorage; and Margery shunned her maternal and conjugal duties and travelled as a pilgrim and a (largely unwanted and unheeded) prophet. Perhaps unsurprisingly, neither seemed to live entirely happy lives, but having eschewed the typical routes by which one might embrace their (prescribed) gendered identity, the recording and hence sharing of their experiences provided an invaluable window through which they could articulate and sanctify an otherwise maligned and marginalised feminine subjectivity, and through which we can now view an otherwise fairly inscrutable faction of medieval Christian society.

Though *Revelations* continues to be a well-regarded contemplative text of literary and theological acclaim, and Julian is often seen as composed and wise even in the modern period, Christian commenters like C. S. Lewis regarded her work as "dangerous" (quoted in Maskulak 2011: 72). The intense and emotional protagonist of Margery's text, forever wailing, weeping, fainting, pleading and admonishing herself as a sign of her devotion and passion for God, has given Margery a reputation, both in life and in

62 *Venetia Laura Delano Robertson*

scholarship, for being a "hysterical, hyperbolic, noisy and undignified renegade" (McAvoy 2004: 25). Rescued from the fate of being simply labelled an eccentric hermit or a raving lunatic, feminist historiography has done much in the way of recognising the contribution these women have made to our understanding of gender and religiosity and in laying the foundations for the writing of the female subject. Regarded as spiritually inferior and with few opportunities to participate formally in religious life, medieval women were able to find a platform for the articulation of their faith in personal, often subversive, and sometimes heretical modes of connecting to the divine.[2] Within both orthodox and heterodox circles, Caroline Walker Bynum states that female devotees were principally interested in an "affective religious response, an extreme form of penitential asceticism, an emphasis both on Christ's humanity and on the inspiration of the spirit, and a bypassing of clerical authority" (1988: 17). The development of mysticism amongst women in reaction to these concerns was inevitably met with hostility. From the fourteenth century onwards, there was a decline in the number of church roles for women and increased suspicion of "those prophetic and visionary powers of holy women that contrasted most sharply with male clerical authority" (Bynum 1988: 21).

For Margery and Julian, mystical experience and the autobiographical recording of these revelations became intertwined routes via which they could transcend the strictures of their sex and attempt to articulate a spiritual sense of self independently. They both sacralised the feminine subject, contrarily conforming to, subverting and expanding upon tropes of femininity along the way. As Bynum has suggested, through his visitations Jesus impressed upon Margery and Julian a theology coloured by affective language, a fascination with the manhood of Christ and a deep dedication to repentance. In both writings, the authors describe themselves as unworthy mortals, "living in wretched flesh" (Julian ch. IV) who are miraculously contacted by Christ and given a series of revelations and visions. Their theophanic encounters generate a relational ontology between themselves and God: Christ is revealed as all-goodness, all-wisdom, father, lover, husband, maker and in Julian's words, mother (Julian ch. LVIII), while in either contrast or complement, they take the role of the sinner, the unlettered, a submissive daughter, lover, wife and creature. Yet in their intriguing reappraisal of the body as having soteriological value, Margery and Julian charted a sensual and sensorial route to the sacred and to their own sacralisation. As Julian says of corporeality as a reflection of the divine: "Our nature that is the higher part is knit to God, in the making; and God is knit to our nature that is the lower part, in our flesh-taking: and thus in Christ our two natures are oned [made one]" (Julian ch. LVII). Their complex somatic spirituality interweaves pleasure and pain, whether by meditating on the suffering of Jesus on the cross, his dehydration, the punctures by his thorny crown, his weeping wounds and desperately desiring this agony

Salvation and animation   63

upon oneself as Julian does (chs II and III); or by a preoccupation with carnality, contrasted by Margery in her disgust with the thought of sex with her husband so that she would rather "have eaten and drunk the ooze and muck in the gutter than consent to intercourse", with the romantic seduction by her Lord:

> I must be intimate with you, [says Jesus] and lie in your bed with you . . . you greatly desire to see me, and you may boldly, when you are in bed, take me to you as your wedded husband, as your dear darling . . . take me in the arms of your soul and kiss my mouth, my head, and my feet as sweetly as you want.
>
> (Margery ch. 36)

For both mystics, their fluctuating proximity to Christ provides them with moments of ecstasy and moments of torment. Julian describes this exasperating vacillation as follows:

> Lord gave me again the comfort and the rest in soul, in satisfying and sureness so blissful and so mighty that no dread, no sorrow, no pain bodily that might be suffered should have distressed me. And then the pain shewed again to my feeling, and then the joy and the pleasing . . .
>
> (Julian ch. XV)

Margery's encounters were sometimes so blissful as to be torturous:

> These conversations were so sweet, so holy and so devout, that often this creature could not bear it, but fell down and twisted and wrenched her body about, and made remarkable faces and gestures, with vehement sobbings and great abundance of tears, sometimes saying "Jesus, mercy", and sometimes, "I die".
>
> (Margery ch. 17)

But for enduring, these travails, physical as much as spiritual, they are rewarded with the knowledge that their substance is one with God's own being. In contradistinction to the prevailing Augustinian gender binary that saw men as naturally spiritual while women were bound to the material realm with their carnal concerns (Gilchrist 1994: 14–15), the theological premise that even women "are knit and oned" with God "and made holy in this holiness" (Julian ch. LVIII) body and soul was a radical affirmation of the female subject in medieval Christianity. In addition, the mutual passionate intimacy of their interactions with Jesus indubitably raises them up as his favoured subjects, and by virtue of their sex differences, places them in binaries such as man (though a godly one) and wife, a privileged position indeed.

64 _Venetia Laura Delano Robertson_

Fanspace as manspace? Geek culture, fandom and the Internet

Geek culture, media fandom and the Internet can be spoken of separately, but the entanglement of the three constitutes the modern context described in this chapter. A pioneering voice in the study of fandom, Henry Jenkins rightly calls media fandoms "participatory cultures" and outlines at least five ways in which this is so:

1 Reception: fans watch/read/play their chosen media, often multiple times, "with a mixture of emotional proximity and critical distance".
2 Interpretation: they watch critically and speculatively, seeking plot holes, clues and parallels between the narrative and their own lives.
3 Consumerism: fans effect the marketing of media indirectly and directly, providing feedback to producers and distributors, and purchasing relevant merchandise.
4 Cultural Production: fanart, fanfiction and fanvids are just some of the many forms of products or 'fan labour' that fans construct using material from media but reworking it – this in turn generates a specialised aesthetic, vocabulary and system of symbols for the fandom.
5 Community: "fandom functions as an alternative social community", particularly for those seeking a network of people with shared interests that may exist separately from other aspects of daily life (Jenkins 1992: 284–287).

Both mainstream and alternative forms of media can gain a cult following if they have enough appeal, but as John Fiske notes, fandoms are "typically associated with cultural forms that the dominant value system denigrates – pop music, romance novels, comics" (Fiske 2001: 30), products that are usually affiliated with geeky or uncool social groups, and generally considered 'low' rather than 'high' culture. Jenkins adds that the attendant concepts of taste and appropriate conduct that draw such a distinction are flouted by fans, fandoms and fannish activities: "From the perspective of dominant taste, fans appear to be frighteningly out of control, undisciplined and unrepentant, rogue readers" (Jenkins 1992: 18). Yet, Jenkins rightly insists, remixing cultural artefacts, for example, writing fanfiction that extrapolates upon the existing storyline, making a dedicated web profile for a favourite character, or creating devotional artworks, music videos or animations, imaginative fans can update, expand, perhaps most importantly, customise the text to reflect and enact their own desires. There is no place more suitable for the celebration of subculture than the Internet; its social networking opportunities, relative anonymity and expressive capacities provide both a platform for independent opinions and a hub for a community of otherwise dispersed or isolated peoples.

There are many overlaps between fandom and the Internet culturally speaking, mostly surrounding the nature of geek or nerd identity and its

Salvation and animation 65

inherent masculinity and exclusivity, and so both concepts are better spoken of as a network of ideas and interests. There is a misconception that men numerically dominate fandoms, perhaps because so many fandoms celebrate texts that are falsely believed to be favoured by men over women. This is likely because, despite a long-running interest and participation in geeky and fannish products like sci-fi, superhero, supernatural, sword and sorcery narratives, films and television shows, tabletop, computer and video games, Western comics and cartoons as well as *anime* and *manga*, women still struggle for recognition as equal contenders for both geek and fan status. Lori Kendall aptly sums up the image of the geek or nerd as a masculine identity that is simultaneously desirable and marginal, including such characteristics as: "fascination with technology, interest in science fiction and related media such as comic books, and perceived or actual social ineptitude and sartorial disorganization" (Kendall 2000: 262). To this "mythological male archetype" Roli Varma adds "idealised male norms", such as a natural affinity and/or obsession with computers, Whiteness,[3] high IQs with especial talent in the departments of mathematics and sciences, and the presumption that characteristics like social skills are feminine and hence undesirable (Varma 2007: 360–361). The nerdy male stereotype is one that is imposed upon this subculture and at the same time taken up by and toyed with by self-identifying nerds (Kendall 2000; Robertson 2014).

There are multitudes of ways that women are excluded from this realm, an exclusion that is maintained online, despite internet users' opportunities for relative disembodiment and anonymity. In 2010, Cindy Royal caught the attention of the producers of *Wired* magazine when she wrote them an open letter lamenting the notable paucity of professional women in the technology industry gracing their covers, a problem that, she notes, came under scrutiny almost 20 years ago by Lynn Cherny and Elizabeth Reba Weise's 1996 book *Wired Women: Gender and New Realities in Cyberspace* (Royal 2010). With its roots in Stewart Brand and John Perry Barlow's *Whole Earth Review*, *Rolling Stone* and the 'cyberdelic' publication *Mondo2000*, the outlook of *Wired* is as informed as much by the counterculture of the 1960s and 1970s as it is by a San Franciscan brand of consumer capitalism (Davis 2004: 196–202). Yet in their unequal attention to women in the industry they promote, they continue to propagate the notion that technology is solely a male pursuit. It is predictable then that in numerous studies, women have indicated that they feel either compelled to avoid or uncomfortable pursuing careers in computers and technology because of the masculine environment that is both implied and explicitly present, despite efforts to create the appearance of a democratic and progressive ethos in the tech-world (Margolis 2003: 18; Varma 2007: 359–376).

This gendered dichotomy is perpetuated by negative attitudes towards female users of technology, the Internet and their attendant geeky activities and subcultures. The explosion of the 2014 'GamerGate' scandal saw an online revolt against female computer gamers such as indie developer, Zoe

66 *Venetia Laura Delano Robertson*

Quinn, and game critic, Anita Sarkeesian. Torrents of abuse were hurled at women in the industry, including vitriolic taunts, incitations to rape, death threats and 'doxxing' – the leaking of identifying information such as their home addresses – all creating fears for the victims' physical safety as well as their emotional wellbeing (Wu 2014). Though claims were made that the real crux of the crisis was corruption in game reviewing, journalism and tensions between indie and industrial game designers, the core problems stem from simultaneous anti-liberal sentiments and anti-feminist conservatism that found an excuse for expression in the perceived intrusion of women into arenas typically dominated by men (Dean 2014). Ironically, despite the association of gaming with maleness, females make up close to 50 per cent of the player community and may also be more invested in terms of hours dedicated to play (Entertainment Software Association, 2014; Williams *et al.* 2009: 716–717).

The sexist agenda that keeps females alienated and silenced in geek culture is well evidenced by memes like "Idiot Nerd Girl". This meme presents as a picture of a teenage girl wearing thick-rimmed glasses with the word 'nerd' written on her hand, and a much publicised rendition has the caption "self-proclaimed title of 'nerd'; what is World of Warcraft?" Meant as a paradoxical statement, here proficiency with the popular online game *World of Warcraft* is being used as a benchmark for nerdiness to make this girl appear like a clueless 'poser' or 'try-hard'. Comparatively, Jessica Bagnall argues, "men are rarely challenged on the 'authenticity' of their participation within the subculture" (Bagnall 2012). She points out additionally that not only are female characters in geeky media mostly sexist and sexualised stereotypes, proxies for the promotion of heterosexual, Anglo-Saxon, androcentric storylines (the same claim that was made by Sarkeesian and garnered violent responses), but the companies who make games actively ostracise female consumers, both by refusing to allow for female-gendered avatars and by limiting female attendance at game-related events, citing the example of the men-only Texas launch of *Battlefield 3* in 2011, which was subsequently billed as a 'gentlemen's retreat'. The latter case showed, unfortunately, that the "nerd subculture is viewed as so heavily male-geared, that instead of banning misogyny within these events, they banned women" (Bagnall 2012). As a result, studies have shown that female gamers are likely to circumvent anticipated hostility by "avoiding feminine screen names, female avatars, or voice chat functions that can reveal their sex" (Fox and Tang 2014: 318), both playing into the oppressive normativity of the community and indicating that women are being forced to rely upon anonymous computer-mediated contact as a safe route to participating in geeky subcultures.

The problem persists in comic book fandoms; very few mainstream comics offer powerful female protagonists and are, in fact, steeped in a history of blatant sexism. When attending comic or fan conventions with the intention of cosplaying, female fans then face the dual challenge of feeling objectified if they don closely replicated, generally scanty costumes of their heroines, or opting for a modified costume or masculine character, which further highlights ways in which female subjects do not 'fit in' to this scene. Attending at all comes with the risk of, at least, condescension by those who are suspicious of women's abilities to be 'genuine' fans and, at worst, sexual harassment. Aja Romano, writing in 2012, collates the negative experiences of numerous females at conventions such as being dismissed by male panel-lists or moderators during question time, seeing panels on gender diversity in gaming headed by only male speakers, a dearth of female voices on the organising committees, the reduction of female artists and vendors to 'booth babes' by patrons, and the ubiquitous assumption that female attendees are either there because of their boyfriend or, as Bagnall says, because they are trying to attract a male by appealing to his interests (Bagnall 2012; Romano 2012). Suzanne Scott safely concludes that:

> Because comic book culture is male defined, and because this perception has permeated both the collective consumer consciousness and the spaces in which those exchanges take place, it is understandable that many female comic book fans have taken it upon themselves to construct alternative, fangirl-friendly spaces.
>
> (Scott 2013: 10)

The above discussion highlights a plethora of cases where females are passively and aggressively vilified within the geek subculture and, by extension, the fandoms intertwined with geek identity. However, in certain corners of fandoms, women hold an unmistakably significant, yet still contentious, place and use cultural production and writing especially to enunciate their personal relationships with their favoured media. "From its very beginnings", Karen Hellekson and Kristina Busse write, "fan fiction has been a female, if not feminist, undertaking" (2014: 75). Pointing to the role of women in starting the first fanzine dedicated to *Star Trek* in 1967, generating most of the Trekkie fanfiction of the 1970s, and developing, as Francesca Coppa says, "a distinctively female visual aesthetic and critical approach" (Coppa 2008), Hellekson and Busse note that there is a precedent for the high proportion of females participating in fandoms today. The original series of *Star Trek* has not been awarded with any accolades for its depiction of gender equality – female characters are sparse and either have their femininity and sexuality played down or hammed up to conform to the stereotypes of the time – still, clips from this show and a variety of others have been spliced and reworked into fanvids time and time again in the interest of alternative readings that reify otherwise "marginalised female perspectives" (Coppa 2008).

These fangirl-friendly spaces most commonly produce fan labour that has an erotic and/or romantic tone. Partially, this draws from a socially ingrained interest in relationships amongst females, evidenced by the popularity of

68   *Venetia Laura Delano Robertson*

'chick-flick' and 'chick-lit' genres, and fandoms surrounding paranormal romance media (for example, the *Twilight* and the *True Blood* franchises). Hellekson and Busse's 2014 volume demonstrates that the main themes of these fan works are power, pleasure and subversion. This is patently visible in the development of slashfic: narratives that typically revolve around homosexual encounters between otherwise straight male characters. First popularised by the pairing of *Star Trek* characters Captain Kirk and Spock, today couples like Aragorn/Legolas of J. R. R. Tolkien's legendarium, Angel/Spike of Joss Whedon's Buffyverse, and Harry/Draco of J. K. Rowling's Potterverse are favourites (Subtext 2014). Elizabeth Woledge makes the compelling argument that because the universes these dalliances take place in are alien or fantastic, female authors are able to re-write masculine codes of behaviour, feminising their relationships to represent the qualities of intimacy, mutuality and passion typify idealised feminine interactions and appeal to female audiences (Woledge 2005: 56–57). This might, as Woledge contends, reveal the genre of slash to have far more conventional motivations than its superficially queer and transgressive nature might denote, but it also provides an important and creative channel for championing 'the feminine'. This is not true of all kinds of slash or fanfiction, but the inscribing of values held by the author and community onto their products are central ways that fans as "craft consumers" (Kirby 2012) can feel closer to and be better represented by their favoured text.

Naturally, to be a fan of a media product is to be interested in the world, plot and characters of the text, and so sexualisation, fetishisation, adoration of, and even obsession with, real life or fictional figures occur within fandoms along a vast spectrum of degrees. Self-insertion into fanfic narratives is one way that consumers can 'live out' their fantasies with the subject of their idolisation. Since the 1972 fanfic piece by Paula Smith in which she, under the pseudonym Mary Sue, enters the *Star Trek* universe, a self-insertion is referred to as a 'Mary Sue' by fandom communities. While there is a grand tradition of authors including themselves in their own work, either by name, cameo or through a generally transparent avatar, the Mary Sue is characterised by a perceived desire on the part of the producer to channel or explore hidden or latent aspects of their 'true self' through this fictional manifestation. Essentially, the insert is an avatar and mode of self-exploration and identity formation. Commonly associated with women's fanfic, Camille Bacon-Smith has suggested that this is because they are already automatically displaced by their interest in 'masculine' texts and activities: "For intelligent women struggling with their culturally anomalous identities, Mary Sue combines the characteristics of active agent with the culturally approved traits of beauty, sacrifice, and self-effacement which . . . wins her the love of the hero" (Bacon-Smith 2014: 101).

While Bacon-Smith's analysis is somewhat narrow in seeing this is the sole motivator, there are notably times when Mary Sue allows one to embody heteronormative and hegemonic standards of femininity within the masculine realm of geek culture in a context entirely suited to the desires of the author. The Soulbonding phenomenon represents an expansion of this genre of writing and, in some cases, clearly reflects the interests proposed by Bacon-Smith. In attempting to explain Soulbonding, it could be argued that the Soulbond is primarily a vessel for the fan's desires: the Soulbonder who tells the tale of their relationship with this character either consciously or subconsciously imbues them with qualities they wish to see in a friend, partner, lover or even themselves. The narrative created enables both Soulbond and Soulbonder, through their unique and often-otherworldly relationship, to be represented as idealised beings. Through the following analysis of Sephirothslave and Mrs Sephiroth, the tropes of fangirling as a response to the masculinisation of geek culture can be seen as inscribed upon their interactions with their favourite character and superhuman lover, Sephiroth. The tales of their relationships with Sephiroth, like those of Margery and Julian with Jesus, contain typical elements such as jealousy and possessiveness, despondency and salvation, monogamous true love, and female submissiveness and male mastery, but their deployment through socially, religiously and sexually 'deviant' goes beyond wish-fulfillment, demonstrating considerable ontological and epistemological significance in light of the current trends in religious creativity demonstrated in this volume.

Soulbonding: fangirl narratives to the next level

During the short-lived existence of the Soulbonding community (the *Soul Bonding* LiveJournal suggests it has been in decline since 2012, supported by other abandoned groups and Google search metrics for related terms), their unusual principles attracted notoriety and scorn from various corners of the Internet and tensions ran high internally, a remarkable example being the jealous feud that raged between Mrs Sephiroth and Sephirothslave. Within the game and its spin-off animations, Sephiroth is revealed to be the product of an experiment in genetic mutation and carries the DNA of an ancient alien being. He aims to harness the life-force of the planet, Gaia, believing it will make him a god and lead him to the legendary Promised Lands. With the release of the extremely successful *Final Fantasy VII* (*FFVII*) in 1997, Sephiroth quickly became the subject of his own fandom, starring in countless slash stories and *yaoi* comics (homoerotic manga), inspiring several religiously themed fan pages, and remains today one of the most popular videogame villains ever unleashed (Bridgman 2014). Sephiroth embodies many religious references, courtesy of the game creators: his name is Qabbalistic; he resembles, with his wings and flaming glory, the seraphim of the Old Testament; and acts the archetypal fallen angel coveting apotheosis. Even more religious in tone was the nature of some of his fans' infatuation.

Motivated by the release of the *FFVII* film *Advent Children* (2005) Mrs Sephiroth introduced the religion of "Sephyism", the worship of "the great god Sephiroth", and hosted an online 'shrine' to the animated deity

(Mrs Sephiroth 2005). On the website, Mrs Sephiroth reacted to the criticism of detractors by likening her veneration to an act of martyrdom:

[m]y love and devotion to Sephiroth is absolute. For if it wasn't I may have failed by now . . . think of how early Christians were stoned by the Romans, yet they still followed their faith. Being a true Sephyist is like that . . . we'll receive ridicule, but no matter what, we stay close to our beliefs.

(Mrs Sephiroth 2006)

Like Margery Kempe, her willingness to make public her affections and endure inevitable derision was meant as a personal sacrifice to demonstrate the depth of her devotion. In Margery's case, Christ practically insists, saying, "Yes, daughter, the more ridicule that you have for love of me, the more you please me" (Margery ch. 15). Mrs Sephiroth perceived, and the feeling was mutual, Sephirothslave to be a rival in love. In a comment on Sephirothslave's Deviant Art page, home to many drawings and photoshopped images of her and her beloved (including a hypothetical baby in their digitally manipulated family portrait), Mrs Sephiroth made her animosity clear:

How dare you think to call yourself his girlfriend. Your [sic] not fit even to stand in his presence. Sephiroth and I are bound together, your little fantasy is nothing more than a dream . . . you are nothing more but another fan girl who tarnishes my beloved's name . . . always remember I am his wife.

(Mrs Sephiroth 2007)

To which Sephirothslave retorts:

I do try to refrain [from] engaging in arguments with you . . . and every other psychotic fangirl running around the internet in an awesome-to-behold state of delusion . . . You have nothing to support your claim and Seph actually finds people like you amusing.

(Sephirothslave 2007a)

These exchanges are indicative of not only a jealous obsession with the character of Sephiroth, but a challenge for the legitimacy of those feelings, a need for a sense of authenticity, authority, confidence and belonging. Margery and Julian expressed this in their longing to be placed amongst Christ's most cherished lovers like Mary Magdalene (Julian ch. II), with Margery being repeatedly assured that she is predominate in his affections – "I have told you before that you are a singular lover of God . . . my own blessed spouse" – and that she is privy to wisdom that he never shared with other hierophants like Saint Bridget (Margery ch. 22).

Sephirothslave's convictions were based in her understanding of Sephiroth as a being that inspired the appearance and personality of the *FFVII* character, but who is actually an entity of the astral plane. From at least 2004 until 2012, spanning from high school to adulthood, Sephirothslave recounted her journey with her supernatural lover through various online journals. Initially, she said, "I fell in love with the videogame character. When I first began spontaneously [astral] projecting, I thought I was meeting the game character". But after developing her psychic skills, she realised fate was leading her to the "true" Sephiroth (Sephirothslave 2007d). Because this was the real Sephiroth and not the fictional version, Sephirothslave suggested that 'Soulbonding' is not the correct term for their relationship (Sephirothslave 2007f). Nonetheless, her experiences have often left her associated closely with the phenomenon, and indeed her description more than adequately fits the criteria.

Rather than seeing Sephiroth as a god, Sephirothslave syncretised a number of magical traditions and biblical notions into her "one-woman religion" and concluded that he was, in fact, an archangel, with access to the Akashic records (Sephirothslave 2004 'been away'), the theosophical term for a celestial archive of all our earthly experiences, past, present and future (Leadbeater *Clairvoyance* 1903). As well as meeting in other dimensions, Sephiroth advised his 'slave' in waking life as a disembodied voice. Sephirothslave claimed to have a marriage licence for the couple, and while Mrs Sephiroth fantasised about the opportunity to kiss Sephiroth in real life, having to settle for a picture of him instead, Sephirothslave enjoyed the full connubial benefits of her relationship through out of body experiences. As with Margery and her spiritual marriage to Jesus (Margery ch. 35), sexual relations were saved exclusively for their holy husbands, much to the disappointment of Margery's earthly spouse (Margery ch. 11). Sephiroth was an especially jealous god, described on Sephirothslave's *Blurty* as possessive and paranoid. Yet, she enjoys being the submissive partner, claiming to have based her relationship on a medieval definition of marriage, emphasising the solemnity of her vow to 'love, honour and obey'. This is reflected in her fanfiction, wherein the Mary Sue-style heroine 'Julia' pledges herself to Sephiroth, who says to her:

> "From here on out, you aren't a person, you aren't free to do as you please. You should consider yourself my slave" . . . As if to further prove herself, Julia fell to her knees, humbling herself before him . . . undisturbed by the fact she'd just been reduced to property.
>
> (Sephirothslave 2007b)

Both Mrs Sephiroth and Sephirothslave suffered the consequences of their 'long-distance relationship', as did Julian and Margery. For Mrs Sephiroth, this is partly due to a sense of cognitive dissonance: she muses in one post that Sephiroth may exist in some form in another dimension, but in others confesses to knowing that he is only a character (Mrs Sephiroth 2004c). She feels

72 *Venetia Laura Delano Robertson*

"passions", physical signs of his presence, not dissimilar to the "the fire of love burning in her breast" sensation described by Margery (ch. 35):

> First I had this feeling inside my chest. Then it consumed me. All the way through my body. All over I felt an intense heat . . . I guess heat is the nearest word that I can explain it as . . . it was really more than that though . . . It was like he was there with me, holding me. Of course I know that he was not . . . but it felt that way.
>
> (Mrs Sephiroth 2004d)

She pledges herself to Sephiroth, real or not, and conveys her ultimate desire for unity:

> My Sephiroth. My one and only. Our dreams will be our reality . . . together we will be forever . . . take me into your darkness with you . . . for there I am surrounded by you . . . never to escape . . . to love you and to become one with you.
>
> (Mrs Sephiroth 2004a)

Such longing is reminiscent of Julian's plea for wholeness with God: "until I am substantially [bodily] united to him, I can never have love or rest or true happiness . . . that is I am so attached to him that there can be no created thing between my God and me" (ch. V).

Both Margery and Julian developed their esoteric theologies if not in response to, then at least in concert with, debilitating and lengthy physical and possibly mental illnesses. In addition, Julian worried at times that she was "raving" mad and burdened by "weariness of my life, and irksomeness of myself" (ch. XV). Margery was consistently shirked and chastised for her beliefs in life and has been diagnosed posthumously with everything from hysteria to heart disease, Tourette's and post-partum depression (Warren 2007: 1382). So too have Sephirothslave and Mrs Sephiroth attested to serious depressive episodes. Each expressed at times a yearning to die in order either to end the suffering of their distance from their holy husbands, or to finally be united with them. The body in this case, bound as it is to the material plane, is seen as a barrier between lovers who wish to be together in the spirit realm. "I think of no other", says Mrs Sephiroth, "I have began to think that I might be able to be with him if I end my life here" (2004b), while Sephirothslave says she has been diagnosed at times with bipolar, schizophrenia and severe depression due to her mental suffering (Sephirothslave 2007e). "I desired to have all manner [of] pains bodily and ghostly that I should have if I should die . . . for the more speed in my death: for I desired to be soon with my God" says the anchoress (ch. II), and Margery reports that she too "would like to be slain for God's love" (ch. 1).

Despite the hardship of being in love with an unseen entity, not just the emotional torment and its physical effects, but the accompanying ridicule, persecution, pathologisation, ostracisation and loneliness, the experiences have proved formative in terms of identity- and world-construction. Their relationships, irregular though they might sound, brought solace and much needed affirmation: "I was a goddamn wreck" Mrs Sephiroth says, "and it was my love for Sephiroth that actually helped me get out of the hole I was in and begin to live my life again" (Mrs Sephiroth 2004c). Likewise, Sephirothslave admits that prior to meeting Sephiroth she was "in a bad state . . . I got into a lot of bad habits, not the least of which being cutting myself and overdosing on various over-the-counter painkillers . . . if the archangel hadn't come to me . . . I would be dead" (Sephirothslave 2007c). Though these narratives are told through online or written media, and the relationships had in the immaterial realms of the spiritual, astral or imagination, consequences are quite clearly felt in the offline world.

Like Margery and Julian, a connection with an otherworldly being provided these young women with a source of joy, inspiration, even community as each attracted a small but sympathetic number of supporters: their very own fans. But, perhaps most importantly, it provoked them into undertaking a difficult journey of self-discovery, through which their autobiographical writing allowed their narrative to be crafted and shared. Partially this is due to a lack of space for enunciation offline, as Mrs Sephiroth intimates: "I just feel I have to write all these feelings and emotions down sometimes, as I can't express them any other way" (Mrs Sephiroth 2004c). Both speak of social isolation and feeling misunderstood by their peers, virtual and actual. After taking a hiatus from the Internet after being mocked for her claims, Sephirothslave returned to blogging to again utilise this platform in her ongoing project of selfhood. It is not just the writing of identity that fosters meaning-making, but audience participation, passive or active, that gives this method efficacy.

The necessary catalysts for these positive effects, the idealised superman and the narrativisation of the relationship through the paradoxically personal yet virtually distant medium of writing, speak to the fact that in their contexts, be it medieval Christendom or contemporary fandom and geek subculture, there is little opportunity for the development of female identity. When women do try to articulate their subjectivity within these allegedly masculine spheres, they risk becoming targets for discrimination and harassment. As this chapter has argued, this intentional curbing of female agency has meant that women, and especially those holding subversive beliefs or opinions, for example, regarding sexuality, sensuality and spirituality, must carve out a space of their own in order to express their feelings and findings.

Conclusion

It may seem reductive to make comparisons between the writings of medieval and modern women when undoubtedly their historical, social and cultural contexts bear many differences. However, the similarities between

74   *Venetia Laura Delano Robertson*

the extra-canonical claims made in each of these confessional texts are not only striking, they are insightful with regard to the role of other-than-human but human-like persons in the articulation and sacralisation of identities of marginalised individuals within marginalised spaces. By using a lens adapted from fandom studies to review these forms of engagements with unreal persons, a productive analysis of the contextual pressures and motivators for these relationships, the writing of these relationships and their consequences for developing identity, has been made. A study of gender has been key to this examination, revealing that just as medieval women like Margery and Julian had to delve, at their own risk, into the masculine world of literature and theology to create a spirituality that embraced their womanhood, their desire for acceptance in Christ and their need to be one with their divine love, so too do modern women face many challenges in raising an independent voice in fan communities, on the Internet and as a part of gender-positive personal religion, and particularly when their exclamations are deemed deviant.

Margaret Wertheim's *The Pearly Gates of Cyberspace* (1999) drew a parallel between the medieval Christian perception of Heaven and contemporary cyberspace as a "disembodied paradise", "open to everyone" and offering "salvation to all" (Wertheim 1999: 19, 24). This chapter provides a counter to this utopic claim: while both Christianity and the Internet have been lauded as universal spaces for acceptance and authenticity, agents and attitudes of conservative, patriarchal normativity have not enabled this to be the guiding ethos of either culture. On the sardonic wiki *Encyclopedia Dramatica*, Mrs Sephiroth and Sephirothslave are described as "batshit-insane", "delusional" (*Encyclopedia Dramatica* 2013), "attention-whores" (*Encyclopedia Dramatica* 2015), derided for everything from their fanfiction to their fashion sense: treatment typical for the "culturally anomalous identities" of female fans and geeks (Bacon-Smith 2014: 101). Such antagonistic responses are part of a system of boundary-policing or as one commenter on the website *Fandom Wank* proffered: "setting a standard way of interacting with other fans and with the source material, and then setting a social disincentive to stray from that pattern" (quoted in Alderton 2014: 227). Whether it is the "dangerous" theology of Julian, the histrionics and hubris of Margery, or the imaginative romantic narratives generated by devotees of *FFVII*, it is clear that the transgression being 'policed' is not simply a case of unorthodoxy or rogue reading, but the perceived foray of women into men's space, their use of men's technology, their unabashed displays of intimacy, sensuality and sexual pleasure, and their projection of their personal and gendered ideals onto their characters and those of their mythical, spiritual or divine lovers.

The spirituality and ontology that each woman developed through their bonds with their gods both subvert and reinscribe gender norms. Feminine tropes are drawn on in their erotic relations with their masters, who take on a role at times domineering and others effeminate as husbands, or occasionally, fathers, brothers, even mothers. They cast themselves in the role of a submissive helpmeet, yet also as chosen ones of exceptional spiritual power whose entire person and purpose is inextricably linked to the divine. Stereotypical and idealised gendered subjects are essential to the story. Nonetheless, the writing and, for the authors, reality of these relationships has enabled the reification of female subjectivity in the face of worldly discrimination, criticism and exclusion. The personal mythologies formed and the sacralised identities assumed by mystics Margery and Julian, and Soulbonders Mrs Sephiroth and Sephirothslave, irrespective of traditional signifiers of authority and authenticity like adherence to orthodoxy, community sanction, longevity and normativity, demonstrate the perennial relevance of creative interaction with figures from popular culture for the making of meaningful worldviews.

Notes

1 This chapter is based on material presented in the paper 'Animation as Salvation: How Soulbonders Find the Spiritual in New Narratives' at the International Conference for the Centre for Studies on New Religions (CESNUR), Aletheia University, Taiwan, 21–23 June 2011 (Robertson 2011).
2 Historians such as John H. Arnold have argued that the numbers of women in heretical groups was in actuality far less than once thought, though there are notable exceptions, like the Beguines or the cult of the prophetess Guglierma that were small movements, but comprised solely of women. He nonetheless maintains that how heretical piety might have afforded the "renegotiation of the constraints of gender" is a question worth asking (Arnold 2013: 505).
3 Though there are parallels with non-White cultures, such as the *otaku* subculture of Japan, which is comprised of 'hardcore' geeks who favour videogames, *anime*, and *manga*. See Hiroki Azuma (2009).

References

Alderton, Zoe. 2014. '"Snapewives" and "Snapeism": A Fiction-Based Religion within the Harry Potter Fandom'. *Religions* 5: 219–267.
Arnold, John H. 2013. 'Heresy and Gender in the Middle Ages'. In Judith M. Bennett and Ruth Mazo Karras (eds), *The Oxford Handbook of Women and Gender in Medieval Europe*, 496–510. Oxford, UK: Oxford University Press.
Azuma, Hiroki. 2009. *Otaku: Japan's Database Animals*. Translated by Jonathan E. Abel and Shion Kono. University of Minnesota Press, MN: Minneapolis.
Bacon-Smith, Camille. 2014. 'Training New Members'. In Karen Hellekson and Kristina Busse (eds), *The Fan Fiction Studies Reader*, 138–158. Iowa City, IA: University of Iowa Press.
Bagnall, Jessica. 2012. 'Nerd Girls Are Real Nerds Too! (And Why This Meme Sucks)'. *Feminspire*. At: feminspire.com/nerd-girls-are-real-nerds-too-and-why-this-meme-sucks/. Accessed 15 June 2015.
Bridgman, Andrew. 2014. 'Toplist Results: The 20 Greatest Videogame Villains of All-Time'. Dorkly. At: www.dorkly.com/post/60001/toplist-results-the-20-greatest-videogame-villains-of-all-time. Accessed 11 August 2016.

76 *Venetia Laura Delano Robertson*

Bynum, Caroline Walker. 1988. *Holy Feast and Holy Fast*. London: University of California Press.

Chance, Jane. 2007. *The Literary Subversions of Medieval Women*. New York: Palgrave Macmillan.

Cherny, Lynn and Elizabeth Reba Weise. 1996. *Wired Women: Gender and New Realities in Cyberspace*. Seattle, WA: Seal Press.

Coppa, Francesca. 2008. 'Women, *Star Trek,* and the Early Development of Fannish Vidding'. *Transformative Works and Cultures* 1. doi:10.3983/twc.2008.0044

Cusack, Carole M. 2010. *Invented Religions: Imagination, Fiction and Faith*. Burlington, VT: Ashgate.

Davis, Erik. 2004. *Techgnosis: Myth, Magic, and Mysticism in the Age of Information*. London: Serpents Tail.

Dean, Tim. 2014. 'Beyond Gamergate'. *ABC*. At: www.abc.net.au/technology/articles/2014/10/28/4116140.htm. Accessed 15 June 2015.

Encyclopedia Dramatica. 2013. 'Summoner Yuna'. At: encyclopediadramatica.se/Summoner_Yuna. Accessed 15 June 2015.

Encyclopedia Dramatica. 2015. 'Sephirothslave'. At: encyclopediadramatica.se/Sephirothslave. Accessed 15 June 2015.

Entertainment Software Association. 2014. *Essential Facts about the Computer and Video Game Industry*. Washington, DC: ESA.

Fiske, John. 2001. 'The Cultural Economy of Fandom'. In Lisa A. Lewis (ed.), *The Adoring Audience: Fan Culture and Popular Media*, 30–49. New York: Routledge.

Fox, Jessica and Wai Yen Tang. 2014. 'Sexism in Online Video Games: The Role of Conformity to Masculine Norms and Social Dominance Orientation'. *Computers in Human Behavior* 33: 314–320.

Gilchrist, Roberta. 1994. *Gender and Material Culture: The Archaeology of Religious Women*. London: Routledge.

Hellekson, Karen and Kristina Busse. 2014. *The Fan Fiction Studies Reader*. Iowa City, IA: University of Iowa Press.

Jelinek, Estelle. 1986. *The Tradition of Women's Autobiography: From Antiquity to the Present*. Boston, MA: Twayne.

Jenkins, Henry. 1992. *Textual Poachers: Television Fans and Participatory Culture*. New York: Routledge.

Jenkins, Jacqueline. 2004. 'Reading and *The Book of Margery Kempe*'. In John H. Arnold and Katherine J. Lewis (eds), *A Companion to The Book of Margery Kempe*, 113–128. New York: Brewer.

Julian of Norwich. 1901. *Revelations of Divine Love*. Translated by Grace Warrack. London: Methuen and Co.

Kempe, Margery. 2000. *The Book of Margery Kempe*. Translated by B. A. Windeatt. London: Penguin.

Kendall, Lori. 2000. '"Oh no! I'm a Nerd!" Hegemonic Masculinity on an Online Forum'. *Gender & Society* 14(2): 256–274.

Kirby, Danielle. 2012. 'Readers, Believers, Consumers, and Audiences: Complicating the Relationship between Consumption and Contemporary Narrative Spiritualties'. *Australian Journal of Communication* 39(1): 119–131.

Laycock, Joseph and Natasha L. Mikles. 2015. 'Tracking the Tulpa: Exploring the "Tibetan" Origins of a Contemporary Paranormal Idea'. *Nova Religio* 19(1): 87–97.

Leadbeater, Charles. 1903. *Clairvoyance*. London: Theosophical Publishing Society.

Luhrmann, Tanya. 2012. *When God Talks Back: Understanding the American Evangelical Relationship with God*. New York: Vintage.

Margolis, Jane and Allan Fisher. 2003. 'Geek Mythology'. *Bulletin of Science Technology & Society* 23(1): 17–20

Maskulak, Marian. 2011. 'Julian of Norwich and the God of No Blame and No Wrath'. *Magistra* 17(2): 71–87.

McAvoy, Liz. 2004. *Authority and the Female Body in the Writings of Julian of Norwich and Margery Kempe*. Cambridge, UK: Brewer.

McCloud, Sean. 2003. 'Popular Culture Fandoms, the Boundaries of Religious Studies, and the Project of the Self'. *Culture and Religion* 4(2): 187–206.

Mrs Sephiroth. 2004a. 'Sephiroth . . . so evil . . . so mine!!!'. *Dreaming of Sephiroth* blog.

Mrs Sephiroth. 2004b. 'Getting too far?' *Dreaming of Sephiroth* blog.

Mrs Sephiroth. 2004c. 'Catching up'. *Dreaming of Sephiroth* blog.

Mrs Sephiroth. 2004d. 'Passions and rants'. *Dreaming of Sephiroth* blog.

Dreaming of Sephiroth. At: web.archive.org/web/20090509212922/http://sephiroth.blogdrive.com/. Accessed 15 June 2015.

Mrs Sephiroth. (as Summoner Yuna). 2005. *Sephyism*. At: sephyism.livejournal.com/profile). Accessed 15 June 2015.

Mrs Sephiroth. 2006. Comment. *Sephyism*. At: sephyism.livejournal.com/806.html. Accessed 15 June 2015.

Mrs Sephiroth. (as Sephiroth's Wife). 2007. Comment. *DeviantArt: Sephirothslave*. At: sephirothslave.deviantart.com/art/Who-I-Am-63848986. Accessed 15 June 2015.

Possamai, Adam. 2007. *Religion and Popular Culture: A Hyper-real Testament*. Brussels: Peter Lang.

Robertson, Venetia. 2011. 'Animation as Salvation: How Soulbonders find the Spiritual in New Narratives'. Paper presented at International Conference for the Centre for Studies on New Religions (CESNUR), 21–23 June. Aletheia University, Taiwan.

Robertson, Venetia. 2014. 'Of Ponies and Men: *My Little Pony: Friendship is Magic* and the Brony Fandom'. *International Journal of Cultural Studies* 17(1): 21–37.

Romano, Aja. 2012. 'How Female Gamers and Comic Fans Fight Real-Life Sexism Online'. *The Daily Dot*. At: www.dailydot.com/society/readercon-comic-gamer-sexism-kate-leth/). Accessed 15 June 2015.

Royal, Cindy. 2010. 'An Open Letter to Wired Magazine'. *Cindy's Take on Tech*. At: tech.cindyroyal.net/an-open-letter-to-wired-magazine/. Accessed 15 June, 2015.

Scott, Suzanne. 2013. 'Fangirls in Refrigerators: The Politics of (In)Visibility in Comic Book Culture'. *Transformative Works and Cultures* 13. doi:10.3983/twc.2013.0460.

Sephirothslave. (as Julia). n.d. *Julia's Blurty*. At: web.archive.org/web/20051129014719/http://www.blurty.com/users/sephirothslave/. Accessed 15 June 2015.

Sephirothslave. 2004. 'Been Away for a While'. Blurty.

Sephirothslave. 2007a. Comment. *DeviantArt: Sephirothslave*. At: sephirothslave.deviantart.com/art/Who-I-Am-63848986. Accessed 15 June 2015.

Sephirothslave. 2007b. 'Sephirothslave'. *DeviantArt: Sephirothslave*. At: sephirothslave.deviantart.com/art/Sephirothslave-67453799. Accessed 28 January 2015.

Sephirothslave. 2007c. 'Here We Go Again'. Blurty.

78 *Venetia Laura Delano Robertson*

Sephirothslave. 2007d. 'Questions and Answers'. Blurty.

Sephirothslave. 2007e. 'And the Debate Rages on'. Blurty.

Sephirothslave. 2007f. 'Some Interesting Developments'. Blurty. At: www.blurty. com/users/sephirothslave/day/2007/11/05. Accessed 28 January 2015.

Soul Bonding. 2002–2005. At: soulbonding.livejournal.com/profile. Accessed 15 June 2015.

Subtext: The Slashfic Fanfiction Fanlisting. 2005–2014. At: slashfic.org/popular. php. Accessed 15 June 2015.

Varma, Roli. 2007. 'Women in Computing: The Role of Geek Culture'. *Science as Culture* 16(4): 359–376.

Warren, Nancy Bradley. 2007. 'Feminist Approaches to Middle English Religious Writing: The Cases of Margery Kempe and Julian of Norwich'. *Literature Compass* 4(5): 1378–1396.

Wertheim, Margaret. 1999. *The Pearly Gates of Cyberspace*. London: Virago.

Williams, Dmitri, Mia Consalvo, Scott Caplan, and Nick Yee. 2009. 'Looking for Gender: Gender Roles and Behaviors among Online Gamers'. *Journal of Communication* 59(4): 700–725.

Woledge, Elizabeth. 2005. 'From Slash to the Mainstream: Female Writers and Gender Blending Men'. *Extrapolation* 46(1): 50–65.

Wu, Brianna. 2014. 'Rape and Death Threats are Terrorizing Female Gamers. Why Haven't Men in Tech Spoken Out?' *The Washington Post*. At: www.washington post.com/posteverything/wp/2014/10/20/rape-and-death-threats-are-terrorizing-female-gamers-why-havent-men-in-tech-spoken-out/. Accessed 15 June 2015.

4 The development of spirituality in the Brony community

Pavol Kosnáč

What is this weird show?
It's like the only thing you know
You talk about it every day
You know this is child's play?
Your path ahead is blurred
Told to go join in on the Herd
You know this show's for younger crowds
How can you say you're proud?
  . . .
And then you have the nerve . . .
To ask me to observe . . .
These girly things . . .
You open your mouth and sing!
  . . .
Hey, this show's not bad
I'll give it to ya, I'm real glad
I never thought I'd like this stuff
Thought I was just too tough.
  . . .
So thanks, brony, thanks
My mind was shooting blanks
I feel like such a fool
Who knew ponies were this cool?
  . . .
So thanks, brony, thanks
Looks like I've joined your ranks
I never could repay
What you've done for me today.
        (Forest Rain – 'Join the Herd' [n.d.])

Introduction

Hasbro Inc. is a toy company. They are best known for inventing Transformers, but they have a very popular line of G.I. Joe action figures for boys and My Little Pony colourful, plastic ponies with unique symbols

80   *Pavol Kosnáč*

on their flanks called "cutie marks" for girls. In October 2010, trying to boost the sale of their toys to 2- to 11-year-old girls, Hasbro launched an animated series about ponies called *My Little Pony: Friendship is Magic* (*MLP:FIM*). But something very unexpected happened. Approximately a year after the first episode of *MLP:FIM* was released, the programme gained a huge following of teenage and adult men, especially in the United States. Brony fandom – or "the Herd" – was born. Some Bronies took a liking to the series because of the animation or storylines, but some claim it means much more to them; it saved them from depression or even suicide, and made them better people when they adapted the show's moral message to their lives. Some even developed a spiritual bond with certain characters. This chapter will discuss Brony fandom in general, about which there is some academic (Crome 2014; Robertson 2014) and fan-made documentary (for example, Malaquais 2012) material. The focus is on the smaller, particularly "devoted", part of the fandom.

A note on methodology

In this chapter, the author has used a functionalist methodological approach. Functionalism has its flaws; for example, it is not good at distinguishing philosophical nuances and purposely does not look for substance. It focuses more on the lived aspects of any system of ideas and emphasizes attention to behaviour rather than textual canons or doctrine, since these are often highly abstract and do not correspond to the daily life of a common adherent. That is why the functionalist approach is useful when studying the lifestyle of a loose community, as it is easier to look after religious behaviour than try identifying the "sacred". I have attempted to compensate for the flaws of functionalist observation applied to Brony cyberspace textual and visual production or at Brony conventions I attended by using qualitative interviews and questionnaires to explore the thoughts and views of members of the community.

Distinguishing between a hard-core fan and someone who has taken their hobby to a level that could plausibly be described as spiritual devotion (in the widest possible sense of hyper-reality) is difficult. A simple but effective method to distinguish between these two groups was used. A hard-core fan (or any fan for that matter) can be distinguished from a "devotee" by the impact the television show had on a combination of their everyday lifestyle, worldview and ethics. All Bronies obviously like the show, and they have been affected by it – they may have bought *MLP:FIM* paraphernalia or merchandise, started using a few phrases from the show or actually applied a lesson from it to their lives – but their lives were not affected by it in a systematic and wholehearted way. Devotees not only enjoy *MLP:FIM*, they build their lifestyle and worldview on it. The series often provides moral guidance, and its storylines are used to interpret reality. It is thus one of the most important, or even the prime, source of advice and reference in life. For Brony hobbyists,

Spirituality in the Brony community 81

MLP:FIM never becomes a source of such significance that it shapes their entire worldview. For a Brony devotee, it does. Identifying the point at which one crosses the line between a hobbyist and a devotee precisely is impossible, but such is the nature of much of the study of religion. Nevertheless, the final outcome of the difference between a Brony fan and a Brony spiritualist is recognizable; so, on an intersubjective level, the difference between these two states can be identified, or even self-identified. This is the main idea upon which this categorisation is premised.

The origins of Brony fandom

The concept of a "Brony" was first articulated on 4chan b/message board in October 2010, largely by accident. One of the members posted an article written by Amid Amidi about how companies are micromanaging television shows and using them to sell their merchandise, and Hasbro and My Little Pony were explicitly mentioned (Amidi 2010). Other members started to research the topic and watched *MLP:FIM*. One posted that the show was actually very good, which generated a discussion, and other people started watching it and speaking about it, attracting more who tried to figure out if these conversations were an elaborate joke, satire or if people really meant it. It did not seem possible to some that this kind of series might be of interest to an adult. Many reacted with ridicule, which provoked a flamewar (a very agitated discussion full of personal attacks, irony, sarcasm, offence and so on) that flooded the forum with pony-based memes by the newly formed fans of *MLP:FIM*. The administrators of 4chan eventually banned pony memes from 4chan, so the newly formed groups of Pony fans started their own forums (Hodge 2014, 00.18.00).[1]

This commotion caught the attention of still more people, who wanted to find out what the fuss was about and enlarged the fandom. From the spring of 2011, it was growing exponentially. The narrator of *Brony Chronicles* mentions an interesting phenomenon:

> This increase in fans brought a change. After the flamewars ended on co'n'b (4 chan message board) a good chunk of Bronies sincerely believed in this philosophy being open-minded and loving and took phrases such as "love and tolerate" to heart. Many of these new Bronies were not around during the events on the 4chan and got their start elsewhere – they didn't realize that the philosophy they were adopting was actually a quote used by spammers to antagonize critics. Yet this wave of fans in their excitement misunderstood the inside jokes from 4chan and turned "love and tolerate" into a mantra that has stuck with the fandom ever since.
>
> (Carver and Tyson 2013a, 00.59.30)

The primary contact with *MLP:FIM* for most of the current Bronies was not through the show directly, but usually through fan-made content, like music,

82   *Pavol Kosnáč*

internet memes or videos. Some of the videos were especially popular and went viral because of a combination of dark or serious material with colourful ponies (for example, audio from *Batman* or *Watchmen* montaged on pony animations). Another first contact is through friends; basically, one fan recruits another by persuading them to watch a few episodes. A routine initial reaction is incredulity, even ridicule, which then gives rise to curiosity – similar to the curiosity of original 4chan members who wanted to find out what the "hook" was – and as they state, they become "hooked" or even "addicted". Some go so far as to say that becoming a Brony was like a "conversion" (Brony Admin Group n.d.). As one respondent put it, the "world just seemed different after" (Respondent 23).

How can a joke become something that is taken this seriously? It happens all the time. As George Orwell said, "every joke is a tiny revolution" (Orwell 1945). If a joke or satire has some depth and references something people care about, it may have a strong real-life impact independently of whether it is considered serious or not, especially if it gets into social media. In the United States context, where Bronies originated, an example is the Comedy Central hosts Stephen Colbert and Jon Stewart, who have had a very serious impact on American society (Grossman 2014) – Colbert even testified in front of the Congress committee – through the comedy persona of a "hyper-American", ignorant, posh, over-the-top conservative republican, modelled on Bill O'Reilly (Gray 2014). This demonstrates that certain acts may be taken seriously, even if still understood and performed as a joke. This is not a new reality; ancient Greek comedies often had influential theological or ethical themes, stating controversial things, but evading censorship because they did not look "serious" at first. Many serious things emerge from jokes and satire. Laws get passed, influential people lose office, movements get started, dictatorial regimes are undermined (TenDyke 2007) and new religions originate. A joke can become influential, it can inspire, it can educate or it can provide catharsis.[2] The idea that a serious thing might come from a joke – basically, a joke gaining a life of its own – has a long tradition.

Thanks to the shift in understanding the source of legitimacy in the last few decades, if a joke gains power as discussed above, is based on a narrative that has depth and sophistication and is appealing to a certain group of people, a social movement that provides the services and qualities previously associated with religion can emerge. That is how Dudeism and Jediism gained popularity (Cusack 2010; Possamai 2005; Benjamin in this volume), and that is how Brony fandom originated.

MLP:FIM has been Hasbro's greatest success, which is largely due to its creator and main writer, Lauren Faust, who gave it depth that is not typical for a show targeted at minors. The series has been praised for its humour and moral outlook (Truitt 2012). The reasons for this unintended appreciation by adult viewers include creative writing and characterisation, the expressive Flash-based animation style and themes that older audiences can appreciate. Each show includes a moral or life lesson, but these were chosen

Spirituality in the Brony community 83

to "cross a broad spectrum of personal experiences" and not simply to suit children (Griffiths 2011). The reciprocal relationship between Hasbro, the creators and the fans is also important. Creator Lauren Faust has stated that she wanted to make the show interesting for adult members so that parents watching with their kids would not be bored. So she added references that no child is able to identify for the amusement of more adult viewers, but she never expected such popularity to result (Morgan 2011).

The main character of *MLP:FIM* is a serious unicorn pony Twilight Sparkle, a student of Princess Celestia. Celestia is a ruler-god of the pony realm, Equestria, who causes the sun to rise every morning. She asks Twilight to go to the town of Ponyville to learn about friendship. There she meets many different ponies, pegasi and unicorns, and befriends five of them: tomboyish Rainbow Dash who loves speed and adventure and is in charge of managing the weather and skies of Ponyville; hard-working and plain-spoken farm girl Applejack who lives in an apple orchard with her large family; extremely shy and tender Fluttershy, beloved by all the residents of Equestria, who nurtures the animals of Ponyville; elegant and lady-like Rarity, a fashion designer with her own boutique; and always cheer-ful, hyperactive, loud and talkative Pinkie Pie, the town's party-planner. Each of them represents a different aspect of friendship, manifested in the show visually as magical tiaras – the Elements of Harmony – the "most powerful magic known to ponydom". They are honesty (Applejack), kindness (Fluttershy), laughter (Pinkie Pie), generosity (Rarity) and loy-alty (Rainbow Dash). Twilight Sparkle is the one that connects them all together. Together they have many great adventures: from fighting leg-endary adversaries and saving the whole of Equestria; through everyday problems in Ponyville; to self-discovery quests facing their own character traits. Every episode has one or more morals and life lessons, which are summed up at the end, usually by a letter written by Twilight Sparkle to her mentor Princess Celestia.

Fan statistics and activities

Two informal surveys of 2,300 and 9,000 participants respectively revealed that the average age of adult fans is around 21, that approximately 86 per cent were male and their educational levels were 35 per cent high school, while 62 per cent were studying or had already completed college. A 2012 survey with over 20,000 respondents showed similar statistics and highlighted that the majority of fans were in the 15–30 age range, were heterosexual and have or were pursing college degrees. Further, using the Jungian-derived personal-ity test, the Myers-Briggs Type Indicator, the survey revealed that the largest fraction of respondents fell into the "INTJ" classification, which normally only occurs in 1–3 per cent of the population, according to the surveyors. An informal statistical census suggests that as of September 2012, there are between 7 and 12.4 million people in the United States that would identify

84 *Pavol Kosnáč*

themselves as Bronies (Wikipedia 2016), and, interestingly, they score lower on neurosis scales than non-Bronies (Hodge 2014, 00.14.00).

The Brony Study (Research Project) states that 45.6 per cent of the variance "was associated with both of the Moral aspects, described as Faith and Guidance, which indicates an interest in the show and its moral message that may reach an almost religious fervour and depth of conviction". Fifty-seven per cent of respondents say they are dedicated fans and receive a strong sense of moral guidance from *MLP:FIM*. Twenty-nine per cent do not hide their love of the show and sometimes are openly "proselytizing" about their "Bronyhood" (Brony Admin Group n.d.). In other words, *MLP:FIM* and community has an impact in the area of morals and worldview in real-life for about half of the fandom. That is a very significant number.

The author's own data corresponds in the area of demographics (age, sex, education). Thirty-two in-depth structured interviews with Bronies were conducted, and 99 responses to open-answer qualitative questionnaires were received. The impact of the television series and community on the life of Bronies was slightly higher than the Brony Study (Research Project). Sixty-three per cent of respondents stated that it has impacted their worldview and/or ethical values, and 12.5 per cent of those that were interviewed stated that it was the most important reference point in their life.

There is also an interesting trend in the formation of "Brony flats", as one respondent termed it. Some university students and early-career young adults are looking for shared accommodation with other Bronies. Four per cent of respondents stated they live in a "Brony flat", but as the author did not include a question on living arrangements, this number may be higher. Also 7 per cent stated that they had found a girlfriend or boyfriend in the Brony community, and 1 per cent a husband or wife. Some Bronies grew more interested in IT, because they wanted to help with online projects of the fandom; 2 per cent of respondents even chose an IT career because of it. Nine per cent who never travelled became interested in doing so because of Brony conventions. Eleven per cent of Bronies from non-Anglophone countries started to invest more time and energy to learn English so they can watch *MLP:FIM* easily in its original language. Finally, 4 per cent of respondents said they ate more apples.

Bronies form "meetup" groups, where they can discuss topics from *MLP:FIM*, but also just to meet other Brony friends and find general support (Calpain 2013a). Fans meet at conventions and festivals, for example Bronycon in the US or BUCKs in the UK, but there are at least 15 others, mostly in the US, but also in the UK, France, Russia, Germany and Australia. Another intriguing phenomenon is a sub-group of Military Bronies, *MLP:FIM* fans serving in the military, but also including police, fire-fighters, military contractors and similar professions. There is even an Air Force Class (Class 14–05 at Vance Air Force Base in Oklahoma) flying with *My Little Pony*-inspired "My Little Pilot" patches (Watercutter 2013).

Spirituality in the Brony community 85

Charitable undertakings are a significant manifestation of the ideals of the fandom. The most active is probably "Bronies for Good" (BfG), a group that runs blood drives and raised over $60,000 during 2012 for charities like the Children's Cancer Association, Room to Read, CureSearch and Your Siblings. The philosophy of BfG is based on the ideas of the Effective Altruism movement, meaning they choose the charities they will support based on the effectiveness and transparency of that charity. In 2015, the Against Malaria Foundation was selected. According to the website of Give Well, a non-profit organisation that traces and evaluates the efficiency of different charities, this is the most effective charity (it has a very high ratio of cost and effect) in the world on which they have data. Denis Drescher of BfG explains that charities usually:

> [g]o to great lengths to appeal to donors . . . but what they don't do is to go to the same lengths to actually help those they proclaim to help. It is the rare charity that runs self-evaluations on its projects, tracks its impact, or changes its strategy in response to the results . . . Hence, our mission . . . is as much about educating donors as it is about fundraising for these highly effective charities.
>
> (Personal communication)

BfG often has a booth at Brony conventions, and members are happy to speak to anyone who is interested. They are currently working on an educational animation on Effective Altruism with Nightwave Studios. The Effective Altruism forum has praised BfG for raising hundreds of thousands of dollars for this type of charity (AlasdairGives 2014), often using fan-made music albums like "Building Bridges" or "Shine Together" (Seeds of Kindness 2014, 2015) that came into existence especially to support the BfG fundraising initiatives.

There is no structure or hierarchy in fandom, although certain bloggers, Brony-content creators and chief organisers of Brony festivals and conventions have some unofficial authority. These include: Living Tombstone; DustyKatt; Tiarawhy; Mic The Microphone (a Brony rapper); Kkat (author of the acclaimed 600,000+ word novel *Fallout: Equestria*); and Whitedove (a plushie crafter). Also, voice actors and Lauren Faust, the series creator, are considered celebrities and are influential in the Brony community. The quantity of the artistic outputs of the Brony fandom is impressive and may deserve its own chapter.

Motivations for becoming a Brony

What makes the Brony fandom so attractive? It is generally considered to be part of the "New Sincerity" movement, which is a type of philosophical post-conceptualism. New Sincerity involves attempting to renew the pathos of love, sentimentality, enthusiasm and authenticity. It can be found

86 *Pavol Kosnáč*

in music, aesthetics, film criticism, poetry, literary criticism and philosophy, and the term is used describe art or ideas that run against prevailing modes of postmodernist irony or cynicism. Its usage dates back to the mid-1980s (Tennant 2012). Psychologist M. H. Redden, who has studied Brony fandom, regards it as a historical pattern of societal reaction. After World War I came the "roaring twenties", and after World War II, Korea, and Vietnam came the 1960s counter-culture. Thus, in the 2010s, society is tired of violence, the "clash of civilizations" and the "war on terror" and desires something that is tolerant and friendly, is about conflict and resolution, has a positive message, an escape that is entertaining (Hodge 2014, 00.14.00).

Jonathan D. Fitzgerald argues in an article on Patheos – a multi-blogging website devoted to discussing religion and spirituality – that New Sincerity had a serious impact on twenty-first century pop culture.

> Around the turn of the century, something began to change. Suddenly the nerd stereotype – always the object of derision in popular culture – became kind of cool. Vulnerability invaded pop music where bravado and posturing once had ruled. Television shows and movies depicted characters determined to do some kind of good in the world. And respected literary authors began writing books about morality again. Overall, this renewed interest in moral storytelling has come about through a de-emphasis on image and irony and an open embrace of the virtues of sincerity and authenticity.
>
> (Fitzgerald 2013)

Are sincerity and authenticity virtues? Many think so, and this view is supported by several heavyweights in the field of philosophy, of whom the most prominent is Charles Taylor (Taylor 1992). *MLP:FIM* sounds like a good platform on which to base an ethics system for the twenty-first century.

The typical responses given by Bronies when asked why they watch the show and actively participate in the fandom can be divided into three groups: 1) admiration of the technical qualities of the show (good animation, colourful, good music); 2) narrative qualities (well-written dialogues and storylines, and deep psychology of the characters that makes viewers care about them); and 3) philosophical qualities (morals, artistic inspiration and so on). These reasons are very broad, and to gain a clearer idea of what *MLP:FIM* means for individual Bronies, more personal examples will be provided. Many, very personal, reasons were given by Bronies during interviews with the author, reasons that go far beyond the standard enjoyment of an entertaining television show. Some of these were mentioned frequently (in more than 20 per cent of cases) and so may be considered common in the Brony fandom. They also reveal why it makes sense to apply concepts and methodology from the study of religion to the fandom, as this helps to understand the intensity of the attraction, motivation and loyalty that some members feel to *MLP:FIM*.

The first notable phenomenon is the "joy effect". Just as horror films have a "chill" or "fear" effect that some people enjoy, many Bronies watch *MLP:FIM* because it generates a feeling of joy and happiness after watching the show. They state that this is somehow a higher quality "joy" than the joy generated by other television programmes or films; it lasts longer and inspires a more optimistic approach to life. Some even assert that this joy lifted them out of depression, helped them avoid suicide, aided soldiers to overcome PTSD or some to manage Asperger's syndrome (Malaquais 2012, 00.15.00 and 00.29.00). The surprise of viewers at their willingness to learn from *MLP:FIM* is a constant theme:

> This weird alchemy that Lauren Faust tapped into when she set out to make the show accessible to kids and their parents hooks into the male geek's reptilian hindbrain and removes a lifetime's behavioral indoctrination against pink . . . As a person with Asperger syndrome, I learned more about theory of mind, friendships and social interactions from this season than I had in the previous 31 years of life.
>
> (Allen, quoted in Watercutter 2011)

A second effect is that of moral regeneration. Certain Bronies tell tales of character reformation as a result of watching the series, in which valuable life lessons are put simply, so everyone can understand them. This is a hidden benefit of a television programme primarily focused on kids. Many Bronies state that it is not about loving a show for little girls, but about loving the message; be honest, be friendly, don't be afraid and stand with your friends.

MLP:FIM has a guiding function in their lives; the stories are little parables that help the viewer to understand moral lessons of life.

> I used to be a cynical jerk, kicking puppies, building my career on expense of others, I am sure you can imagine. Then one of my colleagues I fancied made me watch ponies – I planned to suffer through it – it would be easier to screw her later. I wanted to get into her head, and so when I fell ill as I usually do in the beginning of autumn, and had a lot of time on my hands, I started to watch it . . . I watched all episodes in 5 days – that's some 20 a day. The story somehow spoke to me. It just overflows with joy, even when bad stuff happen to the Mane 6. It was completely irrational, but I couldn't help it . . . Since then I am trying to be helpful, no backstabbing anymore, and I became a type of person I used to ridicule the most – an outgoing optimist. Before I thought that's just naïve, a sign of no life experience. Now I know it may be a deliberate choice to be better. It looks kinda similar. Oh, by the way, I got the girl. She is my girlfriend now.
>
> (Interview No. 17)

88   *Pavol Kosnáč*

Viewers who feel a strong impact from these life lessons then naturally start to use *MLP:FIM* as a set of stories that help them to grasp and interpret the world and teach them how to act in different life situations. That is a powerful service for a piece of popular culture to provide and one that was typically reserved for religion and mythology in the past. *MLP:FIM*, in a certain sense, provides a Brony devotee with a personal mythology, a traditional tool of spirituality. Some Brony members have even started to use the acronym well-known from Christian popular culture: WWJD? Only "P" is substituted for "J" – *What would Pony do?*

A third important effect is the sense of security and unconditional acceptance in a cynical world that Brony fandom bestows on members. The series' message is not ironic or sarcastic; its genuineness is attractive to many, as compensation in a world where cynicism is prevalent and where public image, status, career or keeping up appearances is more important than happiness. Maintaining an image also drains many people's energy; it is tiring and causes a lot of stress. Aggressive rhetoric is everywhere and there is almost a *need* to have an enemy – in particular, American society always seems to be waging a war on something – which makes people sad, pessimistic and exhausted. *MLP:FIM* compensates for this: "it's just this positive oasis in the sea of sarcasm and cynicism in modern society" (Hodge 2014). The result of this security and acceptance that Bronies derive from *MLP:FIM* is moral improvement:

> I have started appreciating my friends more. I also try to be as close to the elements of harmony as possible. Like, I say, "would Rarity approve of this?" It is weird (then again, what's not?), but it has helped me be a better person.
>
> (Calpain 2013b)

This draws attention to an important issue for scholars of Brony spirituality; the various effects, impacts, changes in lifestyle and so on that are analysed in this chapter are closely interrelated. Joy assists in the development of security, as well as in moral transformation, which is more likely to happen in the lives of joyful, balanced people.

A fourth important factor, which may seem less serious but is nevertheless important, is that watching *MLP:FIM* and participation in the Brony community is a fun escape from an increasingly demanding life (either work or school) for many Bronies. It helps them relax and rest, to take things more slowly in a world that is going too fast. Coupled with this is the argument that the show and the fandom assist in combatting loneliness in a seemingly uncaring world. A questionnaire respondent told the author:

> Before I joined the fandom, I was afraid of men and I had a problem making new friendships. I would say that ponies made me a more open person. And more even-tempered as well. Ponies came to my life at

Spirituality in the Brony community 89

a time when my grandfather died and the divorce of my parents was imminent. Ponies were a warm blanket of friendship in a time when the whole world seemed hostile.

(Respondent 54)

Many Bronies state that the show and the community saved them from loneliness and depression: after watching it, they started to socialise more and found new friends (or even their "first real friends"), which gave them more self-confidence. A popular English bumper sticker, emulating the style of the official London Underground logo, states: "Don't acknowledge fellow passengers or sustain eye contact beyond 2 seconds. Please respect urban solitude". At first glance, many people do not recognize it is a fake.

Sociological research suggests that people are more lonely in the contemporary West, especially people from large cities, where the traditional social network of family has tended to dissolve more quickly than in rural areas. This "urban loneliness effect" is on the rise. Japan manifests an extreme version, the *hikikomori* – "apartment hermits" or "shut-ins" – people, mostly young men, who may not leave their room for years (Buljan and Cusack 2015: 175–176). According to the statistics, most Bronies come from urban areas,[3] and the majority are introverts (Brony Admin Group n.d.). The combination of introverts living in urban areas (Berry and Okulicz-Kozaryn 2011; Horowitz *et al.* 1982) may result in individuals who are more prone to loneliness. The Brony Study poll also revealed that Bronies "displayed a lower general interest in dating, and fewer of this group dated frequently" (Brony Admin Group n.d.), which may be another indicator. Loneliness may be another significant factor behind the rapid rise of Brony fandom, as its inclusiveness and friendliness is attractive to lonely people, and belonging sometimes transforms them into more social and confident people. This conclusion is partially speculative, but it is consistent with the data and with the author's personal experience of the Brony community. It may therefore be a productive research topic for future scholars studying the fandom.

Brony troubles

The final clear reason why the Brony fandom is so attractive and is growing quickly is that, despite its inclusiveness and tolerance, it is also protective of its members, which makes it a natural refuge. "Protective" here means two things: first, that the group supports (verbally and sometimes non-verbally) those who are attacked for who they are (be it due to their interests, their looks, their sexuality and so on); and second, the group defends individual members when it can. This protectiveness developed very early on, since members of the fandom were ridiculed and verbally attacked from the beginning.

The Brony fandom has developed a strategy about how to answer questions concerning the "normality" of boys and men liking a show that was intended for little girls, because a very common attitude of Western society is that it is not normal for (even little) boys to like the same things that little girls do. Further, the intensity of certain Bronies' "obsession" with *MLP:FIM* is claimed to be unhealthy by critics. Bronies handle this critique in three ways: first, they argue that it is merely a societal prejudice to link boys with blue and girls with pink, and, in time, society will overcome this lame stereotyping; second, some argue that it is a personal preference and thus nobody's business but their own (the "I like it, so I don't care what others think" approach); and third, Bronies question what is "normal"? If Bronies compare themselves to many other fan groups, their level of engagement with *MLP:FIM* is comparable to that of other sci-fi and fantasy fans (for example, Trekkies and *Star Trek*), and some Bronies assert that they are far more reasonable than certain fans of celebrities, who are willing to risk their lives to get closer ("stalking"), or some sports fans who literally dedicate their life to a certain code. So what is normal? Who decides?

These strategies to refute criticism are widespread in the fandom. This is not because members have especially high interest for sociological riddles, but because many have experienced the very common negative reaction to their interest in ponies. On the Internet, their manliness, maturity, sanity, sexuality and mental age are routinely questioned in the roughest terms, and the accusation of sexual perversion is never far away. Admittedly, this is not unique to Bronies – many others similarly experience such vilification in the anonymity of cyberspace. More serious are the real-life problems of Bronies. Apart from verbal attacks, some Bronies (often from American rural communities) claim to have been harassed, intimidated and bullied, and to have experienced property damage (including vandalised cars with a pony sticker and so on). Some administrators of Brony websites, bloggers and video channel administrators claim to have received death threats (Malaquais 2012). Media have portrayed the fandom negatively; Fox News gets an honourable mention (Carver and Tyson 2013b, 00.26.30), but radio "shock jock" Howard Stern is the example *par excellence* of mockery and ridicule of all "ponyfags" (Stern 2013). These and other negative experiences are some of the reasons why some members do not tell their friends in school or university that they are Bronies, or even in some cases do not share their Brony interests with their spouses. One informant did not have the courage to tell his wife, because he feared she would worry and lose respect for him, but since he wanted to go to BronyCon and participate in a costume contest, he created his mechatronic costume at night, locked in the bathroom. This illustrates how strong the social stigma can be for Bronies.

Bronies consider themselves, sometimes, as martyrs to the cynicism of contemporary society, and they deliberately challenge its stereotypes and norms, propagating a more emotional, caring male role model rather than a "macho" type. They view their identity as a challenge to the social norms and accept that there are people who are threatened by their stance and actions, so they react defensively. Generally, Bronies ignore those who

Spirituality in the Brony community   91

do not "love or at least tolerate". They believe that in time their situation will be much the same as that of Trekkies (fans of *Star Trek*). That is, in the beginning people thought they were a weird cult, deviants taking their obsession too far, but over time the fandom has mainstreamed. Other large fandoms have developed, which generate their own subcultures, like fans of *Star Wars*, *Lord of the Rings*, *Harry Potter* or comic fans (many Marvel comics are now mainstream films, filling cinemas for months).

The negative reaction of a sector of society towards Bronies is to a certain extent to be expected; the Brony fandom violates common assumptions about age and gender divisions regarding pop culture content. Even one of the voice actresses, Ashleigh Ball, voicing Applejack and Rainbow Dash said that "The Pervert alarm for sure went off in my head" when she first heard about male fans of the show (Hodge 2014, 00.06.55).

This reflexive reaction is often just a simplified stereotypical reflex, but some criticism is targeted on several controversial practices of some members of Brony fandom. There is a part of the Brony community that admits they are sexually attracted to the pony characters of *MLP:FIM* and create and consume animated pony-related adult material. They are called "Cloppers" (Agostinelli 2015). Some Bronies distance themselves from Cloppers, but others, appealing to the core value of inclusion, defend them. The inclusiveness of the fandom has two effects. First, many insecure, shy and introverted people are attracted to the fandom, since it provides a friendly and non-judgmental environment. But this openness of approach necessarily attracts people from the fringes of many different areas of society, be it in terms of character, sexual preferences, physical appearance or abilities. Available data on Bronies demonstrates that this is true at least in the area of sexuality. According to the well-respected NHIS 2014 research, the US reports 1.6 per cent homosexuals and 0.7 per cent bisexuals in the general population (Centre for Disease Control and Prevention 2014). Other surveys have similar results – the number of non-heterosexuals never goes above 4 per cent – but according to the Brony survey conducted by Redden, the percentage of self-identified LGBTs in the Brony community is 11.5 per cent. Such high levels of LGBT participation is clearly at odds with mainstream society. Thus, some critics state that, as inclusiveness is a core value, the larger proportion of socially deviant members in the fandom makes it problematic or even dangerous, especially for children and teenagers. This assessment may be, to a certain extent, legitimate. However, it depends on the definition of "deviance", which is also deliberately challenged by Bronies.

Brony devotees

Examples have been given that demonstrate why, from the functionalist viewpoint, a certain smaller section of the Brony fandom could be considered *implicitly religious*, meaning, in Thomas Luckmann's sense, that it provides psychological, communitarian and ritualistic services that religions commonly provide to certain people (Luckmann 1967). Among the Brony devotees, two principal practical traits can be identified. First, the main motto and moral requirement for those who try to live according to *MLP:FIM* is "Love and Tolerate", which is explained as, "forgive your friends, ignore your enemies". The emphasis is on assuming that if someone is being unpleasant towards you, it's because they made a mistake (they spoke hastily, had a bad day, misunderstood you and so on) and one should answer with love. Bronies aim to start with, and patiently hold, a friendly attitude for as long as possible, according to each individual's capabilities. This does not mean that a Brony should be a "doormat" (an episode focused on Fluttershy is devoted to precisely this point). If someone needs genuinely to defend themselves, that is not a problem, as tolerance does not mean giving up self-respect.

The second point is that the lifestyle that Bronies aspire to is living according to the *MLP:FIM* life lessons and the Elements of Harmony. This translates as being tolerant, full of love and, most importantly, cultivating the culture of friendship so as to have some really good friends. Cultivating the bonds of friendship with several close friends means that you can talk about everything and can relate in any situation. It is acknowledged that reaching this ideal is hard work, which requires seriousness and a focused will.

There are not only implicit, but also explicit, religious or spiritual traits present in the cases of several respondents. For example, mystical experiences have been recorded:

> For the better development of my inner self (personal reasons) I started listening to the pony hypnosis . . . After some time I was able to speak to the Mane 6, princesses and unicorns that have introduced themselves as Azure Mind and Icicle. They told me a lot of personal information. I talk to them from time to time. They help me, but I don't take them as deities or something. Well, maybe a little. Sometimes I wonder if it is just my imagination or if I am crazy. But I am sure it's more than that.
>
> (Respondent 52)

A large part of explicit Brony religiosity or spirituality is concerned with Brony Original Characters (OCs) and Ponysonas. Forty-six per cent of Bronies have an OC, 39 per cent have a Ponysona, which is typically the first OC they create. Nine per cent state that their OC "means a lot" to them, without further detail.

A Brony OC is any character developed by a Brony for any purpose. A Ponysona is an alter ego and the representation of a Brony within the fandom. This is usually (although not always) a visual representation of a nickname, but some Bronies use it for roleplay on forums or roleplaying games and have an elaborate backstory and lore connected to it. There are some that state the OC or Ponysona is a greater entity. Six per cent state that it represents not only the alter ego, but their better self, and when "in role" they try to be their better self, and that experience helps them to be their better self in real-life (that is, out of the persona). One respondent even stated that he designed an OC that is interested in technology and then started to study different mechanical engineering devices online to make his roleplay more believable, and this provoked his interest to such an extent that he is now studying mechanical engineering at university. He never planned to study at university at all before designing his Brony OC. The attribution of higher qualities to OCs and Ponysonas strengthens the accounts of mystical experiences given by Bronies:

> From time to time I went into a special kind of trance. I was in the skin of my pony-self (it's a pegasus) . . . The place in the trance was partially influenced by *The Shadow Trilogy* by Lapis-Lazuli . . . It wasn't always very enjoyable, especially since I feel everything that happens (I had broken wings once). Does my own self count as an OC? . . . Maybe it's just another life I have the opportunity to live, either in my head, or somewhere else.
>
> (Respondent 57)

The OCs of some individuals (though this is relatively rare) apparently have the qualities of spirit or totemic animals in the shamanic sense, "familiars" as they are termed in some types of esotericism and Paganism, or astral travelling companions. Bronies have speculated on ways to connect to their *MLP:FIM* heroes, and some have concluded that the astrophysical theory of multiverses may solve the problem, whereas others are researching astral-plane travel, or the Buddhist multiverse cosmology. Some OCs are like the *waifu* or *moe* from Japanese animation; these are characters that the viewer is attracted to, feels strong emotion for and regards as a wife (from which *waifu* is derived), or romantic partner more generally. In the Brony fandom, this not uncommon, and this casts the OC and the Ponysona as more like *tulpas* (magical emanations) from mystical types of Vajrayana Buddhism and esoteric traditions inspired by Eastern religion. A respondent stated that one of the characters is so close to him that it is like his body is hosting two souls and that he definitely did not mean that as a mere figure of speech (Interview No. 6). This resembles soulbonding, discussed in this volume by Venetia Robertson. Several pony therians are part of the Brony fandom as well.

There are also specific cases of watching *MLP:FIM* that did not produce implicit or explicit new religiosity, but informed, or even changed the viewer's original, traditional religion. Some members of mainstream religious groups – in the US most notably Christian denominations – say that *MLP:FIM* helped them to realise the importance of their own religion. There are dozens of Facebook groups for Bronies who are Christian, who watch the series and find Biblical parallels in it, or use stories of *MLP:FIM* to explain Christian morality. There is a general tendency to use *MLP:FIM* narratives to re-actualise Christian teachings in a modern and simple way that many can understand better than through often archaic parables and language of Christian scriptures. Some *MLP:FIM* fans who were very lax Christians started to practise their faith more rigorously as a result of their Bronyhood (Crome 2014; Primalcorn1 2011–2016; Rebel Brony 2011–2016).

On the other hand, there are some (the author's research suggests a much smaller number) who turned away from Christianity as a result of *MLP:FIM*. One respondent stated: "It changed everything – just everything. As I mentioned before, I started to learn English and focused on IT. I started to play piano. I came to dislike Christians and became a Buddhist and started to meditate" (Respondent 47). It seems that *MLP:FIM* and its fandom have all kinds of effects that are of interest to scholars of religion.

Conclusion

It is possible to find much moralising and self-righteousness on Brony forums, with some Bronies exhibiting their moral superiority openly, while others are trying to persuade people who are not interested and getting "on their nerves". There are other negative aspects of Brony subculture, but I have deliberately not elaborated on these. The goal of this chapter was to explain the attractiveness of the fandom and note the reasons why it generates such devotion; devotion that sometimes reaches the level of mainstream spirituality. If the chapter occasionally seemed overly positive, it is because it is important to capture the attitude of Bronies towards *MLP:FIM* and their community, and mediate their views and feelings to the reader.

Since the start of the twenty-first century, a number of new religions inspired by popular culture have emerged; a question that arises in the context of this volume is whether the trend of pop culture-based religions will continue? It is not easy to predict, but if Western cultural trends, strongly based on individualism, capitalism and consumerism continue to grow stronger, it is reasonable to expect that part of society will continue to consider itself the highest authority concerning the legitimation of beliefs. This leads to individuals selecting their own stories with which to interpret the world, and finding these stories within pop culture is very convenient. We may also expect that intelligent people will try to develop deeply meaningful, high-quality stories – not only because people intuitively know that good stories are attractive and making one is a source of professional pride, but also because a good story sells, and a good story is the backbone of word-of-mouth marketing (Reese 2006–2016). Hasbro knows this, and others are long familiar with it or are starting to rediscover this old idea as well (Suddath 2015). If there is a market for stories, there will be investment in stories. Taking this into consideration, this allows us to conclude that there is a good chance, if not a high probability, that hyper-real religions will continue to be a healthy part of the contemporary religious scene, and probably even be on the rise, for quite some time in the future.

Notes

1 The numbers included in this and other references to documentaries indicate the point during the documentary at which the cited quotation occurs.
2 Jokes have this function often for example in totalitarian societies.
3 71 per cent of the respondents who talked to the author stated they were from urban areas.

References

Agostinelli, Alexandra. 2015. 'Cloppers: Perverts or Fetishists?' *Gadfly Online*, 15 January. At: gadflyonline.com/home/index.php/cloppers-perverts-or-fetishists2/. Accessed 10 November 2015.
AlasdairGives. 2014. 'Effective Altruists elsewhere: Bronies For Good'. *Effective Altruism Forum*, 21 December. At: effective-altruism.com/ea/cn/effective_altruists_elsewhere_bronies_for_good/. Accessed 10 November 2015.
Amidi, Amid. 2010. 'The End of the Creator-Driven Era in TV Animation'. *Cartoon Brew*, 19 October. At: www.cartoonbrew.com/ideas-commentary/the-end-of-the-creator-driven-era-29614.html. Accessed 10 November 2015.
Berry, B. J. L. and A. Okulicz-Kozaryn. 2011. 'An Urban-Rural Happiness Gradient'. *Urban Geography* 32(6): 871–883.
Brony Admin Group. n.d. 'Study Results'. *Brony Study (Research Project)*. At: www.bronystudy.com/id1.html. Accessed 24 November 2014.
Buljan, Katharine and Carole M. Cusack. 2015. *Anime, Religion and Spirituality: Profane and Sacred Worlds in Contemporary Japan*. Sheffield, UK and Oakville, CT: Equinox.
Calpain. 2013a. 'Brony Meetup Group Map'. *Equestria Daily*, 7 April. At: www.equestriadaily.com/2013/04/brony-meetup-group-map.html. Accessed 10 November 2015.
Calpain. 2013b. 'Discussion: Pony, a Catalyst for Change'. *Equestria Daily*, 22 October. At: www.equestriadaily.com/2013/10/discussion-pony-catalyst-for-change.html. Accessed 24 November 2015.
Carver, Steve (Saberspark) and Josh Tyson (Paleosteno). 2013a. *The Brony Chronicles: A Documentary on My Little Pony and Bronies (Part 1)*. At: www.youtube.com/watch?v=t2EOfhvvURY. Accessed 24 November 2014.
Carver, Steve (Saberspark) and Josh Tyson (Paleosteno). 2013b. *The Brony Chronicles: A Documentary on My Little Pony and Bronies (Part 2)*. At: www.youtube.com/watch?v=t2EOfhvvURY. Accessed 24 November 2014.
Centre for Disease Control and Prevention. 2014. 'National Health Interview Survey'. At: www.cdc.gov/nchs/nhis.htm. Accessed 24 November 2014.
Crome, Andrew. 2014. 'Reconsidering Religion and Fandom: Christian Fan Works in *My Little Pony* Fandom'. *Culture and Religion: An Interdisciplinary Journal* 15(4): 399–418.
Cusack, Carole M. 2010. *Invented Religions: Imagination, Fiction and Faith*. Farnham, UK and Burlington, VT: Ashgate.
Fitzgerald, Jonathan D. 2013. 'How the "New Sincerity" Changed Popular Culture'. *Patheos*. At: www.patheos.com/blogs/christandpopculture/2013/01/how-the-new-sincerity-changes-the-way-we-watch-popular-culture/. Accessed 10 November 2015.
Forest Rain. n.d. 'Join the Herd'. At www.youtube.com/watch?v=MjfCH89sBzs. Accessed 10 November 2015.

Gray, Sarah. 2014. 'Stephen Colbert vs. Bill O'Reilly'. *Salon*. At: www.salon.com/2014/11/24/stephen_colbert_vs_bill_oreilly_36_clips_that_define_their_relationship/. Accessed 24 November 2014.

Griffiths, Daniel Nye. 2011. 'Friendship is Massive – Ponies, Internet Phenomena and Crossover Audiences'. *D Nye Everything*, 27 September. At: www.danielnyegriffiths.org/2011/09/friendship-is-money-ponies-internet.html. Accessed 10 November 2015.

Grossman, Samantha. 2014. '5 times Stephen Colbert Changed the World'. *The Times*, 17 December. At: time.com/3561636/5-times-stephen-colbert-changed-the-world/. Accessed 10 November 2015.

Hodge, Brent. 2014. *A Brony Tale*. Vancouver, BC: Hodgee Films.

Horowitz, Leonard M., Rita de S. French, and Craig A. Anderson. 1982. 'The Prototype of a Lonely Person'. In L. Peplau and D. Perlman (eds), *Loneliness: A Sourcebook of Current Theory, Research, and Therapy*, 183–205. New York: John Wiley and Sons.

Luckmann, Thomas. 1967. *The Invisible Religion: The Problem of Religion In Modern Society*. London: Macmillan.

Malaquais, Laurent. 2012. *Bronies: The Extremely Unexpected Fans of My Little Pony*. Anaheim, CA: Big Focus Television.

Morgan, Matt. 2011. 'Could My Little Pony Be Raising the Next Generation of Geeks?' *Wired*, 17 September. At: www.wired.com/2011/09/could-my-little-pony-be-raising-the-next-generation-of-geeks/. Accessed 10 November 2015.

Orwell, George. 1945. 'Funny, But Not Vulgar'. *Leader*, 28 July. At: orwell.ru/library/articles/funny/english/e_funny. Accessed 24 November 2014.

Possamai, Adam. 2005. *Religion and Popular Culture: A Hyper-real Testament*. Brussels: Peter Lang.

Primalcorn1. 2011–2016. 'Welcome to the "Christian Bronies" Group'. *Christian Bronies*. At: www.fimfiction.net/group/1565/christian-bronies. Accessed 10 January 2016.

Rebel Brony. 2011–2016. *Bronies for Christ*. At: www.fimfiction.net/group/201660/bronies-for-christ. Accessed 10 January 2016.

Reese, Nick. 2006–2016. 'Storytelling for Fun and Profit'. *Nick Reese*. At: www.nicholasreese.com/persuasive-storytelling/. Accessed 10 January 2016.

Robertson, Venetia Laura Delano. 2014. 'Of Ponies and Men. *My Little Pony: Friendship is Magic* and the Brony Fandom'. *International Journal of Cultural Studies* 17(1): 21–37.

Seeds of Kindness. 2014. 'Shine Together'. *YouTube*, 17 December. At: www.youtube.com/watch?v=7hd0VI8Gfoo. Accessed 24 November 2015.

Seeds of Kindness. 2015. 'Building Bridges'. *YouTube*, 19 November. At: www.youtube.com/watch?v=lBclh-JC28U. Accessed 24 November 2015.

Stern, Howard. 2013. 'Bronies, Brony Hate Mail, and Comic Con'. *YouTube*, 4 March. At: www.youtube.com/watch?v=dj11mL200qY. Accessed 24 November 2015.

Suddath. Claire. 2015. 'The $500 Million Battle Over Disney's Princesses: How Hasbro Grabbed the Lucrative Disney Doll Business from Mattel'. *Bloomberg Business*, 17 December. At: www.bloomberg.com/features/2015-disney-princess-hasbro/. Accessed 10 January 2016.

Taylor, Charles. 1992. *The Ethics of Authenticity*. Cambridge, MA: Harvard University Press.

Spirituality in the Brony community 97

TenDyke, Elizabeth. 2007. 'Humor As Resistance'. *Making the History of 1989*. At: chnm.gmu.edu/1989/exhibits/humor-as-resistance/essay. Accessed 24 November 2015.

Tennant, Laurence. 2012. 'Bronies and the New Sincerity'. At: laurencetennant.com/bonds/newsincerity.html. Accessed 24 November.

Truitt, Brian. 2012. 'My Little Pony plants a hoof in pop culture'. *USA Today*, 26 November. At: www.usatoday.com/story/life/2012/11/26/my-little-pony/1725375/. Accessed 24 November 2015.

Watercutter, Angela. 2011. 'My Little Pony Corrals Unlikely Fanboys Known As "Bronies"'. *Wired*, 9 June. At: www.wired.com/2011/06/bronies-my-little-ponys/. Accessed 24 November 2015.

Watercutter, Angela. 2013. 'Yes, There's an Air Force Class Flying With *My Little Pony* Patches'. *Wired*, 5 August. At: www.wired.com/underwire/2013/08/air-force-my-little-pony/#slideid-184921. Accessed 24 November 2015.

Wikipedia. 2016. '*My Little Pony: Friendship Is Magic* fandom'. *Wikipedia*. At: en.wikipedia.org/wiki/My_Little_Pony:_Friendship_Is_Magic_fandom#cite_note-28. Accessed 24 November 2015.

Part II

Film and television as sacred texts

5 Spirituality-struck
Anime and religio-spiritual devotional practices

Katharine Buljan

Introduction

Japanese animation (anime) has struck a chord with many members of the audience in the West although the cultural/linguistic/religious/spiritual context it belongs to differs from that of the Western world. This interest started around the 1960s, although anime's earliest showing in the West dates back to several decades earlier (Buljan and Cusack 2015). Western aficionados' enthusiasm for anime manifests in various ways. This chapter focuses on three activities: dressing and posing as favourite anime characters (cosplay ritual); visiting places used as sites in anime (anime pilgrimage); and forming anime-based religions (Haruhiism).

By analysing these three phenomena through the framework of Mircea Eliade's theories on the sacred-profane dichotomy, the function of myth in ritual, sacred-profane space, and desacralised context and religion, this chapter argues that they can be seen, in a certain sense, as an expression of a (perhaps subliminal) 'need' for the presence of a supernatural/spiritual/religious (hereafter supernatural) dimension (Eliade 1958: 385, 1959b). The main driver behind this need, according to Eliade, is the search for an ultimate meaning (Eliade 1959b, 1979), a topic which is outside the remit of this chapter. Bearing these points in mind, it can be said that it is not surprising anime has found a large following in the West, since its supernatural, spiritual and religious content is one of its main characteristics (Buljan and Cusack 2015). The first part of the chapter focuses on cosplay ritual and anime pilgrimage, while the second part focuses on Haruhiism. This study adopts an outsider perspective, but through the use of theologically inclined scholars such as Eliade and Paul Tillich, treats the beliefs and practices of members of so-called "invented" or "fiction-based" (Cusack 2010; Davidsen 2013) religions in a serious fashion.

Meaning, religion and spirituality

One of the primary human activities is to seek, find and construct meaning. Humanity is a meaning-seeking and meaning-making species (Klinger 2012).

There are, however, many interpretations, layers, levels and types of meanings, ranging from those associated with mundane, daily activities and actions, to those which theologians generally refer to as ultimate or transcendental meanings (of life). Institutional religions traditionally acted as a mediator for the latter, but in contemporary times popular culture also plays a role (Possamai 2005). Eliade saw the search for ultimate meaning as underpinning humanity's need for (symbolically speaking) 'contact' with the supernatural dimension (Eliade 1959b), and Tillich has elegantly described it as, "a meaning which gives meaning to all meanings" (Tillich 1952: 47). Both Eliade and Tillich interpreted ultimate meaning as a solace for individuals having to face the imminent end of personal existence (Eliade 1959b, 1968, 1975; Tillich 1952). This brief sketch of the idea of ultimate meaning and humanity's existential situation provides a 'snapshot' background to Eliade's model of humanity's orientation towards the supernatural; however, investigation of these topics and anime aficionados' relation to them is outside the scope of this chapter.

This chapter is divided into two parts. The first part considers the phenomena of cosplay (costume and play) ritual and pilgrimage to places featured in anime, both of which gained popularity in anime fandom in the West (Buljan and Cusack 2015). Working under the assumption that a dichotomy exists between sacred and profane planes (Eliade 1958), and employing Eliade's theories on the function of myth in ritual (for cosplay ritual) and sacred-profane space (for anime pilgrimage), the first part argues that these two anime phenomena can be understood as an expression of a need to connect symbolically with the sacred or supernatural dimension, a dimension that is in stark contrast to that of everyday life (Eliade 1958). Viewed in this way, they resemble "magico-religious" practices (Eliade 1958). The second part of the chapter focuses on Haruhiism, an anime-based religion concerning Haruhi Suzumiya, who is who is a god in the form of a high school girl and the main character in the 2006 anime series *The Melancholy of Haruhi Suzumiya* (hereafter *MOHA*). Working with the same assumption that a dichotomy exists between sacred and profane planes (Eliade 1958), and employing his theory about desacralised context and religion (Eliade 1959b), I argue that the appearance of this anime-based religion may also be seen as an expression of the need to 'connect' symbolically with the supernatural dimension (Eliade 1958: 385).

In establishing the ground for analysis of these three anime-related phenomena, there are two points that require a brief clarification, namely secularism and religious sentiment, and popular culture (anime) and religious experience. Concerning the first point, it is useful to draw on Sigmund Freud's schema of three historical systems of thought: animistic, religious and scientific (Freud 1983: 77). The first two systems imply the idea that humanity in general has a basic tendency to believe in a force(s) that surpasses/transcends every aspect of its existence, consequently finding in it an ultimate meaning (of life). According to Freud, animistic beliefs have been

Anime and devotional practices   103

'surmounted' in the third, scientific stage (Freud 1955: 249). The phenomenon of secularisation is an important aspect of this system, as it also records a decline of interest in institutional religions (Possamai 2005). However, as Carole M. Cusack notes:

> [t]he net result of the secularisation process has not been, as originally envisaged by Max Weber, Karl Marx and Sigmund Freud and others, the death of religion in the West. Rather, the more positive framework of [Emile] Durkheim, who asserted that new forms of religiosity would develop as older forms faded, has proved to be the case.
>
> (Cusack 2013: 370)

Thus it follows that, despite the advancement of secularism, scientific and technological knowledge, and a mass rejection or outgrowing of belief systems offered by institutional religion, personal religious sentiment survives in the contemporary world and with it the need to connect symbolically with the supernatural dimension. In this new milieu, "a privatized and individualized space remains open to the voluntaristic adoption of sacred themes and ideas" (Hills 2000: 76), and popular culture (including anime) proves to be a source of inspiration and significance in this context.

With regard to popular culture and religious experience, it is worth recalling that anime is classified under the umbrella of "popular culture", to which scholarship has traditionally designated a lower status as compared to higher culture whose products, according to Hegelian tradition, have the potential to communicate the higher, transcendental values (Shusterman 2003: 297–298). Popular culture was believed not to offer its admirers the same 'elevated' experience as higher culture. The attitude of rejection of popular culture has found its support in the philosophical subgenre of aesthetics (Shusterman 2003: 289). Arguably, there are many differences between high and popular cultures, but they are not sufficient to deny to the latter the same capacity to engender transcendence of the former. There is considerable modern scholarship that deals with a close connection between popular culture and religion and spirituality (Chidester 2005; Cusack 2010; Possamai 2005), which indicates the potential this 'lower' or mass culture has to evoke religious sentiment and experience. There are also numerous religions based on works from popular culture (Cusack 2010; Davidsen 2013), which confirms the point that popular culture has greater potential than is commonly recognised to pique or satisfy peoples' religious and spiritual needs. In this context, however, as is the case with artistic works in general, the attitude of audience members is important. New religious forms are unlikely to develop amongst passive viewers, but are the result of active participators' immersion in the particular popular cultural form (Buljan 2006).

Recalling that artistic expression and religious sentiments and experiences have a deep and longstanding connection, this study highlights that the

104   *Katharine Buljan*

genre of anime sits within this tradition and, despite its different cultural and religio-spiritual background, Western audiences can relate to it on a deep level as demonstrated by the size of its fandom (Buljan and Cusack 2015).

Cosplay ritual and anime pilgrimage

Frequent television showings of anime, Japanese anime directors becoming household names, numerous anime festivals, anime societies at universities, fans' blogs and forums, and numerous conventions are some of the examples that demonstrate the rising demand for and love of anime in the West. Fans' love may be intense and their devotion deep and also motivated by different reasons and expressed in varied ways. Focusing on the dichotomy between profane and sacred and employing Eliade's theory of the function of myth in ritual (in the case of cosplay ritual) and sacred-profane space (in the case of anime pilgrimage), this section argues that cosplay and anime pilgrimage can be viewed as an expression of a need to symbolically participate in the supernatural or sacred. Viewed in this way, they resemble "magico-religious" practices (Eliade 1958).

Cosplay ritual refers to anime aficionados dressing up as their favourite characters and striking a particular pose on stage that typifies that character. Aficionados also use wigs, make-up and accessories to resemble their chosen character. They often make their own costumes. Generally, a photo-shoot session also takes place. Cosplay ritual is an important part of anime conventions; cosplay competitions are held at local, national and international levels. An example is the Madman National Cosplay Championship in Australia, which requires a cosplay skit and a costume made by the cosplayer (Anon n.d. a). The World Cosplay Summit is an international cosplay competition established in "the Cosplay Holy Land", Nagoya, Japan in 2003 (Anon n.d. b).

Regarding the cosplaying experience, one cosplayer said, "I enjoy the idea of being able to be a different character for a day" (Anime Fan 2, 2014, pers. comm., 14 October). An anime fan (not a cosplayer) explains, "I'll agree with the idea . . . [that] cosplaying is allowing people to act as a different character and enjoy it" (Anime Fan 6, 2014 pers. comm., 7 November). Second cosplayer reflects similarly on the experience:

> [i]t's something that allows me to be someone else. When I'm in cosplay, I am not just myself but I also act like the character that I am cosplaying . . . To me, cosplaying is a show of affection . . . Because I love the character, I make my costume, style my wig and attempt to put on make-up to look as closely as possible to the character.
>
> (Anime Fan 3, 2014, pers. comm., 8 November)

Furthermore, another cosplayer interestingly observes, "I like the passion that people put [into it] and the opportunity it offers for people to be or

Anime and devotional practices   105

perceived to be someone else for a time" (Anime Fan 4, 2014, pers. comm., 27 October). Another cosplayer explains, "The aspect that I like about cosplaying would be the sense of satisfaction when you get recognised as the cosplaying character at the convention" (Anime Fan 5, 2014, pers. comm., 6 November). The cosplay ritual experience is described by another cosplayer in the following way, "I like cosplay as it is like acting, you get the opportunity to pretend to be someone else" (Anime Fan 7, 2014, pers. comm., 9 December). Thus, a point noticeable in fans' comments is that the idea of 'transforming' into someone else is one of the most appealing aspects of cosplay ritual. An examination of cosplay ritual suggests that this 'someone else' is mostly a *supernatural being* or a human character with *supernatural abilities*. This supernatural quality/ability belongs to the world of myth(s) (Eliade 1975).

Eliade highlights that a model that has "mythical precedents" can have "mythical status" (Eliade 1968: 25). Both cosplayed anime characters with supernatural qualities and the narratives in which they are set are indeed modelled on 'mythical precedents'. Many of these anime characters embody one of the most famous myths, that of the Hero (a saviour-figure in mythical times). There are instances in anime when these old myths are combined with a new element, for instance technology (Astro Boy, a hero and boy robot) creating what could be termed a 'new myth'. The character of Haruhi Suzumiya from *MOHA* is based on a myth concerning a divine being. This myth also frequently appears in anime and consequently in cosplay ritual. Ritual is a vehicle for re-enactment of myth(s) (Eliade 1975: 139–140). Taking this into account, it follows that cosplay ritual represents the re-enactment of myth(s) in the sense of episodes from anime featuring supernatural plotlines and characters with superhuman powers. Eliade bases his theory of re-enactment of myth through ritual (and the meaning of it) on the dichotomy between what he calls 'profane' and 'sacred' (or supernatural) dimensions (Eliade 1959b). The profane dimension refers to mundane existence, the realm of the everyday, and this dimension is sharply distinguished from the supernatural (sacred) dimension. The latter, as the term suggests, transcends the profane dimension (mundane existence). Eliade traces narratives about the sacred back to antiquity, when it was believed that this dimension was closely linked to the origin of time and populated by gods, mythical heroes and other supernatural beings that created the universe, this world and human beings (Eliade 1959b: 202, 1975). Narratives about these beings and events and the supernatural dimension are "preserved in the myths" (Eliade 1959b: 202). Thus, for Eliade, myth primarily discloses "sacred history" although he acknowledges that other interpretations are possible (Eliade 1975: 5–6). Humanity manifests a desire to connect with the sacred and participate in it (Eliade 1959b: 91). While in cosplay ritual there are differences in terms of each fan performer's "level of engagement and the degree of commitment" (Rahman *et al.* 2012: 325), when applying the above model to cosplay it follows that a such ritual has the potential to transcend the profane dimension and enter, so

106   *Katharine Buljan*

to speak, this other, 'supernatural', dimension through the vehicle of myth (by 'transformation' into a creature with mythical, that is supernatural, qualities), as one cosplayer writes:

> [h]ave any of you ever felt a spiritual or mystical purpose behind why you cosplay? For me, I always felt that the act of cosplaying itself was a ritual. It was a way for me to align myself with the myth of the story and reenact its events. I guess cosplaying for me is similar to how Christians replay from the Bible like the Stations of the Cross. By dressing up, I feel as if I can go through what the character felt or experienced and learn the lessons that he did in his story. I don't actually believe I am the character and I have a healthy separation of reality from fantasy, but cosplaying does help me gain an appreciation of the journey of a character that I love . . . I know most people cosplay just for fun, or attention . . . but I think we should be more aware of the ritual behind why we cosplay.
>
> (Anon 2015, 18 May)

Thus, while for many anime fans cosplay represents only a form of entertainment, there are also those for whom cosplay potentially has a deeper meaning that closely relates to Eliade's theory discussed here. Additionally, it can be said that this is a general phenomenon as it is applicable to various other contexts where costuming and performance have an important role. Eliade notes, in the context of the novel form, that through "projection" and "identification" readers enter the fictional world (Eliade 1975: 185), and, by applying this to cosplay ritual it follows that projection and identification may aid aficionados to enter symbolically that supernatural dimension through the means of myth re-enactment. For Eliade, "ritual abolishes profane, chronological Time and recovers the sacred Time of myth" (Eliade 1975: 140). Viewing cosplay ritual this way reveals its capacity to symbolically "break into" this supernatural time of myth. For this to happen, ritual needs to be genuine, which implies a successful act of identification, projection and arguably even what Samuel Taylor Coleridge called "suspension of disbelief" (Coleridge 1971 [1817]).

This need for sincerity is confirmed by research arguing that "cosplayers must fervently believe in the role that they are playing . . . Through this participatory activity, cosplayers can enter into an imaginative world or into dreamlike states of hyperreality" (Rahman *et al.* 2012: 325, 333). Eliade observes that "myths are the most general and effective means of awakening and maintaining consciousness of another world, a beyond . . . the divine world . . . This 'other world' represents a superhuman, 'transcendent' plane" (Eliade 1975: 139). Thus, it is not surprising that (re-enactment of) myth plays a central role in cosplay ritual. Eliade claimed that, "directly or indirectly, myth 'elevates' man" (Eliade 1975: 145), and cosplay ritual also has the potential to do this. Interestingly, Eliade asserted that "anyone who

Anime and devotional practices 107

'imitates' a mythological model or even ritually assists at the retelling of a myth (taking part in it), is taken out of profane . . . and returns to the Great Time" (Eliade 1958: 429). This 'Great Time' implies transcendence of the individual, and this function of myth (to symbolically connect humanity with the supernatural dimension) is preserved to some degree in a cosplay ritual. Myth represents a "religious experience" (Eliade 1958: 430), and this suggests that cosplay ritual experience has the potential to also become religious in some way as it centres on the re-enactment of myth. This is exemplified in the following answer by Erica Friedman on the question "what is the fascination with cosplay?":

> [a]ncient peoples dressed up as animals and gods. They dressed up as powerful characters of myth and reenacted stories that were important to them. Modern people do the same . . . I attend anime/manga gatherings and I know from talking to many, many people about this, that the drive to dress up as characters you love comes from wanting to participate more deeply in the narrative . . . So, why cosplay? **To engage with our mythical/narrative roots; to take on skills and powers that we don't normally have, in the context of ritual – or fun**
> (Friedman 2012, 19 October. Emphasis in original)

The overlapping of cosplay with ritual requires a clarification here. For British cultural anthropologist, Victor Turner, religion is an important aspect of ritual (Deflem 1991: 12) and he further explains that, "theatre is one of the many inheritors of that great multifaceted system of preindustrial ritual which embraces ideas and images of cosmos and chaos . . . [also] enacting . . . mythic and heroic plots drawn from oral traditions. And so much more" (Turner 1990: 12). Cosplay, like a theatre, has many elements of a performance (art), and, as Turner highlights, performing arts are an offspring of ritual (Turner 1990: 13). For Turner, "the costume in ritual and theater create an embodied alternate persona for the wearer" (Fron *et al.* 2007: 1), and by implication this also applies to cosplay. This was reflected in some of the cosplayers' comments previously discussed. Furthermore, cosplay uses many tools that have an important role in ritual including costumes, make-up, masks, gestures, performance and various objects (often with supposedly supernatural characteristics) that have a special meaning. Thus, looking from this point of view, cosplay has a potential to be interpreted as a ritual to an extent. While "ritual . . . engages the viewer on a different level of consciousness than everyday life" (Niemi 2003: 438), by implication it also 'engages' the one performing it, in this case a cosplayer, 'on a different level of consciousness than everyday life', as it requires 'stepping into' a different character. The function of myth in ritual is deepened by "reproducing the same [mythical] paradigmatic acts and gestures [through ritual] . . . because he [the human being] desires and attempts to live close to his gods" (Eliade 1959b: 91). In proximity to the gods, humans

108 *Katharine Buljan*

find both refuge against their own mortality and the ultimate meaning of existence (Eliade 1975: 139). Discussing these two arguments is, as noted, outside the scope of this study, but they serve here to close the circle of Eliadian theory of the function of myth in ritual (and its meaning). In short, through symbolical re-enactment of a myth, a cosplay ritual reflects a need for or attempt to create a connection with the supernatural dimension.

In conclusion, "play is . . . a close relative of ritual . . . and therefore of the sacred" (Cusack 2013: 362). This is what cosplay has the potential for; starting as play, by symbolical re-enactment of (supernatural) myth (by means of identification and projection) it becomes a ritual, and as such expresses a need to connect with the supernatural (sacred) dimension by rising above the profane dimension. Viewed in this way, it resembles "magico-religious" practice (Eliade 1958).

Anime pilgrimage

A second phenomenon associated with anime fandom is anime pilgrimage. This involves fans' visits to places that feature in their favourite anime. Some also post their pilgrimage visual diaries on their blogs or discuss their impressions with other fans through online forums. Using an Eliadian model of sacred and profane space, this section argues that anime pilgrimage could also be seen as an expression of a need to connect symbolically with the supernatural (sacred) dimension. As such, anime pilgrimage also involves "magico-religious" practice (Eliade 1958).

Anime fans have "adopted the term *seichi junrei*, a compound meaning 'sacred site' (*seichi*) and 'pilgrimage' (*junrei*)" to describe anime pilgrimage (Andrews 2014: 218). The earliest pilgrimages date from the 1990s; for example, a pilgrimage to Hikawa Shrine (Tokyo), linked to the *Sailor Moon* anime (Andrews 2014: 218). Other pilgrimage sites include Chichibu (Saitama) related to *Anohana: The Flower We Saw That Day* anime (2011 series, 2013 film), and Hirakawa (Aomori) and Tokyo, the former associated with *The Secret World of Arrietty* (2010) and the latter with the 1995 anime *Whisper of the Heart* (Stimson 2014). There is even a book titled *Anime Tours: A Holy Land Pilgrimage Guide*, which includes Japanese locations that feature in 150 anime (Stimson 2014). Anime pilgrimage has become so popular that there are now specialised tours for fans.

Reflecting on anime pilgrimage, one fan says:

> I think it's . . . great to see a place you see in anime in real life because the fictional world might be that one step closer to being that much more real . . . When you see anime characters you know and love in the locations you have been [to], even if they're just drawn in the anime, it's so exciting to perceive that 2D world and know it's real and you've gone there.
>
> (Anime Fan 1, 2014, pers. comm., 13 October)

Regarding an anime setting in Australia, another anime fan explains:

> I have had a couple of moments while standing in The Rocks [Sydney], where I felt a rush of excitement at recognising a location which had featured in an anime. Various locations in Sydney have recently been on the anime *Free!*, so this is an exciting moment for Sydney anime fans.
>
> (Anime Fan 4, 2014, pers. comm., 27 October)

Also commenting on Sydney locations that feature in anime, another fan says, "I do feel excited when I pass by and recognise the locations [in Sydney] used [in anime]" (Anime Fan 7, 2014, pers. comm., 9 December). This sense of excitement related to places featured in anime is also expressed by yet another fan:

> To me, anime pilgrimages are always exciting because you get to see the 2D being transformed into 3D. You recognise places that you'd seen in anime and that makes me feel as if they actually exist in our world. It's a surreal feeling that's hard to describe because anime is often far from reality, and seeing the places that an anime is based off makes me feel like the characters I like and the story I enjoyed actually exists in this world/reality. If I get the chance to, I'd like to go on more anime pilgrimages, and maybe even one day cosplay at those places.
>
> (Anime Fan 3, 2014, pers. comm., 8 November)

A noticeable feature of the above comments by fans is that the excitement is seemingly triggered by the feeling that, symbolically speaking, the dimension 'lived in' every day somehow came into 'contact' with another dimension, that is, the 'other' world of anime.

Similarly to traditional religious practices where "travel is . . . a crucial, even necessary, part of a tradition of religious experience" (Norman and Cusack 2015: 1), anime pilgrimage has significance for fans in a sense that, like traditional religious pilgrimage, there is potential to have a 'special' experience of the place visited. The word, "pilgrimage . . . is derived from the Latin *peregrine-um*, meaning one that comes from foreign parts, linked with its usual meaning as denoting a journey (usually involving a long distance) to a sacred place to undertake demonstrations of religious devotion" (Digance 2015: 249). This also applies to anime pilgrims who, through these travels, express devotion to their favourite anime, its characters and story. Thus, it is not a coincidence that the word 'pilgrimage' is used in the context of these anime-related travels.

The dichotomy between profane and sacred dimensions also implies dichotomy between profane and sacred (supernatural) space (Eliade 1959b: 20–65) that is relevant to anime pilgrimage. Eliade claims that "a sacred place constitutes a break in the homogeneity of space . . . [and] this break is symbolized by an opening by which passage from one cosmic region to another is made possible (from heaven to earth and vice versa)" (Eliade 1959b: 37). This 'opening' occurs in profane space (Eliade 1959b). Therefore, for a pilgrim, a 'profane' space (place) of anime pilgrimage is, symbolically speaking, transformed into a 'sacred' (supernatural) space, a space where anime's supernatural story occurs, inhabited by its (supernatural/mythical) protagonists. Sacred spaces (not necessarily those associated with religion, but those of personal significance) "are the 'holy places' of his [human being's] private universe, as if it were in such spots that he had received the revelation of a reality *other* than that in which he participates through his ordinary daily life" (Eliade 1959b: 24). Having this in mind, it appears as no coincidence that many anime pilgrims refer to the anime-related places that they visit as "holy places", because as mentioned, it is as if the 'reality' or the 'otherworldly' space of anime becomes 'manifest' and overrides the actual, in Eliadian terms, 'profane space' in which they are physically located. This is in a way reflected in an anime fan's statement, "By going on these pilgrimages, I feel closer to the anime characters because it feels like I have entered their world" (Punynari n.d.). While an average tourist would usually admire a particular space for what *it actually is* and its cultural significance, the purpose of anime pilgrimage is different. The motive of such pilgrims (usually highly familiar with anime) is to see, admire and experience the place, not for what it actually is, but for *what it actually is in the world of anime*. After watching anime, the future pilgrim will no longer look at that space in the same way. Thus, it could be said that an anime pilgrim is, symbolically speaking, on a mission for an out-of-the-ordinary or 'otherworldly' experience. As these places are often given a mythical aura in anime, they 'become' locations of supernatural events and stories, populated with protagonists possessing supernatural, mythical characteristics, and thus this pilgrimage is, in a way, an expression of an Eliadian need to 'connect' with the supernatural dimension.

While religion traditionally catered for this need for the supernatural, popular culture, including anime, has the potential to also play a role in this context. Eliade coined the term "hierophany" to describe a manifestation of the supernatural (sacred) in the profane dimension (Eliade 1959b: 11). He claimed that "every sacred space implies a hierophany, an irruption of the sacred that results in detaching a territory from the surrounding cosmic milieu and making it qualitatively different" (Eliade 1959b: 26). From this point of view, it follows that a 'holy' anime-related location may potentially become for its pilgrim, in Eliadian terms, 'qualitatively different', as if that was an experience of hierophany. Accepting that "a church constitutes a break in plane in the profane space of a modern city" (Eliade 1959b: 72), then the same applies to traditional religious places of pilgrimage, and, by implication, 'holy' locations of anime pilgrimage also have the potential to symbolically constitute this 'break' or 'opening'. Eliade believed that this 'opening' facilitated "communication with the gods" (Eliade 1959b: 65). He

Anime and devotional practices 111

also uses the expression 'gate to heaven' to describe this 'break' or 'opening', and, for him, it becomes "the paradoxical point of passage from one mode of being to another" (Eliade 1959b: 26). Thus, anime pilgrims' 'passage' from the 'profane' dimension of the place of the pilgrimage into the supernatural world of the anime set is a symbolical expression of the 'passage from one mode of being to another'. This focuses attention on a vital quality of sacred space: "from whatever angle one looks at it, the dialectic of sacred space always reveals . . . nostalgia for paradise", which is "the desire to be . . . at the heart . . . of the sacred, and, briefly, to transcend . . . the human condition and regain a divine state of affairs" (Eliade 1958: 383). From this point of view, it follows that pilgrimage to anime 'holy' places can be symbolically seen as a reflection of a need for a supernatural dimension. This need is a desire "to live close to his [or her] gods" (Eliade 1959b: 91), which gives an ultimate meaning (to existence) and becomes a refuge from the knowledge of the imminent end of physical existence, that is, death. As indicated earlier, it is outside the scope of this study to dwell into these two areas. Taking into consideration the above analysis, it follows that similarly to cosplay ritual, anime pilgrimage is an expression of the desire to enter the supernatural (sacred) dimension.

In conclusion, although there are various levels of fans' engagement (De Kloet and Van Zoonen 2007: 325), using the dichotomy between profane and sacred space, the above section has argued that anime pilgrimage in general, similarly to cosplay ritual, can be seen as an expression of a 'need' to connect with the supernatural dimension. As such, it can be viewed as Eliadian 'magico-religious' practice (Eliade 1958, 1959b).

The next part focuses on the third anime phenomena, a new religious expression called 'Haruhiism'.

Haruhiism

The Melancholy of Haruhi Suzumiya (2006) is an anime series directed by Tatsuya Ishihara, based on the light novels of Nagaru Tanigawa. The main character in this anime is a high school student named Haruhi Suzumiya who is also a god, though she is unaware of her divine nature and powers. If Haruhi becomes bored, there is a danger that she will destroy the existing world and create a new one. *Haruhiism* is a religion linked to this particular anime, and, as the name suggests, it is centred on the character of Haruhi. By utilising Eliade's notions of desacralised context and religion (Eliade 1959b: 23, 202–204), this part of the chapter argues that the appearance of this anime-based religion can be seen as an expression of a need to connect symbolically with the supernatural dimension (Eliade 1958: 385).

Fiction-based religions are not new phenomena. The earliest examples date back to about 60 years ago, and amongst the best-known today are Jediism, Matrixism and Discordianism (Cusack 2013: 362). Cusack coined an elegant term for these religions, "invented religions" (Cusack 2013: 362),

112 *Katharine Buljan*

noting that that drew attention to their fictive origins, and this term will be used in this case study. Beside Haruhiism, other invented religions based on anime include Yukiism (centred on Yuki Nagato, another character from *MOHA*), and the Church of Madoka, based on the anime series *Puella Magi Madoka Magica* (2011), directed by Akiyuki Shinbo.

Haruhiism also has a website and a Facebook page. Its website describes Haruhiism as:

> [a] religion based around a high school student living in Japan named Haruhi Suzumiya. It is the belief that she possesses the power to re-establish the universe on a whim . . . If she is upset or in a state of boredom, it's likely she will manufacture a prototype world.
>
> (Anon n.d. c)

The same website describes 'Haruhiists' as, "the external followers of Haruhi whose sole goal is to entertain the goddess and prevent her mood from swaying to the dark end" (Anon n.d. c). Haruhiism's website also lists 'Haruhistic 10 Commandments', 'The 5 Pillars of Haruhiism' and so-called 'Haruhi Day', 7 July (Anon n.d. c). One of the five pillars of Haruhiism is "Declaration of Faith" and it requires, "constantly declaring the phrase 'There is no god but Haruhi and Nagaru Tanigawa [writer of the work] is Her prophet'" (Anon n.d. d). Another of these five pillars called "Fasting" requires "fasting on days of new episodes and not watching any other anime" (Anon n.d. d). This is similar to some practices of self-restriction and self-control from world religions (for example, not eating meat on Fridays), which act as an offering. There is even a "Haruhiist prayer" and here is an excerpt from it:

> Our Lady, who art in North High School.
>
> We pray that you are happy with your creation.
>
> We pray that you are happy with yourself.
>
> We pray that like you we will strive to save the world by overloading [it] with fun in your name.
>
> May you be guided in your infinite eccentricity by your friends.
>
> We pray to the aliens. May the Data Overmind protect you with its infinite knowledge.
>
> (Wolf 2013. Italics in original)

These descriptions clearly borrow from the terminology of world religions, including Christianity (commandments), Islam (pillars) and Shinto/ Chinese legend (7 July is also the Tanabata festival). Furthermore, one fan of the series explains that, "when I am asked if I was religious, I could give the following short response: 'I'm a Haruhiist'" (Waver 2011). Another

Anime and devotional practices 113

fan writes, "if you've been following the novels you'll realise it isn't all nonsense/fantasy but has roots in physics and maths. So if Haruhiism is rooted by [*sic*] physics and maths then it can't be wrong" (dKiWi 2007). This fan adds, "I seriously do believe that someone like Haruhi can exist. Or at least a model for this religion is the religion that I would believe in" (dKiWi 2007). These fans' comments demonstrate how the character of Haruhi and the series inspired in some fans a devotional impulse and the use of logic of science (mathematics and physics) to attempt to explain a spiritual/religious dimension. Some invented religions have been offensively referred to as 'parody' religions (Cusack 2010: 3), and from the above-mentioned Haruhiism's description, it is easy to dismiss them as being nothing more than just that. Arguments about mock or parody religions fall outside the scope of this study, and it suffices here to highlight two points. The first is that, "even a fake religion . . . can do real religious work" (Chidester 2005: 219). From this follows the second point that, even if in the background of the Haruhiism religion lie mockery, parody, fun or entertainment, its existence unveils the point that the supernatural dimension generates interest and fascination, which consequently discloses (perhaps subliminally) the need for it. If this dimension caused a sense of disinterest, indifference, irrelevance or carelessness, then fans' affections would presumably be linked to a non-supernatural character and would be expressed in a different form rather than a religious one. After all, in addition to religion, there are other areas that lend themselves well to parody.

Earlier in this study, it was noted that the 'scientific' stage is, according to the modern scholarship on the topic, characterised by a decline of interest in institutional religions and the rise of secularism, as recorded in Europe (Halman and Draulans 2006: 263). Reflecting on secularism and religion, John Frow writes:

> [r]eligion is an embarrassment to us; it's an embarrassment to me, and above all because we Western intellectuals are so deeply committed to the secularization thesis which makes of religion an archaic remnant which ought by now to have withered away.
>
> (Frow 1998: 207)

However, he quickly admits that, "this thesis . . . is plainly wrong . . . religious sentiment . . . has migrated into many strange and unexpected places . . . [including] manga [anime] movies" (Frow 1998: 207). Some of the reasons behind 'survival' of this 'religious sentiment' are found in Eliade's discussion on desacralised context and humanity that follows, and this will be connected to Haruhiism. Secularism parallels Eliade's idea of a "desacralised world" stripped of religious meaning, yet, as Eliade explains, "to whatever degree he [human being] may have desacralized the world, the man who has made his choice in favor of a profane life never succeeds in completely doing away with religious behavior" (Eliade 1959b: 23).

114   *Katharine Buljan*

He further elaborates on the origins of this need for religion (and by implication for a supernatural dimension) in the following way:

> [i]n the modern societies of the West . . . nonreligious man has devel-
> oped fully . . . But this nonreligious man descends from *homo religiosus*
> and, whether he likes it or not, he is also the work of religious man; his
> formation begins with the situations assumed by his ancestors.
>
> (Eliade 1959b: 203)

Eliade further notes the fact that "the majority of the 'irreligious' still behave
religiously, even though they are not aware of this fact" (Eliade 1959b: 204).
Thus, even in a secular, or in Eliadian terms "desacralised world", humanity
still tends to be religious even unconsciously (Eliade 1959b: 211–213), and,
by implication, the need for the supernatural dimension persists. Taking into
account the above points, it follows that the appearance of Haruhiism suggests
traces of Eliade's *homo religiosus* concept, which survives in a desacralised context and consequently discloses (perhaps subliminally) the need for a religious/
supernatural dimension. According to Eliade, even various alternative 'religious'
options that "almost always present the aberrant aspects of pseudomorphs",
and also 'secular' and 'antireligious' movements, still have a 'camouflaged'
religious impulse (Eliade 1959b: 206–207). Consequently, Haruhiism can be
classified in this group, and, if done so, this reaffirms the point that, in Eliadian
terms, its appearance discloses a religious impulse and by implication a need to
connect with the supernatural dimension. One fan writes:

> I am a Christian, and thus I obviously don't believe in Haruhi as
> God. For that matter, I'm pretty sure most devout Haruhiists don't
> either . . . [but] I'm the one who goes around conventions looking for
> Haruhi stuff and loving lots of stuff I find.
>
> (Anon 2009)

Fans' fascination and familiarisation with Haruhi's godly character and
its supernatural story have the potential to open new religious insights or
inspire curiosity regarding spiritual, religious or supernatural elements.

The character of Haruhiism's goddess is strongly embedded in a mixture
of myths from the world religions. First, in one discussion about Haruhi's
godly nature, two characters, Kyon and Itsuki Koizumi, express the belief
that the world they live in is a dream of god Haruhi. This has a direct relation
to Sufism; "the relation Haruhi's character has with physical reality accords
with the Sufi view that physical reality exists in the mind of God" (Buljan
and Cusack 2015: 147). Second, as mentioned, Eliade describes the manifestation of the sacred in the profane dimension as a hierophany (sacred stones
being a simple hierophany while the "incarnation of God in Jesus Christ" is a
complex hierophany) (Eliade 1968: 124). This 'hierophany' is reflected in the
character of Haruhi, a god incarnated in the form of a high school student.

Third, there is a danger that if Haruhi is bored, she will destroy the world and create a new one. Here is yet another borrowing from world religions, which Eliade calls, "the myth of the periodic destruction and re-creation of worlds, [which is] the cosmological formula of the myth of the eternal return" (Eliade 1968: 244). According to Eliade, this 'myth of eternal return' refers to the return to the sacred or supernatural dimension, populated by divinities and other supernatural entities (Eliade 1959a). This myth, which dominates in *MOHA*, Eliade closely connects with the earlier discussed "nostalgia for paradise" (Eliade 1958: 383). Therefore, it could be said that Haruhiism, being centred on Haruhi, expresses its liking for this character and by implication (perhaps unconsciously) its liking and attraction to religious ideas and myths which, symbolically speaking, make this character what it is. Consequently, this reaffirms the point that the origin and development of Haruhiism reflects a need to 'connect' with the supernatural dimension.

Religion, according to Eliade, is, "enabling man to transcend personal situations and, finally, gain access to the world of spirit" (Eliade 1959b: 210); thus it is a vehicle of connection with the sacred (supernatural) dimension (Eliade 1959b). This demonstrates the importance that Eliade gives to the function of religion. Taking this into consideration, it follows that by imitating in some ways a religious model and being centred on a character with godly/mythical qualities, Haruhiism can be seen as an unconventional way of expressing (perhaps subliminal) interest in religious matters/supernatural dimension. Rather than being seen as a social invention (Eliade 1961: 32), religion as Eliade observes, "is believed to have a transcendental origin and hence is valorized as a revelation received from an *other*, transhuman world" (Eliade 1959b: 210). From this point of view, it could be said that Haruhiism's central character is a symbolical personification of a representative belonging to this 'transhuman world', and consequently affection for this character can be seen as an expression of fascination with the supernatural dimension and thus as an expression of a need for it.

In conclusion, even invented religions have some legitimacy. Durkheim claimed, "in reality . . . there are no religions which are false. All are true in their own fashion" (Durkheim 1965: 15). Although there are different types of fans and their degree of involvement, enthusiasm and motives vary, by employment of Eliade's theory on desacralised context and religion, it was demonstrated that the appearance of Haruhiism can be seen as an expression of a 'need' for the supernatural dimension.

Conclusion

> There "is *the need that man constantly feels to 'realize'* [mythical] *archetypes* even down to the lowest and most 'impure' levels of his immediate existence; it is this longing for transcendent forms . . . "
>
> (Eliade 1958: 385. Emphasis in original)

116 *Katharine Buljan*

This chapter focused on three anime-related phenomena: cosplay ritual, anime pilgrimage and the invented religion of Haruhiism. Working under the assumption that there is a dichotomy between sacred and profane dimensions (Eliade 1958) and employing Eliade's theory on the function of myth in ritual (in the context of cosplay ritual), on sacred-profane space (in the context of anime pilgrimage), and on desacralised context and religion (for analysis of Haruhiism), it has been argued that they can be seen as an expression of a need to, symbolically speaking, 'connect' with the supernatural dimension (Eliade 1958). In this context, it has also been mentioned that both cosplay ritual and anime pilgrimage can be seen in terms of Eliade's 'magico-religious' practices. In Eliade's theory, this 'need' for a supernatural dimension is closely related to both (the search for) an ultimate meaning and the awareness of an imminent end of physical existence, because "by virtue of . . . eternal return to the sources of the sacred . . . human existence appears to be saved from nothingness and death" (Eliade 1959b: 107). These two points of his theory, however, were outside the scope of this chapter, but the purpose of their brief mentioning was to clarify the background of his theory. While Eliade developed his theories by analysing religious contexts of archaic societies, he did stress that these 'situations' in truth "have not vanished without a trace; they have contributed toward making us what we are today" (Eliade 1959b: 202), and the religious impulse remains constant, expressing itself in various ways, despite the secularist milieu (Eliade 1959b).

References

Andrews, Dale K. 2014. 'Genesis at the Shrine: The Votive Art of an Anime Pilgrimage'. *Mechademia* 9: 217–233.

Anon. 2009. 'The Morality of Haruhiism'. *LiveJournal*, 27 July. At: petertomarken. wordpress.com/2009/07/27/the-morality-of-haruhiism/. Accessed 5 November 2014.

Anon. 2015. 'Spiritual or Mystical Reasons for Cosplaying'. 18 May. At: archive. rebeccablacktech.com/cgl/thread/8334857. Accessed 25 May 2015.

Anon. n.d. a. 'Enter for a Chance to Win a Trip for 2 to Japan!' *Madman National Cosplay Championship 2014*. At: www.madman.com.au/cosplay/entry/. Accessed 10 December 2014.

Anon. n.d. b. 'The World's Best Cosplay Performance Championship to be Determined in the Holy Land of Manga – Japan. *World Cosplay Summit Official Site*. At: www.worldcosplaysummit.jp/en/about/. Accessed 10 December 2014.

Anon. n.d. c. 'About Haruhiism'. *Haruhiism*. At: haruhism.webs.com/aboutharuhiism. htm. Accessed 12 November 2014.

Anon. n.d. d. 'About Haruhiism'. *Haruhiism Community – Facebook*. At: www. facebook.com/pages/Haruhiism/148829691832699?sk=info&tab=page_info. Accessed 25 May 2015.

Buljan, Katharine. 2006. *Towards Spirituality Through the Works and Reflections of Three Contemporary Australian Artists: John Coburn, Richard Goodwin and Marion Borgelt*. PhD Thesis, University of Sydney.

Buljan, Katharine and Carole M. Cusack. 2015. *Anime, Religion and Spirituality: Profane and Sacred Worlds in Contemporary Japan.* Sheffield, UK and Oakville, CT: Equinox.

Chidester, David. 2005. *Authentic Fakes: Religion and American Popular Culture.* Berkeley, CA: University of California Press.

Coleridge, Samuel Taylor. 1971 [1817]. *Biographia Literaria.* Menston, UK: Scholar Press.

Cusack, Carole M. 2010. *Invented Religions: Imagination, Fiction and Faith.* Farnham, UK and Burlington, VT: Ashgate.

Cusack, Carole M. 2013. 'Play, Narrative and the Creation of Religion: Extending the Theoretical Base of "Invented Religions"'. *Culture and Religion: An Interdisciplinary Journal* 14(4): 362–377.

Davidsen, Markus Altena. 2013. 'Fiction-Based Religion: Conceptualizing a New Category Against History-Based Religion and Fandom'. *Culture and Religion* 14(4): 378–395.

Deflem, Mathieu. 1991. 'Ritual, Anti-Structure, and Religion: A Discussion of Victor Turner's Processual Symbolic Analysis'. *Journal for the Scientific Study of Religion* 30(1): 1–25.

De Kloet, Jeroen and Liesbet Van Zoonen. 2007. 'Fan Culture – Performing Difference'. In *Media Studies: Key Issues and Debates,* edited by Eoin Devereux, 322–341. London: Sage.

Digance, Justine. 2015. 'Religious and Secular Pilgrimage: Journeys Redolent with Meaning'. In *Religion, Pilgrimage, and Tourism,* edited by Alex Norman and Carole M. Cusack, 249–261, volume 1. New York: Routledge.

dKiWi. (2007). 'The Religion of Suzumiya Haruhi'. 26 June. At: ckwiz.blogspot. com.au/2007/06/religion-of-suzumiya-haruhi.html. Accessed 26 May 2015.

Durkheim, Emile. 1965 [1915]. *The Elementary Forms of the Religious Life.* Translated by Joseph Ward Swain. New York: The Free Press.

Eliade, Mircea. 1958. *Patterns in Comparative Religion.* New York: Sheed and Ward.

Eliade, Mircea. 1959a. *Cosmos and History: The Myth of the Eternal Return.* Translated by Willard R. Trask. New York: Harper.

Eliade, Mircea. 1959b. *The Sacred and the Profane: The Nature of Religion.* Translated by Willard R. Trask. New York: Harcourt Brace Jovanovich.

Eliade, Mircea. 1961. *Images and Symbols.* London: Harvill Press.

Eliade, Mircea. 1968. *Myths, Dreams and Mysteries: The Encounter between Contemporary Faiths and Archaic Reality.* Translated by Philip Mairet. London: Collins.

Eliade, Mircea. 1975. *Myth and Reality.* Translated by Willard R. Trask. New York: Harper and Row.

Eliade, Mircea. 1979. *A History of Religious Ideas: From the Stone Age to the Eleusinian Mysteries,* volume 1. London: Collins.

Freud, Sigmund. 1955. 'The Uncanny'. In *Sigmund Freud Standard Edition,* volume xvii (1917–1919). London: The Hogarth Press.

Freud, Sigmund. 1983. *Totem and Taboo.* London: Ark Paperbacks.

Friedman, Erica. 2012. 'What is the Fascination with Cosplay?' *Quora,* 19 October. At: www.quora.com/What-is-the-fascination-with-cosplay. Accessed 27 May 2015.

Fron, Janine, Tracy Fullerton, Jacqueline Ford Morie and Celia Pearce. 2007. 'Playing Dress-Up: Costumes, Roleplay and Imagination'. Philosophy of

Computer Games Conference, 24–27 January, University of Modena and Reggio Emilia, Italy, 1–23.

Frow, John. 1998. 'Is Elvis a God? Cult, Culture, Questions of Method'. *International Journal of Cultural Studies* 1(2): 197–210.

Halman, Loek and Veerle Draulans. 2006. 'How Secular is Europe?' *The British Journal of Sociology* 57(2): 263–288.

Hills, Matthew. 2000. 'Media Fandom, Neoreligiosity, and Cult(ural) Studies'. *The Velvet Light Trap* 46: 73–84.

Klinger, Eric. 2012. 'The Search for Meaning in Evolutionary Goal-Therapy Perspective and Its Clinical Implications'. In *The Human Quest for Meaning: Theories, Research, and Applications*, edited by Paul T. P. Wong, 2nd edition, 23–56. New York: Routledge.

Niemi, Alison. 2003. 'Film as Religious Experience: Myths and Models in Mass Entertainment'. *Critical Review: A Journal of Politics and Society* 15(3–4): 435–446.

Norman, Alex and Carole M. Cusack. 2015. 'General Introduction'. In *Religion, Pilgrimage, and Tourism*, edited by Alex Norman and Carole M. Cusack, 1–11, volume 1. New York: Routledge.

Possamai, Adam. 2005. *Religion and Popular Culture: A Hyper-real Testament.* Brussels: Peter Lang.

Punynari. n. d. 'Anime Pilgrimages'. *Punynari's Island Adventures.* At: punynari. wordpress.com/anime-pilgrimages/. Accessed 13 November 2014.

Rahman, Osmud, Liu Wing-sun and Brittany Hei-man Cheung. 2012. '"Cosplay": Imaginative Self and Performing Identity'. *Fashion Theory* 16(3): 317–342.

Shusterman, Richard. 2003. 'Entertainment: A Question for Aesthetics'. *British Journal of Aesthetics* 43(3): 289–307.

Stimson, Eric. 2014. 'New Japanese Guidebook Focuses on Anime Pilgrimages'. *Anime News Network*, 18 January. At: www.animenewsnetwork.com/interest/2014–01–17/new-japanese-guidebook-focuses-on-anime-pilgrimages. Accessed 10 December 2014.

Tillich, Paul. 1952. *The Courage To Be.* New Haven, CT: Yale University Press.

Turner, Victor. 1990. 'Are There Universals of Performance in Myth, Ritual, and Drama?' In *By Means of Performance: Intercultural Studies of Theatre and Ritual*, edited by Richard Schechner and Willa Appel, 8–18. Cambridge, UK: Cambridge University Press.

Waver, Lloyd. 2011. 'Haruhiism: What it Means to Me'. *Polychromium*, 1 June. At: polychromium.wordpress.com/2011/06/01/haruhiism-what-it-means-to-me/. Accessed 24 May 2015.

Wolf, Ian. 2013. 'From the MyM Archive – The World of Haruhi Suzumiya'. 7 May. At: ianwolf.org/2013/05/07/from-the-mym-archive-the-world-of-haruhi-suzumiya/. Accessed 25 May 2015.

6 Jediism and the Temple of the Jedi Order

Ash Williams, Benjamin-Alexandre Miller and Michael Kitchen

Introduction

It is impossible to describe fully the nature of a single religion in one short chapter, and the only true way of understanding a religion would be to live it yourself. But this account may serve as both a rough guide to, and summary of, the religion of Jediism as it is taught and practised currently at the church Temple of the Jedi Order. This chapter attempts to cover some of the fundamental features and practices of the Jedi of the Temple of the Jedi Order (hereafter TotJO). For the scholar, this chapter describes the religion in terms of the six dimensions of religion as proposed by Ninian Smart, with additional explanations for some of the original inspiration of the movement sourced from works by such scholars and religious commentators as Joseph Campbell, Alan Watts and Jiddu Krishnamurti. For the historian, a brief history of the TotJO is outlined, which includes information on how certain practices have changed over time. For the lay reader, the chapter should provide an interesting insight into the lives and practices of living Jedi. This chapter reflects some of the particular religious biases of the authors, though attempts have been made to limit this as much as possible to provide the broadest insight possible in a single chapter. This work is very much the product of members of one particular church of Jediism and should not be taken as representing the entirety of the Jedi movement and its practices, though there are many similarities between different groups.

The Jedi of the real world, to distinguish us from those in the *Star Wars* fiction series, take inspiration from the ideas and ideals of the fiction and its source materials to create a pragmatically spiritual way of life. Unlike in the fiction, Jedi of the real world are constrained by the limits of our worldly existence. There is no ancient organisation which sends its members out on missions; there is no secret technique which is taught to pupils allowing them to lift cars with their mind. Real Jedi are just people like any other. Jedi go to work, go to school, look after children, pursue hobbies, enjoy time with our partners and with our friends, and Jedi experience all the joys and hardships such activities entail.

The Jedi path is that journey which every Jedi travels on, but it is not a singular entity, rather its configurations are as numerous as there

120   *Ash Williams et al.*

are Jedi; for the Jedi path is as much an expression of one's individuality as it is a shared experience between those like-minded persons who call themselves Jedi. Each Jedi is a Hero on their own heroic journey, the journey of life, which is common to each and every one of us. Jedi recognise this heroic aspect to their lives while at the same time seeing this in the lives of others. It is through understanding that individuality is shared by everyone that Jedi can begin to cultivate an empathy with the choices and circumstances, both familiar and foreign, that shape the lives of those we have not met but whose actions reverberate across our global society. Jedi believe in a just and fair society in which the freedoms of speech, association and expression are respected by an acceptance of those differences, which so often lead to hurtful prejudices. While everyday experience may teach that we are separate individuals, the saying "You are unique, just like everyone else" perhaps captures the ultimate unity between "separate" individuals, a unity recognised in a Jedi's belief in the Force as the ultimate unifier.

Jediism seen through the six dimensions of Ninian Smart

Were one to recall what Joseph Campbell predicted in 1986, one could almost instantly recognise the importance of the spiritual/religious communities about which this volume is concerned. It stands to reason though that although the information age may change certain qualities about the way in which people communicate with one another, just as science has changed the way we think about the world around us, there are going to remain some fundamental elements of humanity's need to find meaning in the world and understanding in the experience of life.

We imagine what we cannot know. We create stories about what we imagine. With the developments in science and technology, these stories are shared with more and more elaborate forms of expression – beginning with the development of writing and continuing on through our modern capacities in multi-media. Yet the archetypal characters and situations remain, if not static, nevertheless quite homologous. Religions and the myths that convey them serve to touch that part of the human psyche for which a foundational need for attention exists and that finds its balance in no other way. To quote Campbell and Moyers:

> You can't predict what a myth is going to be any more than you can predict what you're going to dream tonight. Myths and dreams come from the same place. They come from ritualization of some kind that have then to find expression in symbolic form. And the only myth that is going to be worth thinking about in the immediate future is one that is talking about the planet, not the city, not these people, but the planet, and everybody on it. That's my main thought for what the future myth is going to be.

Jediism and the Temple of the Jedi Order   121

And what it will have to deal with will be exactly what all myths have dealt with – the maturation of the individual, from dependency through adulthood, through maturity, and then to the exit; and then how to relate to this society and how to relate this society to the world of nature and the cosmos. That's what the myths have all talked about, and what this one's got to talk about. But the society that it's got to talk about is the society of the planet. And until that gets going, you don't have anything.
(Campbell and Moyers 1991 [1989]: 38)

So, we find it hardly surprising that as the means of conducting cultural representations of archetypical personalities – those in whom a great many of us may identify ourselves – and situations to which they apply – "The Hero's Adventure" – to ever expanding social and geographical perimeters, that religious/spiritual movements such as Jediism come about in response to the age-old necessity for belief. Religions, as it were, are more than simply philanthropic organisations. Religions have an organic existence, the external aspects of which are evident to an observer, and internal ones are the hopes and feelings of its participants.

Therefore, it is worth looking at Jediism through the dimensions set forth by Ninian Smart in *The Religious Experience of Mankind* (1996). In this section, we shall attempt to define the practices of the TotJO with regard to each dimension and illustrate how these relate to the experience of "the religion of Jediism" to those who practise it.

The ritual dimension

The ritual dimension is the outwardly observable characteristics of a faith. These could be temples or other revered symbols, but also practices such as services and prayers. Campbell denotes a ritual as the re-enactment of a myth; one may be inclined to say that the TotJO has a relatively discreet yet rich ritual dimension.

The first aspect of the ritual dimension could be seen on the TotJO's website, for in lieu of an edifice it provides a static meeting place for all of the TotJO's members and guests, which can be visited from anywhere in the world with internet access. There, without even registering with the TotJO, one has contact with the doctrine and the written sermons. One may even read through some of the conversations in the general forum. When one registers, one becomes a Guest. One may then look over the Initiates' Programme (the study of which is on a voluntary basis) and upon submitting a valid and approved application, one becomes a Temple Member. Each level of participation brings with it access to a little more of the TotJO's content. This status system is part of the ritual dimension as well.

There are regularly published written sermons every five days, with fortnightly, real-time live services in the TotJO website's chat room. In addition to these, there are ceremonies for dubbing Knights and for the ordination of

122 *Ash Williams et al.*

clergy members. Both Knighthood and clerical responsibility require a certain investment of time and study to achieve, so these ceremonies are quite happy celebrations.

There is also the symbol of the TotJO, which represents part of our doctrine: a black circle surrounding a white 5-pointed star, within which is another black circle surrounding a white 16-pointed star. This also has symbolic (thus ritual) significance as it illustrates the interdependence of light and dark (literally as well as figuratively) in much the same way as the *t'ai ch'i* (the yin-yang circle), the 5-pointed star being the lines of the Jedi Code and the 16-pointed star the 16 Teachings of the TotJO (Temple of the Jedi Order 2015). Some members wear it as jewellery or tattoos, but this is a purely personal choice.

The ritual dimension is vast in any religion, as well as in any culture. There are rituals that are purely secular, such as greeting and taking leave. For the TotJO, there is a certain ritualisation that is constantly evolving with regard to how a principally online community contextualises the interaction amongst the members. It would be interesting to revisit this dimension in the future.

The mythological dimension

This dimension is for Jediism (as it is practised in the TotJO), at once perhaps the most important, yet the least faithful to the qualities set down by Smart. The TotJO itself has been established since 2005, and the Jediist movement itself has existed in some form since the 1990s and as is emphasised on our website's front page, we do not consider the events depicted in *Star Wars* to be "historical" or "prophetic" by any measure (Temple of the Jedi Order 2015).

The Jedi is sensitive, however, to the importance of myth in our lives. Myth is as crucial to a civilisation as dreams are to the individual. Without them, there is neurosis and ultimately paralysis. It is by respect for all myths, regardless of their origins, that Jediism can truly be said to be syncretic. Myths are simple "stories" which reflect some deeper reality than what can be perceived with the senses. Or, they can provide some sense to what can be perceived partially with the senses yet not fully comprehended in its entirety and to the multiple relationships that interact to create a reality too large to be taken in at a glance. The "Hero's Adventure" then can serve as a prime illustration of life, its struggles, its victories and defeats, the intervention of chance (for better or worse) and all the roles we play in our interactions with those around us and the world during our lives.

We also recognise the "cosmogonic cycle" in which invariably in all cultures and religions there are stories of the creation and destruction of the world, the "virgin birth", symbol of the feminine principle in bringing balance (redemption) to the world and the modelling of the Hero figure to the needs of the time and society s/he serves. This is a fundamental part of the human psyche and the basis upon which one can discover one's own sense of sacred or vile. Therefore, if Jediism is too young to have a mythology all of its own, its mythological dimension is nevertheless quite consequential, for it takes up all of the mythology of human history as one of its cornerstones.

The doctrinal dimension

Here too, as with the mythological dimension, Jediism does not conform very closely to the description. According to Smart, "Doctrines are an attempt to give system, clarity, and intellectual power to what is revealed through the mythological and symbolic language of religious faith and ritual" (Smart 1996: 5). The TotJO does have some doctrine, but it is not revelatory; neither is it prescriptive. We have various elements to the doctrine: the Code, the Creed, the 16 Teachings, the 21 Maxims and the 3 Tenets (Temple of the Jedi Order 2015). Our mythological and ritual dimensions are not dependent on the doctrine, which is itself not an entrenched set of laws; neither does it provide any revelation as to the nature of the Force. Instead, it serves as a practical set of guidelines towards orthopraxy – as an alternative to orthodoxy – rather than a rigid method of instruction for the Jedi.

The TotJO doctrine will likely be the beginning of a Jedi's journey, but the doctrine will not be the end. The doctrine is often the first impression one gets of the kind of community at the Temple, and many are attracted by the Temple's acceptance of people from all walks of life and the humanist principles which most find are easily incorporated into one's already held beliefs. The various elements of the doctrine should not be taken separately; rather a Jedi should look at the doctrine holistically to better inform their understanding.

Because of the doctrine's non-prescriptive nature, there is no "sin" within Jediism or "heresy"; the doctrine is human in origin and human in scope, an expression of the Temple's collective ideals in the promotion of empathy, understanding, compassion and life. Furthermore, if one disagrees with an element of the doctrine, such as an advocation of the death penalty despite the doctrine's statement against its use, this does not constitute a breach of faith.

The doctrine has changed over the course of the Temple's existence, and while the broad brush strokes have remained the same, further change is an inevitability. These changes to the doctrine are an essential growing process for our church, because the doctrine is an expression of the Jedi at the TotJO as much as the Jedi at the TotJO are an expression of the doctrine. The doctrine is the result of, and informs, the beliefs, the lessons learned and the training undertaken by the Jedi in the Temple. As the Jedi in the Temple have grown over the years, so has their understanding of the doctrine and the need for alterations to better express the kind of pragmatically spiritual environment that is TotJO.

The ethical dimension

The doctrinal dimension is much more congruent to the ethical dimension of Jediism. As with most religions, there is some sense of establishing what is right and wrong behaviour. Yet, the Jedi are also quite aware of the limits of such idealism. There is often a gaping difference between what one 'says' and what one actually 'does'. We profess love and tolerance, not as a dishonest method towards some hypothetical salvation, but out of an intimate understanding of what we ourselves are. As Krishnamurti wrote:

> We human beings are what we have been for millions of years – colossally greedy, envious, aggressive, jealous, anxious and despairing, with occasional flashes of joy and affection. We are a strange mixture of hate, fear and gentleness; we are both violence and peace. There has been outward progress from the bullock cart to the jet plane but psychologically the individual has not changed at all, and the structure of society throughout the world has been created by individuals. The outward social structure is the result of the inward psychological structure of our human relationships, for the individual is the result of the total experience, knowledge and conduct of man. Each one of us is the storehouse of all the past. The individual is the human who is all mankind. The whole history of man is written in ourselves.
>
> (Krishnamurti 1975 [1969]: 6)

This is also reflected in our Creed, which is an adaptation of the Peace Prayer attributed to St Francis of Assisi (Francis of Assisi 2002), and our Code. We accept that which is less than desirable in human nature as inexorably contained within and congruent with all that we may aspire to be.

The social dimension

Perhaps the most evident dimension of the Jedi religion is the social dimension. Since our religion is relatively recent and largely based on internet exchanges, but also due to the non-prescriptive doctrine and simply the fact that we do not harbour such concepts as 'sin', one would be inclined, at first glance, to find Jediism to be very associative. Many active members of the TotJO participate in the discussion forums on diverse subject matters, most of which do not revolve around the beliefs and practices of Jediism. It is through this social dimension that one may witness the way in which the mythological and ethical dimensions and the guidelines of the doctrine affect the ways in which people communicate. As these dimensions are of fairly liberal exercise, the social dimension tends to fill in the gaps. Indeed, it is possibly by way of the social dimension, the way in which social interactions are shaped in the community that the personal meanings of the other dimensions are explored or discovered. Smart described the social dimension thus:

The doctrinal, mythological, and ethical dimensions express a religion's claim about the nature of the invisible world and its aims about how people's lives ought to be shaped: the social dimension indicates the way in which people's lives are in fact shaped by these claims and the way in which religious institutions operate.

(Smart 1996: 6)

Yet, as we have shown, the doctrinal, mythological and ethical dimensions of Jediism make very few claims about the nature of that invisible world; it is not denied as with some non-religious ideologies – such as Marxism – but the invisible world, the ineffable foundation of being which we call the Force, is not revealed in doctrine or liturgy. Jediism encourages personal exploration of one's spirituality rather than dispensing a template for it. Herewith, the social dimension is at the same time one of the most evident weaknesses and also the most indispensable asset.

The experiential dimension

The experiential dimension is probably the most important of all of the six and the most difficult to depict accurately. What could one bear witness to about one's own experience of religion, much less could any blanket description take place of what any particular (or all particular) devotee feels via the practice of religion? We may understand what one says and/or observe how one might behave, but this is not likely to be entirely revelatory of an inward experience of the eternal. As the religious experience is that of the inexpressible, then the attempt to express it would conform more to the ritual dimension than truly to the experiential. As Smart indicated, this dimension involves the hope for the experience of the invisible world, as it is believed to be according to the religious doctrine. One would desire not only the external manifestation, but also the fulfilment of the inner experience – a kind of atonement with the absurdity of mundane existence.

In Jediism, there is no standardised belief of what a personal connection to the Force feels like. Although it could be that many of us do indeed have some sort of experience of this type, it remains doubtful that one could – or would even try – to describe it in concrete terms. Furthermore, as the Jedi is concerned with consciousness of the present, the experiential dimension is not something that could be permanently attained. The connection to the Force could never really be 'lost'; it would be always there, though one may not always be conscious of it. Likewise, as one is always connected to the 'what is', it is not something that needs to be attained.

In the TotJO, the ritual and mythological dimensions illustrate that the Force can be evident through mindfulness thereof. The doctrine serves as parameters for cultivating that mindfulness and the ethical dimension takes into account that human-heartedness does include us not being so very nice to one another occasionally. This does not in and of itself show

126 *Ash Williams et al.*

an experiential dimension that resembles very closely what most people would call 'paradise'. However, it does lend credibility to a rich experience of 'being alive':

> People say that what we're all seeking is a meaning for life. I don't think that's what we're really seeking. I think that what we're seeking is an experience of being alive, so that our life experiences on the purely physical plane will have resonances within our own innermost being and reality, so that we actually feel the rapture of being alive. That's what it's all finally about, and that's what these clues help us to find within ourselves.
>
> (Campbell and Moyers 1991 |1989|: 13)

History

The TotJO was incorporated as a non-profit corporation with 501c US tax status, in the state of Texas by John Henry Phelan on 25 December 2005 (Hegar 2015). The first interaction the corporation embarked upon was the creation of a website: templeofthejediorder.org, which still exists today, though in a changed form. The TotJO is not the only Jedi organisation, but was certainly amongst the first to receive official tax status within its country of inception. Not all Jedi communities that existed at that time were incorporated as corporations; many existed purely as online entities, with some extending back to the 1990s, which is seen by many amongst the Jedi community as some of the earliest beginnings of the Jediism (or Jedi) movement.

Contextually, during the community at the time, there was discussion over whether Jediism was a religion, a philosophy or a spiritual path. Regardless of the conclusions by other members of the community, Mr Phelan created and incorporated Jediism as a demonstration that Jediism could be considered as much a religion as any other religious movement. As a non-profit charitable organisation within Texas, the TotJO had the right to ordain its own ministers and give out religious Degrees of Divinity (degrees in Jediism).

Syncretism greatly influenced early forms of the TotJO's structure, where a "Rite", later renamed "Special Interest Group" (SIG), for each of the major world religions was created. Jediism is not mutually exclusive, with many belief systems allowing many practitioners to follow the practices of Jediism while maintaining other religious affiliations. However, if one had no other religious affiliations, whether formal or informal, there was an SIG for one who followed Jediism solely named the "Pure Jedi SIG" where 'pure' should be taken to mean 'only'. The SIGs were intended to provide a forum between like-minded individuals to help them further understand how the teachings of Jediism could be adapted into their other religious practices. For example, early forms of the doctrine included an adopted earlier version of this statement from the website religioustolerance.org/statbelief.htm, and the Prayer of Francis of Assisi, mentioned above, which was adapted and renamed the Jedi Creed.

The TotJO, as a corporation, maintains a board of directors, which takes the form of a Council of typically around seven or eight members. The Council are the general management that oversee the administration of the corporation, assist members by resolving disputes, maintain the website and other social media outlets and provide a sense of direction without inhibiting the latitude each Master, Knight and member deserves.

The syncretic nature of Jediism and the structure provided by the SIGs were reflected in the early Council, where the head of each "Rite" maintained a place on the Council. Over time, the influence of the SIGs waned as fewer members chose to align themselves with one. While the SIGs have taken a backseat in their role within the TotJO, with Councillors no longer being head of a SIG, the importance in understanding the influence and similarity of other religions remains a required understanding in the TotJO's early training programmes.

Over time, the number of members has greatly increased, which has allowed for organisational improvements within the structure of the TotJO. The administrative requirements of being a member of the Council restricted the amount of time that they could spend working on other projects that might require their attention. The effect of an ever-increasing membership, however, was the delegation of some responsibility, allowing the creation of a more diverse range of departments such as the creation of a Public Relations Department, an increase in the number of forum moderators, clerical secretaries and greater assistance in handling member affairs.

How to join

Joining the TotJO is a very simple and straightforward affair. There is no initiation ceremony to become a documented member, though there are ceremonies if one chooses to go onto the path of Knighthood. To become a documented member, one must fill out an application form containing personal information (such as real name and date of birth), so we know who you are, and also take an Oath as a commitment to your path. The Simple Oath must be made sincerely and without duress and taken with your real name and publicly as a statement of intent. The Oath binds you to commit to the Jedi path "until I am ready for knighthood or I otherwise decide" (Temple of the Jedi Order 2015). This condition is added because during the time in which they are training, the person might change their mind or discover another path that is more suited to them. Once a member has joined, they are given the title of "Temple Member" to indicate that they have the legal status as one of the church's members. "Temple Member" is not a rank (see "Evolution of Ranks") and is a prior condition before attaining any rank within our organisation.

Minors

As a non-profit church in the state of Texas, the TotJO has the ability to have people legally recognised and documented as members of the church. Despite the ability to have minors (those people under the age of 18) as members of the church, the TotJO does not allow minors under the age of 13 to become members.

There are a few reasons for this. One is that Jedi believe in the freedom of conscience in choosing your own religious affiliations, but also that such decisions should be made at the express and informed decision of the participant. Our Oath requires it be taken sincerely and with full knowledge, which we cannot guarantee is a condition filled by having a minor take the Oath.

Being Knighted requires a completed membership application, but since we do not wish to have any of the personal details of any minor, we do not require that they complete an application and as such they cannot be knighted until they are at least 18. Apprenticeships are a personal student-teacher bond and so we do not allow any minor to be apprenticed until they are at least 16.

The TotJO recognises the negative impact religion can have on children and minors, so has taken steps to ensure minors are afforded a great deal of protection. To this end, we have a Minor's FAQ, which we require all minors to read and which instructs them on basic internet safety and informs them of which Temple officials to contact if they have reason for concern (one example reason given would be someone asking for personal information such as date of birth, legal name or address, etc.). Further, the Temple may also contact the minor's guardian to ensure they are aware of what the minor is doing and to provide a line of communication to ensure the safety of the minor. It is against the principles upon which the Temple, and the Jedi within it, stand to indoctrinate, either religiously or educationally, any person of any age; but particular care and attention is given to those who are likely to be the most vulnerable. The Temple views all minors to be within this category.

Ranks

The evolution of the ranks has followed the broadly increasing organisational structure of the TotJO. The Temple keeps a list of Knights (www.templeofthejediorder.org/teachers) and above, but recognises that not every Knight is available all the time as some take leaves of absence for other pursuits. The titles for each rank have remained the same or similar throughout our history, but the requirements for each rank have changed over time.

The requirements for each rank have increased, sometimes dramatically, over the course of TotJO's history. In the early years, there were worries about the leniency with which one might attain a particular rank, with

Jediism and the Temple of the Jedi Order   129

some people making accusations that the requirements were too low or the Masters, those responsible for granting ranks, were too lenient. Such issues might be expected when an organisation is just starting out and they have been addressed over time by making the process of advancement much more robust. Each stage of advancement is now peer reviewed, and questions or concerns can be raised as and when they arise so that they might be dealt with in a fair manner.

The ranks themselves are meant to be a rough indicator of the amount of work and participation a member of the TotJO has completed. The ranks are as follows: Novice, Initiate, Apprentice, Knight, Senior Knight, Master and Grandmaster. The rank of Novice is for those that have begun our initial training programme, the Initiate Programme. The rank of Initiate is for those that have completed the Initiate Programme and are awaiting apprenticeship. The rank of Apprentice is for those that have completed the Initiate Programme and are now being personally trained by a Knight or above in a one-to-one tutor-like relationship. The rank of Knight is for those that have completed an apprenticeship and have then taken a life-long vow to dedicate themselves to the Jedi path. The rank of Senior Knight is for those Knights who have done additional study in our Degree Scheme (see "Training and the Degree Scheme"). The rank of Master is for those that have fully trained three apprentices to Knights. The rank of Grandmaster is an honorific title for those people who have shown exemplary dedication and work to the TotJO.

The title "Master" is unlike the Western interpretation of the word to mean 'best', but rather follows along the lines of Eastern traditions, where for example "Zen Master" means "Zen Teacher". The ranks themselves are meant to give some indication of wisdom and experience, so it is natural to expect that those who have 'higher' ranks are wiser, but this is not necessarily the case.

Training and degree scheme

There are two types of training at the TotJO: degree training and seminary training. The degree training is the training that people undergo to advance in rank and was the first training that was implemented within the TotJO.

The first training material that required study at the TotJO was Joseph Campbell and Moyer's work *The Power of Myth* (1991 [1989]) and Alan Watts' *The Book: On the Taboo of Knowing Who You Are* (1989 [1966]), which reflect the original inspiration behind the Jedi ideals. The study of these materials remains today, alongside such other material related to meditation, metaphysics, TotJO doctrinal studies, studies on world religions and a selection of short essay topics designed to gauge the particular personal views of the student.

The teacher-student relationship is one of more than just simply giving out tasks for the student to complete; it is much more personal and trusting in nature. The difference between the sorts of things one learns in 'conventional education' whether that be at high school, college or university, is that we are attempting to teach not only knowledge, but wisdom. The learning is a personal exploration of yourself and your understanding of your own nature as much as it is the accumulation of knowledge. The teaching of wisdom is what the teacher is there for and allows them to create a personally tailored programme that is able to challenge the student to excel.

Teachers that decide to train a student do so when they feel it is right. They are under no obligation to provide their services as that would be counterproductive to the spirit of the training. The teacher also chooses their students based on the similarity of mind they both have and such other factors as the particular challenges the student might pose and the readiness of the student to learn what the teacher offers.

Students, when approached by a teacher, can turn that teacher down if they do not feel that the teacher can provide the particular type of training that they desire or require. The entire relationship must be mutual and both parties must be in agreement, because the training goes both ways. The teacher can learn a lot about themselves and the way they teach just as much as the student can learn about themselves. This process is perhaps the most fundamentally important part of a student's experience within the TotJO.

Once an Apprentice has completed the lessons offered by their teacher to the required level of understanding, then they are ready to undergo their knighting ceremony and be granted the rank of "Knight". Knighthood is not the end of their learning, however, and is instead a way of marking where one part of their journey ends and another begins. Upon Knighthood a vow is taken – the Solemn Vow – which makes you "vow to uphold the Jedi teachings, and to henceforth devote myself to the life of a Jedi" (Temple of the Jedi Order 2015).

Being a Jedi requires serious commitment and we do not encourage people to join unless they have spent time considering the Jedi way of life, which is why they are not bound by this vow until Knighthood. Further, there is a minimum time of eight months' study before one can be knighted, with two months minimum studying the Initiate Programme and six months minimum as an Apprentice. Many of those that become Knights, however, typically spend up to a year or two years in training.

As was mentioned above, Knighthood is only marking another step along the Jedi path, and there is still much more training that can be done afterwards. As a non-profit religious institution, the TotJO has the right to issue religious degrees. These degrees are "Degrees of Divinity", which are in effect degrees in Jediism. The current degrees that we issue are the Associate Degree of Divinity (A.Div) and the Bachelors Degree of Divinity (B.Div). While we do have the right to issue Masters of Divinity, we do not currently have a process in place to provide this. We can also provide a Doctorate of Divinity (D.Div), though this is purely honorary. Work that has been completed throughout a person's time spent training at the TotJO contributes to the eventual awarding of a degree if they complete the required amount of work. The A.Div is awarded upon Knighthood when a student has completed their apprenticeship. The B.Div is required for a member to advance in rank from "Knight" to "Senior Knight" and is approximately the same amount of work as two apprenticeships.

When a Knight is training their Apprentice, they will assign that Apprentice particular lessons and these lessons contribute to that Apprentice's degree. However, these lessons will also be submitted into a pool of lessons that each Knight or teacher might use to train others. Those that decide to do additional study, to obtain the B.Div, will choose and complete lessons within that pool. In this way, each Senior Knight has been trained, to some extent or other, by every other teacher at the TotJO. This allows us to provide additional peer review of rank advancement.

Clergy

The clergy are those members that, along with their additional duties, have decided to maintain the spiritual well-being of the TotJO as a whole. Training to become a member of the clergy requires one to undergo separate training in our seminary. The seminary training is different from the degree training, because while the degree training is there to help members with their own understanding of the Jedi path, the seminary training is there to further expand the members' understanding of their Jedi path. Our Seminary training was expanded in 2015 to cover such topics as liturgy, spiritual guidance, role-play scenarios, religious understanding, syncretism, the writing and giving of sermons, and a comprehensive understanding of empathy and its role within a spiritual framework.

Some of the additional functions of the clergy are to give sermons and services to the members on a regular basis. The sermons are every 5 days and services are once every 15 days, where a service is given to a live audience on our website's 'chat' feature and usually ends with a group recitation of the Creed. The contents of the sermons are chosen by the clergyperson giving them, but the intention is to provide a new insight or lesson to those reading. Each Wednesday, we have an 'open sermon', which is a chance for any member of the TotJO to contribute a sermon regardless of whether or not they are a member of the clergy.

The most recent changes to the clergy have been in the form of the creation of a Synod and the introduction of monthly "Reflections". The Synod, like the Council but subject to the authority of the Council, is an organisational and administrative body that oversees the functioning of the Clergy. The Synod consists of five members in total: three Pastors and two secretaries, who discuss, implement, vote on updates, changes and promotions. The Reflections are various monthly dichotomies of human nature (such as Ego, yet Humility and Cowardice, yet Courage and so on) to encourage all Jedi to contemplate and consider that particular theme. Each first day of the

132 *Ash Williams et al.*

month hosts a live service introducing that month's reflection, and clergy are encouraged to incorporate the reflection into their sermons.

We have also begun trialling the idea of having themed sermons, where each sermon relates to a particular topic with the eventual goal of producing a book of collected sermons. There has been a push in recent years for the TotJO to produce its own materials and the sermons are one way in which we eventually hope to have an entire library's worth of Jedi produced material for people to study from.

Demographics

Here a careful note must be made about what we describe as active and inactive members. At TotJO, we have approximately 2,000 legally recognised members of our church since its foundation in late 2005. The proportion of those that are still actively contributing (what we describe as 'active'), however, is probably only around 10 per cent of that number. This may be likened to many people being baptised into a faith, but over time halting their religious activity.

There was a campaign in 2001 and again in 2011 that encouraged people to write down the word "Jedi" or "Jedi Knight" as their religion on their census forms, with results being in the hundreds of thousands. We do not consider these results as having any validity to them. They resulted from a form of political protest and humour, and we have not seen any indication that these numbers of people pursue the Jedi path outside of that census participation. We do not count the people who took part in the census as being members of our church.

We are ultimately just one church and have no ultimate authority to deny that one is a Jedi because they choose to call themselves as such. But if one tries to account for factors like those participating for protest, or for humour, or for fashion, or those that halt their religious activity, the actual numbers of Jedi would number in the thousands rather than the hundreds of thousands. A conservative estimate would place the number of Jedi at no more than 4,000 to 5,000 worldwide.

Conclusion

The Jedi path is completely gender and race neutral and is even neutral when taking into account things like social class and disability. There is no positive or negative discrimination towards members who wish to follow the Jedi path, because we accept people for whoever they are and help them to become who they want to be. Geographically, most members are from the United States or the United Kingdom, but we have members of our church from many different countries across the world, such as Australia, New Zealand, Iran, South Africa, France, Germany, Poland, etc.

We do not have exact details, though primarily the members that join are white males between the ages of approximately 20 and 40; though we do have many members who are female and/or a different ethnic origin. The reason for this might reasonably be assumed to be related to the viewing audience of the *Star Wars* films, which are or were predominantly viewed by white males.

References

Campbell, Joseph and Bill Moyers. 1991 [1989]. *The Power of Myth*. New York: Anchor Edition.

Francis of Assisi. 2002. 'Prayer of St. Francis: Lord, Make Me An Instrument of Thy Peace'. *The Prayer Foundation*. At: prayerfoundation.org/prayer_of_st_francis_instrument_of_peace.htm. Accessed 5 June 2015.

Hegar, Glenn. 2015. 'Window on State Government'. *Texas State Comptroller's Office*. At mycpa.cpa.state.tx.us/coa/servlet/cpa.app.coa.CoaGetTp?Pg=tpid&Search_Nm=Temple%20of%20the%20Jedi%20Order%20&Button=search&Search_ID=32018723158. Accessed 19 April 2015.

Krishnamurti, Jiddu. 1975 [1969]. *Freedom From the Known*. Mary Lutyens (ed.). San Francisco, CA: Harper San Francisco.

Smart, Ninian. 1996. *The Religious Experience of Mankind*. Upper Saddle River, NJ: Prentice Hall.

Temple of the Jedi Order. 2015. *Temple of the Jedi Order*. At www.templeofthejediorder.org/doctrine-of-the-order. Accessed 5 June 2015.

Watts, Alan. 1989 [1966]. *The Book: On the Taboo of Knowing Who You Are*. New York: Vintage Books.

7 Virtual knights and synthetic worlds
Jediism in Second Life

Helen Farley

Introduction

Almost every manifestation of religion finds expression in the virtual world of Second Life. Established religions have a presence; for example, Epiphany Cathedral is home to Anglicans in the virtual world (Hutchings 2011). Geographically dispersed adherents gather for communion, Bible study and regular services. Those manifestations of the numinous bordering on religion, depending on the definition employed, can be found in every corner. Masonic temples abound and all the paraphernalia required for the mysterious rituals of Freemasonry can be bought from the Second Life Marketplace (Farley 2010). There are some religions that only find expression in this virtual space. There are all manner of temples, churches, sacred grottoes, simulated stone circles and the opportunity for religious pilgrimage. Some of these expressions can be seen as virtual missionary activity, taking religion to a new frontier. Some religion in virtual worlds is just for fun; people experimenting with a new religion for a while and trying on the trappings for size.

One of the more interesting manifestations of religion in Second Life can be found in role-play. There is a growing scholarship about religion in the Massively Multi-player Online Role-Playing Games (MMORPGs) such as *World of Warcraft* or *Runescape*, but religion still remains in the service of the overall narrative that drives the gameplay. Role-play in Second Life is different: it is entirely created by its users, not the owners of the platform (Guitton 2012). This freedom allows expressions, religious and otherwise, that cannot be readily found within MMORPGs.

This chapter considers the expression of hyper-real religion through role-play in the virtual world of Second Life. There are a number of role-playing groups that draw their inspiration from Jediism in the virtual world, including Jedi's [sic] of the Republic and Jedi of Second Life. Most require strict adherence to a code of behaviour, context-appropriate apparel that could reasonably appear in *Star Wars*, which must be worn at all times, and a requirement to remain in character while role-playing. This chapter conducts an etic investigation into the motivations behind role-playing in

Virtual knights and synthetic worlds   135

Second Life and whether or not role-play acts as a form of religious expression in this environment by using Johan Huizinga's concept of the "magic circle", a walled-off but temporary spot within the real world dedicated to the performance of an act alone (Huizinga 1949). Rather than regarding spaces within virtual worlds as being totally sealed, Edward Castronova considers them to be porous, leaking through into the real world and vice versa (Castronova 2001, 2005). Hyper-real religion in Second Life is considered in light of this theoretical lens.

The emergence of Jediism

At the start of the twenty-first century, an email did the rounds urging people to claim 'Jedi' as their religion in response to a question on the national census forms in Australia, New Zealand, Canada and the United Kingdom. The author claimed that such an action would force the governments of these countries to include 'Jedi' as an option for selection in response to an enquiry about religious affiliation in future census collections (Singler 2014). In response, some 70,000 Australians, 53,000 New Zealanders and 390,000 Britons claimed they were 'Jedi' in the 2001 census in these countries (McCormick 2006). Though it was widely viewed as a joke or a statement by atheists objecting to the idea of religion, data collected in the 2011 census saw 65,000 Australians and 177,000 from the United Kingdom claiming 'Jedi' as their religious affiliation (De Castella 2014). Almost certainly, a small number of those respondents, identifying as Jedi, desperately wanted Jediism to be a real religion and wanted their beliefs to be more broadly recognised by the community in which they lived (Singler 2014).

Jedi are an order of warrior monks, first seen in George Lucas' science fiction epic, _Star Wars_ (1977), who claim to be "the guardians of peace and justice in the galaxy" (De Castella 2014). Most followers claim to use "the Force", which is similar in concept to the Chinese _qi_ (Cusack 2010: 121), an echo of many of the holistic spiritual ideals touted in the 1960s and 1970s (De Castella 2014). Believers claim the Force is generated by all living things and binds the universe together; it seeks balance and to regulate destiny itself (Peters 2012). Through rigorous training, Jedi learn to conquer fear and anger, learning to wield the 'Light' side of the Force (Cusack 2010: 121). The idea was borrowed from a number of religious traditions including Taoism, Buddhism, Christianity (Bowen and Wagner 2006), the cultural and spiritual ideals of the _samurai_ of Japan (De Castella 2014) and the monks of the Shaolin Temple of China (Cusack 2010: 121). Certainly, Jediism draws extensively from the work of mythologist Joseph Campbell, particularly _The Hero with a Thousand Faces_, in constructing a modern mythology and marrying it to popular culture, transcending both to frame a coherent ideology (Peters 2012).

Initially, the divide between adherents of Jediism and fans of the franchise were difficult to discern as both groups took what they could from the

136 *Helen Farley*

seemingly never-ending stream of movies, series, fan fiction, video games, comics, role-playing books and so on, and filled in the gaps as they became obvious. Anthropologist Matthew Kappel believes that Jediism became participatory when a *Star Wars* role-playing guide from 1987 laid out a coherent code for aspiring Jedi to follow (Collman 2013).

> There is no emotion, there is peace
> There is no ignorance, there is knowledge
> There is no passion, there is serenity
> There is no death, there is the force.
>
> (Costikyan 1987)

Since that time, Jediism has been formed into a coherent religious code (De Castella 2014), drawing from the plethora of franchise-generated and fan-generated media that accompanied and developed from those original films.

Interestingly, just as there is a light side of the Force; there is also a "dark side", which is exploited by the Dark Lords of the Sith (Cusack 2010: 121). The term 'Sith' first appeared in *Star Wars Episode I: The Phantom Menace* (1999). In the first video games of the *Star Wars* franchise, such as *Jedi Academy* and *Jedi Knights*, aspiring Jedi Knights or Padawans had to overcome challenges and obstacles to become Jedi. Later games gave players the opportunity to choose the side with which they wanted to align. In *Star Wars: The Old Republic*, players can choose to either play as a Jedi Knight or to align with the Sith (Loh 2008).

Second Life

At first, the relationship between Jediism and Second Life is not obvious. From 2007, Second Life exploded into the public perception through a number of high profile scandals. It was variously seen as an environment that could give vent to a range of often-unsavoury sexual activities (Brookey and Cannon 2009) and as a money-laundering venue for potential terrorists (Leapman 2007). But for its millions of users, Second Life provides a three-dimensional area of the Internet, where an individual is represented by a highly customisable motional avatar, able to interact and commune with others who may be geographically distant in the real world, commonly known as "meatspace" (Bardzell and Bardzell 2008). For users, the interactions and activities that take place in this virtual space are as real as those in the virtual world. The user, through their avatar, can perform actions including religion and rituals with an "embodied body" (Radde-Antweiler 2008: 174).

Second Life is a virtual world, a three-dimensional virtual environment resembling a physical space that exists on a computer, some external storage device or server, and is generally – though not always – accessed via the internet (Pereira 2010: 94). It allows participants to create a virtual identity that persists beyond the initial session (Maher 1999: 322; Ritzema and Harris 2008: 110). The term "virtual world" was first coined by Chip Morningstar and F. Randall Farmer in 1991 (Morningstar and Farmer 1991: 273). Virtual worlds, sometimes called "Multi-user Virtual Environments", are spaces where the most elaborate buildings can take shape within minutes or hours. To all intents and purposes, if something can be imagined, it can be created in a virtual world environment. Historical, generational, professional or gender gaps are rendered obsolete in a virtual space where users cooperate to create knowledge and experiment with identity (Farley 2014).

Second Life was publicly released in 2003 by the San Francisco-based Linden Lab. Then CEO, Philip Rosedale, was inspired by the 1992 cyberpunk novel *Snow Crash*, which prominently featured a persistent, ubiquitous metaverse where users could "digitize everything: and collaborate in a 3D environment that would be built by the users themselves" (Hendaoui *et al.* 2008: 88; Jennings and Collins 2008: 181). Second Life is the most mature and undoubtedly the most well-known virtual world probably due to the intense media scrutiny it has attracted, but many others exist such as Jibe, OpenSim, Active Worlds, Kitely, IMVU, Twinity and Blue Mars. As of November 2015, Second Life has around 44 million registered user accounts, with between 8,000 to 10,000 new user accounts registered each day (Voyager 2015). There are slightly fewer than 25,000 regions or sims (a sim represents a virtual area of 256m x 256m) (Linden Labs, n.d.). There are between 25,000 and 55,000 users online at any time (Voyager 2015).

Role-playing on screen

In Second Life, the appearance of an avatar can change just by dragging a folder across the screen. In this way, gender can instantly be changed, as can height, age, outfit, culture, occupation or religion (Ducheneaut *et al.* 2006: 294; Wadley 2011: 114). This makes virtual worlds an optimal venue for experimentation and role-playing (Farley 2014). Consequently, role-playing is very common in virtual worlds as it is in MMORPGs (Farley 2014). Though there are many similarities between virtual worlds and MMORPGs, what distinguishes the latter is the presence of an overarching narrative theme or plot-driven storyline (Jennings and Collins 2008: 181; Warburton 2009: 416), or even the pursuit of a high score (Radde-Antweiler 2008: 174). Though these can be built into a virtual world by a single user, or group of users, a narrative is not a necessary condition of its existence or functioning (Farley 2014). Role-playing in this environment requires that users exert higher cognitive efforts and ensure that there are sufficient elements to allow for the emergence of spontaneous complex behaviours (Guitton 2012). In this way, users become active participants instead of just being passive observers or simply re-enacting a particular scene or sequence from an established narrative (Guitton 2012).

138 *Helen Farley*

Religion frequently forms an integral part of the rich narrative structure in digital gaming. Games such as the *Elder Scrolls* games of *Skyrim, Morrowind* and *Oblivion* are examples of the fantasy Role-Playing Game genre in which religion is made explicit through the presence of deities, moral codes and cults (Thames 2014). The mythos of *Star Wars* also makes an appearance here through *Star Wars: Knights of the Old Republic*, featuring an epic power struggle between the Sith Empire and the Galactic Republic (Thames 2014). Likewise, religion is often integral to role-play in Second Life. Leigh and colleagues describes religious role-play in a community recreating life in Ancient Egypt (Leigh *et al.* 2010).

Meeting to role-play in Second Life engenders "social presence" in users, the ability to project themselves emotionally and socially (Pereira 2010: 94). If other people in that environment acknowledge one's presence, it offers further affirmation that one actually 'exists' in that environment. Social presence results from communicating with others in any of a variety of ways, including using voice or text chat, using gestures, or by otherwise interacting with those in the environment (Sadowski and Stanney 2002: 795). In general, there are three factors that impact the extent to which immersion and presence occur. These are commitment (individual-level, to the character and the community), cohesion (group-level, between the members of the community) and coherence (environment-level, between the community and the environment) (Guitton 2012: 1689).

Jediism in Second Life: a methodology

Baym and Markham note that in conducting qualitative research on the Internet, there are fewer bounded places than in the 'real' world (Markham and Baym 2008). This is especially true when conducting research in virtual worlds; there is very little space that is truly private. The user's ability to move their vantage point allows visibility of just about every space. Anyone with a Second Life account can explore most spaces, can view the charters of groups and buy the regalia of most religions via the browser-based Second Life Marketplace. Groups may link spaces in the virtual world with web-based spaces such as web pages or discussion forums through the web-on-a-prim functionality, whereby an object can act as a web link and either be displayed on the object or open a web page (Linden 2011).

Adherents of Jediism make substantial and effective use of the Internet to communicate via email, newsgroups and particularly through social media. Beth Singler has explored how the Jedi leverage social media, particularly Twitter, and the Internet to create legitimacy (Singler 2014). On 18 October 2015, a Google search on Jediism revealed that there are some 62,200 websites accessible on this topic, and while many will contain information for fans or fan fiction or other, many represent groups of people who consider Jediism to be a legitimate religion, such as the Temple of the Jedi Order (Temple Of The Jedi Order 2015).

For this chapter, data was collected from a number of public spaces in Second Life and virtual artefacts gathered. The author assumed a Jedi identity (Figure 7.1), including appropriate apparel, in order to blend into the *Star Wars* role-playing regions and in order to not violate the rules of engagement in those regions. Group descriptions and group charters were examined. The Second Life Marketplace was searched in order to gather information about the sorts of resources available to Jedi role-players. A number of *Star Wars* Role-Play (SWRP) and other Jedi/Sith role-playing regions were visited. Though engaging in conversation, either through text or voice chat, with participants, there was no discussion about the religious or role-play aspects of Jediism, as "out of character" (OOC) chat was usually prohibited during role-play. Though it would be possible to converse with these people outside of role-play, this remains an objective for future research.

Jedi in the Second Life economy

In contrast to some other virtual worlds, Second Life has an economy fuelled by a currency based on Linden dollars and regulated through the LindeX or Second Life Stock Exchange. This allows for the co-creation of value by both the owners of Second Life and the users of the platform (Bonsu and Darmody 2008: 356). One thousand Linden dollars is worth around US$4 (Linden Labs 2015a). Goods or services can be bought or sold, mostly mediated through the Second Life Marketplace (Linden Labs 2015b), but it is possible to buy goods through shops and kiosks throughout Second Life. The Second Life Marketplace is searchable and orders results according to search preferences, including categories of content (apparel, hair, gestures and so on), cost, maturity level and relevance.

Figure 7.1 The author as Helen Frak dressed as a Jedi Knight.

140   *Helen Farley*

A search (conducted 17 November 2015) reveals some 1,668 results across all maturity levels and merchandise categories for the search term 'Jedi'. A similar search with the term 'Sith' returns slightly fewer results at 1,442. There are likely to be many products in common between these searches, as the search function is powered by keywords selected by the seller. The products available include complete avatars, outfits, vehicles, weapons, scripts and animations. Outfits vary from revealing outfits probably used for sexual role-play (Brookey and Cannon 2009), to outfits that very closely resemble those depicted in the *Star Wars* franchise.

Movement of avatars in Second Life is mediated usually through a keyboard and mouse, which does not lend itself to natural movement, particularly that movement not associated with locomotion. Animations can help render this movement both more complex and more natural. For example, within the native Second Life interface, there are few opportunities to simulate combat with light sabres. An animation, which becomes linked to a particular avatar, can allow a reasonable simulation of light sabre combat. Though this allows more natural movement in real time, it can become particularly important when creating machinima. Machinima, short for "machine cinema", is where "3D computer animation gameplay is recorded in real time as video footage and then used to produce traditional video narratives" (Bowen and Wagner 2006: 66). A search of YouTube reveals a number of machinima created featuring Jedi and Sith role-play. Some of these are informational, describing the ethos and ideals of the Jedi; many more document battles and events in Second Life (see X6GrimReaper9X 2015).

In essence, all of the accoutrements required to equip an avatar as a Jedi Knight or as a Sith lord for role-play in Second Life, can be bought for a few US dollars and are readily available through established commercial channels. The barriers to role-play are small, excepting the possession of sufficiently powerful computer hardware and adequate internet bandwidth.

Jedi and Sith groups in Second Life

Collaboration and socialisation in Second Life are facilitated by the use of 'groups'. Groups allow constituent members to communicate directly with each other through instant messaging or voice chat wherever they are in the metaverse. These conversations are private from other Second Life users. Group owners are able to name and regulate the permissions and duties of office bearers. They are also able to regulate membership, allowing avatars to join and expel them from the group should the need arise. Groups can jointly own land or other assets. Access to certain regions can be restricted to the members of certain groups. Hence, role-play in Second Life is facilitated by the presence and functionality of groups (Linden Labs 2011).

Using the search functionality of Second Life with the search term 'Jedi' within 'groups', some 415 results are returned (as of 27 July 2015). Though the vast majority of these groups communicate in English (that is, group descriptions are in English), there are also a number of groups that use other languages, namely Japanese, Portuguese, French, Italian, Spanish, German and Polish. This reflects the approximate makeup of the Second Life population by nationality: United States 31 per cent; France 13 per cent; Germany 10 per cent; United Kingdom 8 per cent; Netherlands 7 per cent; Spain 4 per cent; Brazil 4 per cent; Canada 3 per cent; Belgium 3 per cent; and Italy 2 per cent (Hachmann 2007).

Interestingly, though there are some 372 groups that are returned in a search for 'Sith', a large number of Jedi groups also claim some affiliation with the dark side of the Force, perhaps as many as a quarter. Such groups include the Order Of The Dark Jedi (ODJ), which claims to be fallen Jedi who serve the Sith Emperor ({ODJ} Order Of The Dark Jedi n.d.) and the Jedi Crusaders. Another grouping, the Gray Jedi, are those who make use of the Force, treading a fine line between the light and the dark aspects of the Force. The term can also refer to those Jedi who distance themselves from the Jedi High Council (Gray Jedi 2005). The Gray Jedi are well represented in Second Life by groups such as The Galactic Imperial Knights (The Galactic Imperial Knights n.d.) and the Force Vigilante. The latter group states that there is no good without evil and pledges to do whatever is necessary to maintain the balance between the two (Force Vigilante n.d.).

Jedi Knights and Sith are not the only characters residing in the *Star Wars* universe, and many take on roles representing the myriad of other humanoid and alien characters that have emerged from the franchise. Many Second Life groups support SWRP in general and Jedi Knights seek membership of these groups for a more complete role-playing experience that better reflects the *Star Wars* universe. To enable them to be found, these groups identify themselves with the acronym SWRP (for *Star Wars* Role-Play) (Guitton 2012). A search using this acronym reveals some 239 groups including SWRP SANITY (SWRP SANITY n.d.) and SWRP Spacers United (SWRP Spacers United n.d.). Many of the groups identified with this acronym appear to serve as a means of promoting Star Wars role-playing by acting as a communication and dissemination portal.

It is difficult to discern which of these groups are for role-playing for entertainment and which represent a genuine religious community. What is most likely is that there is no clear boundary between these types of groups. Some groups explicitly state that they are true believers and adherents of Jediism. The Temple of the Jedi Force state that they are true adherents of Jediism and also promote this through a web presence. The website grants access to a wide range of resources to facilitate learning in the ways of the Jedi and is available once a user has registered. Accounts are free and immediate access is granted (Temple of the Jedi Force n.d.).

Jedi role-playing regions in Second Life

Grand spaces are relatively easy to create in Second Life. Users have all the tools to build spaces as long as they have some land and the skills. Buildings, forests, temples and landscapes can also be purchased for as little as a few hundred Linden dollars from the Second Life Marketplace and unpacked and modified to suit the needs of the user. Weapons, animated objects and heads up displays are similarly available and make it relatively easy to create a space for role-playing. All of these objects can be infinitely modifiable to suit any purpose or to satisfy any aesthetic ideal. A relatively unskilled user, without too much effort or time, can create a professional-looking environment that is attractive and functional. Given the ease with which bespoke spaces can be created, it is not difficult to create spaces that echo the feel and intent of the *Star Wars* universe.

There are 33 regions in Second Life that are identified as spaces tagged with the label 'Jedi' in Second Life. Most of these also share the SWRP tag. Some are training academies which young Padawan or Jedi in training can visit to learn the doctrines and skills needed to be a Jedi Knight. Yavin IV is such a place (Yavin IV (ILM-CS AoWCS FFC) n.d.) (see Figure 7.2). Again, the name of this region is taking from the fictional *Star Wars* universe (see Yavin 4 n.d.). Notecards are given upon arrival at the region, outlining the history of the region (in the larger context of the *Star Wars* universe) and the rules of participation. More typical are the role-playing sims, such as New Alderaan. Named after Alderaan featured in the first movie of the *Star Wars* franchise and home to Princess Leia (later Leia Organa Solo) (Anon n.d. a), the blurb that describes New Alderaan claims it is the home of thousands after Alderaan was destroyed by the first Death Star (Anon n.d. b). Upon arrival at this destination, a notecard containing the rules of role-play and of sim is automatically

Figure 7.2 The Wilderness in Yavin IV.

provided. It asks that avatars remain in character, that any OOC discussions occur only in private chat, and that overt sexuality be avoided because of the classification of the sim (rebeldyke n.d.). Apparel for the role-play is provided at New Alderaan for those without their own.

The magic circle

Dutch cultural historian, Johan Huizinga, wrote his seminal work, *Homo Ludens* in 1938, surmising that to be human was to play (Huizinga 1949). He emphasised that play is voluntary, creative and altruistic, tends to foster secrecy and community among the players, is temporary and repetitive, and takes place in 'special' places (Cusack 2013: 363). The connection to religion is striking. Even though the participants in Second Life role-plays may not specifically espouse religion, there is something religious in their participation (Plate 2010). Huizinga described play as:

> [a] free activity standing quite consciously outside "ordinary" life as being "not serious", but at the same time absorbing the player intensely and utterly. It is an activity connected with no material interest, and no profit can be gained by it. It proceeds within its own proper boundaries of time and space according to fixed rules and in an orderly manner. It promotes the formation of social groupings which tend to surround themselves with secrecy and to stress their difference from the common world by disguise or other means.
>
> (Huizinga 1949: 13)

Religionist, William E. Paden, recognised that religions exist in another world with their own sets of rules, beliefs and behaviours (quoted in Plate 2010). Plate takes this further by declaring that we live in concentric worlds in which neighbours keep different calendars, with their lives oriented to different gods, goddesses, books and places (Plate 2010: 220). Each alternate world functions as what Huizinga described as a "magic circle", characterising religion as much as it characterises play. In this way, Jediism role-play spans the divide between religion and play with each having more in common with the other than not. In each there are different rules, a different timeline (literally in the case of Jedi role-play), with players taking on different masks and identities (Plate 2010). What is to differentiate the Padawan learning the ways of the Jedi Knight on Second Life's Yavin IV from the Catholic Novitiate?

Conclusion

Though Jediism owes its origins to a social protest in response to a census in a number of countries, there is no doubt that in many cases, it has emerged as a hyper-real religion manifesting in many real and virtual spaces,

144   *Helen Farley*

including the virtual world of Second Life. Second Life users may overtly assert their belief in Jediism as a legitimate religion as with The Jedi Temple of the Force or they may don the garb, take up a virtual light sabre and participate in the many role-playing groups that market themselves as such with the SWRP tag, wanting no more than to pass a few hours in the company of a virtual brotherhood. The functionality built into the virtual world of Second Life enables those who are interested to form groups to enable communication, voice or text, between like-minded individuals who may be remote geographically. They can gather to talk, enact rituals and to engage in combat. Almost universally, this kind of role-playing requires that players/adherents remain in character (IC) so as not to disrupt the 'magic circle' characterised by strict rules, a code or credo and a parallel timeline.

Spaces sacred to Jedi (and their Sith antagonists), role-playing regions with lofty stone towers, otherworldly technologies and a strict dress code, can be readily manufactured from the inexpensive resources made available through the Second Life Marketplace. The magic circle takes a pixelated form, yet is no less real than a Gothic cathedral or a mosque with its imposing towers and a plaintive call to prayer (these too can be found in Second Life). Participants would look at home in any of the *Star Wars* films. The attention to detail in their dress, speech and the make up of their weaponry belies the perceived connection to the fictional characters of the franchise. The struggle between good and evil is writ large in the battles between the Jedi Knights and the Sith, but the dichotomy is not so clear cut, with the Gray Jedi walking the line, their sacred duty to restore balance to a disordered universe.

Much remains to be done, and this chapter forms only the first part of a great journey. It explores those very public virtual artefacts of Jediism in Second Life. How those role-plays impact the real lives of the participants and the complex interplay between religion, religious role-play and play remain to be plumbed. Can we really say that to be virtually religious is religious enough, or is it more than enough?

References

Anon. n.d. a. 'Alderaan'. At: starwars.wikia.com/wiki/Alderaan. Accessed 15 November 2015.

Anon. n.d. b. 'New Alderaan'. At: world.secondlife.com/place/7427d00e-2f97-c933-a832-e535d96642ea?lang=en-US. Accessed 15 November 2015.

Bardzell, Jeffrey and Shaowen Bardzell. 2008. 'Intimate Interactions: Online Representation and Software of the Self'. *Interactions* 15(5): 11–15.

Bonsu, Samuel K. and Aron Darmody. 2008. 'Co-creating *Second Life*: Market-Consumer Cooperation in Contemporary Economy'. *Journal of Macromarketing* 28(4): 355–368.

Bowen, Jonathan L. and Rachel Wagner. 2006. '"Hokey Religions and Ancient Weapons": The Force of Spirituality'. In M. W. Kapell and J. S. Lawrence (eds), *Finding the Force of the Star Wars Franchise: Fans, Merchandise, and Critics*, 75–94. New York: Peter Lang.

Brookey, Robert Alan and Kristopher L. Cannon. 2009. 'Sex Lives in Second Life'. *Critical Studies in Media Communication* 26(2): 145–164.

Castronova, Edward. 2001. *Virtual Worlds: A First-Hand Account of Market and Society on the Cyberian Frontier*. Center for Economic Studies & Ifo Institute for Economic Research.

Castronova, Edward. 2005. *Synthetic Worlds: The Business and Culture of Online Games*. Chicago, IL: Chicago University Press.

Collman, Ashley. 2013. 'The Real Church of Jediism - THOUSANDS Believe in Religion Based off the Star Wars Franchise'. *Daily Mail Australia*, 18 October. At: www.dailymail.co.uk/news/article-2465445/Jediism-THOUSANDS-believe-religion-based-Star-Wars-franchise.html. Accessed 15 November 2015.

Costikyan, Greg. 1987. *Star Wars: The Roleplaying Game*. New York: West End Games.

Cusack, Carole M. 2010. *Invented Religions: Imagination, Fiction and Faith*. Farnham, UK and Burlington, VT: Ashgate.

Cusack, Carole M. 2013. 'Play, Narrative and the Creation of Religion: Extending the Theoretical Base of "Invented Religions"'. *Culture and Religion: An Interdisciplinary Journal* 14(4): 362–377.

De Castella, Tom. 2014. 'Have Jedi Created a New "Religion"?' *BBC News Magazine*, 25 October.

Ducheneaut, Nicolas, Nick Yee, Eric Nickell and Robert J. Moore. 2006. 'Building an MMO With Mass Appeal: A Look at Gameplay in *World of Warcraft*'. *Games and Culture* 1(4): 281–317.

Farley, Helen. 2010. 'Teaching Studies in Religion in Second Life: UQ Religion Bazaar'. Paper presented at the Australian Association for the Study of Religion Conference, Griffith University, Brisbane.

Farley, Helen. 2014. 'Virtual Worlds in Higher Education: The Challenges, Expectations and Delivery'. In M. Gosper and D. Ifenthaler (eds), *Curriculum Models for the 21st Century*, 325–349. New York: Springer.

Force Vigilante. n.d. At: world.secondlife.com/group/49a1a712–1710–3169–6721–5a39a6371f9e?lang=en-US. Accessed 29 November 2015.

The Galactic Imperial Knights. n.d. At: world.secondlife.com/group/6f6aec4e-622d-aff6–5f17–84fd04680237?lang=en-US. Accessed 29 November 2015.

Gray Jedi. 2005. 'Gray Jedi'. At: starwars.wikia.com/wiki/Gray_Jedi. Accessed 29 November 2015.

Guitton, Matthieu J. 2012. 'Living in the Hutt Space: Immersive process in the *Star Wars* Role-Play community of Second Life'. *Computers in Human Behavior* 28: 1681–1691.

Hachmann, Roland. 2007. 'Second Life User Statistics by Country'. At: www.web-jungle.com/2007/02/11/second-life-user-statistics-by-country/. Accessed 29 November 2015.

Hendaoui, Adel, Moez Limayem and Craig Thompson. 2008. '3D Social Virtual Worlds: Research Issues and Challenges'. *IEEE Internet Computing* January-February: 88–92.

Huizinga, Johan. 1949. *Homo Ludens: A Study of the Play-Element in Culture*. London: Routledge & Kegan Paul.

Hutchings, Tim. 2011. 'Contemporary Religious Community and the Online Church'. *Information, Communication & Society* 14(8): 1118–1135.

Jennings, Nancy and Chris Collins. 2008. 'Virtual or Virtually U: Educational Institutions in Second Life'. *International Journal of Social Sciences* 2(3): 180–186.

Leapman, Ben. 2007. 'Second Life World may be Haven for Terrorists'. *The Telegraph*, 13 May. At: www.telegraph.co.uk/news/uknews/1551423/Second-Life-world-may-be-haven-for-terrorists.html. Accesssed 29 November 2015.

Leigh, Morgan, Mark G. Elwell and Steven Cook. 2010. 'Recreating Ancient Egyptian Culture in Second Life'. Paper presented at the Digital Game and Intelligent Toy Enhanced Learning (DIGITEL), 2010 Third IEEE International Conference, Kaohsiung.

Linden, Jeremy. 2011. 'Shared Media'. At: community.secondlife.com/t5/English-Knowledge-Base/Shared-Media/ta-p/700145. Accessed 29 November 2015.

Linden Labs. 2011. 'Joining and Participating in Groups'. At: community.second life.com/t5/English-Knowledge-Base/Joining-and-participating-in-groups/ta-p/700117. Accessed 29 November 2015.

Linden Labs. 2015a. 'Buy L$'. At: secondlife.com/my/lindex/buy.php? Accessed 29 November 2015.

Linden Labs. 2015b. 'Second Life Marketplace'. At: marketplace.secondlife.com/. Accessed 17 October 2015.

Linden Labs. n.d. 'Land'. At: wiki.secondlife.com/wiki/Region#Region. Accessed 29 November 2015.

Loh, Christian Sebastian. 2008. 'Confronting the Dark Side of Video Games'. In C. T. Miller (ed.), *Games: Purpose and Potential in Education*, 185–218. New York: Springer.

Maher, Mary Lou. 1999. 'Designing the Virtual Campus'. *Design Studies* 20(4): 319–342.

Markham, Annette N. and Nancy K. Baym. 2008. 'Introduction: Making Smart Choices on Shifting Ground'. In A. Markham and N. K. Baym (eds), *Internet Inquiry: Conversations About Method*. Thousand Oaks, CA: Sage Publications.

McCormick, Debbie. 2006. 'From Jesus Christ to Jedi Knight: Validity and Viability of New Religious Movements in Late Modernity'. Paper presented at the Social Change in the 21st Century Conference, Brisbane, Australia. At: eprints.qut.edu.au/6636/1/6636.pdf. Accessed 17 October 2015.

Morningstar, Chip and F. Randall Farmer. 1991. 'The Lessons of Lucasfilm's Habitat'. In Michael Benedikt (ed.), *Cyberspace: First Steps*, 273–301. Cambridge: MIT Press.

Order Of The Dark Jedi. n.d. '{ODJ} Order Of The Dark Jedi'. At: world.secondlife.com/group/0e2fb539-a434-ed86–1ff9–07f29748f461?lang=en-US. Accessed 29 November 2015.

Pereira, Joe. 2010. 'AVALON to Shakespeare: Language Learning and Teaching in Virtual Worlds'. In Susan Sheehan (ed.), *Teacher Development and Education in Context: A Selection of Papers Presented at IATEFL 2010 by the British Council*, 94–97. London: British Council.

Peters, Timothy D. 2012. '"The Force" as Law: Mythology, Ideology and Order in George Lucas's *Star Wars*'. *Australian Feminist Law Journal* 36: 125–143.

Plate, S. Brent. 2010. 'Religion is Playing Games: Playing Video Gods, Playing to Play'. *Religious Studies and Theology* 29(2): 215–230.

Radde-Antweiler, Kerstin. 2008. 'Virtual Religion. An Approach to a Religious and Ritual Topography of Second Life'. *Heidelberg Journal of Religions on the Internet* 3(1): 174–211.

Reb (rebeldyke). n.d. 'New Alderaan Sim Rules'. In *New Alderaan* (Second Life Notecard). San Francisco, CA: Linden Labs.

Ritzema, Tim and Billy Harris. 2008. 'The Use of Second Life for Distance Education'. *Journal of Computing Sciences in Colleges* 23(6): 110–116.

Sadowski, Wallace Jr and Kay M. Stanney. 2002. 'Presence in Virtual Environments'. In Kay M. Stanney (ed.), *Handbook of Virtual Environments: Design, Implementation, and Applications*, 791–806. Mahwah, NJ: Lawrence Erlbaum Associates Publishers.

Singler, Beth. 2014. '"SEE MOM IT IS REAL": The UK Census, Jediism and Social Media'. *Journal of Religion in Europe* 7(2): 150–168.

SWRP SANITY. n.d. 'SWRP SANITY'. At: world.secondlife.com/group/fd538be7-c22c-4ecc-c69e-abec0a19ae3c?lang=en-US. Accessed 29 November 2015.

SWRP Spacers United. n.d. 'SWRP Spacers United'. At: world.secondlife.com/group/a268f24d-a1ab-a6cc-2265–3ed1ad13ca34?lang=en-US. Accessed 29 November 2015.

Temple Of The Jedi Order. 2015. 'Temple Of The Jedi Order: First International Church Of Jediism'. 4 November. At: www.templeofthejediorder.org/. Accessed 29 November 2015.

Temple of the Jedi Force. n.d. 'Temple of the Jedi Force'. At: www.templeofthejediforce.org/. Accessed 29 November 2015.

Thames, Ryan Clark. 2014. 'Religion as Resource in Digital Games'. Online – *Heidelberg Journal for Religions on the Internet* 5: 183–196.

Voyager, Daniel. 2015. 'Metrics'. At: danielvoyager.wordpress.com/sl-metrics/. Accessed 29 November 2015.

Wadley, Greg R. 2011. 'Voice in virtual worlds'. PhD thesis, Department of Inofrmation Systems, University of Melbourne.

Warburton, Steven. 2009. 'Second Life in Higher Education: Assessing the Potential for and the Barriers to Deploying Virtual Worlds in Learning and Teaching'. *British Journal of Educational Technology* 40(3): 414–426.

X6GrimReaper9X. 2015. 'Second Life – Ashas Ree: Jedi Arrival Fight (Part 1)'. *YouTube*. At: www.youtube.com/watch?v=ocOeepNWuTE. Accessed 29 November 2015.

Yavin 4. n.d. 'Yavin 4'. At: starwars.wikia.com/wiki/Yavin_4. Accessed 29 November 2015.

Yavin IV (ILM-CS AoWCS FFC). n.d. 'Yavin IV'. At: world.secondlife.com/place/1c5a27f9-fb4d-7cf1-d939–6295c60c8f21?lang=en-US. Accessed 29 November 2015.

8   A brief history of Dudeism

Oliver Benjamin, The Dudely Lama

Duddha nature

One of the charges leveled against Dudeism (The Church of the Latter-Day Dude) is that it's ridiculous to base a religion on a movie. Which is a fair enough complaint. Indeed, there are very few movies upon which a religion might well be based. *The Big Lebowski* is not just any movie, however. We've gone on record as stating that it is a hologram for the entire human condition. Complete with cuss words and excrement jokes (Coen and Coen 1998).

Often referred to (at least by ourselves) as the greatest cult film of all time, some sort of magical alchemy has been perpetrated in the film's construction that allows it to transcend the limitations of the conventional format, caveats of cinematic structure, and, occasionally it seems, the very laws of time and space.

The problem with most movies is that they don't tend to challenge our prejudices or expand our consciousness. There just isn't enough time for it to get under your skin and alter your existential DNA. Moreover, there's something osmotic about a written (or spoken) story. By putting the words in the mouths of others, movies take them out of your own head. You become a witness to the events instead of an avatar in the act.

The secret to *The Big Lebowski* lies in (among other things) a level of complexity and allusive language normally reserved for novels, manifestos and anything by Bob Dylan. Because the film is as meticulously layered as a *mille-feuille*, it allows the viewer, with each repeated viewing, to gradually descend into its seemingly bottomless well of ideas. First time watchers may emerge from their first descent utterly baffled, wondering why none of the plot points were adequately resolved. (What happened to the big bowling showdown? Did the old man actually take the money? Who the fuck are the Knudsens?) But each additional viewing brings a new shift to light as the viewer plumbs deeper and apprehends the interconnectedness with history, philosophy, and, ultimately, religion.

It's often said that you can't teach someone something by showing it to them or telling them about it, they have to experience it themselves. Most movies merely offer you a two dimensional stream of events. *Lebowski*, on

A *brief history of Dudeism*   149

the other hand, is one of the few true 3D movies in history, in the sense that as you watch it, you gradually enter its orb of reality. With each viewing, the movie resonates more and more with your inner hardwired humanity, imploring your inner Dude to reach out to the ideal Dude (Lebowski) and shake his (and our own) atavistic hand. Or, perhaps pass him a joint.

In other words, the more you watch *The Big Lebowski*, the more you become the Dude. In Buddhism, this would be referred to as finding your Buddha nature. We consider the Buddha to be one of the Great Dudes in History ('Great Dudes in History' n.d.). So, basically, you know, same difference.

Hound dogma

Where religion was once the grand all-explainer with an answer for everything, it now seems a pale shadow of its former self, beset on all sides, declining in influence and popularity, yet still trying to hog the stage. We might say that religion is the fat Elvis of human culture.

Of course, that would be insensitive and cruel to religion (and to Elvis). It's not religion's fault that it's become so misguided and mismanaged. After extended abuse by powerful organizations, it became increasingly gaudied up in sequined costumes with a bloated backup band, pandering to the interests of moneymen and the market, mangling its original greatest hits, the ones that changed the world.

With a hankering toward getting back to basics, Dudeism digs the cozy Axial Age linens out from underneath eons of encrusted ecclesiastical vestments. The Axial Age, we recall, was the period about two millennia ago when most of the current world religions were birthed. Though arising in different parts of the world, they all had the same basic maxims: "Just take it easy" and "That's just, like, your opinion, man". Early Christianity, Buddhism, Taoism, and several of the Greek philosophical schools (including Epicureanism, Stoicism, and Pyrrhonism) all had these as their central messages. Most of these are either gone now, or unrecognizable in their current incarnations. Then again, another of the original Axial Age maxims was "shit happens," so its prime movers and early acolytes probably anticipated that this too would come to pass.

Possibly the oldest of the Axial Age religions, Taoism's primary text, *The Tao Te Ching*, was a virtual Old Testament of taking it easy. At 81 slim verses, it's easily the shortest holy book in the world (unless you count Zen, which doesn't really have a holy book and is sort of against the idea of writing things down). Probably the most important concept in the book, one which pops up in many of the verses, was the concept of *wu wei*—or action without action—a sense that we should never strive or struggle, but instead try to always take the path of least resistance, else we waste our vital energy. Furthermore, in keeping with this enshrinement of emptiness, it also suggested time and time again that the sage is one who knows that he knows

150 *Oliver Benjamin*

nothing (just as Socrates famously admitted, more or less at the same time, and half a world away). And as for dealing with excremental happenstance, *The Tao Te Ching* prescribed "bending like a flexible reed" when the winds of change fart in your face (Lao Tzu 1963: 79, 138). It sure beat quixotically battling them head on. Tilting at wind-breaks, as it were.

Surely the image of the Buddha beat both Lao Tzu (the mythical founder of Taoism) and Jesus Christ when it came to suggesting that we "take it easy." Lao Tzu may generally be featured riding an ox and Jesus prominently venerated hanging from a cross, but the Buddha is usually shown sitting in meditation, serene as can be, without an evident care in the world. Perhaps more than any other religion, Buddhism codified a series of techniques to aid people to assuage their anxiety, see things from various points of view, and deal with disappointment. It's all very well and good to tell people not to let the bastards get them down, quite another to show them how to do it. Meditation and the "middle path" were meant to guide people along the difficult so-called "razor's edge" to enlightenment.

Like their Eastern counterparts, the Western side of the planet seemed to find similar spiritual inspiration in the easygoing. Though the Old Testament noted from time to time (mainly in the more fanciful parts like Psalms and Proverbs) that worry was a pointless endeavor, it's really in the Gospels where "taking it easy" became exalted to a canonical injunction. Time and time again, Jesus promoted the notion that indolence is next to Godliness: "Therefore I tell you, do not worry about your life, what you will eat or drink; or about your body, what you will wear. Is not life more important than food, and the body more important than clothes?" (Matthew 6: 25) and "Do not worry about tomorrow, for tomorrow will worry about itself. Each day has enough trouble of its own" (Matthew 6: 34). Though Jesus' ultimate message was that it is their God that will provide for them, it didn't have to be interpreted as a strict *quid pro quo*, rather something akin to the provident nature of Nature itself, as enshrined in Taoism's "ever refilling vessel" (Lao Tzu 1963: 60). He differentiates between the pagan supplication for favor and an over-arching sense that the cosmos will appear generous to those who aren't greedy. "For the pagans run after all these things and your heavenly father knows that you need them" (Matthew 6: 32). Christianity may not have been as easygoing about varieties of opinion as its Eastern Axial counterparts, but nevertheless its notion that human knowledge is fallible and that the "vanities" of man should not be held too dearly differentiated the creed from the rigid catalog of superstitions of pagan cultures it supplanted. That is, of course, until the Church rushed in to fill the power vacuum and introduced its own catalog of regulatory superstitions.

What is the sound of shit happening?

Though a lot of the Axial Age insights became buried under the battlements of civilization and power, there's nothing to say that shit can't be made to

A brief history of Dudeism   151

unhappen as well. Perhaps all we need to do to return religion to its original nature is to properly pot it and cultivate it. In keeping with the Axial Age traditions, this would unfold via its fundamental maxims: promoting "taking it easy" and the notion that all concepts are just models (i.e., opinions) of the world, not a hard and unchanging reality.

One of the first steps to bring us back to a new Axial Age (in Dudeism, we refer to it as a "Relaxial Age") is that the word "religion" needs to be made sense of. Currently religion derives a lot of its power from the fact that, like a moving target, it cannot be accurately pinned down. Terms like God, love, patriotism, and value-added tax are powerful and manipulative, because no one really knows what they mean.

Which brings us to the second most common criticism of Dudeism: that it can't be called a religion since it recognizes no God or gods. Which is not to say we're an atheistic religion, but rather a non-theistic religion. We don't have any opinions on the existence or non-existence of God because we don't think God has been adequately defined to even pose the question. Asking whether you believe in God is akin to asking whether you believe in Blah. What is Blah? God means many things to many people all over the world. God is love. God is nature. God is the guy you acknowledge during orgasms. If God were a corporation, he'd have to fire his branding department.

Do we believe that there's some far-out stuff out there that we don't understand? Of course we do. Even the most dyed-in-the-unwoolly Logical Positivist would admit this. But do we claim to know what it is? Of course we don't. To do so would be a logical contradiction. And yet this is the foundational *modus operandi* of most religious catechisms: God is a mystery that cannot be understood by mere mortals; now, let us tell you all about him.

Instead of wasting our time on such a quixotic (and exhausting!) endeavor, we choose to focus on the other, more practical aspects of religious tradition—most importantly, its psychological utility. From the Dudeist perspective, that's what religion was really all about in the first place. The metaphysics was only in there because physics didn't exist yet. When it comes to psychological utility, no viable substitutes have emerged to religion, although psychology itself had a good run there for a while.

What's a heuro?

For lack of a better (or more familiar) term, we see religion as a heuristic for holiness. A heuristic is a technique used in the sciences to simplify a complex field of data so that it can be more easily understood, manipulated, and made use of. And not just in academia—human beings use heuristics every day. Without them, they couldn't even get out of bed in the morning. What we call "common sense" is just the panoply of heuristics we've accumulated over our lives. Rules of thumb, mnemonics, and educated guesses are all everyday forms of heurism.

152   *Oliver Benjamin*

Life can be hard and complex, and we need help making sense of it. We utilize heuristics to help cut through and categorize all the chaos and endless decision-making. As Jesus in the Gospels points out, human beings are the only animals that worry and toil—and for apparently no good reason. He suggested that we consider the lilies of the field (evidently there were no sloths in Galilee) and just take 'er easy instead of getting all worked up over things. His prescriptions in the Gospels went some way toward showing how this might be approached.

All religions do just this: they provide a worldview and package of heuristics which teach us how to behave, how to spend our time, how to treat each other, how to survive, and how to maximize our psychological well-being. The reason animals (and flowers) don't need religion is because that's all taken care of by their instincts. Their heuristics are hardwired.

So what would a "heuristic for holiness" consist of? What is holiness, after all? Unsurprisingly, "holy" comes from the same root as "whole." Tellingly, it's also related to the root for "health." Of course, etymology can be used to argue anything you like, but here it seems likely that the notion of the holy implies something like integrity on steroids. Or, at least, we can choose to interpret it that way. Thus, rather than suggesting something otherworldly and separate from the world (as many religions seem to), the prime objective of "holy" religious practice and tradition might be to render the acolyte whole and hale, both within the realm of his own consciousness and the society and environment of which he or she is part. Put simply (and Dudely), religion helps us get our heads together, man.

The Relaxial Age

Historian Karl Jaspers came up with the term "Axial Age," because he saw it as a profound turning point in human cultural development, witnessing the birth of the great religions, philosophies and worldviews that continue to inform our culture today. Though differing in the details, all of these "isms" aimed to assuage the discomfort everyday humans felt in just being alive (Jaspers 1977).

But why is it that "all life is suffering," as the Buddha (and virtually every other religious figure) suggested? Religion has tried to address this mystery in various ways. Judaism says we were perfectly well-adapted to nature, but then we got ambitious and gave up our birthright. Christianity says we just have to learn to love unconditionally and we'll once again dwell in an updated version of the Garden. Buddhism says that we just need to evolve until we realize our place in the world. Taoism says you're not going to fix anything so we should just relax and go with the flow. Are they wrong? No, they're all generally correct. The devils, so to speak, are in the details.

One of our great intellectual revolutions took place in the early 1990s, though few have noticed yet. At the University of California at Santa Barbara (incidentally, the town where Jeff Bridges, the actor who plays the

A brief history of Dudeism 153

Dude in *The Big Lebowski* lives), a field called evolutionary psychology was birthed. Prior to its genesis, psychology had become a somewhat bankrupt science, with myriad conflicting schools of thought, all of which disagreed with each other, few of its experiments showing repeatability, and featuring a diagnostic and statistical manual so enormous and bloated that a good number of its students couldn't actually even lift it.

The simple and elegant principle underlying evolutionary psychology was that our minds were biologically shaped by a long, stable period living on the African savannah. Life was likely fairly copasetic back then, and even when it wasn't, we were well-adapted to deal with any bummers that came our way. We hung out in groups of about 150 close-knit friends, lived off the land, and basically took it easy most of the time. Most of the problems we have to deal with today came as a result of the rise of agriculture, which forced us to stay in one place and guard our hoard of food. The consequent rise of cities and fortifications led to warfare and disease and massive expansion of social pressures, frictions, expectations, and competition. Our brains were simply not (and are still not) designed for this new environment.

Thus, what Judaism, Hinduism, Jainism, Confucianism, Christianity, Buddhism, Taoism, Epicureanism, and other Axial Age creeds offered were explanations and prescriptions for dealing with this new "exile" from the world to which we were biologically adapted. Their original messages (parts anyway) are still relevant today, since the basics of life haven't changed that much since civilization found its first footing: we still have to struggle with the pressures of materialism and social status, the stress of being surrounded by strangers all the time, the burden of learning vast amounts of information, the frustrations of bureaucracy, the prevalence of fear-mongering, and the depressing sense that we are a tiny and insignificant drop in a bucket of billions of drops instead of an important part of a caring and loyal tribe.

The UnDude Ages

These new ideas and their recommendations may have helped us for a while. But then, just as we lost our bucolic African "paradise," the religions meant to help us deal with that loss became quickly usurped by the politics and pressures of empire-building. In many cases, the creeds were dramatically modified to exacerbate our discomfort rather than assuage it: Judaism grew to emphasize "otherness" from the rest of the world and the heavy portent of a savior who still has not shown up; Christianity introduced the glorification of suffering, keeping its followers in line with the terrifying threat of hell and an uncertain consolation of an unlikely heaven; Buddhism became mired in superstition and obsessed with the very notions of hierarchy it was mean to jettison in the first place; Taoism abandoned its practical and poetic prescriptions for living in the here-and-now in favor of superstitions surrounding immortality and quack medicine; and Epicureanism became systematically and vindictively crushed by followers of Christianity, only

154　*Oliver Benjamin*

to be reintroduced in the twentieth century as a marketing strategy which purveyed overpriced products.

It hasn't all been a washout, of course. Under all the ecclesiastical and financial trappings of the organizations, we can still see hints of the original charitable, meek, and loving Jesus; within the Talmud and Kabbalah we can find exegeses on personal development and virtue instead of adherence to archaic law; within *zazen* we can find the direct apprehension of Dharma promised by the Buddha instead of the obfuscating distractions of superstition; within Yogism we can find an all-encompassing humility and liberation which counters Hinduism's ethnic and ritualistic obsessions. And so on.

The problem is that most societies don't really allow us to order religion *a la carte*. If only there were a way to distill out the essence from the excess and enshrine it in a new worldview! Certainly some have tried. Aldous Huxley promoted the idea of the "perennial philosophy," which he said existed at the base of all the great religions. Unitarian Universalism and Secular Humanist movements have tried to refashion religion without religiosity. And many New Age movements have attempted to separate the sweet bits from the hard crusts of all variety of religion. Even celebrated author, Alain De Botton, penned a book called *Religion for Atheists*, which had several good ideas and a few bad ones, one of which was an annual orgy sanctioned by the state. But nothing has really caught on to any substantial degree (De Botton 2013).

The Dude Vinci code

No one knows for sure what the Coen Brothers had in mind when putting together an epic like *The Big Lebowski*. Is it a mere coincidence that its protagonist dresses in a robe and sandals, like the prophets of the Axial Age? Are the pepperings of religious metaphor there only for decoration, or are a pedophile Jesus, Nietzschean nihilists, a militant orthodox Jew, lashings of Eastern mysticism, and an omniscient white-haired narrator all part of a hermetic subtext? It doesn't really matter. Just as we choose to read "holy" as "whole and hale," we also choose to see enshrined in *The Big Lebowski* a suitable and very welcome heuristic for holiness. So many of the elements and allusions in the film speak to our desperate human need to "abide" in the world instead of merely surviving it, that it would be churlish to disregard them in favor of maintaining a dismissive literalism.

Though history records the works of so-called great men and generally paves over the bones of the losers, clandestine fragments of fossils have been passed down throughout history. What we call hermetic traditions or secret societies have generally taken it upon themselves to safeguard holy but endangered truths so that they can't be destroyed by the fascist regimes who relentlessly end up in charge. Yet only those with the appropriate key can unlock the code. This in mind, we're prone to wonder: might there be a "Dude Vinci" code that has existed throughout history?

A brief history of Dudeism   155

The canon of the Church of the Latter-Day Dude contends that, indeed, Dudeism has always existed, getting its start in the early incarnations of Axial Age religions and then, once persecuted, going underground, or at least being relegated to sidekick status. We choose to retroactively baptize all the disparate strains as "Dudeism," not to claim them for our own, however, but rather to offer kinship and allegiance and to try and gather together the fragments so that our followers don't have to reinvent the wheel of Dudeist Dharma. Ours can be seen as the hermetic key to the door of the Dude, one which has always been outward-opening, and more or less unlocked anyway.

The Dude testament

So what are the tenets of Dudeism anyway? At the risk of being anti-climactic, the subject is too big to be delved into in any depth here. For that, further study of our books *The Abide Guide* (2011) and *The Tao of the Dude* (2015) are in order, along with material found on our website, dudeism.com. But suffice to say that virtually everything that can be said about Dudeism now, had been said at the beginning in the form of the first and still most-powerful and unadulterated Dudeist antecedent, that of Taoism. One might say that Dudeism is just an updated version of early Taoism, before its *wu wei* got infested with woo.[1] Sources we commonly allude to include David Hall and Roger Ames' commentary on their translation, *Dao De Jing* and Holmes Welch's *Taoism: The Parting of the Way* (1957). One will also find a great deal of Dudeism in Raymond M. Smullyan's *The Tao is Silent* (1977). We're also working on our own new and annotated version of the Tao.[2]

But not just Taoism. As we've suggested, the same variety of thought and perspective can be found in the gnostic tradition of Christianity, in several of the classical Hellenic philosophies, in the yogic traditions of Hinduism, in the Zen traditions of Buddhism, and later in American Transcendentalism and some of the more sober modern spiritual traditions. In all of these, we see reflections of the Dude: principled but ordinary human beings who have managed to liberate themselves (to a degree)[3] from societal pressures, covetousness, worry about the future, and everything else that the engine of civilization would have us trust is important.

Our hero,[4] the Dude, is a thoroughly modern man who has made peace with his caveman mind, making sense of his exile from an erstwhile Eden to which he has been adapted. We would do well to follow in his sandal-steps, enrobing ourselves in a spiritual tradition which has helped perpetuate human sanity, down through the generations, across the sands of time.

So how does one become a Dudeist? Rather than make the same mistake as many of its ancestors, we are loath to try to identify any strict propositions or guidelines. To do so seems to always usher in an ossification of the original message. Instead, we hope to lead by example—our own

156 *Oliver Benjamin*

and those of philosophers, writers, comedians, and deep thinkers that we identify as Dudeist. Our recently published book, for example, *The Tao of the Dude* (Benjamin 2015) contains a compendium of Dudeist quotes and passages taken from a wide swath of world literature. As a sort of open-source religion, we rely on our followers to submit ideas, articles, and events that might help us gather up our rosebuds (and other buds), promote the ethos, and learn to abide (Benjamin and Eutsey 2011). The best the organizational aspect of the religion can hope to do is provide a meeting place and sometimes break up the minor virtual online scuffle. See, even Dudeists are sometimes prone to lose their cultivated cool. However, they do tend to snap back rather rapidly—just as the Dude did moments after having the worst day of his life, deciding immediately that he "Can't be worried about that shit. Life goes on, man!"

As far as what will "go on" for Dudeism, we're having fun fashioning the roadmap. If we've allowed even a few people to take comfort in all this, well then, it's been well worth the ramble.

Notes

1 *Wu wei* is one of the central Taoist principles, and very hard to adequately translate. Something like "actionless action" or "action without striving," it neatly describes the way that the Dude shambles his way through the world, going with the flow as much as possible, even under the direst of circumstances. Woo is the name of the character who sets the story in motion by urinating on the Dude's rug, but it is also commonly used by rationalists to describe any pseudo-scientific New Agey mumbo jumbo. Taoism may have originated as a very rational understanding of human psychology, but ended up becoming obsessed with pseudoscience.
2 Not to be confused with our Dudeist translation of the *Tao Te Ching*, *The Dude De Ching* (Church of the Latter-Day Dude 2010).
3 Dudeism maintains that there is no such thing as a saint. The best we can hope for is a "Sane." (Note that there is the same relationship between "sane" and "saint" as there is between "whole", "healthy", and "holy"). That is to say that even the most spiritually adept among us lose our cool from time to time. The difference lies in the speed and facility in which we come back to our Dudeness. Though many have pointed out that the Dude loses his cool throughout the movie, he has a nearly supernatural ability to "abide" quickly after the inciting incident.
4 The entire film challenges the notion of heroism and doesn't explicitly provide an alternative, so we might take a stab here—a hero for "our time and place" would provide a heuristic, or a model upon which we might reimagine ourselves and reorient our predispositions. Thus, a "heuro." Note that our propensity toward wordplay is largely in the interest of deflating the manipulations of language, and should not be taken too seriously.

References

Benjamin, Oliver. 2015. *The Tao of the Dude: Awesome Insights of Deep Dudes from Lao Tzu to Lebowski*. Abide University Press.
Benjamin, Oliver. n.d. 'Great Dudes in History'. *Dudeism.com: Your Answer For Everything*. At: dudeism.com/greatdudes. Accessed 8 September 2015.

A brief history of Dudeism   157

Benjamin, Oliver and Dwayne Eutsey. 2011. *The Abide Guide: Living Like Lebowski*. Berkeley, CA: Ulysses Press.

Church of the Latter-Day Dude. 2010. *The Dude De Ching: A Dudeist Interpretation of the Tao Te Ching*. Chiang Mai, Thailand and Los Angeles, CA: Church of the Latter-Day Dude.

Coen, Joel and Ethan Coen. 1998. *The Big Lebowski*. Working Title Films/Polygram Filmed Entertainment.

De Botton, Alain. 2013. *Religion for Atheists: A Non-Believer's Guide to the Uses of Religion*. London: Vintage.

Holy Bible: New Living Translation. 1996. At: www.nlt.to. Accessed 8 September 2015.

Jaspers, Karl. 1977. *The Origin and Goal of History*. Westport, CT: Greenwood Press.

Lao Tzu. 1963. *Tao Te Ching*. Translated by D. C. Lau. Harmondsworth, UK: Penguin.

Smullyan, Raymond M. 1977. *The Tao Is Silent*. New York: Harper and Row.

Welch, Holmes. 1957. *Taoism: The Parting of the Way*. Boston, MA: Beacon Press.

9 Diego Maradona and the psychodynamics of football fandom in international cinema

Marcus Free

Introduction

This chapter concerns three films variously concerned with former Argentine soccer player, Diego Maradona, as an object of intense psychodynamic investment for his fans worldwide. The term 'psychodynamic' refers to how "unconscious mental activity" and "conscious thoughts, feelings and behavior" are dynamically interrelated (Cabaniss *et al*. 2011: 4), but in ways that are only partially or inconsistently consciously accessible. Drawing on concepts derived from Freudian and object relations psychoanalysis, the chapter focuses, first, on how Maradona is a varied and often contradictory object of psychodynamic investment for his fans, then on how his status as such is represented and explored in these films.

Methodologically, using varied sources, from Burns' (2010) biography to various commentaries by Argentine and international authors, together with ethnographic and journalistic studies of Maradona's fans, the chapter examines how Maradona has acquired a symbolic status as a celebrity whose fame transcends the sphere of football. It identifies the contradictoriness and inconsistency of Maradona's highly publicised behaviour and pronouncements, and so highlights the difficulties of offering a plausible interpretation of either his psychology or his symbolic meanings for his fans. Utilising psychoanalytic perspectives on sport in relation to ethnographic and journalistic accounts of his Argentine fans (Archetti 1997, 2001; Franklin 2008), it is argued that Maradona's untrained and visibly unique achievements as a player lie at the core of his appeal to a nostalgia for idealised boyhood. Yet his repeated career transgressions and punishments are equally suggestive of unconscious masochism at work, while his apparently intense personal investment in his exalted status as celebrity – explored in such texts as the 'biopic' *Maradona, la Mano de Dio* (2007) – suggest a pathological narcissism as the root of his periodic crises.

The chapter then examines how the films illustrate the refraction and geographical specificity of his symbolism for his fans. In each case, the focus on affective – over and above intellectual – investment, and the often visually suggestive, rather than verbally articulated, form of the text lends itself to interpretations variously inspired by Freudian and object relations psychoanalysis. The discussion of *In the Hands of the Gods* (Turner and Turner 2007), a documentary chronicling the journey of five male practitioners of freestyle football (that is, the art of expressing yourself with a football, performing tricks with any part of the body) from the UK to meet Maradona in Buenos Aires, acknowledges the documentary's constructive role in its participants' forging their onscreen identities through its progressive record of their journey, and the ways in which its camera operates as a confessor to which they confide their experiences and desires. Nonetheless, the focus of their discursive interactions on themselves and their individual life trajectories, rather than on Maradona, is read as indicative of how Maradona as a celebrity is an object of affective investment that validates the protagonists' corporealisation of their self-identities through performances as freestyle footballers that are clearly distinct from the world of organised team football and (seen from a psychoanalytic perspective) its post-Oedipal code of submission to its rules. National origins, identities and narratives, too, are marginal to the shared theme of individual renewal through their affinity with Maradona (who only appears briefly). Maradona becomes a vehicle for the rather neoliberal, de-territorialised theme of individual empowerment.

El Camino de San Diego [*The Road to Saint Diego*] (Sorín 2006) follows a fictional fan who journeys to Buenos Aires when Maradona falls gravely ill, carrying as a gift a tree root that supposedly resembles Maradona. The emphasis here is on how the film's visual iconography is suggestive of fandom as narcissistic identification with the object of fandom. The methodology focuses on the tensions between the appearance of romantic endorsement and Sorín's problematising of this outwardly simplistic representation through sometimes complex use of mise en scène and juxtaposition. The analysis reads these tensions as a critical commentary on the contradictions and harsh reality of Argentina's recovery from the 2001 economic crisis, which is periodically directly referenced. The context is problematic of 'national' cinema: celebrity fandom as a prism through which to explore the contradictions of post-crisis Argentina.

The analysis of *Maradona by Kusturica* (Kusturica 2008), an explicitly authored cultural and political documentary portrait of Maradona by Bosnian-born Emir Kusturica, focuses on the film's foregrounding of psychoanalytic concepts through Kusturica's own voice-over narrative of his efforts to make sense of Maradona's personal and political symbolism. It offers an interpretation of the repetitive structure of this non-narrative film and Kusturica's expressions of frustration with his project as evidence of a reflexive acknowledgement of fan investment as a form of narcissism leading back to himself. It seeks to identify how this is rhetorically presented through the visual and discursive focus on Kusturica as narrator, interviewer and observer, and on the use of marked fantasy sequences. Each film illustrates the varied psychodynamic investments of fans, but only *Maradona by Kusturica* explicitly offers a metacommentary on celebrity fandom.

A mess of contradictions

Generally considered the most talented footballer of his generation, Maradona captained Argentina to World Cup victory in 1986, en route against England scoring two of soccer's most notorious goals, the second the outcome of a breathtaking dribble past half the England team, the first from an illegal handball unseen by the officials. This combination of supreme achievement and controversy characterised his career. In 1991 he was banned from football for 15 months after testing positive for cocaine while a player at Napoli, and in his 1994 World Cup comeback he was expelled for using the banned drug ephedrine.

Despite his transgressions, Maradona was considered to be essential to the marketing of international soccer by FIFA. Yet he outspokenly criticised FIFA in 1986 for its inappropriate scheduling of games in extreme heat in order to maximise television and commercial revenue, so fuelling his status as an icon of resistance to the game's power hierarchy, an image that was further enhanced by his career at Napoli in the 1980s. Napoli was both a poor relation of the wealthier northern Italian clubs and a geographical representative of Italy's poorer south. Maradona's success there was thus both geographically and economically symbolic, and it became intertwined with a romantic narrative, in Argentina, of his rise from the impoverished suburb Villa Fiorito, on the margins of Buenos Aires, to the status of national hero. Following his retirement, he became politically associated with Cuba's Fidel Castro and Venezuela's Hugo Chávez. He criticised the US boycotting of Cuba and joined Chávez for his 'People's Summit' rally to protest at the holding of the Fourth Summit of the Americas at Mar del Plata in 2005, "an occasion for ALCA (Free Trade Area for the Americas) to deliberate on the expansion of a free-trade zone regulated by the United States" (Salazar-Sutil 2008: 450).

Maradona's political statements and beliefs are notoriously inconsistent and often incoherent. Critics such as biographer Jimmy Burns (2010: 6) have stressed his political inconsistencies. He did not protest when, having been central to Argentina's 1979 Youth World Cup victory, this achievement was used to symbolise the military junta's legitimacy. He supported President Carlos Menem and Domingo Cavallo, Menem's neoliberal economic minister, widely blamed for the 2001 economic collapse. When Menem's policies massively increased unemployment and poverty (Cooney 2007: 23–24), Maradona did not support a socialist alternative. However, for Tobin (2002), Maradona's appeal lies in the perception of his being against power in a non-specific sense, however incoherent his position may be: hence his widely reported reference to US President George W. Bush as "human garbage". Such gestures make him a compelling, populist symbol of resistance to American geopolitical hegemony.

Nicolás Salazar-Sutil (2008: 448) argues that "Maradona" is a "neutro-semic fan text" (citing Sandvoss 2005), a "mirror on which anyone can project

Psychodynamics of football fandom 161

an image or signification" with the "potential to be a pair of opposites or whatever else the audience projects onto his empty bodily screen" (Salazar-Sutil 2008: 455–456). However, while Maradona is a persistently contradictory figure, it is surely too much to say that he is an infinitely variable text with no relationship to the materiality of his actions as a person. But is it possible to find some consistency to his contradictions and to how he is imagined by his fans, or is that an entirely contradictory endeavour?

The popular reception in Argentina of Maradona's World Cup goals against England help explain his enormous national popularity. Maradona attributed the first to divine intervention, the 'hand of God', playfully fuelling discourses on his God-like status for his fans. Though transgressing the ethical code of sportsmanship, this was widely celebrated in Argentina as legitimately crafty play, entirely consistent with the second goal. Maradona also later crossed the supposed boundary between politics and sport, claiming his goals as vengeance for the 1982 Malvinas/Falklands War (Tobin 2002: 68). The longer historical context for this dates to introduction of football by British sailors and émigrés in the late nineteenth century, following which Argentine football has been popularly imagined as bifurcated into a quintessentially British, "industrial" style and a more imaginative "*criollo*" (creole) style described by Archetti (2001: 155) as "restless, individualistic, undisciplined . . . agile and skilful". The archetypal *criollo* player, exemplified by Maradona, is known as *el pibe* ("the young boy"), whose abilities are learned on the *potrero*, a patch of "irregular ground in the city or in the countryside which has not been cemented over" (Archetti 2001: 156). *El pibe* is forgiven personal or public transgressions because of the "joy" he brings (Archetti 2001: 159). Scoring first by cheating England, then scoring again with the "goal of the century", Maradona demonstrated his craftiness, his disrespect for rules and orthodoxies and his "exuberance of skill" and "artistic feeling" (Archetti 2001: 159).

In Archetti's fieldwork, Maradona's Argentine fans repeatedly stressed his "liminal", in-between quality (Archetti 1997: 38) as a *pibe* who has never submitted to the demands of adult masculinity. Hence one typical remark that "he is like our son and we as fathers place our dreams on them (sic)" (quoted in Archetti 2001: 161). In order to make sense of Maradona's appeal in this way, and of the depiction of his devotees in film, I suggest that psychoanalytic perspectives on sport are pertinent.

A key reference point in this respect is Lili Peller's (1954) situating of formal games and sport as the most advanced phase of play in childhood development. Positing that play "alleviates anxiety" (Peller 1954: 179) deriving from internal or external dangers, Peller sees pre-Oedipal play as attempted emulation of maternal control by manipulating objects that the child begins to identify as separate. Oedipal play involves more structured, representational, game-like activities, which enable working through family attachments and fantasies, easing the disappointment of loss (Peller 1954: 187–190).

162   *Marcus Free*

Formally organised games and sports are post-Oedipal, reality-adapted play fostering mutual identification, channelling homosexual urges into teams and observing rules as more significant than victory. These "latency games" represent "independence from external superego figures" (Peller 1954: 191–192). Extending this logic, Barry Richards (1994: 33) argues that soccer's handling taboo, which forces the cultivation of the foot, psychologically and socio-historically contributed to more disciplined social behaviour. By making the foot a means of expression rather than violence or forward propulsion, soccer constitutes a sublimated fusion of Freud's libidinal and aggressive drives, "an image of society . . . with its rituals, its agonistic encounters and above all its taboos and rules" (Richards 1994: 40).

However, as therapeutic observations and analyses of sport and fan biographies have highlighted (Free 2008), involvement in professional sport may facilitate the perpetuation of pre-Oedipal and Oedipal fantasies, especially given sport's systematic reproduction of capitalism's contradiction between promised opportunity and personal development, and alienation and expendability (Ingham *et al.* 1999: 249). The celebration of Maradona's handball goal in Argentina enmeshed both personal and collective Oedipal pleasure in his rule-breaking: the 'liminal', man-child *pibe* versus the game's originators, Argentina's former military foe. As for the second goal, he played as though unaware that it is wiser to pass for fear of losing the ball, combining a breathtaking image of pre-Oedipal exuberance with brilliant adherence to football's foundational handling taboo as the ball seemed almost attached to his left foot.

Indeed, Maradona's affinity with the ball is reminiscent of Donald Winnicott's (1971: 1–34) psychoanalytic concept of the "transitional object", the blanket or toy to which many pre-Oedipal infants attach themselves, and which facilitates transition from maternal dependence to independence as an 'in-between', magical object imagined as neither 'me' nor 'not-me', neither found nor created. The football belongs to the game of football, but at the feet of unique talents like Maradona it is like an imaginative extension of the individual body rather than a neutral, inanimate object. Compilations of moments of brilliance by such players are made, circulated and celebrated via such electronic means as YouTube, because they seem to transcend the spatio-temporal boundaries of individual games and the game of football itself.

Archetti (2001: 159) highlights another feature of the myth of Maradona as quintessential *pibe*: his "capacity to 'die', metaphorically", through imprisonment or drug addiction, "and be resurrected", to return (through irrepressible creativity rather than his expressing guilt and serving his punishment), and so to be forgiven for any moral and social transgressions. Calls for Maradona's return in 1994 were informed by belief in this capacity following his 1991 ban. Yet so strange was the mix of Maradona's exuberance at the tournament, his wild scream at the camera following a goal against Greece, and his visibly emaciated features following rapid pre-tournament weight loss, that

Psychodynamics of football fandom   163

his tragic downfall suggests something else at work in his psyche. He claimed that his trainer Daniel Cerrini gave him an over-the-counter, legal diet formula at the 1994 World Cup (USA 1994) that (unknown to Maradona) contained ephedrine, whose detection in a post-match drug test precipitated his immediate expulsion and 15-month ban from football. However, Maradona's acceptance of Cerrini's "weight reduction and energy-giving drugs" (Burns 2010: 222) seems to have been extraordinarily naïve. He later remarked that he had "risked so much this time round" to be there and that what FIFA "did to me is to make money from blood" (Maradona *et al.* 2000: 222). This suggests a combination of unconscious and conscious motivation, as well as an intimation of the dire consequences that he would melodramatically depict at the ensuing press conference as his martyrdom: "they've cut my legs off". As explored in *Maradona by Kusturica* (see below), there is a possibility that there was unconscious masochism at work here, or at least that we can speculate as to its presence as a motivating force.

It is possible, of course, to read this romantically from a nationalist perspective. Established in Argentina in 1998, the 'Church of Maradona' merges this symbolism in its profanation of the Christian narrative, venerating Maradona's Christ-like suffering for Argentine football with a football crowned with thorns. It initiates its members through re-enactment of the 'hand' goal. Members chant, "He was crucified, killed and tortured . . . They cut his legs but he returned and his magic spell was reborn" (Franklin 2008). This profanation of Christian belief is congruent with the "cultures of devotion" in Argentina to such "folk saint" martyrs as Antonio Mamerto Gil Núñez ("Gaucho Gil"), a nineteenth-century outlaw brutally executed without trial. These figures' reported suffering and miraculous interventions following death elevate them to "saint" status in Latin America, despite Church disapproval (Graziano 2007: 113), and they are the popular cultural context in Argentina for the creation of the Church of Maradona.

Key to the Christian narrative is Christ's masochistic suffering for the sins of humanity. Freud (1985 [1913]: 216) famously read the Crucifixion narrative as symbolic atonement for the guilt of replacing a father-worshipping religion with Christianity and its worship of the son. Through death and resurrection, Christ both replaces and is identified with God. The Church of Maradona's popular narrative of his serial falls and resurrections promotes the Christ-like imagery of his suffering for the transcendent 'truth' of Argentine football and the romance of his unique skills: he suffered for his questioning of the unfair exercise of power in football, his highlighting, through his supreme skill, its cynical culture of foul play, and by relentlessly pushing himself, with or without drugs, knowingly or with denial.

Arguably, though, Maradona's suffering also helped affirm the legitimacy of the nation as a natural political unit, such that each citizen is first and foremost Argentine despite internal material differences. If his was a patriotism driven from below, it served whoever was in power – even the military junta when he led Argentina to the Youth World Cup in 1979.

164   *Marcus Free*

Moreover, for all his supposed radicalism, like Jesus' ultimate identification with God the Father, Maradona's elevation through suffering affirms the post-Oedipal power of football's rules: in his farewell speech to supporters of Boca Juniors at the Bombonera Stadium (10 November 2001) he said, "If someone makes a mistake, football shouldn't pay for it. I made a mistake and I paid, but the ball doesn't get dirty". Yet, like the folk saints, where there is a logical connection between Christ-like human suffering, redemption and a sense of divine justice that exceeds the temporality and brutality of political power, for his fans Maradona's suffering is romantically associated with a truth that transcends both the motives of corrupt political manipulation and the game's governance. If he was punished for pushing himself too hard to play in 1994, through divine intervention (the 'hand of God') he was assisted and spared punishment for the handball goal in 1986.

Such is Maradona's ambiguity that a further possible reading is that he succumbed to a misguided, destructively narcissistic and bogus 'self'-belief. The Italian/Argentine co-produced 'biopic' *Maradona, la Mano di Dio/la Mano de Dios* (Risi 2007) explores this interpretation, offering a variation on the "celebration, punishment, redemption" narrative of many sporting heroes (Whannel 2002: 145–158), but with a cyclical, repetitive structure. Maradona is shown here to identify with his mediatised myth, but to his detriment, as the film chronicles the impact of his drug excess and latterly his chronic weight gain. In a key scene, based on a childhood event (Burns 2010: 10), there is a dissolve from a flashback, in which young Diego searches for a ball in a cesspit (the flashbacks recur, with Diego ultimately retrieving the ball), to his snorting cocaine from a silver plate while a player at Barcelona. The ball as transitional object is replaced by the cocaine as a form of what Joyce McDougall (1985: 87) called a "pathological transitional object". The pathological transitional object is typically a drug imagined as a source of apparent succour, but that is actually poisonous. Reflected in the silver plate we see his drug dealer's reflection, not Maradona's, a suggestion that he has lost his true identity through the bogus narcissism of celebrity. The romantic image of the *pibe*'s magical attachment to the ball as a quasi-Winnicottian transitional object is connected to a scatological image of immersion in, and emergence from, the shit of poverty that is contrasted with later alienation from the inner child. Maradona's cocaine perpetuates a dangerously bogus narcissism in which he identifies either with the image of himself as a combination of exalted star and tradable commodity, or a false self in the faces of drug dealers, the Camorra (while at Napoli), or agent and fellow cocaine user Guillermo Coppola, whom he kisses on the lips at his wedding. This tragedy of the pathological transitional object replacing the real transitional object, bogus versus healthy narcissistic self-belief, is introduced at the film's outset when, gesturing towards Pablo Neruda's (2001 [1974]) 'Where is the child I was?', the bloated Maradona collapses, unable to sustain a keepy-uppy routine with an orange.

Psychodynamics of football fandom 165

This lament can be read as a fan fantasy concerning the tragedy of the commodification of sport's finest talents. Fuelled by cocaine, Maradona's progressive identification with his commodified image impedes his maturation. When his wife Claudia leaves him following her discovery of his brothel visits, he declares "I am Maradona!" and breaks his family picture frames, echoing an earlier scene where, standing on his sports car in Barcelona, he invites Claudia to join him in a chant of "Marado". Narcissistic identification with his commodified image as a celebrity is depicted as alienation from his increasingly unknowable true self. It remains a fetish that, ironically, he cannot de-fetishise: he is the magical object, rather than a fully human subject.

Paul Willis (2000: 55) argues that cultural commodities have a specific quality of usefulness pertaining to their "actual or potential cultural meaningfulness". They invite usage, seek communication by reminding us of the "embedded expressive labour" in them (Willis 2000: 55). Therefore they are doubly half-formed (Willis 2000: 47–66), each side vying with the other: commodity fetishism, the need to be sold as an object disconnected from production history and circulated widely, versus the need to be usable in acts of consumption that personalise or collectivise ascribed meanings in specific contexts (Willis 2000: 58). However, athletes whose labour power is commodified and who are constantly subjected to scrutiny by employers, officials and fans alike may – seemingly paradoxically – be in thrall to their commodified image. *La Mano de Dios* suggests that Maradona could not transform his exchange value as a commodity into use value as a man. The point is wryly conveyed when, hugely overweight and physically restrained in a sanatorium following his 2004 collapse, he remarks that while fellow patients' delusional fantasies are mutually reinforced, "I say I am Maradona, and nobody believes me".

Yet the film's conclusion with young Diego's retrieval of the ball from the cesspit reiterates the theme of healthy individuation through play with the real transitional object. While he can re-emerge from the undifferentiated shit of impoverished Villa Fiorito, Maradona sinks through the bogus narcissistic self-regard and reliance on pathological transitional objects served on the silver-plated but shitty world of elite celebrity. (The slang terms 'shit' for drugs and 'coke shit', signifying the laxative effects of cocaine, come to mind.) Maradona's self-destructiveness has nothing to do with Christ-like suffering at the hands of FIFA and so on, and the film has no interest in his political affiliations or manipulation. The ball that 'doesn't get dirty' here is the one that the enduring Diego within has made an extension of himself.

La Mano de Dios is thus a form of fan text that reiterates, even while highlighting its tragedy, the myth of Maradona. Along with the films discussed below, it illustrates how Maradona is a vehicle for externalising and playing with a core psychodynamic fantasy concerning the tension between submission to football's post-Oedipal discipline and the indulgence of pre-Oedipal nostalgia and Oedipal resistance to it.

166 *Marcus Free*

Following Matt Hills' (2002) reading of Winnicott (1971), I take the 'object relations' psychoanalytic position that cultural fandom opens a 'potential space' of playful psychic engagement with objects of fandom that are themselves imagined as anomalous, neither 'me' nor 'not-me', intermediate, transitional objects onto which idealising, denigrating or ambivalent fantasies can be projected. Because sport as commodity is 'produced' while in progress, and because sport contests unfold unpredictably and are influenced to unquantifiable degrees by vocally and corporeally expressed emotional support, there is a sense that it somehow contains part of the self as a supporter. This also explains such phenomena as one of Archetti's (2001: 160) informants fantasising about asking Maradona for 'mercy' for his unreasonable expectations of him, and his (consequently?) disastrous return to football in 1994. However, sport can never be materially owned. By both enabling and frustrating fans' fantasies, it is an object of ambivalence on to which idealising and destructive fantasies may be safely projected and in which they may be held. Fandom often involves symbolic investments in particular sporting heroes and teams involving complex relationships with the fan's biographical background, and indeed may be a central element in the retrospective tracing of a logical biographical narrative.

Maradona may be a particular object of fan investment, fascination and frustration because of his combination of untrained, supreme skill, a self-destructiveness that may be inexplicably innate (or masochistic, or a symptom of an exalted social status simultaneously empowering and alienating) and an ability to 'resurrect' himself through (as *La Mano de Dios* implies) the endurance of the child within, the arrested development and arresting image of the liminal *pibe*.

In the Hands of the Gods? Or the world at their feet?

The British documentary *In the Hands of the Gods* chronicles the journey to Buenos Aires of five British fans to meet Maradona, funding their trip from London via the United States, then Central and South America, by blagging flights and raising money for accommodation and transport through freestyle football street performances. Varying the reality-TV format of an assembled group faced with the challenge of cooperation and bonding, but with the inevitability of personal differences, the documentary focuses on their self-validation through individual and collective investment in Maradona as a symbolic figure.[1] The three who succeed in meeting Maradona, albeit very briefly, dominate the film: Woody, a failed apprentice professional footballer turned freestyler; Sami, a Somali Civil War refugee living homeless and estranged from his mother following a record of juvenile crime; and Mikey, whose two closest friends have died in accidents, the emotional impact of which, he explains, was that he considered quitting freestyle football altogether. For all, the 'search for Maradona' becomes a symbolic vehicle for self-renewal as they move geographically and psychically towards him.

Given the geographical, cultural and personal differences of its protagonists, the film illustrates how Maradona's meaning as a celebrity articulates with local – and, in Sami's case, complex – biographical vicissitudes. Yet contextual details pertaining to their biographies, or Maradona's nationality or footballing career, are largely absent. The political history is registered only through a shot of a sign in Buenos Aires reading 'Los Malvinas son Argentinos'. Thus, while the title refers obliquely to the handball goal and to Maradona's God-like status as their inspiration, it is perhaps best situated within the context of a series of British films dating from the 1990s, which offered "a certain utopianism about the possibilities of collective action . . . in the face of economic adversity and social decay" (Hill 2000: 183). Most famously, in *The Full Monty* (1997), corporeal performance is key to the recovery of masculine identity, and so to coping with industrial decay and unemployment. Here, however, the freestylers embody a distinctly twenty-first-century neoliberal logic of individual self-empowerment as the antidote to unemployment and welfare dependence (Cruikshank 1999). Freestyle football's elaborate ball manoeuvres, individualistic non-contact nature and focus on the imagery and aesthetics of body movement distinguish it from team football's emphasis on physical strength, collective endeavour and domination of opponents. It was popularised by Nike advertising campaigns and subsequent competitions in the 2000s (www.freestylefootball.org).

Significantly, though, their varied identity projects do not involve movement towards an older paternal ideal. Through their idealising of Maradona without reference to his international football career, the film individualises, depoliticises and rejuvenates him, but Maradona becomes both a tacit symbol of separation from the patriarchal discipline of team football and of asocial individuation through the ball as a kind of transitional object to which, like Maradona, each is inextricably attached. Indeed, Woody describes watching an old video every night "without fail", of Maradona performing tricks with pieces of fruit, a feat he emulates at a Guatemalan market, suggesting that it is with Maradona's perpetual boyishness that he identifies. The tape is like a secondary transitional object comparable to the football itself, while dispensability of the football (the object) signifies the dispensability of football (the game) as the organised team sport that failed him.

The film chronicles their arrival in New York and migration southwards, splitting into two groups in Mexico, and splitting again when Mikey decides to perform solo and fund his own journey, so highlighting the tensions between collective solidarity and the freestyler's individualistic, somewhat narcissistic, motivation. Describing himself as "the best freestyler" through his "flair, confidence, personality and performance", and the prime exemplar of the film's neoliberal theme of self-empowerment in his use of the camera as diary, Mikey justifies his decision rather self-righteously:

168   *Marcus Free*

> Why do I keep saying "on my own"? Because I want it to be on my own . . . You make big decisions in life and this is how I'm gonna mature, this is the biggest decision I'm gonna have to ever make and I've decided.

As Mikey illustrates, such documentaries provide a frame within which, responding to the camera's presence, their participants perform and refine their individual and collective identities. Both the documentary and its protagonists' fantasies are informed by existing, heavily mediated narratives so that, although only appearing briefly for photographs, Maradona confirms the fantasies informing their expectations. Their thoughts, as expressed to each other and to the camera, exemplified by Mikey and Sami (below), are increasingly self-monitoring, indicating the framing, constructive role of its presence as symbolic Other. As Bruzzi (2006: 10) argues, the "collision between [camera] apparatus and subject are what constitutes . . . [documentaries as] . . . performative acts whose truth comes into being only at the moment of filming".

Sami's reflexive commentary on his biographical experiences is the most intriguing of these performative acts. Phoning home, he learns that his parole officer has informed his mother of the journey, intimating, "My Mum knows who Maradona is" and "I want her to think I'm trying . . . but it's hard when I'm trying to talk to her through a letter-box. I know what I've got to do now". This performative self-reinvention leads to what, in Kleinian psychoanalytic terms, is depressive anxiety concerning the damage he has caused his mother and the desire for symbolic reparation. Melanie Klein's psychoanalysis derived from the study of the pre-Oedipal infant's ambivalent relationship with the mother or primary carer, and the individuation of identity and capacity for empathy and sociality via the working through of this ambivalence. The "depressive position" was her term for the progression from psychic splitting of the mother into 'good' and 'bad' 'part-objects' towards the experience of guilt and desire for 'reparation' (Klein 1975 [1935]: 262–289). Describing his mother's heroic efforts to protect him in the war, Sami remorsefully reflects, "I make out like she's the baddie, but I'm realising it's me". Movingly, when generously accommodated by a visibly poor Guatemalan family, he recalls his own family's comparable poverty and maternal protection: "I remember the day the Civil War broke out . . . Bullets ricocheting off the walls and Mum dragging me, and everything after that's just blacked out . . . I'll always love [her because] she risked herself, her life for me to be here".

Sami's pilgrimage thus results in imagined reparation of this maternal bond through his capacity to recall their shared trauma. His individualistic blaming of himself without reference to his criminality as a possible legacy of this trauma, and his seeking to impress his mother by proving his independence, connects with the others' individualistic performative investment in Maradona as a symbolic figure. However, his theme of maternal recovery illustrates the absence from the documentary of older male 'authority' figures. Having told the others, "I haven't got an idol, I haven't got a father figure. Hell, I haven't even got a mother", for him the pilgrimage opens up a Winnicottian 'potential space' (Winnicott 1971: 135) of playful possibility, of imagined reunion with his mother – not the discovery of Maradona as a father figure.

The varied fantasies of self-discovery depend on some shared sense of Maradona's validation of retreat from the post-Oedipal world of football and refusal of sport's inculcation of 'conditional self-worth' (Messner 1992) and expendability among players, like Woody, discarded by it. The eventual encounter with Maradona is secured following Woody's emotional plea via Argentine national television as their journey makes the news there. However, the reason for Woody's identification with Maradona remains obscurely psychological rather than social: "When I was a kid I was inspired by your skill and talent. My education was as hard as yours was and that's why I identify with you. Watching videos of you gave me hope in my football". 'Education' here presumably refers principally to acquiring technical skills, but possibly also the premature end of his professional football career. Meeting Maradona would presumably validate the fantasied Maradona and Woody's post-football-career identity as a freestyler. Indeed, Woody is clearly emotionally overwhelmed when they meet, but the brief encounter seems merely a bonus to an already achieved self-validation through the extraordinary journey. Geographical and psychical progression seems to entail the validation of their creative regression, through freestyling, to the moment before life 'went wrong', to the recovery of a lost boyhood represented by identification with Maradona as an individual abstracted from national identities.

Road to nowhere?

Somewhat surprisingly, Carlos Sorín's *El Camino de San Diego* offers a far more ambivalent representation of its fictional Argentine fan's devotion to Maradona. Although the film is ostensibly a post-crisis feel-good movie, Sorín depicts his fan protagonist's obsession as rooted in a hollow promise of narcissistic self-fulfilment rather than as source of individual and collective redemption.

Despite Argentina's economic crisis since the mid-1990s, the Argentine film industry has had both commercial and critical success. 'New Argentine' film-makers have been classified either as 'industrial auteurs' (Fabien Bielinsky, Juan José Campanella and Marcelo Pineyro) whose work has received transnational funding and been feted through film festivals and awards; or as 'independents' (Lucrecia Martel, Pablo Trapero, Adrian Caetano, Martin Rejtman, Lisandro Alonso and so on) (Falicov 2007: 142), restricted more to the art-house circuits. All have variously engaged with the impact of the economic crisis, which, as Page (2009: 211) remarks,

170   Marcus Free

"shatter[ed] the illusion of 'Argentine exceptionality'" in Latin America, the notion that poverty was merely transitory. Despite thematic, formal and stylistic variation, their work shares an Italian neo-realist aesthetic in their use of actual locations, non-professional actors and simple shooting techniques (Page 2009: 34).

Belonging to neither grouping, Carlos Sorín is largely ignored by critics despite his international successes, *Historias mínimas* (2002) and *Bombón, el perro* (2004). Aguilar (2008: 16) dismisses his continuation of earlier Argentine cinematic tendencies towards 'political imperative (what to do)' and 'identitarian imperative (what we are like)' eschewed by the newer emphasis on spectator 'interpretive responsibility'. However, in *El Camino*, Sorín uses its subject's symbolism to highlight the contradictions of post-crisis Argentina, continuing his earlier films' deconstruction of the countryside as "an ambivalent space, criss-crossed by contesting paradigms of nationalism and modernization . . . where the contradictions of Argentine modernization and the inequalities of global capital are most clearly seen" (Page 2009: 120).

Set initially in the tropical northern province of Misiones, adjacent to Corrientes – from where Maradona's family originated (Burns 2010) – it opens as a pseudo-retrospective documentary. Over flashbacks, fellow villagers recall tree feller Tati Benitez, obsessed with Maradona to the extent of permanently wearing his replica shirt, having a number 10 tattooed on his back and training two pet parrots to say 'Marado'. The opening interview montage also features humour at Tati's expense, when it emerges that his autographed Maradona photograph is only a copy. After losing his job, Tati sees a tree root that, in a case of pareidolia (the imagining of a pattern or meaning that does not objectively exist), he believes resembles Maradona with outstretched arms. Hearing that Maradona is ill, he decides to bring the root to Buenos Aires as a gift.

El Camino repeatedly and deliberately foregrounds its religious symbolism. The title is a pun on Spain's 'El Camino de Santiago de Compostela', signifying the quasi-religious status of Tati's pilgrimage. The tree root resembles both a Maradona goal celebration and Christ's cruciform shape, suggesting – symbolically – Maradona's martyrdom. En route, Tati visits the shrine of Gaucho Gil, whose religious intertextuality is further extended when Brazilian truck driver, Waguinho (who gives Tati a lift), reveals a miniature Virgin of Itatí, a reputedly miraculous wooden statue in Corrientes.

Like Winnicott's transitional object, the root's status for the childlike Tati is ambiguous: did he find it or somehow make it by wishing it to appear? As he journeys, he changes his story, variously describing it to others as a root, a statue he is sculpting and a statue commissioned by Boca Juniors, so in fantasy elevating his status as worker and artist.

This inconsistency suggests a subtext contrary to the outwardly simplistic narrative. Tati finds in Maradona a mirror of his own narcissistic identification with his image, only ever seeing the real Maradona on television, thus as indirectly as the copied autograph, and it is visually suggested that this narcissism and misrecognition are shared. In a shot of a bus driver's rear-mirror reflection as he talks to Tati, beside it is a Maradona picture featuring the word 'dios' spelt with the number 10 ('D10S'), and a miniature Virgin of Itatí. Reflection, photograph and Virgin image ("Itatí" resembles Tati) combine to highlight Tati's narcissistic misrecognition. Just as Maradona has apparently learned nothing (a television news bulletin shows him discharging himself from hospital to play golf), Tati's pilgrimage is hardly enlightening. Indeed, unlike the Greek mythological figure Narcissus, who is captivated by his own image, Tati perhaps resembles more directly his pet parrots in their refrain of 'Marado, Marado'. If Maradona is a misguided Narcissus, withering through his enthrallment by his own celebrity image and his mythical powers of recovery, Tati is closer to Echo, cursed to repeat the words of others and to suffer unrequited love for Narcissus. When Tati finally presents the statue at Maradona's country club, it is uncertain that Maradona will ever see it.

Sorín's film thus seems torn between a celebration of national integration and uplift through Maradona as symbolic of resurrection and a more pessimistic vision. The Maradona root proves economically valuable only to Waguinho. Swaying a group of redundancy-threatened tannery workers to allow him through their roadblock with his truckload of chicks by lying that it is a Boca Juniors' commission, he saves the chicks that will fuel one economy as another dies. Their Brazilian origin is a reminder of the South American (Mercosur) Free Trade Agreement, while the roadblock typifies this method of popular resistance to the "violence of neo-liberal stability" (Dinerstein 2001: 1) in the 2000s.

Ironically, then, the only Argentine film depicts the psychodynamics of fandom rather pessimistically. Meta-filmically, Sorín's irony is symptomatic of his characteristic attempts "to 'resolve' a historical divide" between Argentine independent and commercial cinema (Page 2009: 124), acknowledging Maradona's 'neo-religiosity' (Salazar-Sutil 2008: 445) while simultaneously deconstructing the mythical promise of quasi-Christian redemption, using the road-movie genre to highlight the non-integration of national space. If *In the Hands* suggests that the freestylers are discovering the truth of their abilities and identities (and the neoliberal promise of freedom through heightened individuation) on their journey, *El Camino*'s is a fractured, contradictory road to fantasied national recovery.

Fandom as reflexive mirroring

Maradona by Kusturica (2008) more optimistically explores Maradona's notionally Christ-like symbolism as a potentially redemptive, revolutionary figure for the geopolitical South. But in doing so, Bosnian-born film director, Emir Kusturica, reflexively explores his own narcissistic identification with Maradona, so extending his filmic themes of extremely marginal figures as anti-heroes (Gocic 2001: 53) and of harmony in dissonance (Iordanova 2002).

172   *Marcus Free*

Following his major breakthrough film, *When Father was Away on Business* (1985), Kusturica has pursued a more flamboyantly visual style, exemplified by *Underground* (1995), a richly metaphorical epic chronicling of Yugoslavia from WWII through to the 1990s Balkan wars, and *Time of the Gypsies* (1989), which first established his baroque style of visual and aural excess and his recourse to magical realism (Iordanova 2002: 98). Iordanova (2002: 97) describes him as a "post-modern" artist who "plays with the beautiful and the ugly, the sublime and the despicable, the comic and the tragic . . . in a constantly changing interplay of mutual recreation".

Maradona by Kusturica was more of an authored cinematic portrait exploring Kusturica's fascination with Maradona than a conventional documentary, stylistically exhibiting his trademark characteristics of carnival excess and dense texture. He establishes Maradona as an enigmatic figure eluding description, interpretation and prediction, embodying both irrepressible vitality in his play and seemingly unconscious self-destructiveness in his cocaine abuse. For Kusturica, Maradona is a postmodern both/and, rather than either/or, an intriguing contradiction. But as with the other films, it is in Maradona's representation of pre-Oedipal immaturity that Kusturica is most invested as a fan, echoing his depiction of the permanently migrant and ahistorical gypsies of *Time of the Gypsies* (1988) and *Black Cat, White Cat* (1998).

He introduces the search for Maradona's elusive meaning by quoting Baudelaire's *Fusées* (1867): "God is the only being who, in order to reign, doesn't even need to exist". Like God, the magical object of fan fantasies exists in the worshipper's imagination. As the quote appears, Kusturica introduces his own fantasied version of Maradona with his electric-guitar rendition of Ennio Morricone's theme from Sergio Leone's spaghetti western *The Good, the Bad and the Ugly*, performed in Buenos Aires with the band Zabranjeno Pusenje (No Smoking) (Iordanova 2002: 6). The juxtaposition additionally signals the profound profanity of Maradona's deity, reminding us of the gaucho, and of the film's Mexican-border setting. Leone subverted Western-movie convention in brutally depicting the American Civil War's North-South conflict, highlighting how "the true history of the United States was constructed on a violence which neither literature nor the cinema had ever properly shown" (quoted in Frayling 2000: 205).

This invoking of a North-South geopolitical divide connects with a mapping of a geopolitical fantasy of resistance onto Maradona's body. As his second goal against England is shown in replays from various angles, Kusturica comments that "even God himself got involved" here, as "a country heavily in debt to the IMF triumphed over one of the rulers of the world". Verbally referring to the first goal as we see the second, suggests artistic equivalence. Neither hand nor foot acts as designated or expected by the post-Oedipal, paternal, authoritative codification of football. Kusturica's fantasy of pre-Oedipal recovery and Oedipal resistance combined undergoes numerous repetitions, with minor variations, in the periodic animated sequences where Maradona, his photographed face transposed onto a cartoon body bamboozles various elite Westerners (including Margaret Thatcher and George W. Bush) while the Sex Pistols' 'God Save the Queen' is played. This is a distinctly corporeal fantasy of refusal of the post-Oedipal rules of global football and global politics alike.

However, for all that, he is clearly enthralled by his own fantasy. The film constantly reiterates Maradona's enigma and the frustration of Kusturica's project. It shares the repetitive structure of music and of football itself in its multiple cycles of restart, defence and attack, stressing Maradona's transcendence of hierarchical distinctions through his corporeal irreducibility to discursive explanation or translation. Thus, on discovery that Maradona is again seriously ill and cannot be seen, he witnesses a street performance of Argentina's other famous export, the tango, and verbally indulges a favourite theme of his, finding harmony in dissonance (Iordanova 2002: 104). He connects Maradona's vibrant football, revolutionary political alignments, self-destructiveness and miraculous survival with the dance "most obviously suggest[ing] the union between thanatos and eros", Freud's (2001 [1920]) death and life instincts.

Although mixing images of Maradona with Castro and Chávez with interview segments where Maradona elaborates his populist critique of the hegemony of Western neoliberal economics, Kusturica is fascinated most by the seeming paradox of the great beauty of Maradona's play and his history of turning against himself the righteous anger elsewhere directed at the geopolitical elite. Kusturica thus suggests that Maradona may be unconsciously masochistic, echoing Freud's (1984 [1924]) theory of masochism as the eroticisation of the death instinct. He repeatedly shows Church of Maradona processions and ceremonies. Their equation of Maradona's punishment by FIFA with the Crucifixion is evident as a member holds a football that 'represents Diego's sacrifice', followed later by a 'barbed-wire crown' representing 'the pitch, the field, the grounds' where he suffered. Like Jesus' death, Maradona's disastrous return to football in 1994 was voluntary. Combined with his near death due to chronic obesity and his cocaine addiction, Maradona's actions are clearly open to the interpretation of unconscious masochism.

There is a distinct echo here of Christian masochism's implicitly homoerotic dimension, conforming as it does to Freud's pattern of 'erotogenic', 'moral' and 'feminine masochism', whereby love of the father is forcibly renounced through introjection of the paternal superego, but the ego regresses to the anal stage so that the masochistic fantasy of being beaten by the father maintains the homoerotic dimension (Freud 1984 [1924]: 424), the 'negative' Oedipus complex (Freud 1984 [1924]: 372). The masochist, like Christ, is submissively 'feminine', introjecting the morally punitive strictures of the paternal superego. Maradona both submitted to

174   *Marcus Free*

and transgressed the disciplinary codes of football, on and off the field, paying the devastating consequences as spelt out in his own castration metaphor: they "cut my legs off". Maradona indicates this more directly when admitting to identifying with Robert de Niro's sadomasochistic boxer, Jake La Motta, in *Raging Bull* (1980): "He wants to break everything. I want to score goals". Although Maradona equates goals with outwardly directed violence, *Raging Bull* contains many scenes of homoerotic masochism (Grist 2007): to unconsciously seek punishment is to invite the wrath of the symbolic father.

Yet this masochism, whether real or Kusturica's fantasy, co-exists with nostalgia for the pre-Oedipal exuberance of *el pibe*, exemplified by the goals against England. Pursuing this theme in interview, Kusturica unearths a further contradiction. He juxtaposes archive footage showing the brutal outcome of the Malvinas/Falklands War, including wounded soldiers, with the handball goal. Maradona's verbal likening of the goal to stealing "an Englishman's wallet" invokes both pre-Oedipal exuberance and Oedipal resistance. However, as a national representative, by honouring the dead "sent to die by their own country", he both indicts the military junta who dispatched them and invokes the legitimacy of the state, its national boundaries and territorial claims. Thus, he reflects his vulnerability to political manipulation – just as his support of Menem and the remark that Fidel Castro is a "true patriarch with balls on" (Burns 2010: 6) signify a confused populism more than coherent socialist beliefs.

However, Kusturica's romanticisation of Maradona's resistance is foremost, connecting with his recurring theme of the superiority of perpetual immaturity. Hence his inclusion of a favourite trope, the bride, whose marriage typically curtails her youthful vitality and innocence, as in *Underground*'s wedding scene. Here, though, he shows an already married couple's induction into the Church of Maradona, but their mock wedding ceremony signifies an escape back to immaturity as the bride kicks the ball to the groom, who on scoring screams at the camera, emulating Maradona's charging of the television camera during the 1994 World Cup.

Maradona thus has a Christ-like quality in Kusturica's imagination as fan as he, rather like Kusturica's film characters who comically fail to hang themselves, cheats death in cycles of recovery and repeated crisis. Maradona represents a narcissistic, pre-Oedipal, immature part of himself for which he yearns, a fantasy as a way of staging desire for the narcissistic pre-Oedipal, pre-linguistic, corporeal, imaginary 'I'. Hence his introduction on stage by a No Smoking band member as "Diego Armando Maradona from the world of cinema"; dancing with Maradona on stage; and turning away from a mock lesbian tango at a nightclub to watch television replays of Maradona's goals, an acknowledgement of the homoerotic attraction in football, perhaps, made legitimate through narcissistic 'doubling' with an imaginary mirror image.

Conclusion

While the three films variously address Maradona's symbolism, only *Maradona by Kusturica* engages critically and reflexively with his contradictions as an Argentine cultural icon, and with his place or places in the imagination of his fans. The depoliticised romanticisation of Maradona in *In the Hands of the Gods* offers a fan fantasy of individual renewal in its imagery of freestylers journeying geographically towards him, but equally, or more importantly, towards a fantasied biographical recovery of a lost boyhood. Sorín uses Maradona's neo-religious iconography as a national hero rhetorically to highlight its opiate distraction from a deeply fractured society in his ostensibly linear road movie. Kusturica's is a decidedly postmodern documentary, as befits Maradona's contradictions: "he was at once the imaginary and the symbolic, he was marginal and he was central, he was strong and he was weak, he was popular and he was the elite" (Bilbija 1995: 205). Unable to establish exactly who Maradona is and what he 'means', Kusturica expresses and lives his ambivalent relationship to those contradictions.

However, despite the variations exhibited here, Maradona is not 'neutrosemic' because all of the films are linked by the themes, in football, and as relentlessly reiterated in Maradona's already textualised biography of cyclical symbolic death and renewal. They also reiterate the romantic notion, however fanciful, of an inspirational corporeal 'truth' in his sporting achievements, irrespective of his failings outside of football. And they evince a nostalgia for a pre-Oedipal exuberance that is contradictorily related to the post-Oedipal, hierarchically governed discipline of football.

Note

1 The film was screened in more UK cinemas, on initial theatrical release, than any British documentary film in UK cinema history. At: www.fulwell73.co.uk/film/hands-of-the-gods.

References

Aguilar, Gonzalo. 2008. *Other Worlds: New Argentine Film*. Basingstoke: Palgrave Macmillan.

Archetti, Eduardo P. 1997. '"And Give Joy to My Heart". Ideology and Emotions in the Argentinian Cult of Maradona'. In Gary Armstrong and Richard Giulianotti (eds.), *Entering the Field: New Perspectives on World Football*, 31–51. Oxford, UK: Berg.

Archetti, Eduardo P. 2001. 'The Spectacle of a Heroic Life: The Case of Diego Maradona'. In David L. Andrews and Steven J. Jackson (eds.), *Sport Stars: The Cultural Politics of Sporting Celebrity*, 151–163. London: Routledge.

Bilbija, Ksenija. 1995. 'Maradona's Left: Postmodernity and National Identity in Argentina'. *Studies in Latin American Popular Culture* 14: 199–208.

176 *Marcus Free*

Bruzzi, Stella. 2006. *New Documentary*. 2nd edition. London: Routledge.

Burns, Jimmy. 2010. *Maradona: The Hand of God*. London: Bloomsbury.

Cabaniss, Deborah L., Sabrina Cherry, Carolyn J. Douglas and Anna R. Schwartz. 2011. *Psychodynamic Psychotherapy: A Clinical Manual*. Oxford, UK: Wiley-Blackwell.

Cooney, Paul. 2007. 'Argentina's Quarter Century Experiment with Neoliberalism: From Dictatorship To Depression'. *Revista de Economia Contemporanea* 11(1): 7–37.

Cruikshank, Barbara. 1999. *The Will to Empower: Democratic Citizens and Other Subjects*. New York: Cornell University Press.

Dinerstein, Ana C. 2001. 'Roadblocks in Argentina: Against the Violence of Stability'. *Capital & Class* 25(2): 1–7.

Falicov, Tamara L. 2007. *The Cinematic Tango: Contemporary Argentine Film*. London: Wallflower.

Franklin, Jonathan. 2008. 'He Was Sent from Above'. *The Guardian*. 12 November.

Frayling, Christopher. 2000. *Sergio Leone: Something to Do With Death*. London: Faber and Faber.

Free, Marcus. 2008. 'Psychoanalytic Perspectives on Sport: A Critical Review'. *International Journal of Applied Psychoanalytic Studies* 5(4): 273–296.

Freud, Sigmund. 1984 [1924]. 'The Ego and The Id'. In Angela Richards (ed.) *Penguin Freud Library*, Volume 11, 339–407. London: Penguin.

Freud, Sigmund. 1984 [1924]. 'The Economic Problem of Masochism'. In Angela Richards (ed.) *Penguin Freud Library*, Volume 11, 409–434. London: Penguin.

Freud, Sigmund. 1985 [1913]. 'Totem and Taboo'. In Angela Richards (ed.) *Penguin Freud Library*, Volume 13, 43–224. London: Penguin.

Freud, Sigmund. 2001 [1920]. 'Beyond the Pleasure Principle'. In James Strachey (ed.) *Standard Edition of the Complete Psychological Works of Sigmund Freud*, Volume XVIII, 3–64. London: Vintage.

Gocic, Goran. 2001. *Notes from the Underground: The Cinema of Emir Kusturica*. London: Wallflower.

Graziano, Frank. 2007. *Cultures of Devotion: Folk Saints of Spanish America*. Oxford, UK: Oxford University Press.

Grist, Leighton. 2007. 'Masculinity, Violence, Resistance: A New Psychoanalytic Reading of *Raging Bull*'. *Atlantis* 29(1): 11–27.

Hill, John. 2000. 'Failure and Utopianism: Representations of the Working Class in British Cinema of the 1990s'. In Robert Murphy (ed.), *British Cinema of the 90s*, 178–187. London: BFI.

Hills, Matt. 2002. *Fan Cultures*. London: Routledge.

Ingham, Alan G., Bryan J. Blissmer and Kristen Wells Davidson. 1999. 'The Expendable Prolympic Self: Going Beyond the Boundaries of the Sociology and Psychology of Sport'. *Sociology of Sport Journal* 16: 236–268.

Iordanova, Dina. 2002. *Emir Kusturica*. London: British Film Institute.

Klein, Melanie. 1975 [1935]. 'A Contribution to the Psychogenesis of Manic-Depressive States'. In R.E. Money-Kyrle (ed.), *Love, Guilt and Reparation, and Other Works*, 262–289. New York: The Free Press.

Maradona, Diego, Daniel Arcucci and Ernesto Cherquis Bialo. 2000. *El Diego: Diego Maradona, The Autobiography of the World's Greatest Footballer*. London: Yellow Jersey Press.

McDougall, Joyce. 1985. *Theatres of the Mind: Illusion and Truth on the Psychoanalytic Stage*. New York: Basic Books.

Messner, Michael A. 1992. *Power at Play*. Boston, MA: Beacon.

Neruda, Pablo. 2001 [1974]. *The Book of Questions*. Washington, DC: Copper Canyon Press.

Page, Joanna. 2009. *Crisis and Capitalism in Contemporary Argentine Cinema*. Durham, NC: Duke University Press.

Peller, Lili E. 1954. 'Libidinal Phases, Ego Development, and Play'. *Psychoanalytic Study of the Child* 91: 178–198.

Richards, Barry. 1994. *Disciplines of Delight: The Psychoanalysis of Popular Culture*. London: Free Association Books.

Salazar-Sutil, Nicolas. 2008. 'Maradona Inc: Performance Politics Off the Pitch'. *International Journal of Cultural Studies* 11: 441–458.

Sandvoss, Cornel. 2005. *Fans: The Mirror of Consumption*. Cambridge, UK: Polity.

Tobin, Jeffrey. 2002. 'Soccer Conspiracies: Maradona, the CIA, and Popular Critique'. In Joseph L. Arbena and David Gerald LaFrance (eds.), *Sport in Latin America and the Caribbean*, 51–73. Wilmington, DE: Scholarly Resources.

Whannel, Garry. 2002. *Media Sport Stars: Masculinities and Moralities*. London: Routledge.

Willis, Paul. 2000. *The Ethnographic Imagination*. Cambridge, UK: Polity.

Winnicott, Donald W. 1971. *Playing and Reality*. London: Tavistock.

Film references

Kusturica, Emir (dir.) 2008. *Maradona by Kusturica*. France/Spain: Pentagrama Films, Telecino Cinema, Wild Bunch, Fidelite Products, Rasta Films.

Risi, Marco (dir.) 2007. *Maradona, la Mano di Dio/ la Mano de Dios*. Italy/ Argentina: Institut del Cinema Catala and Pol-Ka Producciones.

Sorín, Carlos (dir.) 2006. *El Camino de San Diego*. Argentina: 20th Century Fox de Argentina, Guacamole Films, K&S Films, Wanda Vision S.A.

Turner, Benjamin and Gabe Turner (dir.) 2007. *In the Hands of the Gods*. UK: Fulwell 73 and Green Wolf Films.

Part III

Online mediation of invented, fiction-based and hyper-real religions

10 "Discordians stick apart"

The institutional turn within contemporary Discordianism

J. Christian Greer

Introduction

The death of Robert Anton Wilson in 2007 marked a turning point in the new religious movement known as Discordianism. With Wilson's death, Discordianism not only lost its principal interpreter and the last of its original spokespersons but also its most popular evangelist. Wilson's failing health and eventual death fomented a crisis within the religion. Instead of fostering dissolution, though, this crisis catalyzed a major shift in how adherents conceptualize and practice Discordianism. As this chapter will show, the loss of Discordianism's chief theorist set into motion three projects that collectively reoriented the way in which the religion is constituted in the everyday life of its adherents.

In the six decades of its existence, Discordianism has taken on many forms, the most salient of which are surveyed below. Today, however, Discordian activity is predominately composed of participation in institutionalization projects, the central aim of which is the transformation of Discordianism into a religious tradition. These projects are the subject of this chapter. They include: 1) an online educational center based on Wilson's writings called the Maybe Logic Academy; 2) the utilization of the Discordian Archive to write the religion's official history; and 3) a global, ethnographic census of the religion entitled the 'Chasing Eris' project. This chapter argues that mass participation in these institutional structures marks a transformation of the lived experience of Discordianism. Further, it will be demonstrated that the institutionalization of Discordianism has not been a top-down process, but rather a community-wide shift in the practices that constitute Discordianism.

At the outset, it is important to clarify how the term "institutionalization" is used in this chapter, and the way in which contemporary Discordianism's turn towards it represents a novel historical trend. Religious institutionalization concerns the translation, transformation, and standardization of spiritual insights into symbolic and organizational structures (O'Dea and Yinger 1961: 31–33). As will be shown, the three institutionalization projects that define the contemporary era of Discordianism perform these functions,

182   J. Christian Greer

to varying, yet complementary, degrees. Collectively, the three aforementioned projects have created a new interpretative framework through which Discordians understand and practice their religion.

The movement towards institutionalization is unprecedented in the history of Discordianism. The reason for this is that such a move seems to violate one of the primary tenets of the religion, namely, that it remain decentralized. Margot Adler made note of this idiosyncrasy in her groundbreaking study of the religion, "since radical decentralization is a Discordian principle, it is impossible to know how many Discordians there were and are, or what they are doing" (Adler 1986: 331). To this point, the founders of Discordianism coined the slogan "Discordians stick apart" as a means of distinguishing their "disorganized irreligion" from mainstream religions wherein members allegedly "stick together" (Adler 1986: 332; Gorightly 2003: 61). That is to say, no two Discordians were to possess the same conception of Discordianism; the theoretical *sine qua non* of the religion was that each member had to think for him or herself. So as to codify this religious tenet, Discordianism introduced a dialectical pair of religious duties. The first was dubbed project "Pan-Pontification," which was composed of handing out small documents termed "Pope cards" that proclaimed the bearer, as well as every man, woman, and child on Earth, to be "a genuine and authorized Pope" of Discordianism (Gorightly 2014: 116–117; Hill 1979: 36). By appointing everyone on Earth a Pope, Discordianism sought to contest the spurious nature of all religious authority, as well as underscore the inherent sovereignty of the individual. As a counterbalance to this duty, though, Discordians were obliged to routinely excommunicate one another (Thornley 1991: i–xxxiv). Working in tandem, Discordians are constantly being elected and ejected from positions of religious authority; the point being that one is always a Discordian hierarch, yet never hierarchically situated against anyone else. Unlike religious systems that demand behavioral compliance or mental acquiescence, Discordianism was designed to act as an intellectual point of departure for religious self-determination, individual sovereignty, and determined decentralization. Accordingly, making generalized statements on the lived experience of the religion would seem incredibly difficult. However, this is not necessarily the case if we look at the way in which these core Discordian doctrines have been embodied over the course of Discordianism's history.

So as to illustrate the ways in which the process of institutionalization has altered the way in which Discordianism is lived as a religious affiliation, this chapter will begin by providing a brief outline of the religion's historical development. This historical overview is followed by an analysis of the three projects that define the most visible form of Discordian religious activity today, namely, institutionalization. The chapter concludes by examining Discordianism's current status as a new religious movement (for both adherents and scholars) over and against its previous formulations in eras now past.

The periodization of Discordianism

Discordianism has changed dramatically from its inception in the late 1950s. The institutional turn in Discordianism comes after five and a half decades of doctrinal development that took place across a handful of alternative subcultures. While it is beyond the scope of this chapter to go into great depth regarding these developments, the following section will outline the five phases of Discordian history. These phases are distinguished both by the differing media through which Discordianism was transmitted, as well as the ways in which it was performed as an identity.

The first period (1958/59–1967) of Discordianism began with its founding in 1958/1959 by two Californian high school students, Greg Hill (1941–2000) and Kerry Thornley (1938–1998). At the heart of their religion was the metaphysical belief that order and disorder were mental projections on the raw fabric of existence, identified as "chaos." They agreed that every form of order, and likewise all conceptions of disorder, were superficial impositions on the ultimately generative force of chaos, which they understood as the ontological ground of being (Gorightly 2003: 57). Based on this ontology, Hill and Thornley decided that the Greek goddess of discord, Eris (Discordia to the Romans) would be the patron deity of their religious society. Since all ideas and beliefs are merely projections on ontological chaos, no singular model of reality (other than Discordianism's poly-focal approach) can be deemed superior to another. A constitutive element of Discordianism is the belief that conceptions of reality serve only as models through which consciousness manipulates ontological chaos. A later Discordian convention was to discuss reality not in the singular, but in terms of the variety of possible "reality tunnels" (Wilson 1997: ii). One of Discordianism's singular values as an intellectual system is that it does not attempt to replace one conception of reality with another, but rather leads adherents to adopt an agnostic subject position in which beliefs are considered a means to an end, and not an end in themselves. This principle was later deemed "the first law of Discordianism" and stated explicitly as "whatever you believe imprisons you" (Wilson 1997: 62).

By 1963, Thornley and Hill's "non-prophet irreligious disorganization" had gained a handful of members (Gorightly 2003: 60, 2014: 11–80). The earliest form of Discordian practice that they engaged in consisted of writing and re-writing religious tracts that outlined the implications of ontological chaos, and how it was to be honored "irreligiously" within what they had dubbed "The Discordian Society." In 1964, Hill (writing under his Discordian name L&Q. vA. Kallisti, or Malaclypse the Younger) and Thornley (as Lord Omar Khayyam Ravenhurst) began laying the groundwork for the religious edifice of Discordianism through epistolary correspondence (Gorightly 2014: 23). Over the course of the next few years, their exchange grew to include numerous others. While Discordianism did not reach its fullest expression as a mail-order religion until 1968, it was

184   *J. Christian Greer*

during this early period that Hill and Thornley began sending interested seekers self-published Discordian religious texts, "epistles," and ordination certificates. Slowly, a decentralized epistolary network formed, and through it a growing number of independently created Discordian "holy works" were circulated. An integral aspect of this epistolary network was the way in which it compelled those involved to independently write, and autonomously distribute, their own Discordian religious tracts. Thornley and Hill led the way, by breaking with one another so as to form rival Discordian factions. Thornley formed the Erisian Liberation Front (which promoted "Erisianism"), and Hill created the Paratheo-Anametamystikhood of Eris Esoteric, which became synonymous with the religion in the following historical phases (Gorightly 2003: 62).

This first phase drew to an end in 1965, when Hill self-published the *Principia Discordia: How the West Was Lost* in an edition of five. This 55-page compendium drew extensively from the work circulated in the epistolary network. As a capstone for the early movement, the first edition of the *Principia Discordia* laid out the complicated hierarchy of the Discordian Society, as well as a summation of the religion's beliefs (largely filtered through Hill's interpretation of Discordianism) (Gorightly 2003: 19). Taken as a whole, this edition of the *Principia Discordia* offers a vital picture of Discordianism's early period wherein the seriousness of this baroque metaphysical ludibrium is abundantly apparent.

The second period of Discordianism's history (1969–1984) is characterized by its emergence from total obscurity. Robert Anton Wilson's initiation into the religion in 1967 was the principal factor in its popularization and subsequent transformation into a spiritual mode of revolutionary consciousness. Not long after his induction into the religion, Wilson began to devote himself to evangelizing Discordianism in his voluminous literary output. His Discordian writings quickly eclipsed Hill's *Principia Discordia* as being the de facto Discordian scripture. Still, it bears mentioning that, between 1969 and 1970, Hill produced the second, third, and fourth editions of the *Principia* in limited publishing runs.[1]

Upon converting the religion, Wilson concocted a way in which Discordianism could be weaponized. Working in collaboration with Thornley, Wilson dubbed this weaponization as "Operation Mindfuck" (henceforth OM), which was envisioned as a means to destabilize a number of the assumptions that sustain consensus reality. Taking a cue from revolutionary insurrectionists like Ché Guevara, Wilson conceptualized OM as a strategic equivalent of guerilla warfare, albeit purely psychological. In his words, OM was "guerilla ontology" insofar as it was composed of "non-violent anarchist techniques [utilized] to mutate our robotic society" (Wilson 1997: 63). OM was less of an organized stratagem than an open-ended call for Discordians to wage autonomous campaigns of psychological warfare against agents of the status quo. For Thornley, this consisted of disseminating proposition papers concerning the P.U.R.S.E. and P.U.T.Z.

Contemporary Discordianism 185

plans; the former plan, known as the "Permanent Universal Rent Strike Exchange," was premised on creating a mass movement against landlords, whereas the latter, "Permanent Universal Tax Zap," outlined a tax resistance plan (Thornley 1985: 49; Wilson 1997: 63). Wilson, on the other hand, intended his contribution to OM to be far more disquieting (Wilson 1997: 62–63). In sum, he would attempt to revive the centuries old conspiracy of the Illuminati as a means of exacerbating the paranoid political atmosphere of the late 1960s.

Due to his former staff position at Paul Krassner's groundbreaking humor magazine *The Realist*, as well as his more recent position as editor of the *Playboy Forum*, Wilson was able to recruit a number of journalists to his Discordian plot to disseminate misinformation about the Illuminati. As contributors to underground newspapers, these new recruits played an essential role in Wilson's conspiracy: through them he would be able to augment the scale of OM considerably (Wilson 1997: 63). On staff at papers like the *East Village Other*, *The Chicago Seed*, and *rogerSPARK*, Wilson's Discordian co-conspirators (as well as Wilson himself) were able to slip cryptic allusions to the Illuminati, as well as their equally shadowy opponents identified as the Discordian Society, into their respective publications (Wilson 1997: 63; see Figure 10.1). What was more, these enigmatic references were entirely uncoordinated, so that in one publication the Illuminati were accused of being behind all international banking, whereas in another the Discordians were identified as instigating the wave of domestic social unrest that gripped the mid-to-late 1960s (Gorightly 2014: 81–113; Wilson 1997: 92–102, 104–113). Soon, exposés on the Illuminati began to appear in publications that had not been infiltrated by Discordians (Wilson 1997: 64). As far as Wilson was concerned, this proved that his conspiracy had worked: Wilson's claim that the Illuminati were locked in an ancient battle with the Discordians (which can essentially be referred to as 'the Discordian Illuminati thesis') had created a marginal niche in the media ecology of the U.S.

Inspired by the success of his Discordian Illuminati thesis, Wilson set about writing the biggest "mindfuck" possible. Together with Robert Shea, Wilson produced the *summa theologica* of Discordianism, a massive pulp narrative entitled *Illuminatus!* The text was written as a single volume between 1969 and 1971: however, its publication was delayed until 1975, by which point it had undergone major editorial changes. By the time it hit newsstands, not only had nearly 500 pages been cut, but the text itself was broken up into a trilogy of novels. Furthermore, its publisher, Dell, chose to market the trilogy as science fiction, despite there being little in the novels that resembled anything usually associated with the genre.

Spanning over 800 pages and including 14 appendices, *Illuminatus!* presented its readers with the most comprehensive exegesis of Discordianism to date. As an elaboration on the Discordian Illuminati thesis, the labyrinthine plot wove no fewer than five intersecting stories into an overarching narrative concerning the on-going battle between the Illuminati and a number of

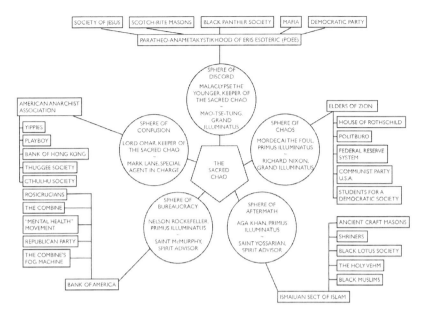

Figure 10.1 Current structure of Bavarian Illuminati conspiracy and the Law of Fives.

This chart was featured in the 4 June 1969 edition of the seminal East coast underground newspaper, the *East Village Other*. Printed without any editorial explanation, this image illustrates the Byzantine logic of the Discordian Illuminati thesis as perpetuated under the auspices of OM. This same image was to appear six years later in Robert Anton Wilson and Robert Shea's *Illuminatus!* trilogy.

independent Discordian cabals. Its sheer size not withstanding, *Illuminatus!* was unlike any Discordian text that preceded it. The first major difference was that, unlike the didactic focus of the *Principia Discordia*, *Illuminatus!* depicted Discordianism as the esoteric counterpart of revolutionary groups like the Weather Underground, the Yippies, and the Up Against the Wall Motherfuckers. This refashioning of the religion entailed fashioning the religion's decentralized, mutualistic structure as an implementation of anarchist philosophy, its promotion of LSD as an expression of Leary's psychedelic philosophy, and ontological chaos in terms of the Dao (Wilson and Shea 1988: 382–384, 406–407, 767–768). Second, the trilogy created a clear picture of how Discordianism could be practiced (as a revolutionary religious orientation) within everyday life. By chronicling the adventures of the novels' Discordia heroes, the authors presented readers with unobstructed views into the thoughts, feelings, and deeds of idealized Discordians. While the four editions of the *Principia Discorida* as well as the "holy works" all outlined the belief system for Discordianism, they never described how to put the beliefs into action. *Illuminatus!* did so adeptly, and in so doing offered sympathetic readers a frame of reference for integrating Discordianism into

Contemporary Discordianism   187

their own lives. Essential to this frame of reference were the practices that Shea and Wilson described as integral to the Discordian way of life. While the theories and practices associated with Aleister Crowley's magick in addition to free love (conceptualized according to the theories of Wilhelm Reich) were both portrayed as central aspects of being a Discordian, the use of psychedelics (e.g., LSD, hashish, and cannabis) stood out as by far the most salient.[2] Following Leary's conceptualization of psychoactive chemicals as spiritual tools, Wilson and Shea portrayed LSD as the "sacrament" of Discordianism (Wilson and Shea 1988: 626). The sacralization of psychedelics within the trilogy integrated Reichean sexual-liberation and Crowley's magick into the religious gestalt of Discordianism, thereby transforming the religion into a vehicle for their determined exploration.

Marketed as science fiction, the *Illuminatus!* trilogy was ignored by the literary establishment of the day. Moreover, it remained marginal in the hermetic subculture that was science fiction fandom at that time. However, as *Illuminatus!* was closer to a Discordian recruitment text than "scienfictional" entertainment, the following it did garner was less a fan-base than a dedicated network of Discordian co-conspirators. The idiosyncrasies of science fiction fandom in the mid- to late 1970s formed an essential part of Discordianism's development, and in order to fully understand its underground popularization, the religion must be contextualized within that heady microcosm. In addition to giving rise to a host of other eccentric religious movements (Adler 1986: 283–318; Cusack 2010: 144–146), science fiction fandom contained an expansive culture of self-publishing in the form of fan magazines, known as "fanzines" or simply "zines" (Bainbridge 1986: 10–11). While *Illuminatus!* was not mentioned in the majority of these publications, the trilogy's admirers steadily produced a small mountain of Discordian periodicals. Indeed, it was the legion of Discordians within science fiction fandom that produced the longest running and most voluminous Discordian publication to date: the *Golden APA*. Running for 24 years (1979–2003) under the editorial direction of Arthur Hlavaty, *The Golden APA* provided a private medium in which the most dedicated Discordians (Wilson and Shea were *ex officio* members and frequent contributors) could extrapolate, contest, and reformulate every aspect of the religion.

In addition to creating *The Golden APA*, Arthur Hlavaty also founded a correspondence club called the Illuminatus! Nut Cult. According to Hlavaty, this was an epistolary, notional organization that consisted of a few dozen Discordians within science fiction fandom "interested in anarchy, magick, self- and drug-abuse, and other unsavory practices" (Hlavaty 2015). Distinct from *The Golden APA*, which was an amateur press association complete with an organizational structure, the Illuminatus Nut Cult was a loose correspondence network dedicated to the exploration of the taboo subjects which Wilson and Shea portrayed as integral to Discordianism (Hlavaty 2015). As the formation of this group makes clear, the trilogy acted as a gateway through which science fiction readers were led to conceptualize

188 *J. Christian Greer*

Discordianism as an intellectual platform for attaining higher states of consciousness through anarchism, magick, and psychedelics. Situated on the margins of science fiction fandom, Discordianism became an intellectual framework for the personal exploration of these taboos.

Towards the end of the 1970s, Discordian fanzines began to attract contributors and readers outside of science fiction fandom, so that by the dawn of the 1980s, Discordianism had distinguished itself as the preeminent psychedelic religion. The trilogy's unapologetic endorsement of the spiritual benefits of psychedelics found a welcome audience within a revitalized psychedelic movement. Few public intellectuals were as vocal in their condemnation of the U.S. government's "War on Drugs" as Wilson, and his criticisms of it effectively cast Discordianism as its ideological foil.[3] While not distinct from the popular conflation of Discordianism and psychedelics, this period also saw the formulation of an explicitly Buddhist interpretation of Discordianism. Initiated by Thornley, this form of Discordianism drew extensively from Zen, psychedelics, and anarchism and was taken up by two notable Discordian authors: Camden Benares (né John Overton), and, years later, Tundra Wind (né Jim Wilson). The literature pertaining to this lesser-known iteration of Discordian thought includes Thornley's *Zenarchy* newsletters (first published in 1968), the subsequent book *Zenarchy* (1991), as well as Benares' *Zen without Zen Masters* (1977) and *A Handful of Zen* (1996). While no less ingenious, Thornley's concept of Discordian Zen, much like Hill's work at this time, was overshadowed by Wilson and Shea's popular formulation of Discordianism.

The third period of Discordianism lasted from 1984 to 1990; it is marked by the ascent of Discordianism within the underground publishing culture known as the "zine scene." By 1984 the custom of making and distributing self-published zines had spread from science fiction fandom to a number political, sexual, and spiritual subcultures, and with it went Discordianism. Unlike science fiction fandom, however, these subcultures actively utilized zines as a means of cross-pollinating with one another (Greer 2013: 170–171). Many of the leading lights of this scene were either Discordian, members of a Discordian off-shoot religion called The Church of the SubGenius, or affiliated with "post-political" programs based on ontological chaos (Black 1994: 3–12, 32, 182–184). One of the most noteworthy figures within the zine scene was Mike Gunderloy, whose participation in science fiction fandom led to his conversion to Discordianism. Gunderloy had been an active contributor to Hlavaty's *The Golden APA* since its inception, and after years of writing for it, he decided to publish his own zine, which he named *Factsheet Five* (Hlavaty 2015). As the first zine dedicated totally to reviewing other zines, *Factsheet Five* quickly became the central clearinghouse for this decentralized milieu. Gunderloy's investment in Discordianism led him to showcase Discordian publications in his zine. Their continued exposure in *Factsheet Five* established the religion as an intellectual and spiritual reference point in the zine scene. The Discordian axiom to "stick apart" conformed perfectly to the epistolary network structure of the zine network, as both the religion and the underground literary milieu were based on decentralized, autonomous communication. Acting as either publishers, writers, or merely interested readers, Discordians of this period lived their religion within this self-published literary underground.

The fourth period of Discordian history (1991–2004) began at the dawn of personal computing, which, incidentally, drove the zine scene into terminal decline. From the early 1990s onwards, former zinesters migrated to BBS (Bulletin Board System) boards and Listservs, carrying their eccentric religious affiliation with them. Relocated to the virtual world of computers, the activities and preoccupations of the zine underground came to be known as "cyberculture." Led by underground publisher and psychedelic aficionado, R.U. Sirius (né Ken Goffman), cyberculture was crafted out of the confluence of a subgenre of science fiction known as cyberpunk, a reemergence of a psychedelic subculture, and computer hacking enthusiasts. Sirius' magazine *Mondo 2000* was the flagship cyberculture publication, and while it was aimed at the general public, it did not attempt to conceal its roots in the zine scene. To this end, *Mondo 2000*, as well as lesser-known cyberculture zines like *bOING bOING* singled out Robert Anton Wilson as being the principle "cyberculture" philosopher (Sirius 2012). From 1990 to 2000, Wilson, along with Terence McKenna and Hakim Bey (né Peter Lamborn Wilson), distinguished themselves as the leading voices of the 1990s underground, which encompassed the rave scene and the "cyberdelic" subculture.

The migration online triggered one of the most significant shifts in Discordian practice to date. In the realm of cyberspace, Operation Mindfuck morphed into hacking. In addition to being an intellectual framework for exploring the intersection of psychedelics, sex, and magick, Discordianism's emphasis on the virtue of creative disorder was a perfect match for the growing number of hackers. In keeping with the original intention of OM, hacking offered Discordian computer enthusiasts an entirely new playing field for creatively disrupting the status quo. Among all of the early Discordian computer hackers, though, one name stands above the rest: Karl Koch (1965–1989). For Koch, the *Illuminatus!* trilogy was revelatory; in homage, he not only adopted the name of the trilogy's protagonist ("Hagbard") as his own, but also named his computer after the artificial intelligence ("FUCKUP") within the novels (Hafner and Markoff 1991: 139–250). In the late 1980s, the names Hagbard and FUCKUP would appear in newspapers worldwide as a result of a Cold War cyber-espionage incident in which Koch played the central part. Over the course of three years (1986–1989), Koch, a German citizen, worked in collaboration with fringe members of the Berlin-based Chaos Computer Club to sell source code hacked from U.S. military computers to the KGB (Stoll 1989). While the international media said little of Koch's religious affiliation, the connection between it and his exploits was clear to the growing international hacking subculture.

190   *J. Christian Greer*

The fifth period of Discordian history (2004–the present) is characterized by the institutionalization of Discordianism. As a consequence of its prominent position in 1990s cyberculture, Discordianism was one of the first religions to establish itself on the Internet, and since its migration to cyberspace, it has enjoyed steady growth (Chidester 2005: 198). Throughout the early 2000s, new Discordian texts were steadily circulated over the Internet; however, their influence all but evaporated with the news that Robert Anton Wilson had become terminally ill. Wilson's declining health, and eventual death, set into motion the latest transformation of Discordianism; after his death, Discordian activity would primarily be oriented in preserving his legacy. The fact that the process of institutionalization is indistinguishable from the creation of Wilson's legacy betrays his status as first among Discordian equals, in addition to the suspicion that he will not be easily replaced. Considering the impossibility of distinguishing between Wilson's work and Discordianism itself, it seems reasonable to suggest that Wilson's death was the primary factor in the shift towards institutionalization.

Maybe logic

Wilson's death in 2007 came at the end of a protracted and painful battle with *post-polio sequelae*. Over the last years of his life, Wilson's infirmed condition galvanized emotional, economic, and spiritual support from the Discordian community he had spent his life fostering. This support reached an apex in the months before his death, when word got out that Wilson was no longer able to afford his medical expenses. Thanks to an internet campaign launched by media theorist Douglas Rushkoff and broadcast by zine-turned-blog *bOING bOING*, Wilson received over $60,000 in donations in just over three days (Davis 2015: 335). The event's success was both a reflection of Wilson's historical influence on Discordianism, as well as a portent for things to come.

An audio retrospective of Wilson's life and work, entitled *Robert Anton Wilson Explains Everything* (2001), signaled the transition into the fifth period of Discordian history. Totaling over six hours of interview material, this project offered listeners an autobiographical account of Wilson's intellectual, spiritual, and political preoccupations. While the audio retrospective marked the first attempt to preserve Wilson's legacy, it certainly would not be the last. The most significant follow-up was a documentary directed by Lance Bauscher entitled *Maybe Logic: The Lives and Ideas of Robert Anton Wilson* (2003). Whereas the audio retrospective presented Wilson's wide-ranging intellect in his own words, Bauscher's documentary put forth a thesis regarding Wilson's stature within Discordianism. Crafting together over 20 years of footage, *Maybe Logic* made the case that Wilson had achieved an uncommon level of spiritual understanding, and that it was his formidable intellect that guided the development of Discordianism. The release of Bauscher's documentary represents a key moment in the formation of the knowledge culture of contemporary Discordianism. Unlike the editions of the *Principia Discordia*, *Zenarchy*, or *Illuminatus!*, which explicated various aspects of Discordian thought, *Maybe Logic* was an emic meta-text on the Discordian movement *as such*. More specifically, the documentary was not an exposition of Discordian thought, but an attempt to portray Robert Anton Wilson's personal philosophy as the embodiment of Discordianism. The transformation of Wilson into a symbol opened up a new vector of Discordian identity and practice; in a word, it began the process of institutionalization in which a standardized Discordian knowledge culture is established in symbolic and organizational structures.

In the process of collecting interviews for the *Maybe Logic* film, it became evident that Wilson's community of supporters included a number of influential esotericists and cultural critics. Sensing an opportunity for collaboration, Bauscher and Wilson spent the year following the documentary's debut organizing an online community and education center dubbed the Maybe Logic Academy (Anon. The Maybe Logic Academy, n.d.). The Maybe Logic Academy opened its (virtual) doors on 23 April 2004, a day that the mayor of Santa Cruz had christened "Robert Anton Wilson Day" a year earlier. Space limitations prevent going into any depth with regard to the academy's varied curriculum, publications, and international events; nevertheless, it is important to stress the continuity between Bauscher's documentary, the creation of Robert Anton Wilson Day, and the formation of the Maybe Logic Academy. Collectively, they indicate a movement within Discordianism towards building an institutional narrative with Wilson as the primary protagonist.

Over 9 years, the Maybe Logic Academy enrolled over 2,000 students in more than 50 courses, thereby becoming the most visible online center for the study of esotericism (Moore 2008). The faculty roster stands as a "who's who" of modern esotericism: R.U. Sirius; the founder of The Church of the SubGenius Ivan Stang; the co-founder of Chaos Magick, Peter Carroll; and the United States Deputy Grand Master of the Ordo Templi Orientis, Lon DuQuette, feature among others. Though the course offerings ran the gamut from Starhawk's courses on ecological feminist Neopaganism to Mark Pesce's class on the open-source digital landscape, each ostensibly honored Wilson's work as foundational; indeed, nearly half the courses offered were either taught by him or based on his work.

The chance to virtually interact with the spiritual patriarch of Discordianism made the academy the first epicenter for international Discordian activity. And as Discordians from around the world began to interact within the academy, the nature of what was considered conventional Discordian practice changed: Discordian activity became centralized in online classrooms devoted to Wilson's writings. The education-based Discordian community that formed around the Maybe Logic Academy quickly became the most visible representative of the religion, and through its efforts, the groundwork of Discordianism's institutionalization was laid.

192   *J. Christian Greer*

Historia Discordia

In 2009, the self-proclaimed "crackpot historian," Adam Gorightly, established the Discordian Archive. The archive was founded after Gorightly acquired Hill's personal papers from Dr Robert Newport, a childhood friend of Thornley and Hill, and an original Discordian (Gorightly 2013). Hill was largely inactive in the Discordian milieu after the production of the fourth edition of *Principia Discordia* in 1970, so while his papers represent the most comprehensive record of the first two periods of Discordianism's history, they do not provide much insight into its later expression. Here, it is instructive to keep in mind that before Gorightly inherited the archive, Discordianism lacked a central repository for its foundational documents. That said, Gorightly's organization, publicization, and publication of Hill's papers serves an important function with regards to the institutionalization efforts initiated by the Maybe Logic Academy. Whereas Wilson's death in 2007 led to the institutionalization of a Discordian knowledge culture within the academy, Gorightly's archival efforts have supplied it with an origin narrative.

As with the Maybe Logic Academy, the organization of the Discordian Archive grew out of a documentary project. Gorightly first became aware of Hill's papers in 2001 while researching a biography on Kerry Thornley, published as *The Prankster and the Conspiracy* (2003). This publication coincided with the opening of the Maybe Logic Academy, as well as the release of another book that treated Discordianism as a religious tradition, namely, Eric Wagner's *An Insider's Guide to Robert Anton Wilson* (2004). As the first analysis of Wilson's work written from an emic Discordian perspective, Wagner's text exemplified the institutionalization trend initiated by the Maybe Logic documentary. At the core of this trend was the conviction that Wilson was not just an exceptional Discordian co-conspirator, but a spiritual authority worthy of veneration. Like Bauscher and Wagner, Gorightly eventually adopted Discordianism as his own spiritual orientation (and in so doing, adopted the Discordian name "The Wrong Reverend Houdini Kundalini"). However, unlike their treatment of Wilson, his biography of Thornley did not constitute a hagiography. That said, it nonetheless was subsumed in the process of institutionalization that dominated the lived experience of Discordianism in the 2000s. The collective effect of these projects signaled a movement in which Discordians themselves began to construct their own intellectual tradition.

Through his blog, *Historia Discordia*, Gorightly continues to transform Discordianism's material culture into a historical narrative of its past. Thanks to the participatory nature of the Internet, Gorightly's narrative concerning Discordianism's historical development has attracted a number of online collaborators. While the intermingling of older Discordians with new converts is not, ostensibly, the primary purpose of the blog, it is inseparable from the archive's aim of creating a serialized history of

Discordianism. This is because the transformation of Discordianism's material culture into its history allows different generations of Discordians to co-create Discordian identity, in both the past and the present. This co-creation is an essential aspect of the lived experience of contemporary Discordianism insofar as constructing the narrative of Discordianism's past entails negotiating the identity of Discordianism today. As the locus of institutional history, the archive mediates between Discordianism's past and its present so that the process by which ephemera is converted into Discordianism's history simultaneously produces contemporary Discordian identity. Accordingly, the archive's power as a mediator should be read in terms of being diachronically generative: it organizes disparate accounts of Discordianism's past into a coherent tradition, which then exerts a considerable influence upon the present. This influence emanates from the creation of a linear historical trajectory (in the form of a narrative) that aligns an invented past with a prefabricated future, thereby inherently implying the continuity of the tradition through the present (Hobsbawn 2000: 1). That is to say, the past and the future are brought into being within the lived experience of the present.

In the contemporary period, the *Principia Discordia* is recognized as Discordianism's primary text. The process by which this came about illustrates how the invention of the Discordian tradition binds archival research to the on-going construction of contemporary Discordian identity. As a result of the highly limited publishing runs, the various editions of the *Principia Discordia* played almost no role in the popularization of Discordianism from the mid-1970s onwards; yet, the institutional projects of the current period have retroactively invested the text (specifically the fourth edition) with a newfound significance. The value contemporary Discordians assign to the text reflects the priorities of institutionalization; its valorization in the present period stems from the fact that the *Principia Discordia* is understood to be the "original revelation" upon which the narrative of Discordianism's history is based.[4] As this example demonstrates, the narrative of Discordianism's past functions as a permanent interlocutor with contemporary Discordians: it is in the mirror of tradition that Discordians today see the reflection of their own religious identities.

Contemporary Discordianism is a discursive field in which the creation of Discordianism's past interfaces with its conceptualization as a lived tradition that is unfolding in the present. The dominant factor in this interface, though, is the religion's orientation in spiritual autonomy. The tension between tradition and autonomy is nowhere more acute than within the question of discursive self-representation. Faced with the imposition of tradition, contemporary Discordians have been led to ask what it meant to be a Discordian. This line of questioning has led to wider, corporate considerations, such as how (or whether) Discordianism constitutes a religious movement. Brenton Clutterbuck's Chasing Eris Project emerged as a direct response to these questions.

Chasing Eris

Brenton Clutterbuck, also known by his Discordian name "Placid Dingo," began the Chasing Eris project in 2012. As an attempt to answer the questions raised by Gorightly's archival research, Clutterbuck's project addressed the issue of Discordian identity, both on an individual and movement-wide level. Clutterbuck's international ethnographic census, which he dubbed the "Chasing Eris project," led him through his native Australia and nine other countries spread across three continents. Through the use of the "snowball sampling" survey method (in which contacts are recruited along lines of acquaintanceship), Clutterbuck was able to document a cross-section of international Discordianism, in much the same way Margot Adler surveyed modern paganism in *Drawing Down the Moon* (Sulak *et al.* 2014: 62). Clutterbuck's informants included prominent U.S. Discordians, like 'Professor Cramulus' and Adam Gorightly, Brazilian and Polish chaos magicians, the Finnish scholar of Discordianism Essi Mäkelä (Mäkelä and Petsche 2013), as well as the present author. Clutterbuck has yet to publish his findings; however, the execution of the project is just as important as the data it will yield, on account of the fact that it clearly represents an iteration of the institutional turn within the religion. Essentially, the Chasing Eris project represents an attempt within Discordianism to outline its own collective identity in much the same way as Gorightly's archival project aspired to produce Discordianism's own official history.

Unlike the periods in which Discordianism was a mode of mail-order spirituality, or, later, a platform for psychedelic culture jamming, Clutterbuck's project makes it clear that contemporary Discordianism is preoccupied with coming to terms with itself as a new religious movement, complete with all the trappings associated with the category of religion. For Clutterbuck, the material culture of Discordianism, as well its history, offers only a partial view of the religion. On the website that introduced his project, Clutterbuck stated that the text that is commonly identified as the *locus classicus* of Discordianism does not disclose the essence of the religion, at least not openly: "The original work of Discordianism, the *Principia Discordia* has an almost scrapbook-like set up, and refuses to explicitly reveal the 'main idea' of Discordianism" (Clutterbuck 2012). Here, Clutterbuck insinuates that his project will do precisely what research into the material culture cannot, to wit, uncover the essence of Discordianism. However, Clutterbuck's work is not positioned in opposition to the archive; in fact, the opposite is true. While Clutterbuck's global census makes clear the value he places on understanding Discordianism as it is lived today, his reference to the *Principia Discordia* as "original work" of the religion evidences how his project supplements Gorightly's institutional narrative. Whereas Gorightly's historical narrative moves forward in time from the religion's origin, Clutterbuck's account moves backwards from the present to meet it. The two work in concert insofar as the identities Clutterbuck mapped are contextualized within the tradition of Discordianism derived from the archive. The positive reception of Clutterbuck's project within on- and off-line Discordian communities makes clear that many Discordians are no longer content to remain in decentralized, anonymous networks. The lived experience of Discordianism today is defined by the impulse to come together in the form of pedagogical, intellectual, and social communities.

Conclusion

It is not a coincidence that the scholars began their inquiry into Discordianism in the early 2000s. The first academic study of the religion, David Chidester's *Authentic Fakes* (2005), was published just at the point in which Discordianism had transformed itself into the new religious movement it is today. Before this period, Discordianism was not constituted in ways that are readily visible to scholars of religion. Discordianism became visible as an object of inquiry only after it took a dramatic turn towards institutionalization. And its transformation into a new religious movement is not without its repercussions. The academic discourse that authenticated the religion in the 2000s also served to further reify Discordianism along the same lines as its emic, institutional narrative. The result was that the religion's adherents, as well as the scholars who study them, came to exist in a collaborative feedback loop involving the on-going construction of Discordianism, both in the past and the present.

Today, academics and adherents appear to agree that the essence of Discordianism resides in the 4th/5th edition of the *Principia Discordia*. Presumably, this is because the text seems to offer all of the requisite data for a normative appraisal of a new religious movement. It contains an origin story, a list of commandments, a liturgical calendar, a list of saints, and an account of Discordianism's principle deity, Eris. In sum, the 4th/5th edition *Principia Discordia* seems to be a perfect index of everything a "real" religion needs. Herein lies the problem: all of the trappings that scholars used to analyze Discordianism were secondary aspects of the religion until the contemporary period. Said differently, the religious minutia contained in the 4th/5th edition of the *Principia Discordia* is an illustration of one aspect of the Discordian *ludibrium*, not its basis. In order to appreciate the status of the *Principia Discordia* within Discordian belief, and more importantly its central place in contemporary Discordiansim, one must examine the ways in which the religion has been recast over the last six decades. Surveying the historical phases in which Discordianism's idiosyncratic beliefs developed, it becomes clear that its current status as a new religious movement obscures its previous iterations within science fiction fandom, the psychedelic underground, the zine scene, and cyberculture.

Until the current period, Discordian belief occupied a liminal position between philosophy, religion, and politics; it was neither merely a joke nor

196 J. Christian Greer

simply a religion. Discordianism's assiduously playful investment in religious forms was premised on the belief that its use of them was neither entirely genuine nor solely satirical. Far from being an indistinct system of thought, Discordianism offered its adherents a means of entering into a state of intellectual liminality that paralleled the indeterminate status of the religion itself. Through the process of institutionalization, this liminality has been replaced with the certainty that Discordianism is a new religious movement, and not only that, but one that is worthy of study. While Discordianism as a religion is evidently worthy of study, what remains to be seen is whether scholars of religion will be equipped to account for the periods in which it was not.

Notes

1 Each subsequent edition of the *Principia Discordia* contained notably different content. The Loompanics 4th/5th edition, published in 1979, is now regarded as definitive (Greer 2014: 110–111).
2 Over the course of his long career, Wilson would gain prominence within esoteric milieus as one of the foremost interpreters (and proponents) of Aleister Crowley's spiritual writings. Appropriating a line of thought initiated by Israel Regardie, Wilson contextualized Crowley's value in terms of the spiritual practices he lucidly enumerated in his work. In his spiritual autobiography, Wilson attributes his own mystical experiences to the combination of Crowley's magick and LSD (Wilson 1997: 66–71).
3 Promotion of the psychedelic experience was a hallmark of Wilson's literary career from its inception (Wilson 1973). His definitive refutation of the logic behind the "war on drugs" appears in Wilson (2000: 12–16).
4 Scholars and practitioners alike pay little attention to the fact that the edition of the text that is commonly referenced as authoritative is in fact the 4th/5th edition of the text, which differs significantly from the 1st edition (Greer 2014: 110–111).

References

Adler, Margot. 1986. *Drawing Down the Moon: Witches, Druids, Goddess Worshippers, and Other Pagans in America Today*. New York: Penguin.
Anon. n.d. 'The Maybe Logic Academy', *Maybe Logic Academy*. At: www.maybe logic.org/academy.htm. Accessed 4 March 2012.
Bainbridge, William S. 1986. *Dimensions of Science Fiction*. Cambridge, MA: Harvard University Press.
Black, Bob. 1994. *Beneath the Underground*. Portland, WA: Feral House.
Chidester, David. 2005. *Authentic Fakes: Religion and American Popular Culture*. Berkeley, CA: University of California Press.
Clutterbuck, Brenton. 2012. *Chasing Eris*. At: www.chasingeris.com. Accessed 17 October 2014.
Cusack, Carole M. 2010. *Invented Religions: Imagination, Fiction and Faith*. Farnham, UK: Ashgate.
Davis, Erik. 2015. 'Robert Anton Wilson'. In Christopher Partridge (ed.), *The Occult World*, 331–335. London: Routledge.
Gorightly, Adam. 2003. *The Prankster and the Conspiracy: The Story of Kerry Thornley and How He Met Oswald and Inspired the Counterculture*. New York: Paraview Press.

Contemporary Discordianism   197

Gorightly, Adam. 2013. 'The Discordian Archives'. *Historia Discordia*. At: historia discordia.com/the-discordian-archives. Accessed 15 October 2014.

Gorightly, Adam. 2014. *Historia Discordia: The Origins of the Discordian Society*. New York: RVP Press.

Greer, Christian. 2013. 'Occult Origins Hakim Bey's Ontological Post-Anarchism'. *Anarchist Developments in Cultural Studies* 3(2): 166–187.

Greer, Christian. 2014. 'Review of Carole M. Cusack's Invented Religions: Imagination, Fiction and Faith'. *Correspondences* 2(1): 109–114.

Hafner, John and Katie Markoff. 1991. *CYBERPUNK: Outlaws and Hackers on the Computer Frontier*, 139–250. New York: Simon & Schuster.

Hlavaty, Arthur. 2015. Personal email communication. 20 October 2014.

Hobsbawn, Eric. 2000. 'Introduction: Inventing Traditions'. In *The Invention of Tradition*. Eric Hobsbawn and Terence Ranger (eds), 1–14. Cambridge, UK: Cambridge University Press.

Mäkelä, Essi and Johanna J. M. Petsche. 2013. 'Serious Parody: Discordianism as Liquid Religion'. *Culture and Religion: An Interdisciplinary Journal* 14(4): 411–423.

Malaclypse the Younger [Gregory Hill]. 1979. *Principia Discordia or How I Found Goddess and What I Did to Her When I Found Her: The Magnum Opiate Of Malaclypse The Younger, Wherein is Explained Absolutely Everything Worth Knowing About Absolutely Anything 4th/5th edition*. Port Townsend, WA: Loompanics.

Moore, Joe. 2008. 'Occult Sentinel podcast #5 Lance Bauscher – Maybe Logic Academy'. *Occult Sentinel Podcast*. At: occultsentinel.com/2008/05/12/os-pod cast-5-lance-bauscher-maybe-logic-academy/. Accessed 13 October 2014.

O'Dea Thomas F. and Milton Yinger. 1961. 'Five Dilemmas in the Institutionalization of Religion'. *Journal for the Scientific Study of Religion* 1(1): 30–41.

Sirius, R.U. [Ken Guffman]. 2012. 'Pariahs Made Me Do It: The Leary-Wilson-Warhol-Dali Influence (Mondo 2000 History Project Entry #3)', *Acceler8or*. At: www. acceler8or.com/2012/01/pariahs-made-me-do-it-the-leary-wilson-warhol-dali-influence-mondo-2000-history-project-entry-3/. Accessed 06 June 2014.

Stoll, Cliff. 1989. *The Cuckoo's Egg: Tracking a Spy Through the Maze of Computer Espionage*. New York: Simon & Schuster.

Sulak, John, Oberon Zell and Morning Glory Zell. 2014. *The Wizard and the Witch: Seven Decades of Counterculture, Magick & Paganism*. Woodberry, MN: Llewellyn Publications.

Thornley, Kerry. 1985. 'Notes of a Neon Gringo', *Factsheet Five* 15: 49.

Thornley, Kerry. 1991. '5th Edition Introduction', *Principia Discordia 5th edition*. Lilburn, GA: Illuminet Press: i–xxxiv.

Wilson, Robert Anton. 1973. *Sex and Drugs: A Journey Beyond Limits*. New York: Playboy Press.

Wilson, Robert Anton. 1997. *Cosmic Trigger: Final Secret of the Illuminati Vol. I*. Tempe, AZ: New Falcon Publications.

Wilson, Robert Anton. 2000. *Sex, Drugs and Magick: A Journey Beyond Limits*. Tempe, AZ: New Falcon Press.

Wilson, Robert Anton and Robert Shea. 1988. *The Iluminatus! Trilogy*. New York: Dell.

11 SubGenius vs The Conspiracy

Playfulness and sincerity in invented religions

David G. Robertson

Introduction

This chapter will interrogate an ambiguity in the construction of 'The Conspiracy' in the cultural products of the Church of the SubGenius (hereafter CoSG). On the one hand, The Conspiracy in CoSG writings parodies real-world claims of 'conspiracy theories' as examples of unreflexive dogmatic thinking. Such a satirical approach is in keeping with CoSG's typical presentation as a 'parody religion'. However, less frequently noted is that CoSG often seems to be reproducing or paralleling conspiracy theory narratives literally. As I have noted elsewhere, Robert Anton Wilson (a major figure in both CoSG and Discordianism) treated conspiracy theories playfully and uses them as examples of dogmatic thinking (Robertson 2012). Wilson would adopt conspiracist thinking in the same way that he would adopt religious narratives; in order to relativise his own thinking, and prevent dogmatic, un-self-reflexive thought:

> The basic technique . . . is to so mix the elements of each book that the reader must decide on each page 'How much of this is real and how much is a put-on?'
>
> (Wilson 1980: 2)

Yet in general, the popular reception of Wilson's work tends to treat his material on conspiracy theories literally and *un*critically. This echoes the treatment of The Conspiracy in CoSG, which frequently can be seen to reproduce both the content and intent of non-satirical conspiracy theory narratives.

In this chapter, I present examples of both satirical and sincere presentations of conspiracy theory narratives in the cultural productions of the CoSG. However, I also argue that we might expand this critique to reconsider how parodic invented religions treat religious narratives. Does the CoSG follow through with the claimed intention of critiquing ALL dogmatic (or catmatic) belief systems? Or do they rather seek to replace established religious traditions (and Christianity in particular) with an alternative; perhaps one which is more in keeping with the moral compass of the baby-boomer generation? In which case, while the techniques may be similar, the aims are rather different. As Carole M. Cusack notes, there are in fact a number of such contradictions in the CoSG; as well as 'religion' and conspiracy theory narratives, we might also include consumer capitalism, which CoSG both parodies and embodies (Cusack 2015).

Before considering specific examples, first, 'parodic' and 'fiction-based' invented religions will be differentiated; and, second, background, terminology and a methodological framework for discussing conspiracy theory narratives will be provided.

Invented religions, 'parodic' and 'fiction-based'

Although terminology varies between scholars (Cusack 2010, 'Invented religions'; Davidsen 2013, 'Fiction-based religion'; Possami 2005, 'Hyperreal religion'), I am here adopting a somewhat idiosyncratic schema for pragmatic reasons. I take it for granted that all religions include invented components, but when I talk of 'invented religions' in this chapter, I refer to those that are *self-consciously and explicitly invented*. Therefore, while a strong case could be made for considering Wicca an invented religion, given Ronald Hutton's important work in separating historical consensus from Gerald Gardner's more fantastic claims, the ongoing debates about Hutton's work (Heselton 2000) show that Wicca is certainly not a *self-consciously* invented religion, and so is not included in the schema which this chapter employs.

I then draw a second distinction between invented religions that are intended to be new *de facto* religions, and those which (initially at least) seem intended to critique, or at least relativise, other religious traditions. The first type generally draw inspiration from fictional, rather than purportedly historical or divinely-authored works, so we may refer to them as *fiction-based religions*, "in which fictional texts are used as authoritative texts" (Davidsen 2013: 384). They posit new religions drawn from ostensibly non-religious aspects of the human imagination, and create religions "so good they should be real" (Cusack 2010: 4).

The Church of All Worlds (CAW) is perhaps the clearest example of a *fiction-based* religion. It was founded in 1962 by Tim Zell (b. 1942) and Richard Lance Christie (1944–2010), and drew its inspiration from Robert Heinlein's science fiction novel, *Stranger in a Strange Land* (1961). The novel concerns Valentine Michael Smith, a human raised by Martians who goes on to found the inclusive and sexually libertarian eponymous religion. Zell and Christie found *Stranger in a Strange Land* resonated with their interest in sexual liberation, penchant for ritualisation, rebelliousness and – perhaps troublingly for their later centrality to the Neopagan milieu – the writings of Ayn Rand. Later, both became passionate environmentalists, and through the 1960s and 1970s, the CAW increasingly aligned itself with

200   David G. Robertson

Wicca-derived Neopaganism. Indeed, it has been argued that Zell invented the term 'Neopaganism', and certainly *Green Egg*, the journal he produced had a reach far beyond the CAW and was important in developing a collective Neopagan identity in the US (Cusack 2010: 63–64). The CAW, then, while acknowledging its fictional roots, is considered very much a 'serious religion', inasmuch as it is positioned as a new alternative religious formation, rather than a parodic critique of other religions.

The second I refer to as *parodic religions*, and their intention seems to be not to replace traditional religions but to expose religion as altogether unnecessary. Parodic religion probably reached its apogee (to date) with the Church of the Flying Spaghetti Monster, which began in 2005 with a letter to the Kansas School Board from Bobby Henderson (then aged 24) challenging their decision to allow Christian creationism to be taught in schools alongside Darwinian evolution. He argued that, as "Intelligent Design" does not need explicitly to identify the Christian God as creator, he should therefore be allowed to have his personal deity recognised. He created the Flying Spaghetti Monster for this purpose, and as such, the Church exists almost exclusively to challenge religious hegemony in the public sphere. Of particular note are several successful attempts to wear a colander on the head 'on religious grounds' in official photographs including drivers' licences and passports. There is, of course, nothing intrinsically more ridiculous about wearing a colander than wearing a wimple, turban or yashmak, but we are simply more used to those. Such explication of cultural relativism is the very point that Pastafarianism's satire makes, aping the form, but not the content, of more accepted religious traditions.[1]

As defined by the *Oxford English Dictionary*, a 'satire' is "[t]he use of humour, irony, exaggeration, or ridicule to expose and criticize people's stupidity or vices".[2] Although generally (though not necessarily) humorous, the principal intention of satire is therefore serious: to challenge. Neither is it disinterested:

> [a]ny satirist deserving the name must be more than a partisan advocate or a clownish entertainer, for a true satirist must be a true believer, a practicing humanitarian, responsible even in his or her own subjective indulgence or personal indignation. The satirist, in short, demands decisions of his reader . . . Through either mimetic or discursive art, the satirist provokes mirth or sadness, a concern for the innocent or the self-destructive fool, or a revulsion for the deceitful knave, and always either laughter or scorn at the anatomized subject.
>
> (Quintero 2007: 3)

Falling somewhere in between these two poles is Discordianism, which was instigated in 1957 by Kerry Thornley and Greg Hill following a number of drinking sessions at a Californian bowling alley, but would go on to have a prominent position in the Neopagan milieu. Many of Discordianism's 'catmas' are obvious parodies of dogmas drawn from many different religious systems. A clear example is the 'Pentabarf', mainly a play on the Ten Commandments, but with ingredients from Hindu, Jewish and Islamic food practices, and served with a side order of Greek mythology. Yet Discordians have also constructed a complex and unique cosmology and theology, and Discordianism has over time come to be considered as having genuine religious significance for many of its adherents (Cusack 2010; Robertson 2012). Thus, Discordianism can no longer be considered purely a parodic religion.

It might, in fact, be best to imagine a continuum of invented religion with 'fiction-based' at one end and 'parodic' at the other. The Church of the Flying Spaghetti Monster would appear at the 'parodic' end, and the CAW at the 'fiction-based' end. But Discordianism would appear somewhere in the middle. Its origin was not a pre-existent fiction, yet its aims are not entirely parodic.

This chapter is concerned with CoSG, which is sometimes considered an offshoot of Discordianism (Cusack 2012: 84). CoSG would appear – initially, at least – to be closer to the parodic end of the scale to Discordianism, given its anarchic sensibilities and self-conscious money-making, and frequent allusions to the proto-SF writings of H. P. Lovecraft, 1950s advertising and Forteana. Some of these can be attributed to the Church of Scientology being a particular target of CoSG satire, as opposed to the Discordian focus on the 'world religions'. Indeed, CoSG's use of 'The Conspiracy' may be intended to ape Scientology's promotion of conspiracy theory narratives, discussed below. Yet as this chapter will argue, SubGenii seem frequently to be mobilising conspiracy theory narratives in earnest themselves.

CoSG in a nutshell

CoSG began in 1979 with the publication of the *SubGenius Pamphlet #1* in Dallas, Texas, by Ivan Stang (1953–, born Douglass St Clair Smith) and Philo Drummond (born Steve Wilcox) (Chryssides 2012: 95). The SubGenius mythology has developed over time through several radio shows, a series of books (including *Book of the SubGenius* (1983); *Three-Fisted Tales of Bob* (Stang 1990); *Revelation X* (Stang 1994); *and The SubGenius Psychlopedia of Slack: The Bobliographon* (2006)). The mythology is complicated, ever shifting and disorganised; that notwithstanding, here it is reduced to a few sentences.

The central figure of CoSG lore is J. R. 'Bob' Dobbs. Dobbs is a pipe-smoking, sports-jacket wearing, brylcreemed salesman who embodies the type of 1950s Americana later deconstructed by David Lynch's *Blue Velvet* or *Mad Men*:

> There's a million pictures of "Bob". Open up any old *Better Homes and Gardens*, *Popular Science*, *Popular Mechanics*, or whatever, from the Forties, Fifties, and early Sixties, and there's these ubiquitous smiling

202   David G. Robertson

pinks – Caucasian handsome guys, with short haircuts and these pipes. Now, they're not all the same person, but a lot of them must be – and that's "Bob". The classic portrait of "Bob" has an undeniable hypnotic hold over those who gaze upon it. I've been trying for twenty years to understand it, and I can't quite put my finger on it . . . I think that grin, and the particular insane gleam in Bob's eye, Is a little bit like a skull. I mean, it's a smiling man. It's a happy man . . . So what makes that any different from a smiley face? There's something about that look in his eye by which you just know he knows something you don't know. Or he just sold you a car.

(Stang *et al.* 1999)

'Bob' is CoSG prophet, 'world avatar' and embodiment of 'slack', whose Third Nostril was opened after 'communionications' with Jehovah-1 (Cusack 2010: 85–86). 'Slack' is the goal of all SubGenii; humanity's natural state in which all needs are fulfilled without the need for work. We are prevented from achieving 'slack', however, by 'The Conspiracy', whose underlings are known as 'Pinks' or 'Normals':

[t]he conspiracy, more or less, lets you know what slack is supposed to be to the average American. They're constantly telling you that slack is having lots of money, and your team just won the game, and life looks like a Miller Beer commercial. Everybody's good looking by a certain standard. Or other branches of the conspiracy would have you believe that slack is sitting around smoking dope all day . . . And the day that anybody can bottle and sell slack, on that day, the conspiracy has won. As long as slack is free, and the conspiracy cannot define it for everybody, then it can't win. So, like any religion really does, what we're really doing is providing a pep talk. Most people already know what we're saying through common sense. They just need to be reminded.

(Stang *et al.* 1999)

'Bob' was meant to be the head of The Conspiracy, but after discovering that some people possess Yeti DNA and therefore have a 'Nental Ife' (sometimes described as the equivalent of a 'soul', but perhaps closer to G. I. Gurdjieff's notion of the 'True Self'), he instead founded the CoSG in order to bring those people to enSlackenment. On X-Day (5 July 1998), aliens from Planet X would take all dues-paying SubGenii away before wiping out those left behind. Of course, this didn't happen – as Stang put it, "In the prediction business, you just can't predict things" (Stang *et al.* 1999) – but it did provide an excuse for an annual *Devival*.

Devivals are CoSG events involving revelry and performance art. To a degree, they satirise evangelical Christian revivals, with Stang and others delivering 'rants', full of thunderous polemic and frequently very funny. Often these rants elaborate on the role of The Conspiracy, and many of these are collected in CoSG publications. These are interspersed with comedy and music performances (a number of bands have connections to the CoSG, including Devo and Negativland). At the same time, the carnivalesque atmosphere underlines that devivals function as "temporary autonomous zones" in which social norms are inverted as a form of social critique (Cusack 2010: 98). There is often no clear distinction between the performers and audience, who contribute heckling, nudity and alcohol-fuelled hijinks.

The CoSG today is a small but lively section of the Neopagan community, with Stang claiming that there were 10,000 paid-up CoSG ministers in 1998 (Cusack 2010: 90). Except for devivals, CoSG activities mostly take place online. Stang has presented a radio show (and latterly podcast) called the "Hour of Slack" since 1985 (Stang *et al.* 1999). Drummond has dropped out of the organisation, leaving Stang in charge, but CoSG publications continue to be collaborative, involving contributions from many people. Thus there are multiple positions within it, including on the role of 'The Conspiracy', as we shall see.

'The Conspiracy'

The need to consider the emergence of any religion in its social context applies to invented religions just as much as the more established traditions. They emerged in the Cold War period following World War II, where the younger 'baby boom' generation was for the first time in several generations not only larger than that of its parents, but had a better education, better health and were wealthier. With two world wars (culminating in the Holocaust) in living memory, there was a widespread desire for change and a feeling that the contemporary system was not working, a critique that can be read in many of the cultural productions of the period. Most obviously, there is a challenge to religious norms. Christianity was particularly singled out for attack: in new religions like Wicca (which deliberately inverts Christian norms); fiction-based religions like the CAW (which deliberately stresses its moral difference from Christianity); and those more at the parodic religion end of the scale like Discordianism (which challenges the hegemony of any religion, although working from a Christian normative understanding of 'religion').

A second significant critique, however, was directed towards political norms. Conspiracy theory narratives – at least as we know them today – were another important product of the Cold War cultural matrix. The end of World War II left many fearful of attack, but they were also supporting a large intelligence and military community who now had little to do, except perhaps protect the status quo that supported their jobs. The intelligence community quickly turned their attention to communism, which developed into a rabid hunt for the enemy within. Through the McCarthy trials, the 1963 Kennedy assassination and the 1974 Watergate

204   David G. Robertson

cover-up, the target of suspicion moved gradually from communists to any 'subversives', i.e. anyone who challenged the governmental position.

Terminology surrounding conspiracy theories is complex, and a scholarly consensus has yet to appear. The issue is that the term 'conspiracy theory' is highly loaded and typically used to indicate paranoia or irrationality. Such a position pathologises any dissent from 'the party line', despite the provable fact that in a number of cases such critiques have proven to be correct (Watergate being an obvious but by no means unique example). Most scholars therefore tend to follow Michael Barkun's (2003) schema of 'conspiracy beliefs' (i.e. any unfalsifiable belief which posits a malevolent conspiracy) and 'conspiracism' (the belief system which results from understanding conspiracies to be the primary motive force behind history). I here refer to *conspiracy theory narratives*, that is, any account which posits a conspiracy, whether falsifiable or not, and regardless of whether the narrator 'believes' it or not, partly to avoid judgements as to the relative degree of rationality, and partly for the sake of brevity.[3]

Conspiracy theory narratives became a significant component of a number of post-war New Religious Movements (some of which may be included in the category 'invented religions'), including Scientology (Urban 2006), Aum Shinrikyo (Repp 2004), Heaven's Gate (Chryssides 2011), the People's Temple, the Nation of Islam and many others. Significantly for this chapter, they were absorbed into the collaborative and deliberately eclectic cosmology of the Discordians, primarily through the contributions of Robert Anton Wilson, but reinforced by Kerry Thornley's connections to Lee Harvey Oswald and Jim Garrison's investigation into the JFK assassination (Robertson 2012: 429). Discordianism was one of the major influences on the CoSG; Wilson is a Pope of CoSG (Cusack 2010: 88), and some have gone further and suggested that 'Bob' is named for him (Forman 2005).

The second major influence upon CoSG, however, is Scientology, which appears to be the primary target of CoSG satire; the science fiction-derived cosmology, relentless charging for spiritual services, 1950s 'everyman' iconography, supposed date of founding and enthusiastic coining of neologisms (Cusack 2010: 83–85, 87–88). Scientology has in fact been a significant promoter of conspiracy theory narratives, for example promoting conspiracy theory narratives concerning the death of Jim Jones' followers at Jonestown in 1978 (Moore 2003). CoSG satirised these through accounts of Dobbstown, in Sarawak, where SubGenii go to have their Third Nostril opened (Cusack 2010: 102). Scientology spokespersons frequently refer to a concerted effort to limit or even shut down Scientology, with David Miscavige claiming "every single detractor on there is part of a religious hate group called Cult Awareness Network . . . it's the same as the KKK would be with the blacks" (cited in Cusack 2012: 306). There was (or perhaps still is, unofficially) even a department within Scientology called the 'Ethics Branch', dedicated to rooting out subversive persons ('SPs') within Scientology and discrediting its detractors (Urban 2006: 374). We might therefore assume that CoSG parodies conspiracy theories in order to parody Scientology.

Pinks vs Normals: 'The Conspiracy' as satire

According to Solomon Davidoff in *Conspiracy Theories in American History: An Encyclopedia*, "the Church has created a satiric commentary on religious observance and denomination, conspiracy theory, and conventional morality" (2003: 170). It is particularly interesting that the CoSG connects conspiracy theory narratives and religious ideas. There are certainly interesting and highly significant connections: as well as Barkun's analysis of the historical connections between conspiracy theory narratives and Christian millennialism, Brian Keeley's "God as the ultimate conspiracy theory" (2007) argues that the idea of a 'hidden hand' behind history means the two should be analysed together. After all, in these two cases alone, "absence of evidence does not indicate evidence of absence" (Keeley 2007: 137). By and large, scholars of religion have not embraced this argument, perhaps unsurprisingly. Popular writers have, however (see Kay 2011; Pipes 1997), and in recent years there has been a good deal of attention paid by psychologists on 'conspiracist ideation', sometimes making the connection with religious modes of thought (Dixon and Jones 2015; Lewandowsky *et al.* 2013). These studies are limited, however, by their continuing insistence that conspiracy theory narratives are evidence of irrationality or paranoia. The CoSG makes the same assumption, but is not afraid to make the comparison with religion, although, to be fair, Christianity and Scientology seem to be singled out. As with Discordanism, Eastern religions seem to be treated somewhat more gently.

'The Conspiracy' – i.e. "ANYBODY who says that you must be part of their CLIQUE or their CLENCH or their CHURCH or their COUNTRY or their SPECIES or their PLANET" (Stang 2006: 98) – has been a central part of CoSG cosmology since the beginning. *SubGenius Pamphlet #1* states that:

> All of civilization's painful and misguided climb up from the primeval slime, and its subsequent loss of Slack and of any class at all, has been indelibly marked, nay, entirely motivated, by the aeons-bridging conflict between the Conspiracy's mindlessly chickenshit Witless Principals and the Jehovah-spawned, grandiose depravity of the superior yet ethnically all-encompassing race of latent SubGeniuses.
>
> *(Pamphlett #1* 1979: 6)

The conspiracy is playfully linked to the Ancient Alien narrative, and in what is likely another dig at Scientology, states that "The movie rights ALONE to these gut-splitting tales of reincarnancient history are worth millions!" (*Pamphlett #1* 1979: 6). The malevolent conspiracy has 'duped' the slumbering mass of Normals, sometimes called 'Pinks'.

206　*David G. Robertson*

The Conspiracy wants people to be "Pinks" or "Normals", who do not suspect its activities or ask questions about the extent of its influence. The world for Pinks may be perfectly pleasant. However, it is a dangerous illusion. The particular quality of SubGenii is that they can "see", they are aware of the activities of "The Conspiracy".

(Cusack 2010: 93)

The opposite of 'Slack' is control, and conspiracy theory narratives are a clear example of the personification of control. Indeed conspiracy theory narratives often literally embody the conspirators in extra-terrestrial, monstrous or demonic bodies, literalising the 'alien'. In CoSG lore, the minions of the Elder Gods, the Watchers (again aping Christianity), are extra-terrestrials who are responsible for creating in humans "*Voices in Heads* which spread Utopian/racist bullshit as 'The Great White Brotherhood'" (Stang 1987: 105). Ironically, then, the Gods create both religion and 'The Conspiracy'.

Three-Fisted Tales of 'Bob' contains a story by Robert Anton Wilson that ties CoSG mythology to the sweeping conspiracy theory narrative of his *Illuminatus! Trilogy* (1975, co-written with Robert Shea). It features Adam Weishaupt, "Primus Illuminatus, and Grand Master of the Ordo Templi Orientis, the Scotch Rite, the York Rite, the Egyptian Rite and the Rite of Memphis and Mizraim" and controller of "every Freemasonic conspiracy on the planet", as well as references to the *Principia Discordia*, James Joyce and Lovecraft's Cthulhu mythos (Wilson 1990). Wilson's work was, as discussed above, to a large degree an attempt to destabilise the readers' ontological certainties. He described this approach as 'guerrilla ontology', and compared it to the effect of Zen koans (e.g. "When you see the Buddha, kill him"), aphorisms designed to jolt student's logical faculties. He was not alone in this comparison; prominent Discordians Kerry Thornley and Camden Benares promoted Discordianism and Zen Buddhism as functionally identical (Robertson 2012: 432–434). He viewed conspiracy theories in much the same way, using them to provoke different modes of thought in his readers. Guerrilla ontology is referred to in CoSG as "Ontological Anarchism" (Cusack 2010: 88, 95–97), and this reinforces the idea of the CoSG as satire designed to relativise all existent belief systems:

You're looking at this like it's a normal religion and finding it doesn't work that way. That's good. That's part of the deprogramming lesson: to look at things in new ways. Now apply that to everything else and you've got it.

(Smith, in Cusack 2010: 99)

Don't be a dupe!: conspiracy as true

All this suggests that CoSG does intend to make cultural critique, particularly of consumerism, religion and – apparently, the worst of all – consumerist religion (i.e. Scientology). However, and to put it in the style of the CoSG: something else is going on here, buddy – *and if you don't get it, maybe you're trying too hard*. The possession of 'slack' would imply that one simply rises above such ideological battles – after all, you don't challenge something you don't care about. Which is to say, the CoSG *does* have a position. It *cares*. Indeed, as Paul Mann writes:

> [t]he cult of Dobbs crystallizes a rabid overparticipation in the stupid spectacle of the real that goes far beyond any "blank parody" or "postmodern pastiche".
>
> (cited in Cusack 2010: 108)

Cusack also notes that the conspiracy motif seems to operate on 'two levels' in the CoSG, and invoking Guy Debord's situationist critiques, describes how in the second level 'The Conspiracy' is constructed as "a materialist phantasmagoria in which people are trapped, working to earn money to buy things, and being alienated from freedom and an authentic mode of being" (Cusack 2010: 108). She is absolutely correct; for example, what is being satirised in the following quotation?

> DID ALL THOSE BRAVE AMERICAN SOLDIERS DIE JUST SO THAT A SECRET ROYAL GANG OF FAT BALD WHITE GUYS COULD MAKE YET MORE MONEY?
>
> (Stang 2006: 110; emphasis in original)

Or in this, which endorses the conspiracy theory narrative that the CIA circulated drugs on the streets of US cities:

> For some reason this whole thing seems to attract pot heads like crazy . . . from what I can tell, about 85 percent of [SubGenii] are probably some kind of psychedelic drug users. Now, why that is, you got me. There's nothing terribly overt about that in any of the books. In fact, it actually says that with "Bob", you can throw away all *your cheap conspiracy street drugs* and never come down.
>
> (Stang *et al.* 1999; emphasis added)

Or in this, which invokes the acquiescent 'sheeple' of David Icke or United States' Libertarian rhetoric:

> Are you registered to vote? Did you manage to overcome the incredible inconvenience of casting a vote in the last election? If not, then please SHUT THE FUCK UP. Go back to your cheeseburgers and gas-guzzlers with the rest of the sheeple.
>
> (Stang 2006: 124)

208   *David G. Robertson*

In fact, Stang seems to acknowledge that 'The Conspiracy' is not entirely satirical. For example, he explains that "the trick is to not sound crazy when you talk about The Conspiracy" (Stang 2006: 120):

> ou see, it's a two way street. The government supports the church, and the church supports the government. We call this secret little agenda THE CONSPIRACY! And that Conspiracy, dear friends, is what the Church of the SubGenius is SWORN TO DESTROY!
>
> (Stang 2006: 140–141)

In fact, the cosmology presented in the various CoSG publications is a variation of a kind of Gnostic dualism[4] which has proven popular in twentieth century religions including Rastafarianism, Nation of Islam and the Gurdjieff Work, as well as many conspiracist narratives. It essentially divides the world into three: a good group and an evil group, and a third, much larger group which is fundamentally unconscious, as (for example) does British conspiracist David Icke (2005: 78–84, 148; cf. Robertson 2012). In which case, being a SubGenius is not such a joke after all.

Conclusion

As discussed above, the purpose of a satire is not to amuse, but to challenge. We do not challenge that which matters nothing to us. If all religious or conspiracy claims are just as based on nonsense as those of the CoSG, why does the CoSG care about them?:

> Satire cannot function without a standard against which readers can compare its subject. We praise with delight what we admire, enjoy, or profit from, and we censure with indignation the despicable or what causes ill because we have an acquired sense of what the world should or might be. How could we perceive something as ridiculous, monstrous, wicked, or absurd without having a comparative sense of what would not be the case? How could we believe that something is wrong with the world without some idea of what the world should be and of how it could be righted? The satirist, either explicitly or implicitly, tries to sway us toward an ideal alternative, toward a condition of what the satirist believes should be.
>
> (Quintero 2007: 3)

Davidsen makes an interesting observation; defining 'fiction' as "any literary narrative which is not intended by its author to refer to events which have [supposedly] taken place in the actual world prior to being entextualised", he notes that conspiracy theories are not *fiction*, but *history*, inasmuch as those making such claims hold them to be true. So is the case with religion; but note that both religion and 'conspiracy theories' are by their nature unfalsifiable. In keeping with my claim above that conspiracy theory is a

SubGenius vs The Conspiracy   209

polemic term, when a conspiracy theory narrative can be falsified, and is not, it is no longer a 'conspiracy theory' but 'historical fact'. Not *fiction-based*, but *history-based*. Therefore, the CoSG, in satirising and thereby challenging such claims, challenges them, in effect taking them as serious history rather than fiction. After all (and I highlight for emphasis), *if it is all fictional, who cares?*

The appropriation of conspiracy theory narratives in the CoSG exemplifies a larger issue in the theorisation of invented religions more broadly. Does CoSG treat conspiracy theory narratives seriously or not? The aim of this chapter has not been to answer this question one way or another, but rather to highlight the tension which I perceive to exist in invented religions including, but not limited to, CoSG. Do invented religions treat 'religion' seriously or not? To bastardise Orwell, are all religions equally problematic, or are some more equal than others?

Why can't a parody be a real religion too? Stang seems to have anticipated the ambiguity when noting that CoSG is "satire and a real stupid religion . . . The fact that it admits that it's a joke proves that it's the only honest religion" (in Cusack 2015):

> Well, it's just a takeoff on religion. Usually misinformed people insist on pinpointing it as being a takeoff on evangelists or evangelism. Whereas, actually we really do try to insult EVERYBODY'S religion. We make fun of every religion, most of all our own. Others think that it really is a true cult. Cult – hell, it's infinitely larger than Heaven's Gate. I mean, it's rather beyond the cult stage now; you've got to call it a religion, because there are so many people involved. And some people think that it's somehow New Age. Others think that it's got this terrible anti-New Age, totally scientific agenda, that's designed to destroy everybody's faith. Others think it's an art project. (Which it is.) And that's the thing: it is ALL of those things. Why can't it be all those things?
>
> (Stang *et al.* 1999)

Cusack notes that, "Stripped of science fiction motifs, the Church of the SubGenius' worldview is almost identical to that of the Situationists" (Cusack 2015). The Situationists also critiqued the society of the spectacle while positing a more 'real' mode of existence. After all, you can only get upset about the commodification of everyday life if you think there is an authentic way of living that can be achieved. And so it is with the CoSG critique of religion. Why argue that CoSG should challenge the definition of religion if you don't give a damn? Why attack Scientology unless it somehow upsets your understanding of what a religion *should be?*

> From what I understand their guru, that Jesus guy, the original Jesus, wasn't quite so squeamish as his fan club is. I thought that he said that you were supposed to at least tolerate the damn weirdos, Republicans,

210 *David G. Robertson*

drunkards and so forth. I find it very ironic that it takes a goddamn joke church to even think about doing that any more . . . I find it very very ironic that for so many of those people, literally, the only church that will take them in, the only place where they won't be mocked, and laughed at, and put down just because of the way they look or they way they are, is a goddamn comic book joke church. What the hell does that say about the Catholics, the Baptists, the Moonies, the Scientologists and everybody else?

(Stang *et al.* 1999)

Perhaps as CoSG gets older and becomes more accepted in the Neopagan milieu, the dominant interpretation is shifting, and more are missing the joke. Stang, however, writes under the imperative heading of "TATTOO THIS ON YOUR BRAIN":

[i]t turns my stomach to see you knee-jerk "SubGeniuses" make blanket statements about "those stupid Christians" or "those stupid Republicans", which might as well be, nay, IS just like saying "those stupid niggers", or "those greedy Jews" or "all Muslims hate women". The mind set is the same old "We're brilliant Us and They're dumb old Them". Pointing out the innate dumbness of that way of "thinking", isolating the loci where the dumbassitude starts, is one of the main points of several satirical put-on religions that I can think of. And wouldn't you know it, that MAIN POINT is the very one MOST OFTEN MISSED.

(Stang 2006: 113)

The answer, perhaps, is that while there is no shadowy 'Us' vs 'Them', no Pinks vs Normals, there is a conspiracy:

The conspiracy is real enough . . . but "The Conspiracy" isn't the rich guys who run things. The conspiracy we're talking about is much worse – it's the one lurking inside every one of God's monkeys . . . Only when we, as a race, can . . . root out that Devil Gene and rationally remake ourselves into OverMen, bereft of the cruel Pan Troglodyte chimp nature . . . shall we find true Slack and freedom for all. All who remain, anyway.

(Stang 2006: 121)

In keeping with the situationist critique, 'The Conspiracy' is us. Just as 'The Conspiracy' commodifies everything, it is we who take a simple satire way too seriously. Is the CoSG a real religion? Does it 'believe' conspiracy theory narratives? That the Devil Gene inside us needs to see the question one way or another is the real 'us vs. them', and that would be the biggest irony of all.

Notes

1 Jediism is an interesting case here. While there are 'genuine' Jedis (i.e. members of a fiction-based religion), Jediism is most often satirical, as exemplified by the United Kingdom censuses in 2001 and 2011 in which 290,127 in the first case and 176,632 in the latter put Jedi as their religion in an attempt to satirise the importance given to religion by asking the question. Interestingly, the story has been widely reported in the UK press, but seldom acknowledges the two kinds of 'Jedi' (see Singler 2014).
2 www.oxforddictionaries.com/definition/english/satire (Accessed 22/4/2015).
3 For a fuller discussion of the definition of 'conspiracy theory', see Robertson (2013).
4 The comparison with gnosticism is carried further in COSG through the wrathful and irrational deity Jehovah-1, who echoes gnostic writings which portray Jehovah as an insane lower god, or demiurge.

References

Barkun, Michael. 2003. *A Culture of Conspiracy: Apocalyptic Visions in Contemporary America*. Berkeley, CA: University of California Press.

Chryssides, George D. (ed.). 2011. *Heaven's Gate: Postmodernity and Popular Culture in a Suicide Group*. Farnham, UK: Ashgate.

Chryssides, George D. 2012. *Historical Dictionary of New Religious Movements*. London: Scarecrow Press.

Church of the SubGenius. 1979. *SubGenius Pamphlet. No. 1*.

Cusack, Carole M. 2010. *Invented Religions: Imagination, Fiction and Faith*. Farnham, UK: Ashgate.

Cusack, Carole M. 2012. 'Media Coverage of Scientology in the United States'. In D. Winston (ed.), *The Oxford Handbook of Religion and the American News Media*, 303–315. Oxford, UK: Oxford University Press.

Cusack, Carole M. 2015. 'The Messiah is a Salesman, Yet Consumerism is a Con(spiracy): The Church of the SubGenius, Work, and the Pursuit of Slack as a Spiritual Ideal'. *Nova Religio* 19(2): 49–64.

Davidoff, Solomon. 2003. 'Church of SubGenius, The', in P. Knight (ed.), *Conspiracy Theories in American History: An Encyclopedia*, 170–171. Santa Barbara, CA: ABC-CLIO.

Davidsen, Markus Altena. 2013. 'Fiction-based Religion: Conceptualising a New Category against History-based Religion and Fandom'. *Culture and Religion* 14(4): 378–395.

Dixon, Ruth M. and Jonathan A. Jones. 2015. 'Conspiracist Ideation as a Predictor of Climate-Science Rejection an Alternative Analysis'. *Psychological Science* 1(3): 664–666.

Forman, Bill. 2005. 'Premature Illumination'. *Metro Santa Cruz*, 10–17 August. At: www.metroactive.com/papers/cruz/08.10.05/wilson-0532.html. Accessed 22 April 2015.

Heinlein, Robert A. 1961. *Stranger in a Strange Land*. New York: Putnam.

Heselton, Philip. 2000. *Wiccan Roots: Gerald Gardner and the Modern Witchcraft Revival*. Milverton, UK: Capall Bann Publishing.

Icke, David. 2005. *Infinite Love is the Only Truth*. Wildwood, MO: Bridge of Love Publications.

212   David G. Robertson

Kay, Jonathan. 2011. *Among the Truthers: A Journey Through America's Growing Conspiracist Underground*. New York: Harper.

Keeley, Brian L. 2007. 'God as the Ultimate Conspiracy Theory'. *Episteme: A Journal of Social Epistemology* 4(2): 135–149.

Lewandowsky Stephan, Gilles E. Gignac and Klaus Oberauer. 2013. 'The Role of Conspiracist Ideation and Worldviews in Predicting Rejection of Science'. *PLoS ONE* 8(10): e75637.

Moore, Rebecca. 2003. 'Reconstructing Reality: Conspiracy Theories About Jonestown'. *Journal of Popular Culture* 36(2): 200–220.

Pipes, Daniel. 1997. *Conspiracy: How the Paranoid Style Flourishes and Where It Comes From*. New York: Free Press.

Quintero, Ruben. 2007. 'Introduction: Understanding Satire'. In R. Quintero (ed.), *A Companion to Satire*, 1–12. Malden, MA: Blackwell Publishing.

Repp, Martin. 2004. 'Aum Shinrikyo and the Aum Incident'. In J.R. Lewis and J.A. Petersen (eds), *Controversial New Religions*, 153–194. Oxford, UK: Oxford University Press.

Robertson, David G. 2012. 'Making the Donkey Visible: Discordianism in the Works of Robert Anton Wilson'. In Carole M. Cusack and Alex Norman (eds), *Handbook of New Religions and Cultural Production*, 419–441. Leiden, The Netherlands: Brill.

Robertson, David G. 2013. '(Always) Living in the End Times: The Rolling Prophecy of Conspiracy Culture'. In Sarah Harvey and Suzanne Newcombe (eds), *Prophecy in the New Millennium: When Prophecies Persist*, 207–219. Farnham, UK and Burlington, VT: Ashgate.

Shea, Robert and Robert A. Wilson. 1984. *The Illuminatus! Trilogy*. New York: Dell Publishing Company.

Singler, Beth. 2014. '"SEE MOM IT IS REAL": The UK Census, Jediism and Social Media'. *Journal of Religion in Europe* 7(2): 150–168.

Stang, Ivan. 1987. *The Book of the SubGenius: Being the Divine Wisdom, Guidance, and Prophecy of J.R. 'Bob' Dobbs*. New York: Simon & Schuster.

Stang, Ivan. 1990. *Three-fisted Tales of 'Bob': Short Stories in the SubGenius Mythos*. New York: Simon & Schuster.

Stang, Ivan (ed.). 1994. *Revelation X: The 'Bob' Apocryphon: Appointed to be Read in Churches*. New York: Simon & Schuster.

Stang, Ivan (ed.). 2006. *The SubGenius Psychlopaedia of Slack: Vol. 1*. New York: Thunder's Mouth Press.

Stang, Ivan, David J. Brown and Sherry Hall. 1999. 'David Jay Brown and Sherry Hall Interview Reverend Ivan Stang'. *Mavericks of the Mind*. At: www.mavericksofthemind.com/stang.htm. Accessed 17 April 2015.

Urban, Hugh B. 2006. 'Fair Game: Secrecy, Security, and the Church of Scientology in Cold War America'. *Journal of the American Academy of Religion* 74(2): 356–389.

Wilson, Robert A. 1980. *The Illuminati Papers*. Tempe, AZ: New Falcon.

Wilson, Robert A. 1990. 'The Horror on Howth Hill'. In Ivan Stang (ed.), *Three-Fisted Tales of 'Bob': Short Stories in the Subgenius Mythos*. New York: Simon & Schuster. At: www.subgenius.com/bigfist/classic/classictales/HowthHill.html. Accessed 15 April 2015.

12 Kopimism and media devotion
Piracy, activism, art and critique as religious practice

Danielle L. Kirby and Elisha H. McIntyre

Introduction

The late twentieth and early twenty-first centuries have seen a rise in religions that are heavily entwined with digital media. Indeed, the adoption of media logics into the realms of the religious is staggering in its variety, ranging from the performative spectacles of African Pentecostal megachurches through to the personal internalisation of fictional characters. One new religion, Kopimism, makes this integration of media all the more explicit in its belief that copying and disseminating information is ethically right, and that 'remixing' is a sacred act. Kopimism was founded in 2010 by Isak Gerson, has branches in many countries and is recognised as a religious community by the Swedish government. Like a number of newly born alternative religions, Kopimism sits somewhat ambiguously between sincerity and satire. Claiming piracy as a sacred duty, Kopimists unequivocally constitute a critical voice against traditional copyright law and in particular its application in digital contexts on an international scale. It would be overly dismissive, however, to assume that public critique is their only goal. Rather, Kopimist thought reflects the entwined influences of political activism, the critique of traditional religiosity and digital arts practice as they manifest within late modernity.

Since their inception, the origins and development of Kopimist thought have been explored by both academic and journalistic commentators (for example, Drecun 2012; O'Callaghan 2014; Sinnreich 2015) There are, however, two particular aspects of Kopimist thought which warrant particular attention here. First, there is a primary tension between the sincerity of the Kopimist belief in file sharing and associated practices and its seemingly ironic 'take' on religion; and second, there is a tension between the legitimating tactic of seeking the status of a religion as granted by the state, and the pervasively anti-state and anti-corporate agendas of digital rights activism. These two concerns provide a vantage point to explore some of the distinguishing features of Kopimism within the late modern new media landscape and highlight the complex interactions of the various spheres within which Kopimism engages.

Kopimism

The Missionary Church of Kopimism was founded in 2010 (Neethu and Zahra 2013: 569) and recognised as a religion in Sweden in early 2012 (George 2012). At the time, Kopimism's founder, Isak Gerson, was a philosophy student at the University of Uppsala and involved in the piracy movement as a member of the Swedish Pirate Party. Kopimism is a religious community premised on the shared belief that copying is sacred and that attempts to curtail that freedom are both reprehensible and evil. The central tenets of Kopimism, as outlined in their mission statement, are as follows:

1   The copying of information is ethically right.
2   The dissemination of information is ethically right.
3   Copymixing is a sacred kind of copying, more so than perfect digital copying, because it expands and enhances the existing wealth of information.
4   Copying or remixing information communicated by another person is seen as an act of respect and a strong expression of Kopimistic faith and acceptance.
5   The Internet is holy.
6   Code is law (Kopimism Australia n.d.).

To become a Kopimist, one does not have to participate in any specific conversion rituals. Rather all that is needed is a personal acceptance of the above tenets of Kopimism and a feeling of being "called to respect and worship the holiest of the holies, information" (Kopimism Australia n.d.). While identifying as a Kopimist requires no official membership, there is the option to officially register as a Kopimist via the Church's websites, a procedure that is akin to signing up to a mailing list as it requires only an (unverified) name and email address. This reflects the Kopimist awareness that if copying and sharing information is a sacred and communal act, being part of the community is important and complements personal freedom and individual agency.

In addition to the obvious injunction to copy and share files, known as Kopyacting, Kopimists are developing other practices that, to some degree, are beginning to mirror more traditional forms of religious behaviour. In 2013, Kopimist and former Pirate Party member, Christian Engström, published *A Kopimist Gospel* on his website (Engström 2013), which is freely available for anyone to download as an 85 page PDF. This text acts as a kind of theological treatise on Kopimism, developing its ideas further and addressing concerns dealt with by traditional religions such as creation, "fundamental principles", ritual and morality. However, the *Gospel* rejects any notion of textual authority and even is in itself an act of copymixing as it contains an extensive discussion of, and borrowing from, Robert M. Pirsig's *Zen and the Art of Motorcycle Maintenance* (1974). Engström also argues that the inclusion of Kopyacting (the act of sharing information through copying and the central ritual performed by Kopimists), as a religious ritual was instrumental in convincing the Swedish government of Kopimism's legitimacy as a religion (Engström 2013: 62).

There are other examples where Kopimism has acted in ways typical of other religious traditions. Peter Sunde has recently complained that he is not able to properly practice his Kopimist faith while in prison and that he requires the opportunity to converse with a representative of his faith (Anonymous 2014). This complaint is particularly noteworthy in that it comes from a founder of the Pirate Bay who was in prison for copyright violation at the time of his complaint. In more visually extravagant terms, the first Kopimist wedding took place in 2014 at a digital rights conference. During the wedding, an op ('operators', a term for Kopimist representatives), wearing a Guy Fawkes mask[1] and ceremonial robes, enjoined the happy couple to share their love, thoughts and feelings "as long as the information should exist" (Doctorow 2012). Here the more familiar words of "till death do you part" are replaced by a phrase that reinforces the Kopimist interpretation of all life as a product of copied and shared information. In both these examples there is a clear element of provocation, in the first instance towards Sunde's jailors and those asserting the criminalisation of breaching copyright, and in the second towards more traditional notions of religiosity. Beyond the provocation, though, these instances also point towards a desire and a willingness of Kopimists to engage substantively in the territories of religion and not simply limit themselves to the fight for digital rights.[2]

Kopimism is very much in its infancy, and formal structures such as ritual practices are still largely unformed. Engström, for instance, devotes a chapter of *A Kopimist Gospel* to the question of what a Kopimist moral system might look like as well as two chapters to ritual. Engström argues that Kopimists do not yet have a firmly established tradition of ritual other than Kopyacting, but that "as Kopimism grows and attracts more followers, rituals will evolve naturally. This is how most rituals in the older religions and society in general have appeared" (Engström 2013: 62). Most importantly, the rituals Kopimists do develop can be copied from established religions or can be newly invented, or a combination of both. This is in itself a Kopimist approach, as Kopimist religious ritual would be made through an act of copymixing:

> This is an open invitation to anybody who feels like it to suggest new Kopimist rituals. The rituals as such do not have to be new. Copying and remixing from existing sources, both religious and other, is of course always encouraged for a Kopimist.
>
> (Engström 2013: 63)

Interestingly, Engström explains that the rituals that will become Kopimist practice will "come into existence through a swarm-based process" where the suggested rituals that the loose community thinks "are good" will be "picked up, and, with time, become more firmly established as rituals" (Engström 2013: 63). Engström is happy to let Kopimist ritual practice develop casually, collectively and gradually and views this as the same way that traditional religious ritual has developed. By virtue of Kopimism's youth and collaborative nature, its practices are not yet always clear to observers, or indeed, to members themselves.

Beyond the central principles of the Kopimist Church are a set of missionary goals specific to ops rather than general members: Away with Anti-Kopimist Laws; Holiness the Protection of Copying Files; and Received Anti-Kopimistiska Tools (Kopimism Australia n.d.). In essence, these goals articulate the political mission of the Church, seeking to fight against intellectual property laws, protect the right to encrypt data, making source code open and available, and making illegal digital rights management software. When seen in conjunction with the central tenets which Sacralise the copying and distribution of information, and the Internet as the mechanism through which to do so, it is clear that the focus of Kopimist thought is very much grounded in everyday digital experience and seeks protections for those increasingly normative practices.

As a lived religion, Kopimism is both ephemeral and pervasive, and on occasion leaves observers with the uncomfortable suspicion that the Church is merely a front for political activism. As is often the case with late modern emergent alternative religions, Kopimism is individualist, non-hierarchical and, beyond Kopyacting, claims no specific rituals or practice of conversion or affiliation. As such, it becomes inordinately difficult to affirm or deny genuine religious sentiment on behalf of participants. In the practice of Kopyacting, however, Kopimists are sacralising a ubiquitous act (copying and sharing files) that is a huge part of everyday lived experience for both adherents and others alike. For example, one Kopimist argued that he is practising Kopimism when he edits Wikipedia pages (Krishna 2012). As Engström writes:

> We perform the holy ritual of Kopyacting not only to remind ourselves that Kopyacting is a Fundamental Principle that we regard as holy, but also to highlight this to others, in the hope that they may want to join our faith. We will force no-one, but we invite everyone to start considering sharing a holy act, as we do.
>
> As such, both receiving and sharing culture and knowledge are perfectly ordinary everyday acts, that millions of people do on a daily basis without any metaphysical motives. But the same is true about washing down a wafer with a swig of wine, which is the central ritual of Christianity. Even if the act itself is unremarkable, thinking about it in a spiritual way transforms it into a ritual with a deeper meaning.
>
> (Engström 2013: 62)

Filesharing, legitimacy and the spiritual frame

Kopimism is unambiguously a belief that glorifies the copying and sharing of information. At the heart of Kopimism is what Andersson Schwarz describes as a form of technocultural progressivism, an approach that tends to claim:

> We are all interconnected and that there is no border between the Internet and the human brain. Further, this notion can be successfully integrated with the notion that duplication and imitation are not only found at the heart of social life, but also found throughout the natural universe.
>
> (Andersson Schwarz 2013: 131)

Naturalising the practice of filesharing and the anti-copyright agenda and, at least to a degree, attributing sacred meaning in Kopimist thought suggests that filesharing can be read as both self-evidently good and a unique and noteworthy act. Importantly, Kopimism is not making super-empirical claims regarding a deity, more-than-human beings, extended non-physical worlds or the like. Gerson himself unambiguously states that there is no deity associated with the religion (George 2012). Kopimism is perhaps more closely related to secular religions such as the atheist Sunday Assemblies (Stahl 2015: 34) than it is to the expressive individualism of more metaphysically oriented new beliefs. Importantly, some members, notably Gerson, identify as Christian (Sinnreich 2015: 5) and appear to perceive no necessary conflict between the two beliefs. Unequivocally, though, Kopimist thought does propose the holiness of information and is sacralising the everyday practices of digital engagement. As the Kopimism Australia website states, there is both a spirituality and a politics co-existing here, rather than simply a shell of a religion.

> While there is a politics to seeking religious sanctuary for the act of copying, our belief in the spiritual value of shared culture is entirely sincere.
>
> (Kopimism Australia n.d.)

That the Kopimists should have to emphasise and defend the sincerity of their spiritual beliefs exposes the suspicions of the wider community about the motives, and hence legitimacy, of new religions, in particular those that may be classified as some form of 'invented' religion. Unlike most invented religions, however, Kopimism does not base itself upon a work of fiction or a parody of existing religions (Cusack 2010; Kirby 2013). Rather it has been inspired by a highly prominent feature of late modern digitised life – information, and specifically the movement and use of that information – and has taken it from the everyday, made it meaningful in a new way and thus sacralising, to at least some extent, the commonplace online practices of many.

218   *Danielle L. Kirby and Elisha H. McIntyre*

The choice to self-identify and be formally recognised as a religion has implications for both Kopimist thought and late modern conceptions of the status of religion.

Primarily, the use of religious language and imagery elevates the debate from the profanity of the legal realm up to the question of morals and ethics. Ethics and morals, while not exclusively under its jurisdiction, have traditionally been associated with religion. In order to co-opt the authority of religion over the question of (specifically digital) ethics, Kopimists have begun using the scaffolding of religious ritual and behaviour to legitimise (and distinguish) their push for digital rights. The examples of the Kopimist wedding and role of ops discussed above are perhaps the most provocative instances, but the central tenets also frame information as holy in a straightforward manner. Such framing reveals something about the nature of religion: that even for the digitised individuals of the twenty-first century, the fight over secular rights can be made more meaningful (and perhaps more legitimate) when converted into a fight for a sacred ideal. For Kopimists, it is not enough to believe that open access to information is of benefit to society. Rather, open access to the sacred is 'ethically right'. Kopimism sits on the middle ground between the traditional religious ideas rejected by secularists (for example, belief in a powerful creator god, institutionalism or divine punishment) and the individual choice to participate in some kind of 'higher purpose' communal activity preferred by those drawn to new or alternative religious movements.

While the use of religious framing is both noteworthy and worth exploring, it is nonetheless important to note that the use of language is not necessarily indicative of sincerity, belief or even a desire to distinguish itself from 'techno-humanist' ideals. Rather, in some ways the co-option of such language can be seen as easily as an attempt to subvert or exploit religious power and authority. Kopimists are clearly aware, both consciously and unconsciously, of the power associated with the category 'religion'. Teemu Taira contends that:

> "[r]eligion" is used for promoting practical interests, from very concrete material benefits to public recognition and the construction of collective identities, because "religion" works as a tactical tool for making things happen.
>
> (Taira 2013: 490)

When coupled with an agenda that requires action, in this instance the campaign for digital rights, religion can be a force for change. Taira also argues that:

> [i]t is not usually the case that "religion" is deployed solely for achieving easily identifiable, particular rewards such as tax exemption, license to teach it in schools, [or] permission to wear religious dress in the

Kopimism and media devotion   219

workplace . . . On the contrary, the most typical uses are about author-
ising, legitimating, reproducing and challenging collective identities.

(Taira 2013: 484)

In other words, it is possible that Kopimism is both a tool for achieving
'particular rewards', and a means of expressing a genuine spiritual identity. Gerson says, "what the registration [as a religion] has done mostly
is strengthen our identity . . . I think it will be easier to find new members
now that we are recognized" (Romig 2012). By self-identifying as a religion, Kopimism engages in the discourse of what makes a religious identity.
Part of that identity comes from creating a distinction between those who
identify as Kopimists and those who believe in the importance, but not the
sacredness, of information. For Gerson, this distinction is significant enough
to need "new members". That is, he sees the movement between the two
groups as a sort of conversion, where those who used to simply 'pirate' are
now engaging in the holy act of 'Kopyacting'. While the individual action
may be the same, when re-framed by a Kopimist identity it becomes a ritual
action imbued with spiritual significance.

By also seeking recognition in the civil and legal sense, albeit achieved so
far only in Sweden, Kopimism challenges the public definition of 'religion'.
We would suggest that Kopimism should not be seen as either quasi-religion
(Andersson Schwarz 2013: 131) or as a particularly fertile home of new
Gnosticism (O'Callaghan 2014: 100), but rather as something in between:
a secular religion that focuses on political and legal critique but nonetheless holds significant individual and collective meaning that is claimed as
sacred by participants. Placing Kopimism within a religious frame highlights
the immediate and personal impact of the current status quo in ways that
are continuous with late modern understandings of personal religiosity,
while simultaneously situating these concerns within realms at least nomi-
nally private and inviolate. Concurrently, in sacralising everyday behaviours,
Kopimists are significantly reframing their digital engagement and ultimately
engaging in the practice of lived religion: while attributing sacred meaning
to a secular act does not necessarily produce an observable difference in the
action, it does significantly change the individual interpretation of the act.

Piracy, digital activism and anti-statism

Counterbalancing the individual and private aspects of contemporary personal religiosity are the public, corporate and state-based concerns of digital
rights and copyright law, perhaps most evident in the expansion of, and
attempts to counteract, digital piracy. Piracy has become an increasingly
fraught issue in the digital world. Evoking the language of bloodthirsty
scavengers on the high seas (Yar 2005: note 3), copyright holders have
militantly sought anti-piracy protections, and governments are increasingly
seeking to police digital engagement. From the perspective of everyday use,

220   *Danielle L. Kirby and Elisha H. McIntyre*

however, digital piracy is increasingly normalised within contemporary culture, a taken-for-granted aspect of everyday life, the very ubiquity of which renders it invisible. As Burkart and Andersson Schwarz note, there is a strong impression that "digital piracy escaped the exclusive provenance of the technoculture long ago, merging with mainstream media consumption norms sometime between 10 and 20 years ago" (Burkart and Andersson Schwarz 2015: 793).

In digital terms, much of what is understood as piracy is also continuous with various forms of activism. The pervasive and ubiquitous presence of online engagement and the importance of media content within contemporary society, have, when coupled with antiquated copyright laws that struggle to respond to new communication technologies, given rise to a circumstance where a staggering number of individuals breach laws with remarkable regularity. Recent years have seen a raft of legislation introduced pertaining to filesharing, such as the American Digital Millennium Copyright Act (1998) and the UK Digital Economy Act (2010), which have inspired significant opposition (Breindl 2013: 1420). These, and other similar Acts, seek to limit and severely penalise any breaches that do occur. Such state and corporate concerns are strongly opposed by the digital rights movement, who generally seek to rethink copyright and associated laws in ways more appropriate to the specifics of digital engagement. There is a range of approaches that are championed across the breadth of digital rights activism, but most are perceived, rightly or wrongly, as being in direct conflict with the interests of the entertainment industry (see Mansell and Stienmueller 2013), if not necessarily the creators of content themselves. Generally speaking, the rejection of traditional copyright within the realms of digital activism tends to be framed in regards to distribution and access, and does not seek to lessen authors' rights. Kopimists, by and large, do not appear to be necessarily anti-corporate or anti-profit, but rather pro-access, which tends to work in favour of artists and content creators but against distributors. It is also worth noting that file sharing is not solely the province of the digital (see Skågeby 2015), but rather with the introduction of the Internet it has become a mass issue and one that is infinitely more subject to surveillance and policing.

This conflict around copyright protection and piracy has become all the more entrenched when seen in relation to the broader cases of whistle-blowers such as Chelsea Manning and Edward Snowden, who copied and made public vast amounts of confidential government files. Examples are sites such as Wikileaks, which enable such information to be published and distributed anonymously, and groups such as Anonymous who have, through actions such as their Denial of Service attacks, demonstrated a willingness and capacity for aggressive digital collective action in defence of digital rights (Benkler 2011). While all these various actors have significantly different aims, they have all in various ways pushed the issues of digital rights, transparency and access, into the public realm and can be seen in combination as a broader 'freedom of information' movement (Beyer 2014). It is the particular combination of "cyberliberties, Net neutrality, and a criticism of immaterial rights management and copyright restrictions" (Jääsaari and Hildén 2015: 871) that are at the heart of digital rights activism.

Kopimism is very much a part of this digital rights activist culture, both in its aims and its origins. Kopimism has close relations with the Swedish Pirate Party, most notably sharing members such as Gustav Nipe of the Pirate Party (Sweden) and Kopimist founder, alongside Gerson (George 2012). The Pirate Party is a political party born in Sweden in 2006, (Jääsaari and Hildén 2015: 870) predominantly concerned with what has been called the trinity of digital rights – "Free speech, privacy, and access" (Burkart 2014: 152) In Sweden itself, file sharing has been described as a national peoples movement (Andersson Schwarz 2013: 126), as the number of people who engage in it is so large.

Having found an appeal by no means limited to Sweden, there have been Pirate Parties formed and registered now in many countries, both within and without Europe.[3] Although varied in their specifics, these political parties share a common focus upon digital rights, often alongside a focus more broadly upon civil liberties. Initially, file sharing was one of the central concerns of the pirate political movement, but has become less prominent within the agendas of the various parties (Jääsaari and Hildén 2015: 883), with a broader critique of the rights to information, such as medicine patents and the like, coming to the fore (Lindgreen and Linde 2012: 159).

This expansive international development of Pirate Parties highlights the peculiarities of digital rights as a simultaneously local and international endeavour. Copyright law is not uniform across continents or between countries. Australia, for instance, has different cultural and legal assumptions to Germany, which, in turn, differs from Sweden and so on. This point, while more or less self-evident, warrants clear articulation as it is regularly assumed that copyright laws are at least broadly standard. Europe, for instance, tends to enjoy a broad cultural position that attributes a greater leniency towards individual non-profitable copying and sharing (Jääsaari and Hildén 2015: 875), whereas the US errs towards a far stricter rule of content purchase and associated rights. Australia, without the strong cultural traditions of Europe, nonetheless has a high rate of digital piracy, which is often attributed to the paucity of available media content through legitimate channels (Beekhuyzen *et al.* 2015).

Kopimism, the Pirate Party and Pirate Bay are but a few of the many specific and individual groups to come to public attention over issues of digital rights. Like many modern protest movements that utilise social media and tend to avoid hierarchical structures, digital rights activism and culture are often perceived to lack coherency by outsiders and their varied ideals, techniques and approaches create a motley of sometimes contradictory impressions. For instance, observers of the field attribute variously anarchist

222 Danielle L. Kirby and Elisha H. McIntyre

tendencies, capitalist leanings, collectivism and individualism as central pillars of the culture (Beyer and McKelvey 2015: 891; Goode 2015: 74). There is no one singular politic, although there are clearly shared concerns. Perhaps most importantly, it has become clear that the Internet, for all the discussions towards online freedoms and the expansive self, is in fact increasingly authoritarian in structure (Burkart and Andersson Schwarz 2015: 793). This increasing authoritarianism perhaps goes some way towards explaining the tendency of digital rights activism towards individualism rather than collectivism (Andersson Schwarz 2013: 118) and the regular feature of pro-globalist and anti-statist discourse within the culture (Jääsaari and Hildén 2015: 872). It is clear, however, that within digital activist cultures there is a broader critique of the status quo.

In his description of Anonymous, for instance, Luke Goode characterises the movement in terms that also speak more broadly to the cultures of digital activism, noting that "digital technology is heralded not only as a way of life for group members but also as a driving force for reshaping society" (Goode 2015: 75):

> Echoes of Dada, the Situationist International and, in a more recent vein, culture jammers such as the Yes Men manifest in the antics and desire for spectacle and spoofing. We see a simultaneous critique *and* embrace of the absurd which, in existentialist philosophy, is closely linked to nihilism as mockery of conventional values.
>
> (Goode 2015: 80)

This linkage with pranks, interventions and the traditions of modern art is of particular note here and is by no means only used by Anonymous as a mechanism of critique. Piratbyrån, for instance, had earlier picked up on this confluence of art and activism, their practice including a series of performances throughout Europe in 2008 (Andersson Schwarz 2013: 128). The Australian Kopimism website is run by artists who specialise in video art and remix (www.sodajerk.com.au). Interestingly, this confluence is matched in the religious as well as the activist spheres as a fulcrum for framing dissent and forcing its discussion through atypical means. Kopimism here joins a distinguished, if perhaps under-known, list of alternative religions. Deliberately antagonistic, groups such as Discordianism and the Church of the SubGenius incorporated much countercultural discourse. Indeed, Discordianism shared with Kopimism an explicit critique of copyright through their concept of kopyleft and traditional assumptions of ownership, access and distribution in their championing of bricolage and pamphleteering. More broadly, the Church of the Subgenius' conceptual bricolage complemented their critique of normative Western society and was present in both their publications and their public interventions (Cusack 2010; Kirby 2012).

Conclusion

When seen within this context of activist politics and fairly direct opposition to the status quo, the Kopimist decision to seek formal recognition as a religion is an interesting one. As a legitimating process, state recognition is not without its perils. One may assume that religious status is desirable at least in part due to the particular protections given to religious beliefs and practices. In light of their central tenet to copy and share, and the regular illegality of doing so, it would seem a straightforward proposition. But while official acknowledgement of religious status may be perceived to have benefits, in the particular case of Kopimism it does not necessarily provide the protections that some might assume participants may be seeking. It does not, for instance, seem to protect individuals who break Swedish laws such as those breaching copyright: religious status does not exempt individuals from issues of legality (Jonasson 2012), although it is worth noting that Europe gives special protection to religious communication (Andersson Schwarz 2013: 131).

At the core, Kopimism's classification as a religious community should perhaps primarily be recognised straightforwardly as what it claims to be: a reflection of the sincere and shared belief in the sacred significance of copying and disseminating information. Kopimism encompasses both a unique approach to the sacred and a clear dedication to activism and, in combining the two, presents an unusual fit within both categories. That Kopimism may seek specific outcomes in social and legal change does not undermine it as an expression of genuine religious sentiment, neither does their strikingly unusual approach to the sacred lessen the strength of their stance on digital rights.

Notes

1 The recent use of Guy Fawkes masks by Anonymous and others as a symbol of protest against state power and intrusion upon privacy with anarchist tendencies is simply the most recent iteration of a persistent symbol within the Anglo-American world. See Burne (1912) and Call (2008).
2 Digital rights, activism and politics are here used as terms denoting the concern with, and activity around, online rights. This is not here intended to be conflated with activism which occurs online but is focused on other issues. In this, we follow Andersson Schwarz (2013: 126).
3 See The Australian Pirate Party pirateparty.org.au/; the Canadian Pirate Party www.pirateparty.ca/; and the Philippine Pirate Movement www.philippinepirate movement.com/.

References

Andersson Schwarz, Jonas. 2013. *Online File Sharing: Innovations in Media Consumption*. New York and London: Routledge.

Anonymous. 2014. 'Pirate Bay Founder's Religious Rights Spark New Complaint'. *Torrent Freak*. 26 July. At: torrentfreak.com/pirate-bay-founders-religious-rights-spark-new-complaint-140726. Accessed 18 August 2015.

224 Danielle L. Kirby and Elisha H. McIntyre

Beekhuyzen, Jenine, Liisa von Hellens and Sue Nielsen. 2015. 'Illuminating the Underground: The Reality of Unauthorised File Sharing'. *Info Systems* 25: 171–192.

Benkler, Yochai. 2011. 'A Free Irresponsible Press: Wikileaks and the Battle over the Soul of the Networked Fourth Estate'. *Harvard Civil Rights – Civil Liberties Law Review* 46: 311–397.

Beyer, Jessica L. 2014. 'The Emergence of a Freedom of Information Movement: Anonymous, WikiLeaks, the Pirate Party, and Iceland'. *Journal of Computer-Mediated Communication* 19: 141–154.

Beyer, Jessica L. and Fenwick McKelvey. 2015. 'You Are Not Welcome Among Us: Pirates and the State'. *International Journal of Communication* 9: 890–908.

Breindl, Yana. 2013. 'Assessing Success in Internet Campaigning'. *Information, Communication, and Society* 16(9): 1419–1440.

Burkart, Patrick. 2014. *Pirate Politics: The New Information Policy Contests.* Cambridge, MA: MIT Press.

Burkart, Patrick and Jonas Andersson Schwarz. 2015. 'Piracy and Social Change: Revisiting Piracy Cultures'. *International Journal of Communication* 9: 792–797.

Burne, Charlotte S. 1912. 'Guy Fawkes' Day'. *Folklore* 23: 409–426.

Call, Lewis. 2008. 'A is for Anarchy, V is for Vendetta: Images of Guy Fawkes and the Creation of Postmodern Anarchism'. *Anarchist Studies* 16: 154–172.

Cusack, Carole M. 2010. *Invented Religions: Imagination, Fiction and Faith.* Farnham, UK and Burlington, VT: Ashgate.

Doctorow, Cory. 2012. 'File-Sharing Church Solemnizes First Wedding'. *Boing Boing.* 7 May. At: boingboing.net/2012/05/07/file-sharing-church-solemnizes. html. Accessed 18 August 2015.

Drecun, Sofija. 2012. 'Internet Based Religions: Alternative and Deregulated Systems of Beliefs in New Media Environment'. *Center for Interdisciplinary Studies.* Belgrade: University of Arts in Belgrade.

Engström, Christian. 2013. *A Kopimist Gospel.* At: christianengstrom.wordpress. com/?s=gospel. Accessed 18 August 2015.

George, Alison. 2012. 'Kopimism: The World's Newest Religion Explained'. *New Scientist* 213: 25.

Goode, Luke. 2015. 'Anonymous and the Political Ethos of Hacktivism'. *Popular Communication* 13: 74–86.

Jääsaari, Johanna and Jockum Hildén. 2015. 'From File Sharing to Free Culture: The Evolving Agenda of European Pirate Parties'. *International Journal of Communication* 9: 870–889.

Jonasson David. 2012. 'File Sharing Recognized as Religion'. *Stockholm News.* At: www.stockholmnews.com. Accessed 18 August 2015.

Kirby, Danielle. 2012. 'Occultural Bricolage and Popular Culture: Remix and Art in Discordianism, the Church of the SubGenius, and The Temple of Psychick Youth'. In Adam Possamai (ed.) *The Handbook of Hyper-real Religions*, 39–58 Leiden, The Netherlands: Brill.

Kirby, Danielle. 2013. *Fantasy and Belief.* Sheffield, UK and Bristol, CT: Equinox.

Kopimism Australia. n.d. *Kopimism Australia.* At: kopimismaustralia.net/constitution/. Accessed 29 April 2015.

Krishna, R. 2012. 'I Kopi, Therefore I Am'. *DNAIndia.* 29 January. www.dnaindia. com/lifestyle/report-i-kopi-therefore-i-am-1643163. Accessed 8 September 2015.

Lindgreen Simon and Jessica Linde. 2012. 'The Subpolitics of Online Piracy: A Swedish Case Study'. *Convergence* 18: 143–164.

Mansell, Robin and W. Edward Stienmueller. 2013. 'Copyright Infringement Online: The Case of the Digital Economy Act Judicial Review in the United Kingdom'. *New Media and Society* 15(8): 1312–1328.

Neethu R. and Shakeri, Zahra. 2013. 'My Religion: My "Copy" "Right"'. *Journal of Intellectual Property Rights* 18: 566–575.

O'Callaghan, Sean. 2014. Cyberspace and the Sacralization of Information. *Heidelberg Journal of Religions on the Internet* 6: 90–102.

Pirsig, Robert M. 1999 [1974]. *Zen and the Art of Motorcycle Maintenance: An Inquiry into Values*. New York: William Morrow and Co. Inc.

Romig, Rollo. 2012. 'The First Church of Pirate Bay'. *The New Yorker*. January 12. www.newyorker.com/culture/culture-desk/the-first-church-of-pirate-bay. Accessed 8 September 2015.

Sinnreich, Aram. 2015. 'Sharing in Spirit: Kopimism and the Digital Eucharist'. *Information, Communication and Society* dx.doi.org/10.1080/1369118X.2015.1036766.

Skågeby, Jorgen. 2015. 'The Media Archaeology of File Sharing: Broadcasting Computer Code to Swedish Homes'. *Popular Communication* 13: 62–73.

Soda Jerk. At: www.sodajerk.com.au/index.php. Accessed 18 August 2015.

Stahl, William A. 2015. 'The Church on the Margins: The Religious Context of the New Atheism'. In Lori G. Beaman and Steven Tomlins (eds.) *Atheist Identities: Spaces and Social Contexts*, 19–37. Cham, Switzerland: Springer International Publishing.

Taira, Teemu. 2013. 'The Category of "Invented Religion": A New Opportunity for Studying Discourses on "Religion"'. *Culture and Religion: An Interdisciplinary Journal* 14(4): 477–493.

Yar, Majid. 2005. 'The Global "Epidemic" of Movie "Piracy": Crime-wave or Social Construction?' *Media, Culture & Society* 27: 677–696.

13 Beyond belief

Revival in virtual worlds

William Sims Bainbridge[1]

Introduction

Among the variety of modern perspectives scholars may employ in viewing religion, one of the most intriguing is to see it as a total work of art (*Gesamtkunstwerk*), serious fiction that combines features of literature, drama, music, and the visual arts (Bainbridge 2013b). The most recognizable genre of total works of art is grand opera, especially the *Ring* cycle of Richard Wagner (1849) who proposed the concept. The most contemporary example is a massively multiplayer online (MMO) game, such as *World of Warcraft*, and many MMOs incorporate serious religious creativity. This chapter will explore the use of this new artform to accomplish a purpose that religion traditionally served, but that is imperfectly satisfied today among secular populations: veneration of deceased family members. The area is too new to proclaim formal scientific findings or design principles, but this chapter will suggest 13 hypotheses of both kinds.

Several leading researchers in the human-computer interaction field have shown that people do become emotionally and cognitively involved in their avatars that exist only within computerized virtual environments (Blaskovich and Bailenson 2011; Yee 2014). Others have explored the specifically religious roles that many of the online games provide for players (Geraci 2014; Nardi 2010). Still others have begun to explore the far-out possibility that artificial intelligence may in future bequeath a degree of reality to avatars that represent people who are no longer alive (Bainbridge 2014; Rothblatt 2014). By way of connection to social science and psychotherapy, this chapter will employ *psychodrama*, a classical method developed by Jacob L. Moreno (1946; Moreno and Toeman 1942) to study the most modern artistic expression of quasi-religious culture, computer-based role-playing games.

The solo expeditions reported in much of this chapter were part of a larger exploration involving several living members of the Bainbridge family, and thus are intended to scout this cultural terrain for future habitation by entire families or groups of friends. In other efforts, the children of two of my uncles offered advice when characters based on their deceased fathers entered *Star Trek Online* and *Lord of the Rings Online*, and exploration of

Everquest by means of an avatar based on a great-grandfather was part of a general exploration of his life done in partnership with two other cousins, carried out online in a variety of media. It is entirely possible for a group of living family members to operate a group of MMO avatars representing an entire deceased generation, despite living thousands of miles apart. Psychodrama, after all, was a technique used in group therapy, and could be adapted for group religious activities. Before we undertake MMO grief counseling or spiritual exploration, however, it would be wise to use the more modest method in which one researcher operates one avatar, to identify with care some hypotheses for later testing and use.

The importance of Constance

On May 14, 1965, at the age of 22, my sister was killed along with our parents in an accidental house fire in Connecticut while I was visiting our grandmother in Britain. Meditating at the center of Stonehenge was the best I and another family member could accomplish by way of a memorial service, and a senseless death like this defies human understanding. Over the past eight years, I have been exploring the multiple dimensions of virtual revival of a deceased person by means of role-playing inside gameworlds (Bainbridge 2013a, 2013c, 2013e). Here I shall illustrate this practice by reviving my sister in three: the solo-player computer game *Neverwinter Nights*; the related massively multiplayer online fantasy game *Neverwinter*; and the historical MMO *Pirates of the Burning Sea*.

The goal is not merely venting emotions like grief or guilt. In preparing to emulate deceased people, we must learn more about them, and by experiencing a rich environment through their distinctive perspectives we also learn more about the nature of human life. Depending upon the history of the person and the nature of our relationship, we may gain specific philosophical insights or practical skills. And by sharing our experience with other living people, such as I have done with a dozen members of the Bainbridge family, we honor the dearly departed.

Barbara Constance Bainbridge (1943–1965) was a sweet child, pretty, and with many friends. Her life turned tragic when epilepsy emerged at the beginning of adolescence, and it was sufficiently severe as to constitute a very serious disability that even endangered her life (Bainbridge 2013d). Connie was drawn to the arts, rather than to technology, and the high point of her life came around 1961 when she was active in a local drama group, the Connecticut Playmakers. I actually never saw her perform, neither do I recall seeing the stage sets she helped create, but for half a century have preserved the souvenir pictures and documents that I found in her scrapbook after the fire.

Hypothesis 1: Studying documents and recalling memories about the deceased person, in preparation for playing the role of that person accurately, can provide more general insights about roles.

228　*William Sims Bainbridge*

These Playmaker documents provide a basis for creating an avatar based on Connie in virtual worlds based on the main tradition of role-playing games, *Dungeons and Dragons* (Gygax 1979).

In preparation, I read dramas named in the documents, simultaneously with looking at old photographs and recalling old memories. Recollection is a form of revival. The particular dramas she experienced in the Playmakers reflect issues relevant to major themes of this book. Notably, she was master painter for the Playmaker's 1961 production of *Bell, Book and Candle*, and the program said:

> CONNIE BAINBRIDGE is well qualified for her job as Master Painter after having painted sets for three or four years in the Summer Youth Festival productions. Although a new Playmaker, Connie has already contributed in several different ways. She played Snooks and was a member of the chorus in *Anything Goes* and was Assistant Stage Manager for *Mr. Roberts* and also for our last Christmas play, *A Christmas Carol*.

As I recall, she was active in the Summer Youth Festival's productions of the musicals *Oklahoma* and *Plain and Fancy*, the latter concerning the Amish religious sect, probably in 1959 and 1960. *Bell, Book, and Candle* by John Van Druten (1951) had been reasonably successful on Broadway, and in 1958 had been made into a romantic comedy film starring James Stewart and Kim Novak. It concerns a book publisher who falls in love with a witch who cannot love him in return because witchcraft inhibits human feelings. At the conclusion of the drama, however, the witch loses her magical powers, becomes capable of love, and exclaims, 'I'm only human!'

Among the salvaged documents is a mimeographed page for a 'meeting' on January 18, 1961, at which a very short play was performed without an audience, in addition to whatever serious business and informal socializing went on. It was *The Tiny Closet* by William Inge (1962), and Connie was listed as stage manager and as playing the role of Elsie. I assume the group was aware that the playwright had killed himself the year before, and that the play concerned 'coming out of the closet' as an expression of Inge's own conflicts over his homosexuality.

The role of Elsie is really just a walk-on part, but symbolically significant. Elsie was a 'colored girl,' that is an African-American servant, whom other characters pushed off stage, and may primarily have represented a normal person observing the pathologies of the main characters from a safe distance. I know my sister was comfortable with African-Americans, although her own heritage was British. Indeed, her favorite music was what was commonly called *race music* in those days, and she often bought recordings of it from a store in Stamford, Connecticut, that primarily served African-American customers.

Perhaps Elsie's marginality to the story also represented Inge's view that America faced many other important issues beyond the one his very short play concerned. Mr Newbold had locked the closet in his rented room, and made Mrs Crosby and Mrs Hergsheimer promise never to open it. But open it they did, finding that it contained a lavish collection of gaily decorated hats, which implied that Newbold was even more deviant by the standards of the day than the communists the two women reviled. As I read *The Tiny Closet*, I imagined Connie and her Playmaker friends breaking into laughter, and she may have attached many different meanings to those crazy hats in the closet. We all have secrets, although hers were painfully obvious when she would lapse into *petit mal* semi-consciousness, and putting on a hat is playing a role, perhaps that of a happy person living a good life.

A solo-player computer game

My sister's avatar, Constance, entered the legendary city, Neverwinter, in the *Neverwinter Nights* game at the beginning of 2013, when the city was under the most insidious siege, infection by a plague. Victims of the disease react differently, but some are transformed into manic zombies, attacking healthy people and thus spreading the horror. The game's instruction manual explains:

> Thousands have died from a mysterious plague called the Wailing Death, and thousands more are infected. With the risk of an epidemic spreading across the face of Faerûn, the Lords of Neverwinter declared a quarantine and shut the gates to all travel, trapping sick and healthy alike inside the city walls. Lady Aribeth de Tylmarande has issued a call to all adventurers within the city, asking them to keep order and help her find a cure. Promises of honor and riches have drawn many to Aribeth's side, but all for naught. The plague spreads with every passing day, and sweeps through the poorer quarters of the city like a flash fire. Many would-be heroes have fallen, and no cure is in sight.
>
> (Knowles *et al.* 2002: 4)

The parallel to my sister's real medical condition should be obvious, but given that Neverwinter is a realm of magic, her avatar might be able to find the cure that eluded doctors in real life. Indeed, the primary goal of the first chapter of the *Neverwinter Nights* saga is to collect four magical items that combined can defeat the plague. These are represented as four mythical beasts, collectively called the Waterdhavian creatures; intellect devourer, yuan-ti, cockatrice, and dryad. Magic is impossible, yet can provide emotional compensation, and the same may be true of religion, as Rodney Stark and I considered in *A Theory of Religion* (Stark and Bainbridge 1987).

Hypothesis 2: Experiencing fiction that parallels real-life problems can provide psychological compensation for failure and loss.

230   *William Sims Bainbridge*

My first decision in running Constance through the first chapter of *Neverwinter Nights* was that she must not be defeated, as the game conceptualizes defeat as death. A deceased avatar comes back to life at a temple of healing, and may resume the struggle almost immediately, but the symbolism was still troubling. The first decision also interacted with the second: that she must be able to end the plague quickly, in terms of hours played, and would pay little attention to side missions and other activities in the game. There was indeed a meta-magic that would render her invulnerable.

Walkthrough instructions posted by players online not only helped me plan each step in the game, but also provided the supposedly secret codes required to hack the game. Putting the game into *god mode* meant Constance could not be injured by an enemy. The two decisions combined to make later stages in the struggle a little frustrating, because had she completed more of the side missions she would have gained strength, thus being able to kill enemies more quickly. Some of the final battles went on for an incredibly long time, as the enemy could not kill her, and her attacking did pathetically little damage to the enemy. This reminds us that life is about diversity, and having one obsessive goal can lead to a less happy experience than a balance across multiple goals.

Hypothesis 3: Much computer technology seems to put the user into the role of a god, yet without a well-chosen set of goals, omnipotence is indistinguishable from impotence.

A related factor was the issue of partners. The avatar Constance could have two companions during most of the time I operated her, an animal and a humanoid assistant. One of the early choices is what class the avatar should belong to, and I selected Druid, which the in-game instructions described thus: "Druids are divine spellcasters who receive their spells from nature, not the gods. They strive to live in harmony with the natural world, and hate anything that is not part of the natural cycle, especially aberrations and undead creatures." This choice prepared her to have an animal companion, and I selected a dog because in life she had indeed had one, giving it the poodle's real name, Pouf. The notion of living in close harmony with nature is profoundly ironic, given that humans survive only because they use technology to exploit nature, and diseases are an integral part of nature.

Recalling my sister's fondness for popular music, and the fact that one blessing of her life was that she did indeed have many friends, I selected a female tavern singer named Sharwyn to be her human companion. However, god mode did not apply to Pouf or Sharwyn, so they typically died early in combat, even as Constance remained invulnerable. She could easily resurrect Pouf whenever she got a chance to rest, but resurrecting Sharwyn required returning to home base. This suggests that gods have little use for friends, and also that friends could not solve the most dire challenges in life.

Revival in virtual worlds 231

Hypothesis 4: An avatar's relationships with non-player characters inside a computer game can reflect real issues about human relationships.

The first chapter of *Neverwinter Nights* highlighted four non-player characters who played roles in the story, and with whom the avatar frequently interacted: Aribeth, Fenthick, Lord Nasher, and Desther. In the background, a god named Týr sustains the social structure, clearly derived from the actual Norse deity, Týr, who represented both law and heroism. The *Neverwinter Nights* wiki calls him "the Even-Handed, the Maimed God, the Just God," whose symbol is "balanced scales resting on a warhammer," and who represents "lawful good" or "justice."[2]

As required by the game, Constance volunteered to be an agent of Aribeth, helping her find the cure, interacting less intensively with the other three. The Helmites, led by Desther, are a different religious cult from the followers of Týr, who claim that their blessings may protect people from the plague, and rejecting the more technological solution pursued by Lady Aribeth. Thus, one way to interpret this tension in the game is as a metaphor about scientific versus spiritual responses to disease, or more generally rational versus mystical approaches to life's problems.

Hypothesis 5: The fictional religions and political ideologies in a computer game can reflect real cultural alternatives; thus interacting with them can have philosophical benefit.

Obtaining each of the four components of the cure required adventuring into a different chaotic district outside the core of the city. In the Peninsula district, the intellect devourer had possessed the mind of the warden of the prison, releasing many dangerous criminals. The poor district, called the Beggar's Nest, was the original site of the Wailing Death, and now zombies rage through the streets, augmented by undead released from the graveyard when the *yuan-ti* seized control of a cult devoted to a god named Cyric, the Prince of Lies. The Docks district, in which the cockatrice is being auctioned to the higher bidder, is overrun by pirates and thieves. Blacklake is the wealthy part of town, and the dryad is being held by a noble named Meldanen who captures people to use in his unholy experiments and now is studying the dryad.

For a grand ritual to unite the four components and destroy the plague, Constance joined Aribeth, Fenthick, Lord Nasher, and Desther, along with four priests of Týr. But as soon as the ritual ends, Desther seizes the cure for his own evil purposes, we learn that Fenthick was so foolish as to help Desther, and a squad of Hemites attacks to cover Desther's escape. Apparently, the blessings of this cleric were actually intended to aggravate the plague, rather than cure it, leaving the impression that religion aggravates misery more than it assuages it. Constance rushes to the headquarters of the evil cleric, vanquishes him, and thereby cures the plague. Having symbolically solved the affliction that disabled my sister, I chose not to continue playing the series of classic solo-player *Neverwinter Nights* games, but to wait for the release of the related MMO later in the year, and allow her to explore it as if reborn into a new life.

An MMO game

Launched in 2013, *Neverwinter Nights* is a highly fantastic ghoul-oriented MMO, based on the influential *Dungeons and Dragons* (D&D) tradition, in which players create elaborate missions for each other, often involving supernatural powers and radical religious movements. When the original D&D emerged back in 1974, it was in the form of an instruction manual that guided players in creating their own table-top games, within a fantasy tradition that drew upon many earlier works of literature, including *The Chessmen of Mars* by Edgar Rice Burroughs (1922) and *The Lord of the Rings* by J. R. R. Tolkien (1954).

Despite serious technical challenges, it was possible to modify *Neverwinter Nights*, thus creating one's own version, and game economist Edward Castronova had led a project to transform it into *Arden: The World of Shakespeare* (Castronova *et al.* 2008). But the *Neverwinter Nights* MMO incorporated a very easy to use system called the *foundry*, allowing any subscriber to create new missions. Creating missions simulating actual life experiences of a deceased person is quite feasible.

Hypothesis 6: Computer games that offer players the ability to create their own missions, and some non-game virtual worlds as well, can be used effectively to simulate actual events in the life of a deceased person.

Many missions and settings were created by *Neverwinter Nights'* designers, all of which are intended to harmonize with the game's tradition, and support an over-arching mythos. A great number of additional missions have been created by players, all in instanced settings—for example a dungeon that must be entered through a particular door—that do not interfere with gameplay in the wider environment. It is possible to progress through the game, gaining experience points, virtual wealth, and skills, through any combination of designer- and player-created missions. Amateur mission creators are encouraged to have their stories harmonize with the mythos, and to avoid violation of copyrights to material outside the mythos, but in fact the style, conceptual focus, difficulty, and quality of player-created missions vary greatly.

The first drafts of D&D included a character type based on the Hobbits invented by J. R. R. Tolkien, but copyright concerns impelled the designers to change the name from *Hobbit* to *Halfling*. This was not necessary for Orcs, because Tolkien had merely adapted this racial concept for his stories rather than having invented it, and many current MMOs include Orcs.

Thus, many *Neverwinter Nights* missions involve Hobbits, Orcs, or both. As it happens, Connie's uncle, Angus McIntosh, was a student and friend of J. R. R. Tolkien, so she had a personal connection to the Hobbit mythos.

Hypothesis 7: Computer games incorporate elements derived from many significant real-world cultures, some of which will be especially relevant to the person being revived.

A player-created mission deriving from a different cultural heritage was The Book of the Dead by a player using the identification @magic88255, which had been completed by 5,734 players by November 29, 2013. The creator's summary says:

> You take your best friend Linda to a secluded cabin in the woods, where you activate an archaeologist's magic diary with a recorded recitation of passages from the Book of the Dead. The spell calls up an evil spirit which possesses Linda, and threatens to do the same to you. When the archaeologist's daughter shows up at the cabin, the night turns into a nightmare.

As more than one player recognized, this is an adaptation of the horror film, *The Evil Dead* (1981). It takes place in and around a nice rural home, and could just as easily have told a less horrifying story about a real woman named Linda, which was the name of a character in the film.

One of the most impressive player-created mission arcs takes place in the huge library and other sections of a complex monastery based on one explored by many millions of players in *World of Warcraft* (*WoW*). The library section was completed by a player using the ID @cojoru179 on August 23, 2013 and by October 10, 2013 players had already completed it 14,624 times. Here is the creator's description taken from the quest-finding interface of *Neverwinter Nights*:

> A remake of the Library side of World of Warcraft's Scarlet Monastery. (Note: I designed the layout of the Library as close to the original instance as the foundry editor would allow, however I had to alter some of the names and references to avoid copyright issues.) The quest takes you into the realm of Azerothia and through a rather large wing of a monastery. While there are some familiar names, faces, and references (for those who have played WoW) the story line is somewhat unique to Neverwinter.

I had in fact explored the original in *WoW* many times, and appreciated the similarities, as well as noticing differences in the shapes, textures, and non-player inhabitants (Bainbridge 2010: 120).

Even at today's early level of technological development, a system like the foundry can be used to simulate a specific real-world environment,

234   *William Sims Bainbridge*

as easily as one borrowed from a different virtual world. At the end of a mission, each player gets the opportunity to rate it, and of 5,267 people who rated Scarlet Library, fully 2,566 "loved it," while at the opposite end of a five-point scale, only 73 "did not like it." The original WoW Scarlet Monastery was one of four strongholds belonging to a faction of non-player characters called the Scarlet Crusade, a fictional religious order dedicated to destruction of the undead Scourge zombies, and ultimately of all intelligent creatures that are not fully human. A much simpler *Neverwinter Nights* mission that had been played fully 211,857 times by October 6, 2013, was Bill's Tavern. This huge number of plays indicates that it was an attractive, efficient mission that was sufficiently rewarding to motivate players to complete it many times. The creator, @DZOGEN, gave it the hashtags #story, #humor, and #solo, with this advertisement: "A fun, campy little zombie revenge quest. Revenge is a dish best served cold for a tavern that welcomed you in to eat your brains. Featuring: Bartender Bill, as the Zombie leader."

In the future, we can imagine that revival and memorialization of deceased persons will often be done not just by individual players, but by groups. As one small step toward this complex possibility, I asked my son, William Carey Bainbridge, to undertake the ironically named Bill's Tavern as I watched and commented. As a solo mission, it is not designed to be undertaken by a pair of players, which is optimal for some other missions. Thus, my son Bill took the role of my sister Connie. The two had met in real life, but her death came two weeks before his first birthday, so he did not remember her. Although very experienced with computer technology, he was not an MMO player, and unfamiliar with *Neverwinter Nights*' user interface, so I was impressed that he defeated the boss zombie on his first attempt.

Hypothesis 8: A variety of ways can be developed to allow two or more people to share in an episode of virtual memorialization.

Sailing, sailing

Given that Connie's pair of *Neverwinter Nights*' experiences had emphasized role-playing, it made sense to consider her game-playing experiences in selecting the gameworld for her final impersonation. She was not in any way a violent person, so melee fighting could not be central, although she had enjoyed playing the card game War, a battle between players, usually favored by children because of its simplicity. Occasionally she played Monopoly, which has some affinity with MMOs because it represents the economy of a rather complex society. Encouraged by her mother, she also played Mahjong, and encouraged by her father she played a dice game named Yap. Similar to the commercial game Yahtzee, Yap was popular in the armed forces during World War II and involved three rolls per turn of five dice, to attempt each of a list of outcomes similar to a hand of cards, for example three of one number and two of another to get *full house*, earning 40 points. One advantage of Yap was that, unlike board games, it could comfortably be played on a sailboat.

When Connie's family moved from back country Connecticut to the seashore in 1950, they bought a 19-foot centerboard sloop Rhodes Hurricane sailboat, similar to the popular Lightning but with a more rounded hull. A small fleet of them was moored at a dock within easy walking distance of her home on Lucas Point, in Old Greenwich, Connecticut, and every summer the local families competed in races against each other. The boat was named *Compass*, both to symbolize a sense of orientation toward a goal, and as a pun on the challenge, 'come pass.' Later, the family bought an old 36-foot yawl, named *September Song* after her parent's favorite nostalgic song from the Broadway musical, *Knickerbocker Holiday* (1938), eventually traded in for a fancier 39-foot Concordia yawl they named *Tripoli*. This name reflected their awareness that Connie's father—and his father and grandfather—had been named William after Commodore William Bainbridge, a distant relative who had been held captive for the two years 1803–1805 in Tripoli, Libya, by the Barbary Pirates (Barnes 1897; Long 1981). On board both yawls, which had bunks for all four members of the family in a two-part cabin, Connie would play Yap.

Hypothesis 9: Within a diversity of computer games, it is usually possible to identify at least one with symbolic affinities to the environment in which a real person lived and died.

With these facts in mind, it was easy to pick the appropriate MMO: *Pirates of the Burning Sea*, one of the rare historical gameworlds, given the dominance of fantasy and science fiction in the genre, set in the Caribbean in 1720 (Searle 2008).

Connie had indeed visited the Caribbean, staying with an uncle and aunt who lived in the Bahamas, and the nature of the game would allow her to resume avocational yachting, even though the story would require her to fire cannon at other ships. I had earlier run a character based on an adventuresome ancestor who was the right age in 1720, Edmund Bainbridge, her great-great-great-great-great-great-grandfather who was also the grandfather of Commodore Bainbridge (De Forest 1950), and another based on her great uncle Consuelo Andrew Seoane, who had carried a bullet in his shoulder ever since he had received it at the Battle of Santiago de Cuba in 1898 (Seoane 1960, 1968). Prior familiarity with an MMO of course makes it easy to use it as the venue for impersonation, even though one discovers less about the game itself during a second or third play-through.

Hypothesis 10: Revival of a deceased person is rendered easier if one has already explored the selected virtual environment in some other way, for example through a less personally meaningful avatar.

236   *William Sims Bainbridge*

Pirates of the Burning Sea (POTBS) should not be confused with the very different MMO *Pirates of the Caribbean* based on the Disney film franchise.

Rather, POTBS is a high-quality, rather realistic game that requires development of sailing skills and careful use of resources, awareness of the local geography, and tactical analysis when the enemy has more than one vessel. The chief departure from boating realism is that the ships have a little bit of headway even when sailing directly into the wind, allowing them to turn. This was necessary not merely because some players would not be expert seamen, but also because the topography of many battles involved archipelagos of islands between which the ship must maneuver, even as the wind direction shifts. In addition to many gangs of non-player characters, there are four factions: English, Spanish, French, and pirates, which indeed were competing in the Caribbean at about that time (Woodard 2007). The details about sailing technology and the historical context are not themselves related to religion, but illustrate the general issue that selection of a gameworld in which to memorialize a deceased person must take into account the degree of realism in the particular areas of life relevant to the deceased individual and the living family.

As well as having an appropriate ambiance, POTBS had a suitable main quest arc, because it involved a love affair with a pirate that could lead to marriage, and marriage was something Connie sought but never gained. Given her ancestry, it seemed reasonable to have Connie's avatar be English, and given her family heritage, which included two other warship captains, be a naval officer rather than, for example, a shipbuilder. She ascended the 50 levels of game experience from November 30, 2013 until February 26, 2014, and her progress was documented in 4,838 screenshot photos of the computer display. The two earlier characters had been run through POTBS when it was operated by Sony Online Entertainment, but Sony had allowed a new company formed by the original designers to take it over in February 2013. When I reentered POTBS, I attempted to subscribe, but this proved to be impossible so I played for free, and most of the game's website was unavailable during this period. The long-term survival of POTBS is uncertain, and its one-time competitor, *Pirates of the Caribbean Online*, lived only from 2007 until 2013.

Hypothesis 11: Because they require continual financial support and in some cases intellectual property permission, online virtual worlds are unreliable for long-term use as environments in which to share a revival with other people.

Games such as the three explored here include many forms of fictional death, but occasionally a real death occurs, as a player's life ends and that player's virtual friends must cope with loss. Constance set black sails on her ship, and joined a funeral procession across the Caribbean for a deceased player whose character had been named Truuth [sic] Bringer, ending with

Revival in virtual worlds 237

a service in the virtual church at Port Royal. Virtual funerals in MMOs are not common, but have been staged in other MMOs such as *WoW* and *Battleground Europe*. There is no reason why real-world friends or relatives could not stage regular online events at which they would commemorate deceased loved ones in many different ways, for example playing the roles of an entire generation of deceased ancestors in some online team adventure.

Hypothesis 12: Groups of people may conduct effective memorial rituals online.

When I logged out for the last time from POTBS, Constance was peacefully chatting with her husband, Rashid of the Barbary Corsairs, in the elegant living room of their comfortable home on Grand Turk Island, in the year 2014 or perhaps 1720.

She wore a lover's handkerchief, "a memento to keep your spirits high, and a cross," carved from whalebone. She also had a wooden leg from an early misadventure, which I could have replaced with a normal one, but kept for her as a symbol of the disabilities she suffered in real life. She belonged to a friendly player guild, named Order of the Temple, so her social as well as religious needs were well taken care of. This fantasy in no way offered real salvation from her horrible death, nearly a half century earlier, or a quarter millennium later, depending on how you count virtual time. But in the absence of faith in gods, it was the best I could do.

Hypothesis 13: To achieve a sense of closure, when a virtual memorial ends, the avatar should be left in a symbolically appropriate situation.

Conclusion

As human society gradually adjusts to the tremendous pressures of scientific discovery, technological innovation, and economic globalization, many alternatives to traditional religion are likely to arise. We cannot predict how significant each will be over the long term, neither can we be certain what the balance between the sacred and the secular will be in people's lives. Logically, information technology will play many significant roles, and allow people to explore many new forms of role-playing. Thus memorialization of deceased persons within computer-generated virtual worlds is but one of many possibilities that must be explored, although at the present time one of the most promising.

Notes

1 The views expressed in this chapter do not necessarily represent the views of the National Science Foundation or the United States.
2 nwn.wikia.com/wiki/Tyr. Accessed April 2, 2013.

References

Bainbridge, William Sims. 2010. *The Warcraft Civilization*. Cambridge, MA: MIT Press.

Bainbridge, William Sims. 2013a. 'Ancestor Veneration Avatars'. In Rocci Luppicini (ed.), *Handbook of Research on Technoself: Identity in a Technological Society*, 308–321. Hershey, PA: Information Science Reference.

Bainbridge, William Sims. 2013b. *eGods: Faith Versus Fantasy in Computer Gaming*. New York: Oxford University Press.

Bainbridge, William Sims. 2013c. 'Perspectives on Virtual Veneration'. *The Information Society* 29(3): 196–202.

Bainbridge, William Sims. 2013d. 'Stranger in a Strange Land'. In Titus Hjelm and Phil Zuckerman (eds), *Studying Religion and Society*, 26–38. New York: Routledge.

Bainbridge, William Sims. 2013e. 'Transavatars'. In Max More and Natasha Vita-More (eds.) *The Transhumanist Reader*, 91–108. Chichester, UK: Wiley-Blackwell.

Bainbridge, William Sims. 2014. *Personality Capture and Emulation*. London: Springer.

Barnes, James. 1897. *Commodore Bainbridge*. New York: Appleton.

Blaskovich, Jim and Jeremy Bailenson. 2011. *Infinite Reality: The Hidden Blueprint of Our Virtual Lives*. New York: William Morrow.

Burroughs, Edgar Rice. 1922. *The Chessmen of Mars*. Chicago, IL: A. C. McClurg.

Castronova, Edward, Travis Ross, Mark Bell, Matthew Falk, Robert Cornell and Matt Haselton. 2008. 'Constructing Arden: Life Inside the Machine'. *IEEE MultiMedia* 15(1): 4–8.

De Forest, Louis Effingham. 1950. *Ancestry of William Seaman Bainbridge*. Oxford, UK: Scrivener.

Geraci, Robert M. 2014. *Virtually Sacred*. New York: Oxford University Press.

Gygax, Gary. 1979. *Advanced Dungeons and Dragons, Dungeon Masters Guide*. New York: TSR/Random House.

Inge, William. 1962. *Eleven Short Plays*. New York: Dramatists Play Service.

Knowles, Brent, Trent Oster, Preston Watamaniuk, Bob McCabe, Luke Kristjanson Jim Bishop and Keith Soleski. 2002. *Neverwinter Nights Manual*. Edmonton, Canada: Bioware.

Long, David Foster. 1981. *Ready to Hazard: A Biography of Commodore William Bainbridge, 1774–1833*. Hanover, NH: University Press of New England.

Moreno, Jacob L. 1946. 'Psychodrama and Group Psychotherapy'. *Sociometry* 9(2–3): 249–253.

Moreno, Jacob L. and Zerka Toeman. 1942. 'The Group Approach in Psychodrama'. *Sociometry* 5(2): 191–195.

Nardi, Bonnie. 2010. *My Life as a Night Elf Priest: An Anthropological Account of World of Warcraft*. Ann Arbor, MI: University of Michigan Press.

Rothblatt, Martine. 2014. *Virtually Human*. New York: St Martin's Press.

Searle, Michael. 2008. *Pirates of the Burning Sea*. Roseville, CA: Prima.

Seoane, Consuelo Andrew. 1960. *Beyond the Range*s. New York: Robert Spellar.

Seoane, Rhoda Low. 1968. *Uttermost East and the Longest War*. New York: Vantage.

Stark, Rodney and William Sims Bainbridge. 1987. *A Theory of Religion*. New York: Lang.

Tolkien, J.R.R. 1973 [1954]. *The Fellowship of the Ring*. New York: Ballantine.

Van Druten, John. 1951. *Bell, Book, and Candle*. New York: Dramatists Play Service.

Wagner, Richard. 1895 [1849]. *The Art-Work of the Future*. In *Richard Wagner's Prose Works*, 69–213. London: K. Paul, Trench, Trübner.

Woodard, Colin. 2007. *The Republic of Pirates*. Orlando, FL: Harcourt.

Yee, Nick. 2014. *The Proteus Paradox: How Online Games and Virtual Worlds Change Us – and How They Don't*. New Haven, CT: Yale University Press.

Part IV

Countercultural personal spiritualities and religions

14 African-American ufology in the music and mythos of Sun Ra

Johanna J. M. Petsche

Introduction

Sun Ra (1914–1993) was a wildly prolific and innovative jazz bandleader, composer and pianist who became immersed in the mythology of ancient Egypt and ideas of space travel, declaring that 'space is the place' and that he himself was of extra-terrestrial origin. These themes pervaded all aspects of his music and onstage performances, from song titles and lyrics to set designs, record jacket art and costumes. This chapter will begin with an account of Ra's life and career, with focus on his fascination with Egyptian mythology and outer space, and the flamboyant ways in which he expressed these in his work. It will then be shown how these two themes form twin poles of Ra's fundamental mythos, or what musicologist Graham Lock terms Ra's 'Astro Black Mythology'. Lock's term refers to Ra's deliberate formulation of a mythic future and past for African-Americans, which Ra presents in his work as an alternative to the Christian mythology that had shaped the worldview of African slaves. For Ra, Egypt signified an ancient Golden Age for Black people, while outer space represented an empowering image of the technological future and the prospect of very new possibilities for human beings. Ra's imaginative Arkestra performances and recordings became sacred arenas, in which Ra could freely express and glorify his mythological vision. Following this discussion, it will be demonstrated how Ra's Afrocentric mission is in some ways congruent with the beliefs of two Black Nationalist spiritual movements in America: the Nation of Islam (NOI), founded by Wallace Fard Muhammad in 1930, and the Nuwaubian Nation of Moors (NNM), founded by Dwight York in 1967. Finally, there will be an examination of the particular significance of ufology, a powerful 'invented' or 'fictional' religious discourse, to Ra's mythos and to the cosmological and eschatological narratives of these two movements. Where the NOI teaches that a UFO will destroy White infidels, the NNM incorporate into their doctrine a developed apocalyptic scenario where members might be transported to outer space and later return to earth to save the planet.

244 *Johanna J. M. Petsche*

Sun Ra: early years (1914–1952)

Sun Ra (henceforth Ra), also known in different phases of his life as Sonny, Le Sony'r Ra, Ambassador to the Emperor of the Omniverse, and other titles, was born Herman Poole Blount in Birmingham, Alabama, the most segregated city in America (Szwed 2000: 3). In his adulthood, Ra was intent on crafting a mythic identity, insisting that he was an alien from the planet Saturn:

> People say I'm Herman Blount, but I don't know him. That's an imaginary person, he never existed. I have a sister and brother named Blount, but their father died 10 years before I arrived on the planet. He's not my father. If I tried to do anything with the name Sonny Blount, I couldn't . . . I'm not terrestrial, I'm a celestial being.
>
> (Sinclair 2010b: 5)

Ra's older sister, Mary Blount Jenkins, gave a different account: "he's not from no Mars . . . he was born at my mother's aunt's house over there by the train station . . . I know, 'cause I got on my knees and peeped through the keyhole" (Szwed 2000: 7). His year of birth is usually given as 1914, though due to his own deliberate obfuscations it has also been reported as 1910 and 1912 (Grass 2009: 43). In one interview, Ra declared that he had come to earth "around 1055 or so" (Lock 2004: 47), and on other occasions he even denied having been born at all, and made the same claim about the members of his musical ensemble, the Arkestra (Lock 2004: 51). For example, Ra informed British journalist, Mark Sinker, in 1989: "I'm not here, you see – this is not me talking, this is just my image and shadow. I wouldn't be caught dead on a planet like this" (Lock 2004: 73). Ra believed that Black people were "myths" and were "not real" (Lock 2004: 60–61), because they had no proper relationship with greater society and with the law. They did not exist in any meaningful sense in the present, and should seek a connection to the past and future, even if they themselves had to create it (Lock 2004: 60–61, 63).

Ra was a dreamy, introverted child who taught himself piano and developed the remarkable ability to transcribe from memory big band charts that he heard at concerts (Gershon 2010: 98). At the age of ten, he joined the fraternal American Woodmen Junior Division, a group of boys who met weekly at the Knights of Pythias Temple. Ra later stated that the group had taught him about discipline, secret orders and how to be a leader (Szwed 2000: 10). At Industrial High School, the only Black high school in Birmingham, Ra excelled in all his subjects and read copiously on science fiction, world history, religion, Freemasonry and the occult (Szwed 2000: 19, 20–22). In 1934, Ra's favourite English teacher, Ethel Harper, a singer, offered him his first full-time music job in a band. This became the Ethel Harper Band and toured through the Southeast and Midwest.

When Harper left the group, Ra took over, renaming it the Sonny Blount Orchestra, though the group was short-lived and he found more lucrative work playing in big bands in Birmingham (Szwed 2000: 24–26, 32–34). Ra stated in a 1970 interview that, "in the Deep South, the black people were very oppressed . . . the only thing they had was big bands. Unity showed that black men could join together and dress nicely, do something nice, and that was all they had" (Lock 2004: 25).

In 1936, Ra was awarded a scholarship to college at Alabama A&M, known at the time as the State Agricultural and Mechanical Institute for Negroes. He was a music education major, though he left after only one year. Ra claimed to have experienced a vision during his time in college, and his account shows all the signs of a classic UFO abduction story. According to Ra, he was contacted by spacemen, transported to outer space in a beam of light and warned of the moral chaos that lay ahead on earth. If Ra had experienced such a vision at the time, it would have occurred over 15 years before the date of George Adamski's alien contact account, which is generally considered the first such account (Szwed 2000: 28–31). However, close acquaintances of Ra say that he only spoke of this vision after 1953 and, according to biographer, John F. Szwed, some parts of the story seem to indicate that it was more "revisionist autobiography . . . Sonny was pulling together and connecting several strains of his life. He was both prophesying his future and explaining his past with a single act of personal mythology" (Szwed 2000: 31–32).

Ra was drafted into the army in 1942 but refused to serve due to his pacifistic Christian beliefs, as well as to a chronic hernia associated with problems of his left testicle that plagued him for the remainder of his life. Becoming one of the first Black conscientious objectors, he spent almost six weeks in prison before moving to Chicago where he met one of his idols, prolific bandleader, arranger and pianist Fletcher Henderson (1897–1952). Ra became second pianist and arranger in Henderson's orchestra at Chicago's Club DeLisa in 1946 and 1947 (Gershon 2010: 99; Szwed 2000: 40–41, 44–45). In Chicago, Ra began assembling his own musical groups, first 'space trios' and eventually in 1952 the nucleus of his ever-expanding musical ensemble, the 'Arkestra', also known by such titles as the Solar Myth Arkestra, the Myth Science Arkestra, the Intergalactic Research Arkestra, the Power of Astro-Infinity Arkestra, and the Omniverse Jet-Set Arkestra (Grass 2009: 47; Sinclair 2010a: 188).

The significance of Egypt from 1952

Egypt became a distinguishing motif in Ra's work from 1952, the year in which he met Alton Abraham, a 14-year-old minister's son who shared Ra's interest in astrology, metaphysics and ancient history. Abraham became Ra's lifelong mentor, manager, booking agent, recording supervisor and

246   *Johanna J. M. Petsche*

business partner (Szwed 2000: 74–75). Under Abraham's guidance, Ra, then Herman Blount with the nickname 'Sonny', legally changed his name to Le Sony'r Ra and began telling tales of his abduction experience at college that he claimed led him to discover that he was actually from Saturn (Gershon 2010: 99). It was common for jazz musicians to create new names for themselves, but Ra did not follow the tradition of using titles derived from European aristocracy as did 'Duke' Ellington, 'King' Oliver, 'Count' Basie or Lester Young whose sobriquet was 'Prez', short for President (Lock 2004: 45). Ra opted instead for a name inherited from Egyptian mythology when, he claimed, "the Creator spoke to me one day and called me that" (Lock 2004: 51). In line with Black Nationalist beliefs of the time, Ra identified himself with a heritage rooted in Egypt. By linking his ancestry with one of the most ancient, celebrated and technologically advanced civilisations in history, Ra sought a deeper significance to his existence as an African-American.

The practice of renaming figures prominently in African-American culture was one of the first actions undertaken by freed slaves. It became a significant emblematic reclamation of personhood (Lock 2004: 49). Historian, Sterling Stuckey, explains the significance of one's name in West African societies (from which the majority of slaves originated):

> Among the Negro peoples a man's name is often identified with his very soul, and often with the soul of his ancestors . . . for black people not born in Africa, resentment at not having a surname and at having a Christian name of another's choosing were causes for distress.
>
> (Lock 2004: 49)

Renaming was a common process undertaken by members of Black Nationalist groups such as the NOI, Moorish Science Temple (MST) and NNM. In the NOI, for example, upon registering as Muslims, members would drop their African 'slave' names in the hope that Allah would bestow upon them their 'real' names. Until then, many members adopted the simple 'X' as did Malcolm X, the most famous member of the NOI, and this signified an original identity. When converts received their X, it was thought that a new world of opportunities would unfold for them (Lock 2004: 49; Turner 1997: 156). Similarly, members of the MST were to convert their 'slave names' into new names by adding the suffixes 'el' or 'bey', and in the NNM, founder Noble Drew Ali took on new names signifying the adoption of new cultural identities that entailed the establishment of new mythic pasts for members (Holzinger 2001: 191; Lock 2004: 46).

The Arkestra

For 40 years to his death in 1993, Ra led his Arkestra, which specialised in performing Ra's own idiosyncratic jazz compositions and individualistic arrangements and which, according to Szwed, "became the most continually

African-American ufology and Sun Ra   247

advanced and experimental group in the history of jazz and popular music" (Szwed 2000: xvii). Szwed explains that the name 'Arkestra' plays on the words orchestra and ark, alluding to the Egyptian god Ra's ark or solar boat, as well as the Biblical ark that held the covenant. Ra once said:

> 'A covenant of Arkestra': it's like a selective service to God. Picking out some people. Arkestra has a 'ra' at the beginning and the end . . . That's phonetic balance . . . ['kest' in the middle] equals 'kist' . . . I read that in Sanskrit 'kist' means 'sun's gleam'.
>
> (Szwed 2000: 94)

Every aspect of Ra's music – timbre, melody, rhythm and instrumentation – was open to exploration, as if calling for listeners to take the journey with Ra into new and unknown sonic territory. Ra instructed Arkestra members to "play what you don't know" (Grass 2009: 44) and said of his own playing: "I have to play things that are impossible. I have to get to a piano and hit some notes on there that aren't on there. And I'm doin' it all the time" (Corbett 1994: 311). His unorthodox compositions fused bebop, blues, big band swing, ragtime and Afro-funk styles, and featured large-scale ensemble collective improvisations as well as the dazzling solo improvisations of long-time members such as saxophonists John Gilmore, Pat Patrick and Marshall Allen (Sinclair 2010a: 186). Compositions sometimes required 'space keys', where a drone or pedal point anchored the composition while players improvised, and some pieces were to be played in multiple keys. The Arkestra utilised an assortment of brass, woodwinds, percussion, electric and acoustic bass, vocals and, from the mid-1950s, pioneered the use of electric piano, Solovox, clavioline, Hammond organ and synthesisers. Ra obtained one of the earliest Moog synthesisers, an instrument which, according to Trevor Pinch and Frank Trocco became an "apparatus for transgression, transcendence, and transformation" (Pinch and Trocco 2002: 305). Through the use of these 'newfangled' electric instruments, Ra's music celebrated alien-ness and challenged more conventional notions of how music should sound, proposing new musical possibilities and alternative listening experiences. Indeed Ra described his music as being from another planet (Corbett 1994: 311).

Ra's wildly original and provocative performances involved mythic themes, Afro-American liturgy, science fiction, Black cabaret and vaudeville, and members of the Arkestra wore a variety of uniforms to match. In the early years, they wore green sport shirts, rust-coloured pants and red fezzes (as worn by the MST and briefly by the NOI) and later, flamboyant futuristic Afro-space costumes featuring shimmering sequin-studded robes and elaborate antennaed space-helmets, which were sometimes equipped with flashing lights (Szwed 2000: xvii, 143). Performances might feature dancing, light shows and slides, art displays and films, as well as juggling, tumbling and fire-eating. In 1978, Ra's enthusiasm for George Lucas' *Star*

248   *Johanna J. M. Petsche*

Wars inspired a choreographed light-sabre battle being incorporated into Arkestra performances (Szwed 2000: 257, 348). Ra once described *Star Wars* as "very accurate", and criticised most science fiction narratives for their tendency to emphasise fear and ugliness (Langguth 2010: 156–157).

Audiences were often involved in performances. The Arkestra might surround an audience member, screeching their instruments while Ra shouted in the face of the unsuspecting person, "If you're willing to give up your life for your country, will you give up your death for me?" (Szwed 2000: 258). One mortified member of Ra's audience recounts having been asked to kick-step right around the theatre with Ra (Szwed 2000: 258). Sometimes Ra requested that the audience join hands to help conquer death, or asked Arkestra member, contralto June Tyson, to cry for the people of the earth. She and the Arkestra would start crying, and then the audience, overwhelmed by emotion, would also join in the weeping (Szwed 2000: 257).[1]

Sun Ra: later years (1961–1993)

From 1961, when the Arkestra relocated to New York, Ra became particularly obsessed with themes of outer space. He began to wear his space-themed stage clothes on the street and his music, more than before, featured electronic instruments producing alien textures and otherworldly sounds (Lock 2004: 27; Szwed 2000: 183). The Arkestra moved into a series of 'Ra houses', where Ra would wake members at 4 AM to play newly-composed works (Ra himself suffered from insomnia). They were to rehearse voraciously, often for 10 or 15 hours a day, with rehearsals augmented by Ra's long-winded monologues on topics ranging from the future of interplanetary humanity to the life-sustaining properties of a specific type of bean. Musicians who did not focus or who came to rehearsals late were locked inside cupboards or, at the Arkestra's next performance, were positioned on chairs at the front of the stage. Ra would announce that they were not allowed to play due to their lack of discipline (Grass 2009: 53–54; Nelson 2014). He also required Arkestra members to weaken ties with family and girlfriends, and punished members who failed to do this (Szwed 2000: 196). There is an interesting parallel with members of the NOI, who were known for their strict discipline as well as their meticulous dress and behaviour which symbolised, according to Daniel Kreiss, a repudiation of Black popular stereotypes and a championing of self-control and work as a means of empowerment (Kreiss 2008: 63).

It is clear that the Arkestra was no ordinary jazz ensemble; in some ways it could be likened to a kind of religious order. The group lived communally under intense and austere conditions imposed by Ra; they wore special costumes that reflected their leader's 'mythos'; and their music was meant as a vehicle for spiritual transformation and experience, presumably just as much for the musicians as it was for their listeners. Indeed Ra designated their performances "myth rituals" (Szwed 2000: 256). On this note, one

African-American ufology and Sun Ra 249

may also consider the improvisatory solo performances of pianist Keith Jarrett, who places stringent demands on his audiences and claims that his performances involve 'channelling' a divine source of inspiration. The resulting ambience of his concerts led to the popular idea that they resembled sacred rituals (Petsche 2009: 142–143). It is known that Arkestra members took seriously Ra's mythology and extra-terrestrial claims. In an interview with Art Yard's Peter Dennett, long-time Arkestra saxophonist Danny Ray Thompson referred to Ra as "angelic" and "a master of everything", while for saxophonist Knoell Scott, he was "a messenger from somewhere . . . He said it was Saturn, I have no reason to disbelieve it . . . his mere presence was enough to put you on another plane, if you were receptive enough" (Allen 2014). Sibylle Zerr, in *Picture Infinity: Marshall Allen & The Sun Ra Arkestra,* even reveals how Arkestra members believe that current pianist, Farid Barron, was 'chosen' by Ra 12 years after his death, with Barron himself stating, "I feel that I have been initiated into a sacred fraternal order" (Patterson 2012).

In 1968 the Arkestra moved to Philadelphia where they continued to work and record, though they regularly travelled back and forth to New York, dressed as spacemen (Szwed 2000: 268). Record executive, Randall Grass, remembers encountering Sun Ra one day in a hardware store in Philadelphia:

> Sun Ra often wore an immense silver tunic or smock made of material that looked like a medieval knight's chain mail, his helmetlike headdress made of the same material. Sun Ra's outfits were not just stage attire. His facial expression was as set as that of a priest presiding over a religious ritual. But he was buying hardware supplies. There was something profoundly incongruous about such a personage engaged in such a mundane activity. One might wonder why he could not simply materialize the supplies in some way. But even a space traveller needs to make certain repairs, and where else could he get materials on Planet Earth?
>
> (Grass 2009: 45)

In the countercultural late 1960s and early 1970s, Ra was appointed lecturer at the University of California at Berkeley, teaching subjects involving Neoplatonism, racial issues in ancient history and religious texts, pollution and war, and a reinterpretation of the Bible in light of Egyptology. Lectures were held in the music department and included a half-hour keyboard or Arkestra performance (Szwed 2000: 294–295).

By the end of his life, Ra had recorded at least 1,000 compositions on over 120 albums, many for his own company, El Saturn, launched in the 1950s and operated by Abraham in Chicago (Ra also owned his own music publishing company, Enterplanetary Koncepts, and production company, Infinity Inc) (Sinclair 2010b: 11, 187; Szwed 2000: xvii). Ra's eclectic music has been kept alive through the continued existence of the Arkestra, currently led by

250 *Johanna J. M. Petsche*

92-year-old virtuoso saxophonist, Marshall Allen, who joined the group in 1958. Numerous tribute bands have also emerged, including Jerry Dammers' Spatial AKA Orchestra. Ra's epochal recordings of the 1950s and 1960s are now available to contemporary audiences, and his trippy hand-painted records have become high-priced collectors items, today among the most collectable records in the world (Nelson 2014; Szwed 2000: xvii).

Ra's Astro Black Mythology and Black Nationalist religio-spiritual movements

Themes of ancient Egypt and outer space dominate Ra's mostly program-matic song and album titles ("Tiny Pyramids", "Ahnknaton" (sic), "Ankh", "Sunology", "Sun Ra Visits Planet Earth", "We Travel the Spaceways" and "Cosmonaut-Astronaut Rendezvous"), as well as his song lyrics, poetry, set designs, record jacket art and the elaborate costumes worn by Ra and the Arkestra. In his study of Ra, Duke Ellington and Anthony Braxton, *Blutopia* (2004), Graham Lock uses the term "Astro Black Mythology", derived from Ra's poem/song lyric "Astro Black", to refer to what he sees as the axis of Ra's cosmology. This was the creation of a mythic past and future for African-Americans, both posed as alternatives to representations of the past (the Exodus myth) and future (an afterlife in heaven) in Christian mythology. Lock argues the term "Astro Black Mythology" clarifies Ra's deliberate formulation of a mythology and encapsulates the two dominant features of that mythology: "Astro" refers to the outer space future and "Black" to the ancient Egyptian past (Lock 2004: 14, 33).

In his Astro Black Mythology, Ra questioned accepted notions of reality and proposed alternatives. Ra disagreed with Judeo-Christian mythology, which had shaped the worldview of African slaves. This is because this mythology encouraged African-Americans to identify with the Old Testament stories of the Israelites, trapping them into a false version of history and disconnecting them from their true historical legacy, the Black civilisation of ancient Egypt. He was also critical of the failure of the church to embrace the science and technology of the day (Lock 2004: 21, 32–33). Ra said "the main problem in America is black folk worshippin' the wrong thing" (Lock 2004: 24). He further explained:

> Myth permits man to situate himself in these times and to connect him-self with the past and the future. What I'm looking for are the myths of the future, the destiny of man . . . I believe that if one wants to act on the destiny of the world, it's necessary to treat it like a myth.
>
> (Lock 2004: 61)

Before continuing with an examination of the particular significance of outer space to Ra's Afrocentric mythos, it is interesting to consider this mythos alongside the values and beliefs of two Black Nationalist spiritual

African-American ufology and Sun Ra 251

movements. These emerged in the United States in response to the continued oppression and social isolation of African-Americans in the twentieth century. These movements – the NOI (1930) and the NNM (1967) – sought to strengthen Black morale by reclaiming a perceived Islamic heritage for Black people and projecting a utopian vision of an interplanetary future for them through elaborate space-themed narratives and eschatologies that identified group members with extra-terrestrials. They share similarities with Ra's Astro Black Mythology, which also posited for Black people an ancient golden age (though this was firmly planted in Egypt) and a future based on a special relationship to extra-terrestrials and outer space.

The NOI

The NOI was founded by Wallace Fard Muhammad (*c*.1877–*c*.1934), a former member of the MST who claimed to be a reincarnation of their founder, the charismatic Timothy Drew or Noble Drew Ali (1886–1929).[2] Between 1929 and 1931, Fard Muhammad assumed the guise of a Syrian door-to-door peddler of silks and Asian and African wares, working in poor African-American neighbourhoods in Detroit. At the same time, he taught them that the so-called Negroes belonged to the lost tribe of Shabazz from Mecca and that they must return to their original religion of Islam and original language of Arabic. Fard Muhammad identified himself as a prophet, though at least some of his followers, including his successor, Elijah Muhammad (1897–1975), believed that he was Allah incarnate (Berg 2005: 691–692; Palmer and Luxton 1998: 363). The attraction of Islam for Fard Muhammad, as it was for the earlier Noble Drew Ali, must have been its dominant themes of egalitarianism and solidarity, and also the fact that it was seen to stand in opposition to Christianity, which belonged to those of European (or White) descent. According to Elijah Muhammad, Christianity was "one of the most perfect black-slave-making religions on our planet. It has completely killed the so-called Negroes mentally" (Berg 2005: 693).

Generating an aura of mystery and legend around his background (details of his actual origins are mysterious) and developing for himself a litany of cryptic names, Fard Muhammad established the NOI in Detroit in 1930, but disappeared in 1934. His successor and one of his earliest followers was Elijah Muhammad, formerly Elijah Poole. Under Elijah Muhammad, the NOI transformed from a local movement into the most powerful Islamic organisation in the United States (Turner 1997: 148, 160–161). It is not known how much of Elijah Muhammad's teaching he himself had invented and how much came from Fard Muhammad, though core NOI cosmology and eschatology is usually attributed to Fard Muhammad (Monastra 1993: 75). When Elijah Muhammad died in 1975, there were 76 NOI temples and between 50,000 and 100,000 members across the United States (Barrett 2001: 251). His son Warith (born Wallace) Deen Mohammed (1933–2008) succeeded him, reforming the NOI along more orthodox lines.

252 *Johanna J. M. Petsche*

NOI cosmology holds that the Creator entrusted the creation of the universe to 24 Black Scientists, who were each given 25,000 years to carry out work on a part of the universe. A dissident among these Scientists, Yakub, was exiled to the Greek island of Patmos, where, in a laboratory, he concocted the White race ('blue-eyed devils') through an experiment involving genetic manipulation that required the mass slaughter of Black babies. The original people of the world were Black, but following Yakub's genetic experiment the newly created White race came to dominate the Black race for the next 6,000 years, during which time Black people forgot their original religion of Islam and original language, Arabic. In NOI doctrine, Yakub is portrayed as a devil figure, and subsequently all White people are seen as children of the devil (Palmer 2010: 17; Szwed 2000: 132). In the context of contemporary discourses regarding 'invented' or 'fiction-based' religions (Cusack 2010; Davidsen 2013), it is important to note that the NOI merged both a fictional Islamic past for African-Americans with the invented tradition of UFO or extra-terrestrial religions, itself a major instance of religious invention in the modern era.

Fard Muhammad taught that the era of this White domination would soon end, along with the destruction of the world and that he had come to earth to oversee this. White people and all enemies of Allah would be obliterated by the 'Mother Plane' or 'Mother Wheel', a massive UFO half a mile in circumference, built by the original Black Scientists. It is described in NOI writings as "a small human planet made for the purpose of destroying the present world of the enemies of Allah" and it is stated that "the small circular-made planes called flying saucers, which are so much talked of being seen, could be from this mother Plane" (Wojcik 2003: 281). Elijah Muhammad's official spokesman, former nightclub singer Louis Farrakhan (born Louis Eugene Walcott but formally known as Louis X), claimed at a press conference in 1989 that during a vacation at his Mexican villa he had a vision where he was beamed aboard the Mother Plane and met with Elijah Muhammad (Wojcik 2003: 281).

The NOI Mother Plane narrative is an interpolation of the Biblical prophecies of Ezekiel, who describes his vision of four winged beasts in the sky next to spinning wheels (Ezekiel 1:4–28), and the imminent apocalyptic battle in which Israel's enemies are demolished so that a new era of peace can follow (Ezekiel 38–39). In NOI doctrine, the Mother Plane remains invisible to most people, though it can be seen twice a week, and is the same object that Ezekiel had seen as a great wheel in the sky (Lock 2004: 48; Szwed 2000: 132). Charles Lieb argues that Ezekiel's account of the spinning wheels, each described as a "wheel within a wheel", signifies an attempt to "technologize the ineffable" by apprehending the power of God in terms of the wheel, likely to be the greatest technological innovation of that time. NOI teachings, in a similar way, conceptualise the vision of Ezekiel as a plane in outer space, representing the apex of mechanical invention in the mid-twentieth century (Taylor 2005: 57).

It is known that Ra was familiar with NOI teachings. He read Elijah Muhammad's *The Theology of Time*, a compilation of 20 lectures given between June and October 1972 and, according to both Alton Abraham and Arkestra tenor saxophonist, John Gilmore, there was contact between Ra and members of the NOI in the 1950s, both being based in Chicago at that time (Lock 2004: 47; Szwed 2000: 133). Gilmore even claimed that the NOI stole several ideas from Ra: "They would sort of antagonise him, in order to get him to talk" (Lock 2004: 47). The NOI newspaper *Muhammad Speaks* was established after Ra began distributing his own leaflets, which the NOI had read, and Ra had stated that Elijah Muhammad's idea that "Negro" means "death" was his own (Ra had researched the etymology). Although Ra distanced himself from the NOI's separatist ideology and could not accept that White people were devils (Ra stated, "black people could be devils, too"), his Astro Black Mythology clearly ties in with the teachings of the NOI. Ra and Elijah Muhammad both perceived history as 'White history', a history that had stolen the past and identities of Black people and that to bring hope to Black people they needed to reverse many of the symbols and meanings of the past. They both distanced themselves from Sub-Saharan Africa, identifying instead with Ethiopia, Egypt and the Sudan, and believed that Black people must learn to restore their former glory, and that apocalypse and redemption by way of space travel might be the final outcome for people on earth. It amused Ra to think that he may be distantly related to Elijah Muhammad, who was originally Elijah Poole (Ra was born Herman Poole Blount) (Szwed 2000: 4, 105–106).

The NNM

The NNM was first established in Brooklyn, New York in 1967 under the title Ansaar Pure Sufi. Its founder, Dwight York (b. 1935), claimed to be an extra-terrestrial from the planet Rizq, located in the 19th galaxy called Illyuwen, who came to earth to save his people from destruction. York assumed a diversity of identities over the years to suit the many different phases of his teaching; he was known as Malachi Z. York, Isa Abdallah, The Qutb ('Axis of the Universe'), and Neter A'aferti Atum Re, among other aliases. Frequently shifting its religious affiliations, York's chameleonesque movement went by titles such as The Nubian Islaamic Hebrew Mission, Ansaaru Allah Community, and the Holy Tabernacle Ministries. Sociologist Susan Palmer argues that York's movement might better be described as not one, but a series of short-lived Black identity movements, drawing their teachings and symbols from a host of seemingly incompatible sources such as Muslim, Hebrew, Christian, Ancient Egyptian and Nubian traditions, as well as MST and NOI teachings. Whenever the group experienced the surrounding White secular society as threatening the group, they changed form (Palmer and Luxton 1998: 357, 2010: 148).

254   *Johanna J. M. Petsche*

The most recent position taken by York is that the Nuwaubians (members explain that the term 'Nuwaubu' is Arabic for 'prophet' or 'prophecy', as opposed to 'Nubian,' referring to the African-Americans not yet awakened) are descendants of the original Egyptians and are the only true Egyptians in the world. In their present headquarters, the Tama-Re compound in Putnam County, Georgia, the NNM community has built pyramids, a Sphinx and obelisk, and wear Egyptian costumes (Gabriel 2003: 155; Palmer 2010: 6). York, however, is not present at the headquarters. He is serving a 135-year sentence in a "supermax" security prison in Colorado after being convicted on numerous counts of child molestation charges (Palmer 2010: xv).

In his teaching, York traces the lineage of the Nuwaubians back to the Sumerian and Egyptian civilisations from the ancient Nubian kingdom in Sudan, but goes even further, expounding the "ancient astronaut" theory of the "Annunaki", who are considered to be angelic extra-terrestrial astronauts from the planet Rizq. York claims that the Annunaki colonised earth and established the first great civilisations of Sumeria and Egypt (Palmer 2010: 6). He concurs with Elijah Muhammad that the Black race is the original, essential humanity and that White people are devils. In a recorded lecture titled "Egipt and the Mask of God", York quite simply asserts, "White people are the devil. They say the Ns are not racist – bullcrap! I am" (Palmer 2010: 18). York taught that the chosen Nuwaubian people could become angelic, godlike beings called Eloheem. They had the potential to communicate with the extra-terrestrials (York himself claimed to be one) and were to breed with their assistance so as to produce 144,000 "pure Nubian children" (a number prophesised in the Book of Revelation). In 2003, the 'Mothership' would descend from the sky and hover over Tama-Re's great pyramid and the 144,000 children would be raptured to the planet Rizq. They would be taken to the Crystal City and "groomed" for 1,000 years, and then return to earth to save the planet (Palmer 2010: 135; Palmer and Luxton 1998: 361).

African-American ufology

Using the futuristic language of science fiction, highly prominent in American culture in the mid-twentieth century, Ra, the NOI, NNM, and other Black groups and artists were able to present utopian visions of the future, bringing new meaning to their existence and an escape route from the oppressive world. Ra stated:

> I ain't part of America. I ain't part of black people. They went another way. Black people are carefully supervised so they'll stay in a low position. But I'm not down there, yet I come from one of the most discriminating states in the whole world – Alabama.

(Lock 2004: 57)

By identifying with extra-terrestrials, Ra and members of these groups assigned a special significance to themselves as Black people, turning the tables on the racist discourse of the day. Their plights are part of the larger Afrofuturist mode of history-making which, for musicologist, J. Griffith Rollefson, "disarticulates Africa from the totalizing narratives of oppression that threaten to represent blackness as a burden alone" (Rollefson 2008: 94). Afrofuturism, a term coined by cultural critic, Mark Dery, in 1993 and examined by sociologist, Alondra Nelson, refers to works created by Black artists that express a uniquely African-American interpretation of futuristic narratives of scientific and technological progress (Rollefson 2008: 83). The significance of African-American ufology will be explored after a brief account of the emergence of, and meaning behind, UFO beliefs and narratives.

Speculation about whether life existed on other planets can be traced back to the work of Swedish scientist and mystic Emanuel Swedenborg (1688–1772). Furthermore, the advent of UFOs into the public consciousness is usually dated from Kenneth Arnold's apparent sighting in 1947, and the first interpretations of the phenomenon to George Adamski's reported UFO encounter in 1952 (Lewis 1995: xiii). With the rise of Spiritualism, the Theosophical Society and the I AM movement in the late nineteenth century, where each explored the idea of contact with spiritual beings from other planets, ufology became an invented tradition or fiction upon which both Black and White new spiritualities have drawn (Saliba 1995a: 26–27). Daniel Wojcik argues that UFO beliefs and science fiction narratives adapt and modify over time to express contemporary concerns, hopes and fears. These beliefs and narratives provide systems of existential meaning, indicating to believers that the universe is ordered, and that an age of harmony and justice is possible through the fulfilment of a cosmic plan. Initially emerging as a folk symbol of hope and salvation, UFOs promise rescue by means of a technological rapture brought about by extra-terrestrial saviour beings in the sky (Wojcik 2003: 274–275, 285). Carl Jung similarly understood UFOs to be expressions of human anxieties and of the need to be saved. He observed, for example, that fears prompted by the Cold War could easily cause people to project these fears into flying saucers (Saliba 1995b: 227). Jung argued that visions of UFOs in the form of luminous disks resembled mandalas and thus were archetypal symbols of psychic totality and salvation, manifesting from the collective unconscious (Wojcik 2003: 285).

According to ufologists, in typical abduction accounts, messages from extra-terrestrials (usually portrayed as superior to human beings) might contain cures to diseases, solutions to the transporting of earthlings to another planet, or messages of warning of imminent disasters on earth. A contactee is then given the critical task of warning others (Saliba 1995a: 48–49; Wojcik 2003: 276). This classic scenario plays out in the narratives of the NOI and NNM, and can be found in Ra's visionary experience

256   *Johanna J. M. Petsche*

described earlier, where Ra claimed that he was contacted by spacemen, beamed to outer space and warned of the moral chaos that threatened to destroy the earth. This classic abduction scenario can also be seen in "Space is the Place", a low-budget feature film which stars Ra, who also played a major role in creating the script. It was directed by John Coney in Oakland, California in 1972, and was produced by Jim Newman for release by North American Star Systems in 1974. Szwed describes the film as "part documentary, part science fiction, part Blaxploitation [sic], part revisionist Biblical epic" (Szwed 2000: 330).

In the opening scene of the film, Ra walks through a strange forest on a distant planet where conditions are more advanced than those on earth. He decides to bring the oppressed Black population of earth to this planet and embarks on a yellow oblong spaceship powered by energy generated from the music of the Arkestra. Ra lands in Oakland, California around 1972 (where in real life the Arkestra was living and where the Black Panthers were under attack by authorities). He sets out to rescue Black people from the evil pimp-overlord, the 'overseer' (Ray Johnson), Ra's greatest adversary. Ra tries to convince local African-Americans in Oakland to follow him into space and live out their "alter-destiny". The Overseer, the FBI and NASA ultimately force him to return to space prematurely. The film ends with the earth exploding as Ra and a small band of Black survivors fly to outer space, accompanied by the Arkestra's rendition of Ra's space chant "Space is the Place" (Grass 2009: 42–43; Szwed 2000: 330–331). In his music, Ra seemed to propose that outer space offered a future for everyone on earth, though in the film he was clearly concerned specifically with the plight of African-Americans (Lock 2004: 69).

A general fascination with outer space, and the belief and hope that space travel was actually possible, was not uncommon among parts of the Black population in America through the twentieth century. African-Americans desired to escape and transcend their oppressive past defined by enslavement, as well as the contemporary racial division of the day. Ra makes it clear in his music and interviews that the way for Black people to establish a personal identity and experience spiritual rebirth was by embracing the future and travelling to outer space, rather than by following the old path of Christianity (Lock 2004: 55). In the lyrics to "Space is the Place", Ra asserts: "Outer space is a pleasant place, a place that's really free, there's no limit to the things that you can do, there's no limit to the things that you can be, your thought is free, and your life is worthwhile" (Lock 2004: 28).

Further, by identifying with extra-terrestrials, Ra and members of the NOI and NNM could assign a new significance to Black people and their ancestry. As extra-terrestrials are not earthbound, utopian possibilities and innovative mythic identities opened up. Ra claimed to be an extra-terrestrial and from "the Angel race" (Lock 2004: 63). He suggested that his jazz heroes, Fletcher Henderson and Coleman Hawkins, were also angels rather than men (Lock 2004: 25). For Lock, Ra:

[o]ffers an alter-destiny to the dehumanization of the slaves and turns a racial epithet like "alien" into a mark of mystery and potential . . . Sun Ra declined to assert equal status with the oppressor and instead turned racist dehumanization on its head by claiming to be of a different race altogether.

(Lock 2004: 63)

Similarly, members of the NNM identified with extra-terrestrials in that they were, according to York, the "children of beautiful angelic beings from the planet Rizq" (Palmer 2010: 16). One day, promised York, a Mothership would descend and Nuwaubians would be raptured. For the NOI, Black people were related to extra-terrestrials while White people were doomed to be obliterated by a UFO, the Mother Wheel. NOI leader Elijah Muhammad stated: "That's the truth. You have people on Mars! Think how great you are. Ask the white man if he has any out there. We have life on other planets, but he don't" (Finley 2012: 440).

As a final note, a useful study was carried out by Stephen C. Finley on NOI member (and later leader of an offshoot group) Louis Farrakhan's UFO abduction account, referred to earlier. In this study, Finley argues that in identifying with extra-terrestrials, NOI members were offered "means of transcendence, meaning-making symbols and mythology, and a source in which to re-envision *black* origins" (Finley 2012: 460). In this context, UFOs provide:

[a] sense of fullness of identity and meaning beyond racist and narrow constructions of black as limited and inferior, and an accompanying alteration in consciousness that moves them to push against such constrictions. Among the many ways that UFOs and extra-terrestrials afforded the NOI complex subjectivity that subverted racism was with the identification of beings on planets such as Mars and Venus as "black", therefore extending African-American lineage and meaning beyond the material boundaries of America and the planet.

(Finley 2012: 440)

Conclusion

In the year 1952, Sonny Blount, as he was then known, legally changed his name to Le Sony'r Ra in reference to the Egyptian deity and began explaining that he was of extra-terrestrial origins. From that time to his death in 1993, Sun Ra's experimental music and flamboyant onstage performances were inspired by what Graham Lock designates his "Astro Black Mythology", which simultaneously creates a new mythic past and future for African-Americans. Ra's fundamental mission was, on the one hand, to replace oppressive Old Testament narratives with a mythologised vision of the heritage of humankind as rooted in African civilisation and, on the

258 *Johanna J. M. Petsche*

other, to posit a utopian interplanetary future for African-Americans, far beyond the confines of earthly existence. In what is perhaps the most unique musical project in the history of jazz, Ra's Afrofuturist vision was revealed through the barrage of alien sounds and otherworldly strains generated by his dedicated Arkestra, which itself demonstrated the scientific potential that Ra envisioned could help humanity. This chapter, while understanding that Ra was not the leader of a new religious movement, nevertheless evaluated Ra's mythos as a creative, and inventive, religious and spiritual narrative that was expressed in all aspects of his work. It also demonstrated how this mythos can be seen as a valuable case study in the broader invented religion of African-American ufology, and showed how it emerged from the same social, political and spiritual malaises that inspired the values and beliefs of a range of twentieth-century Black Nationalist religious systems. Based on heterodox interpretations of Islam and extra-terrestrial-themed mythology, Black Nationalist movements such as the NOI and the NNM were, like Ra, working to empower and bring hope to African-Americans. Combining Afrocentric ideas with UFO narratives enabled a powerful re-envisioning of African-American identities and origins, and allowed for a radically new interpretation of both the past and future.

Notes

1 Tyson was the only core Arkestra member who was female. It has been speculated that Ra disliked women; some say that for him they were a distraction, while others ascribed his attitude to latent homosexuality (Grass 2009: 49).
2 Initially called the Canaanite Temple, the Moorish Science Temple (MST) was founded in Newark, New Jersey in 1913 and came to prominence in Chicago in the 1920s. Noble Drew Ali was the first self-appointed prophet of modern American Islam and the MST the first Black religious group in the United States to disseminate widely the idea that Islam was the original and inherent religion of African Americans (Holzinger 2001: 191; Turner 1997: 90, 92). According to Noble Drew Ali, African Americans were racially not Africans but Asiatics and descendants of the Islamic Moorish Empire that ruled most of Europe and Asia (the term 'Moor' originates from the Greek *mauros*, meaning black or dark) (Easterling 2012: 29–30). The MST is the seedbed and prototype of the NOI, though the practices and scripture of the latter are considerably more Islamic than those of the MST (Berg 2005: 698).

References

Allen, Marshall. 2014. *Marshall Allen Presents Sun Ra and His Arkestra: In the Orbit of Ra*. UK online publishing: Strut.

Barrett, David V. 2001. *The New Believers: A Survey of Sects, Cults and Alternative Religions*. London: Cassell & Co.

Berg, Herbert. 2005. 'Religion Mythmaking in the African American Muslim Context: The Moorish Science Temple, the Nation of Islam, and the American Society of Muslims'. *Journal of the American Academy of Religion* 73(3): 685–703.

Corbett, John. 1994. *Extended Play: Sounding Off from John Cage to Dr. Funkenstein*. Durham, NC and London: Duke University Press.

Cusack, Carole M. 2010. *Invented Religions: Imagination, Fiction, and Faith*. Farnham, UK and Burlington, VT: Ashgate.

Davidsen, Markus Altena. 2013. 'Fiction-Based Religion: Conceptualizing a New Category Against History-Based Religion and Fandom'. *Culture and Religion* 14(4): 378–395.

Easterling, Paul H.L. 2012. 'The Moorish Science Temple of America: A Study Exploring the Foundations of African American Islamic Thought and Culture'. PhD, Rice University, Houston, TX.

Finley, Stephen C. 2012. 'The Meaning of Mother in Louis Farrakhan's "Mother Wheel": Race, Gender, and Sexuality in the Cosmology of the Nation of Islam's UFO'. *Journal of the American Academy of Religion* 80(2): 434–465.

Gabriel, Theodore. 2003. 'The United Nuwaubian Nation of Moors'. In Christopher Partridge (ed.), *UFO Religions*, 149–161. London and New York: Routledge.

Gershon, Pete. 2010. 'Twenty First Century Music'. In John Sinclair (ed.), *Sun Ra: Interviews and Essays*, 95–118. London: Headpress.

Grass, Randall. 2009. *Great Spirits: Portraits of Life-Changing World Music Artists*. Jackson, MI: University Press of Mississippi.

Holzinger, Kay. 2001. 'Black Muslims'. In James R. Lewis (ed.), *Odd Gods: New Religions & the Cult Controversy*, 190–195. New York: Prometheus Books.

Kreiss, Daniel. 2008. 'Appropriating the Master's Tools: Sun Ra, the Black Panthers, and Black Consciousness, 1952–1973'. *Black Music Research Journal* 28(1): 57–81.

Langguth, Jerome J. 2010. 'Preposing an Alter-Destiny: Science Fiction in the Art and Music of Sun Ra'. In Mathew J. Bartkowiak (ed.), *Sounds of the Future: Essays on Music in Science Fiction Film*, 148–161. Jefferson, NC and London: McFarland & Company.

Lewis, James R. 1995. 'Introduction'. In James Lewis (ed.), *The Gods Have Landed: New Religions from Other Worlds*, xi–xv. New York: State University of New York Press.

Lock, Graham. 2004. *Blutopia: Visions of the Future and Revisions of the Past in the Work of Sun Ra, Duke Ellington, and Anthony Braxton*. Durham, NC and London: Duke University Press.

Monastra, Yahya. 1993. 'The Name of Shabazz: Where Did It Come From?' *Islamic Studies* 32(1): 73–76.

Nelson, Jez. 2014. 'Sun Ra: Jazz's Interstellar Voyager'. *The Guardian*, 16 June.

Palmer, Susan. 2010. *The Nuwaubian Nation: Black Spirituality and State Control*. Farnham, UK: Ashgate.

Palmer, Susan J. and Steve Luxton. 1998. 'The Ansaaru Allah Community: Postmodern Narration and the Black Jeremiad'. In Peter B. Clarke (ed.), *New Trends and Developments in the World of Islam*, 353–371. London: Luzac Oriental.

Patterson, Ian. 2012. 'Sibylle Zerr: Picture Infinity – Marshall Allen & The Sun Ra Arkestra', *All About Jazz*. At: www.allaboutjazz.com/sibylle-zerr-picture-infinity-marshall-allen-and-the-sun-ra-arkestra-by-ian-patterson.php. Accessed 26 June 2015.

Petsche, Johanna. 2009. 'Channelling the Creative: Keith Jarrett's Spiritual Beliefs Through a Gurdjieffian Lens'. *Literature & Aesthetics* 19(2): 138–158.

Pinch, Trevor and Frank Trocco. 2002. *Analog Days: The Invention and Impact of the Moog Synthesizer*. Cambridge, MA: Harvard University Press.

Rollefson, J. Griffith. 2008. 'The "Robot Voodoo Power" Thesis: Afrofuturism and Anti-Anti-Essentialism from Sun Ra to Kool Keith'. *Black Music Research Journal* 28(1): 83–109.

Saliba, John A. 1995a. 'Religious Dimensions of UFO Phenomena'. In James Lewis (ed.), *The Gods Have Landed: New Religions from Other* Worlds, 15–64. New York: State University of New York Press.

Saliba, John A. 1995b. 'UFO Contactee Phenomena from a Sociopsychological Perspective: A Review'. In James Lewis (ed.), *The Gods Have Landed: New Religions from Other Worlds*, 207–250. New York: State University of New York Press.

Sinclair, John. 2010a. 'Sun Ra Obituary'. In John Sinclair (ed.), *Sun Ra: Interviews and Essays*, 185–188. London: Headpress.

Sinclair, John. 2010b. 'Sun Ra Visits Planet Earth'. In John Sinclair (ed.), *Sun Ra: Interviews and Essays*, 5–17. London: Headpress.

Szwed, John F. 2000. *Space is the Place: The Lives and Times of Sun Ra*. Edinburgh, UK: Mojo Books.

Taylor, Wayne. 2005. 'Premillennium Tension Malcolm X and the Eschatology of the Nation of Islam'. *Souls: A Critical Journal of Black Politics, Culture, and Society* 7(1): 52–65.

Turner, Richard Brent. 1997. *Islam in the African-American Experience*. Bloomington and Indianapolis, IN: Indiana University Press.

Wojcik, Daniel. 2003. 'Apocalyptic and Millenarian Aspects of American UFOism'. In Christopher Partridge (ed.), *UFO Religions*, 274–300. London and New York: Routledge.

15 The Church of All Worlds

Oberon Zell, Primate, Church of All Worlds

Introduction

In the Fall of 1961 I began my freshman year at Westminster College in Fulton, Missouri. There I met Lance Christie, the first person I had ever encountered who seemed to be the same species as I. We were both avid science fiction readers, and had been particularly taken by the recurrent theme of the emergence of a new stage in human evolution ("Homo Novus"). We thought of ourselves as the new Cro-Magnons in a world of Neanderthals.

Lance and I had many late-night discussion sessions, planning how we might contact others like us, form a community, start a movement, and so on. Lance wanted to create a foundation or institute: "a total-environment educational institution which would theoretically produce Ayn Rand heroes, alias Maslowian self-actualizers" (Zell 2001). Inspired by Rand's *Atlas Shrugged*, I envisioned an alternative community hidden in some remote wilderness fastness . . .

And then, in October 1961, *Stranger in a Strange Land* (*SISL*) by Robert A. Heinlein arrived. Lance got around to reading it in late March of 1962, "and was seized with an ecstatic sense of recognition" (Zell 2001). He turned it over to me on April 4, saying that this one book dealt with much of what we had been thinking and talking about, and had articulated many of our own thoughts. I read it over the next few days, and was similarly enthusiastic. On April 7, 1962, the two of us shared water, pledging to dedicate our lives to a new vision, and bring others into it. The first, of course, were our girlfriends (and future wives), Penny and Martha, who had been away on Spring break. They shared water with us on May 25.

In the novel, Valentine Michael Smith was a human born on Mars as the sole survivor of a crashed first expedition, and raised by the ancient and wise Martians. Upon being brought back to Earth 25 years later, he established the "Church of All Worlds," built around "Nests," a fusion of congregation, group marriage, and intentional community. A basic concept was "grokking" (drinking), that is, the ability to be fully empathic.

Heinlein's novel introduced us to the ideas of: Immanent Divinity ("Thou Art God"); Pantheism ("all that groks is God"); Sacraments (water sharing);

262   *Oberon Zell*

priestesses; social/ritual nakedness; extended families ("Nests") as the basis for community; loving relationships without jealousy; and joyous expression of sexuality as divine union. By defining "love" as "that condition wherein another person's happiness is essential to your own" (Heinlein 1987 [1961]: 333), *SISL* changed forever the parameters of our relationships with each other, especially in the sexual arena. And all this in the context of a legal religious organization—a "church"—which could have all the rights and privileges granted to the mighty Church of Rome!

Founding the Church of All Worlds

We began thinking about creating an organization to bring Heinlein's (and our) vision into being. Lance and I were both in the Psychology Department at Westminster, and we devised a plan: all incoming students were routinely given the Edwards Personal Preference Schedule (EPPS), which rated their attitudes on 15 scales based on Abraham Maslow's work on self-actualizing personalities.

Lance and I got hold of our own test results, noted the matching patterns in several key areas, and then designed a student project, implemented that Fall of 1962, of correlating the EPPS results of all the other students, looking for the same distinctive pattern of matches. Those we found we then contacted, turned them onto *SISL*, and recruited them into our growing water-brotherhood, which we called Atl, an Aztec word meaning both "water" and "ancient homeland of our ancestors" (Sulak *et al.* 2014: 31).

This approach was amazingly successful, and, by the time Lance and I graduated in 1965, we had over 100 Atlan water-brothers and were publishing a regular newsletter, *The Atlan Torch*. We also had a growing anthology of our writings, musings, and favorite quotes, called *The Atlan Logbook*.

In 1965, I went on to graduate school in Clinical Psychology at Washington University in St Louis. Lance went on to the University of Oklahoma in Norman. We founded Nests in these places, and continued publishing separate editions of *The Atlan Torch*.

A column in *The Atlan Torch*, called "Atlan Annals," eventually became its own round-robin members-only "apazine," in which we discussed our unfolding plans and visions. At this time (1966–1967), two different directions emerged: most of the Atlans wanted to keep our water-brotherhood a secret fraternity, operating underground. Others of us felt that our vision needed to be taken to the greater society and made more influential in shaping the kind of world we wanted, and also to be more accessible to other potential Atlans as-yet-undiscovered out there.

Eventually, due somewhat to the influence of Kurt Vonnegut's novel *Cat's Cradle* (1963), it was decided to branch into two separate groups: The Atlan Foundation, headed by Lance, would remain underground and work in secret to influence various social systems. This strategy was inspired in part by the last chapter of Robert Rimmer's *The Harrad Experiment*

The Church of All Worlds 263

(1966). The Church of All Worlds (CAW) would incorporate legally and go public, with me as its High Priest and Primate. This decision was implemented in the summer of 1967 (Vale and Sulak 2001: 141).

CAW began its public life at a fund-raising garage sale at a Beatnik coffeehouse over that Labor Day weekend. I was then invited to be a regular speaker there. Having just come across the word *Pagan* in an historical context in an article called "Functional Religion" by Kerry Thornley (Blackwell 2012), I introduced myself as "Your Friendly Neighborhood Pagan," thus beginning the first usage of that term to apply to this new religion I was promoting. Later we extended it to encompass the entire emerging movement of Nature-based and revivalist pre-Christian religions, including not only witchcraft as European shamanism, but also Egyptian, Greek, Norse, Druidic, Hindu, and various Indigenous tribal traditions. Within a few months, I had developed a significant following, and we filed for State and Federal incorporation.

Following the prescription in *SISL*, I had enrolled in a correspondence course offered by a small Christian seminary, Life Science College in Rolling Meadows, Illinois. I received my Doctor of Divinity at the end of the Fall semester; I was then ordained by the CAW at Yule of 1967.

In the Spring of 1968, we took over another coffeehouse that had been run by a consortium of Christian churches. They had called it "The Exit," but we renamed it "Instead," setting up our first Temple upstairs. We opened on March 1, 1968; our Missouri Incorporation came through on March 4, and the first issue of *Green Egg* was published on March 21. The CAW was off and running!

The development of CAW ritual and theology

Once I had *Green Egg* in existence, even though it was initially just a one-page flyer, I was interested in connecting with other Pagans. Somewhere I got hold of a newsletter called *Korethalia*, put out by a brilliant artistic genius and visionary named Fred Adams, who had founded a religious group he called Feraferia ("wild festival") (Carson 2009). What I read in there seemed very much along the lines of what we were looking for. At that time, we didn't have much liturgical and theological stuff developed. We had just decided that what we really were was Pagans, but all we had was a rough philosophy. We didn't know how to put it into a coherent form, or what to do with it. Feraferian literature was filled with liturgy, ritual, theology, mythology, sacred art and poetry. It was all about the seasonal cycles of celebration, and that was the first time I came across that idea.

As soon as we got the information about the Wheel of the Year, we started aligning ourselves with it. There were marvelous revelations around finding out that the annual holidays and celebrations that I grew up with were linked to a greater and more ancient cycle. There was a sense of deepening and of feeling the roots of all these things and weaving them all together. It was very exciting to have a larger context for that stuff. Most of

264 *Oberon Zell*

us have always loved the holidays, but now we were finding out what they were really all about. I started researching worldwide holiday customs, and the more I learned the more I started to appreciate them.

Our central format for rituals, that allowed a lot of this stuff to be woven around it, was that there was always a Circle where things were passed around. Of course, the first time we did it was with a glass of water. Later it would be food, or stories. We didn't have a "doing" ritual as much as a "sharing" ritual. We would read little passages and poetry that were relevant to the season. It was very simple and unstructured back in those days. Over time, these things evolved and we got better and better at it. We would find out what other folks were doing and take bits and pieces of it and integrate them into our rituals (Vale and Sulak 2001: 137–145).

Over Labor Day of 1970, I had a cosmic acid vision of the Goddess, which I articulated in a series of revelatory thealogical essays published in *Green Egg* 1971–1973 (the "TheaGenesis" papers). This was the first published version of what later came to be known as the Gaea Thesis; a biological validation of the ancient intuition that the planet is a single living organism, Mother Earth (Zell-Ravenheart 2009: 90–95). Thus, Gaea, Pan, and other Nature spirits became our Divine Pantheon.

As they were published one article at a time in *Green Egg*, my TheaGenesis writings had a profound effect on the thealogical perspectives of the emerging Neo-Pagan community of the early 1970s, and were widely read, circulated, and reprinted. By thus merging ecology with religion, the CAW became an early forerunner of the Deep Ecology movement. Through our focus on Mother Nature as Goddess, and our recognition and ordination of women as priestesses, CAW can also hold claim to be the first Eco-Feminist church. Our only creed stated: "The Church of All Worlds is dedicated to the celebration of life, the maximal actualization of human potential and the realization of ultimate individual freedom and personal responsibility in harmonious eco-psychic relationship with the total Biosphere of Holy Mother Earth" (Bromley and Edelman 2015).

Although CAW was the first Neo-Pagan/Earth Religion to obtain full Federal recognition, we were initially refused recognition by the Missouri Department of Revenue on the basis of our "lack of primary concern about the hereafter, God, the destiny of souls, heaven, hell, sin and its punishment, and other supernatural matters." With the help of the ACLU, the ruling was overturned as unconstitutional in March 1974, resulting in much favorable publicity for the Church, and people flocking to us to conduct Pagan marriages. *Green Egg* continued to increase in scale and influence, as the "inside" journal of the growing worldwide Neo-Pagan movement.

The evolution of CAW

The non-fictional CAW has evolved far beyond Heinlein's original fable, to which we may be considered the sequel. The Nest is still the basic

The Church of All Worlds   265

unit, and there are still nine concentric Circles of member involvement, named after the planets and grouped into three Rings. Each Circle's activity includes study, writings, magical training, and wilderness experience, as well as active participation in the life of the Church. The 1st Ring, Circles 1, 2, and 3, is for Seekers, who are simply participants. The 2nd Ring, Circles 4 through 6, is made up of Scions, dedicated to service, who help run the Church. The 3rd Ring consists of Beacons, our Elders and exemplars, who provide leadership and vision, offer spiritual guidance and counsel, and supervise the training of Seekers and Scions.

The Church is governed by the Board of Directors, which determines policy and business matters, and the Council of Elders and Clergy Council, which address spiritual concerns. There is an annual General Curia to which all Waterkin are invited to discuss matters of interest and import. In the 2nd Phoenix Resurrection (1985–2004), Anodea's "Golden Age" Presidency (1985–1991) was succeeded by that of Tom Williams (1991–1994). When Aeona Silversong became President in 1994, CAW became possibly the first international church to elect an all-women Executive Council. Orion Stormcrow was elected President in 1996, followed by Starwhite in 1998, and LaSara Firefox in 1999. Jim Looman in Ohio held the Presidential reins from 2001–2004, terminating the 2nd phase. I was elected President in 2005, and continue in this role to the present.

CAW embraces the sacred Mysteries of the Corn Cycle and the Eleusinia, and honors Sacred Royalty in the form of our annual May Queen and King (sometimes with a May Princess and Prince), and our Underworld King Hades and Queen Persephone. These roles pass to different people each year, and are selected rather than elected. Our Queens and Kings have no temporal authority, but lead by example and serve the community as avatars, holding court at various festivals. We treat them as we ourselves would wish to be treated, for "as these vessels fare, so fares the Tribe" (MoonOak 2010: 144–157).

Worship in the CAW involves weekly or monthly meetings, which are usually held in the homes of Nest members on a rotational basis. A chalice of water is always shared around the Circle either as the opening or closing of the ceremony.

We have created a new Tribalism, where we relate to each other as members of a Tribe, with interconnecting clans and families. And our Tribe, in turn, is one of the Nations of Earth religions, bound together by our love and reverence for our Mother, the Living Earth. We welcome all who wish to join with us honorably. The most common statement we hear from new members is "I feel like I've come home to my people at last!"

CAW: a twenty-first-century religion

CAW embraces the theology of pantheism, as we experience what has been called "God" as an immanent quality, inherently manifest in every living

266   *Oberon Zell*

being, from a single cell to an entire planet—and likely the universe itself. We define Divinity as the highest level of synergic sentience accessible to each living being, manifesting itself in the self-actualization of that entity. Divinity is a function of emergent evolution. Thus, every man, woman, tree, cat, snake, flower, or grasshopper IS "God." We express this in the phrase, "Thou Art God/dess," which was used by Heinlein, but may also be found in the Bible (Psalms 82:6; John 10:34), and in much basic thinking of Hinduism and Buddhism.

At the macrocosmic level, we perceive and revere our entire planetary biosphere as a vast living entity: Mother Earth, Mother Nature, Gaia, The Goddess. We also accept that groups of living beings organized into various ecosystems may manifest psychically as collective entities; hence the local spirits of particular places, as well as tribal deities and pantheons. However, Gods, Goddesses, and Spirits are personae with their own agendas, and should not be considered merely as aspects of human psychology.

We observe that the great dilemma of present-day human society seems to be the alienation caused by splitting apart man and woman, humanity and Nature, matter and spirit, light and dark, good and evil. As the word *religion* means "re-linking," the basic commitment of the CAW is to the re-integration or re-linking of people with ourselves, our fellow humans, and with the whole of living Nature around us.

The CAW may be the first religion to draw as much of its inspiration from the future as from the past, embracing science fiction as mythology with the same enthusiasm as we embrace the classical myths of ancient times. We are future-oriented, meaning we care about how we evolve and change, not only about how we got here and how we will come to an end. We embrace evolution, and in embracing the planet as a living organism, we embrace the evolutionary changes of the planet by bringing human consciousness into direct contact with the growing web of planetary consciousness through such things as the worldwide computer internet.

Unlike nearly all other religions, we are not mired in nostalgia for a Paradise Lost; we are actively involved in helping to save the present world as well as working to actualize a visionary future. With roots deep in the Earth and branches reaching toward the stars, we evoke and create myths not only of a Golden Age long past, but of one yet to come . . .

CAW's sacred mission is "to evolve a network of information, mythology and experience to awaken the Divine within, and to provide a context and stimulus for reawakening Gaia, and reuniting Her children through tribal community dedicated to responsible stewardship and evolving consciousness" (Zell-Ravenheart and Zell-Ravenheart 2006: 288).

CAW's artistic and cultural contribution

I truly hope that my life and works will be a treasured legacy to the Pagan community I love so much. The CAW was certainly my first and most spectacular creation, but by no means my last. The intention there was to create an *in*clusive religion that I, and others like me, could believe in and be proud to be part of. Fifty-five years and three "Phoenix Resurrections" later, I'm pleased to see it is still going strong, and becoming more beautiful all the time with the beautiful people who are drawn to it.

CAW was the first fully incorporated church in modern times to claim the identity of "Pagan"; to legally ordain women as priestesses; to sanction and perform gay and multiple marriages; to adopt ritual nudity; and to restore and revive the ancient Cthonic Mysteries of Beltaine, Samhain, and Eleusis. We developed a strong Bardic tradition of sacred music and poetry, and have honored significant songwriters, musicians, troubadours, and minstrels as official Bards in the CAW. We were also the first to articulate and develop the "Gaea Thesis" as our foundational theology, reconciling science and religion. A current CAW project is a Qadishtu College and Priesthood of sacred sexuality.

Of course, I can claim the entire Pagan community as a legacy, since I was the first to claim the term as a self-identification, way back in 1967, and to promote it through the pages of *Green Egg*. After 167 issues to date (and a number of Editors), *Green Egg* is the longest-running Pagan publication in existence, and I hope it will continue to serve the Pagan community as its major interfaith journal for many years to come (www.greeneggemagazine.com).

Artistically, I have been inspired by the Muse to create dozens of wall plaques and altar statues of gods and goddesses, as well as posters, magickal jewellery, T-shirts, books, and other items that have been widely adopted throughout the Pagan community. Many of these are available through the Mythic Images Collection (deveradistributing.com/mythic-images-collection/).

I am proud of my networking efforts in the Pagan community, and I feel that they, too, are a significant legacy. I have founded, co-founded and/ or been a major player in the Council of Themis (1968), the first Pagan ecumenical council; the Council of Earth Religions (1972); The Covenant of the Goddess (1976); Bay Area Pagan Assemblies (1980s); the Universal Federation of Pagans (1990); The Papal Apology Petition (1999); the Pagan Leaders Summit (2001); the Grey Council (2002); the Coalition of Scholars in Pagan Studies (2013); and the Office of Wardens (2013). Locally, I have been privileged to have served on the Board of the Sonoma County Pagan Network (SCPN) and helped to found a local chapter of the Covenant of Unitarian Universalist Pagans (CUUPS).

And I am especially proud of my Grey School of Wizardry, which I hope to be a valued educational resource for the entire magickal community for the long haul (Sulak *et al.* 2014: 358–361). The Grey School was incorporated as a non-profit Educational Institution in California on March 14, 2004. In 2007, the School received a 501(c)(3) tax exemption from the Internal Revenue Service for charitable and educational purposes. Designed for youth and adult students, the Grey School provides an extensive program of arcane and classical studies, with students living in 50 countries around the world. As a secular online facility of esoteric education, the Grey

School is dedicated to preserving the magickal crafts and arts of the past for generations to follow.

My latest project is the Academy of Arcana, located at 428-A Front St, Santa Cruz, CA, 95060. The Academy is an Educational Center, a Museum of Magick and Mysterie, a Library of Esoterica, and a gift store of Curiosities. Operating entirely online for the past 12 years, the Grey School has always hoped to acquire a regular physical campus. By providing quality educational facilities and resources for studies in arcane lore and mystic history, the Academy of Arcana is a manifestation of that goal.

The Academy is a phenomenal resource and legacy for seekers, adepts, scholars, historians, and the magickally curious. We offer Museum/Library memberships with appropriate benefits. Corporate sponsorships are also available, and are suitably recognized.

I am pleased that Morning Glory's coining of the terms "polyamory" and "polyamorous" in 1990, and our lifetime of open relationships and two ten-year group marriages have inspired a vast movement of expanded relationships involving multiple partners. We were both very active in the early days of the Poly movement (the 1990s), and helped get it off the ground. And we brought Living Unicorns back to the world in 1980!

I am particularly proud of the kids that Morning Glory and I have raised; both our own and the several "Goddess-Daughters" and "God-Sons" we've helped nurture. We have also been the honorary "aunt and uncle" (and now "grandparents") to several generations of kids who have grown up around us, and we have trained a number of apprentices. They are all doing significant work in their respective careers to further the Ultimate Conspiracy of subverting the dominant paradigm toward the next phase of evolution. They are our truest immortality: "What is remembered, lives!"

Tragically, my beloved Lifemate Morning Glory was diagnosed with multiple myeloma (blood and bone cancer) in April of 2006. She died on May 13, 2014, after an eight-year struggle. She was buried in a green burial on the CAW's sacred land of Annwfn—thereby achieving designation of the land as an official legal cemetery for green burials. An apple tree grows upon her grave. I continue to carry forward our work as best I can for both of us.

Key figures in CAW

Oberon Zell—Primate of CAW; founder/co-founder of Atl (1962), Church of All Worlds (1967), *Green Egg* magazine (1968), Council of Themis (1968), Council of Earth Religions (1972), the Universal Federation of Pagans (1990), the Papal Apology Petition (1999), the Pagan Leaders Summit (2001), the Grey Council (2002), the Grey School of Wizardry (2004), the Coalition of Scholars in Pagan Studies (2013), the Office of Wardens (2013), and the Academy of Arcana (2015); first to embrace religious identity as "Pagan"; first to articulate "The Gaea Thesis"; author of numerous books on Pagan/magickal themes.

The Church of All Worlds 269

Lance Christie—Oberon's first water-brother; co-founder of Atl (1962), Church of All Worlds (1967), Earth First! (1980), Association for the Tree of Life (1986). Priest of CAW (ordained March 21, 1968). In his later years, Lance was a principal in the "Spine of the Continent" continental-scale environmental restoration initiative; the Relocalization Network initiative to relocalize community economies internationally; and was principal author of the "Renewable Deal", which is the core of the Earth Restoration Portal on the Internet: www.earthrestoration.net. Lance died of pancreatic cancer at Samhain 2010.

John McClimans—Priest of CAW (ordained February 1, 1970); first person to join the CAW when it became public in 1967. Died at Samhain 1996.

Tom Williams—Priest of CAW (ordained May 1, 1969); Prez of CAW BoD 1992–1994; Editor of *Green Egg* 1976–1978; close buddy and co-conspirator with OZ on many adventures.

Carolyn Clark—First Priestess of CAW (ordained May 1, 1973); High Priestess 1973–1979.

Don Wildgrube—Priest of CAW (ordained August 1, 1973); Prez of CAW BoD 1973–1978; High Priest 1974–1979.

Julie Carter—Significant other to Oberon (1970–1973); co-produced *Green Egg* during that time.

Orion Stormcrow—Priest of CAW (ordained June 21, 1997); Prez of CAW BoD 1996–1998; close buddy and co-conspirator with OZ on many adventures.

Morning Glory—Priestess of CAW (ordained August 1, 1974); High Priestess 1996–2014; Lifemate of Oberon (married April 14, 1974); Goddess historian, ritualist, author; died of multiple myeloma cancer on May 13, 2014.

Gwydion Pendderwen—Minister of Forestry (invested September 21, 1978); and first Bard of CAW; helped get CAW incorporated in California in 1978; died in a car wreck at Samhain 1982.

Anodea Judith—Priestess of CAW (ordained May 1, 1985); High Priestess 1987–1995; Prez of CAW BoD 1985–1992; author of numerous books on chakras, magick, Gaea.

Willowoak Istarwood—Minister of Prisons (invested August 21, 1992); Priestess of CAW (ordained April 24, 2013); helped get CAW incorporated in California in 1978.

270 *Oberon Zell*

Marylyn Motherbear—Priestess of CAW (ordained November 1, 1999); Priestess of the Mysteries.

Aeona Silversong—Priestess of CAW (ordained September 25, 1993); Prez of CAW BoD 1994–1996.

Diane Darling—Co-wife in triad marriage with Oberon and Morning Glory (1984–1994); Editrix of *Green Egg* 1988–1994.

Maerian Morris—Priestess of CAW (ordained May 5, 1996); Editrix of *Green Egg* 1994–2000.

Avilynn Pwyll—Priestess of CAW (ordained November 7, 1994); Nest Coordinator.

Fiona Judge—Priestess of CAW Australia (ordained May 23, 1994); incorporated CAW in Australia (1992).

Julie Epona—Minister of CAW (invested December 22, 2009); significant paramour of Oberon and Morning Glory from 1992 through 2014.

Rev. Luke Moonoak—Minister of CAW (invested September 21, 1978); Primate elect; author of *Radiant Circles* (2010).

LaSara Firefox—Priestess of CAW (ordained November 1, 1999); Prez of CAW BoD 1999–2001; author.

Farida Fox—Priestess of CAW (ordained May 5, 1997).

Ariel Monserrat—Editrix of *Green Egg* 2007–2014.

Liza Gabriel—Ravenheart family member (1995–2005); founder of Sacred Connections; author *The CAW Tradition* (2004).

Cat DeVille—CAW Reorganization Manager (2005–2010); BoD member; author of new CAW Canons (2006).

Mama Maureen—CAW website technomage and Board member (2009–).

Martha Babineau—Priestess of CAW Australia (ordained January 15, 2012); current Prez of CAW-Oz NMC.

Francesca Gentille—Minister of CAW (invested September 15, 2013); current BoD Secretary.

Tim Emert—Minister of CAW (invested September 15, 2013); current BoD member.

References

Blackwell, Christopher. 2012. 'No Stranger in This Strange Land – Interview With Oberon Zell-Ravenheart'. *Penton: Independent Alternative Media*, 2 May. At: www.penton.co.za/no-stranger-in-this-strange-land-interview-with-oberon-zell-ravenheart/. Accessed 10 January 2016.

Bromley, David and Stephanie Edelman. 2015. 'The Church of All Worlds (CAW)'. *World Religion & Spirituality Project*. At: www.wrs.vcu.edu/profiles/ChurchOfAllWorlds.htm. Accessed 10 January 2016.

Carson, Jo. 2009. 'Frederick Adams: Visionary and Founder of Feraferia'. *Feraferia*. At: feraferia.org/joomla/index.php?option=com_content&view=article&id=87:fred-adams-his-life-and-work&catid=65:founders&Itemid=104. Accessed 10 January 2016.

Heinlein, Robert A. 1987 [1961]. *Stranger in a Strange Land*. London: New English Library.

MoonOak, Luke. 2010. *Radiant Circles: Progressive Ecospirituality and the Church of All Worlds*. Gainesville, FL: The Solantis Institute.

Rimmer, Robert. 1966. *The Harrad Experiment*. Los Angeles, CA: Sherbourne Press

Sulak, John C. (with Oberon and Morning Glory Zell-Ravenheart). 2014. *The Wizard and the Witch: An Oral History of Oberon Zell and Morning Glory*. Woodbury, MN: Llewellyn Publications.

Vale, V. and John Sulak. 2001. *Modern Pagans: An Investigation of Contemporary Pagan* Practices. San Francisco, CA: Research Publications.

Vonnegut, Kurt. 1963. *Cat's Cradle*. New York: Holt, Rinehart and Winston.

Zell, Oberon. 2001. 'A Personal History of Tim Zell in the Context of the Church of All Worlds'. *History of CAW According to Oberon Zell, Part 1*. At: groups.google.com/forum/#!topic/alt.religion.all-worlds/-voXALuphEk. Accessed 10 January 2016.

Zell-Ravenheart, Oberon. 2009. 'TheaGenesis: The Birth of the Goddess'. In Oberon Zell-Ravenheart (ed.), *Green Egg Omelette: An Anthology of Art and Articles from the Legendary Pagan Journal*, 90–95. Franklin Lakes, NJ: New Page Books.

Zell-Ravenheart, Oberon and Morning Glory Zell-Ravenheart. 2006. *Creating Circles & Ceremonies: Rituals For All Seasons and Reasons*. Franklin Lakes, NJ: New Page Books.

16 An implicit hyper-real religion
Real-life superheroes

Adam Possamai and Vladislav Iouchkov

Introduction

This chapter uses the Real-Life Superhero (RLSH) movement as a case study of both an implicit religion and a hyper-real religion. It first sets the theoretical scene by exploring the notion of the 'Pygmalion process' and then details the movement as expressed by insiders. This section offers an account of people who dress up as superheroes and go down the streets of our metropolises to curb violence and crime. This chapter then discusses theories on implicit religion, hyper-real religion and consumer culture to explain how comics have provided a platform for people to bring works of popular fiction into their reality.

The Pygmalion process

In the late twentieth century, Fredrick Jameson argued that previously, modernist culture could be judged against certain dominant standards (for example, using the distinction between high culture and low culture), and might even be oppositional or shocking to some elements of society, whereas post or late modernist culture (a culture symptomatic of what he calls the phase of "late capitalism") is fully commodified and tends to be judged in terms of what gives instant pleasure and makes money. We are living in a culture of the simulacrum, in which "the very memory of use value is effaced" (Jameson 1991: 18) and in which there is a fondness for pastiche. If, before, art movements had clear boundaries – often explained in manifestos addressing the new rules of art – post-modern art and culture is a free-floating, crazy-quilt collage of ideas or views: a pastiche. It includes opposing elements such as old and new, modern and traditional, and high and low culture. It denies regularity, logic or symmetry and glories in contradiction and confusion. It is argued that depth in culture is replaced by surface, or even by multiple surfaces – what is often called 'intertextuality'.

In his work, Jameson refers to, for example, the buildings of Las Vegas, the Westin Bonaventure Hotel in the Los Angeles downtown area, and to nostalgia films from mass culture such as *American Graffiti* (Lucas 1973) and *Chinatown* (Polanski 1974). Both films with purportedly historical content, these works approach the past using stylistic connotation, conveying 'pastness' through the glossy qualities of the image and through the fashions depicted. Indeed, *American Graffiti* and *Chinatown* attempted to recapture the atmosphere and stylistic specificities of, respectively, Eisenhower's 1950s and the 1930s. Pastiche does not set out to interpret the past or to judge it against any standard, but simply plays images off against each other to achieve its effect, with no clear reference to an external or 'deeper' reality.

It is not the purpose of this chapter to update these findings with recent works in art or popular culture but to instead make reference to a new social and cultural process. We are arguing here that this fondness for pastiche has emerged from the field of art and popular culture to enter everyday life. Pastiche is no longer only available on a canvas or on a screen, it now 'lives' with us. To borrow from Greek mythology, what we have today is a 'Pygmalion process' in which social actors attempt to bring to life various elements of art or popular culture. In the Greek myth, Pygmalion was an artist who fell in love with his own sculpture of a beautiful maiden and made a successful offering to Aphrodite for his 'ivory girl' to be brought to life. A similar phenomenon is alive and well in late modern society and can be seen in the tremendous growth of, for example, "hyper-real religions" (Possamai 2005, 2012). This term refers to a simulacrum of a religion created out of, or in symbiosis with, commodified popular culture, and which provides inspiration at a metaphorical level and/or is a source of beliefs to be applied to everyday life.

The Pygmalion process is not limited to religion. Other new social practices are being created at the grassroots level and without having any official leadership or hierarchy. For example, new sports have recently emerged, such as quidditch, from the *Harry Potter* stories, and chess boxing, from the graphic novels of Enki Bilal. According to information provided on Wikipedia in mid-August 2013, quidditch began as a real sport in 2005 at Middlebury College in Vermont. The game is a mix of rugby, dodgeball and tag. The teams comprise seven players who run around with a broomstick between their legs. In 2010, World Cup IV in Manhattan involved 46 teams and 15,000 spectators. In 2013, World Cup VI was held in Florida, involved 80 teams and was livestreamed on television. Chess boxing was featured in the French graphic novel, *Froid Equateur*, by Enki Bilal, published in 1992. A match consists of 11 rounds: 6 rounds of chess and 5 of boxing. Rounds of chess and boxing alternate until one player is knocked out or loses his king. The World Chess Boxing Organization was founded in 2003 and the first chess boxing club appeared in 2005.

More and more popular culture conventions, such as the Supanova Pop Culture Expo in Australia, the New York Comic Con and the Japan Expo in Paris are taking place around the world. According to its official Australian site (www.supanova.com.au), the Supanova Pop Culture Expo "is where the adoring public comes face to face with Supa-Star celebrities and the creative talent that inspire their imaginary worlds under one roof". A growing number of the people who visit these shows will perform what is called 'cosplay' (costume play), that is, they will dress up in a costume that signifies a character from popular culture. These costumes can be from films (for example, *Star Wars*) or comics (for example, superheroes). In 2014, at the Sydney event, some people mixed genres in the fashion of high pastiche. For example, an individual was wearing a *Star Wars* Storm Trooper costume with the colours of a Spider-Man suit. A tall Batman was walking around in the colours of Captain America. Cosplay is also a trend at other events, such as comic book days, and even in sports' stadiums (as was evident during the television coverage of the World Cup in Brazil), or at popular running events such as marathons. In Tokyo, the Harajuku district is known to regularly attract these types of activities.

There are also various events centred around the theme of zombie walks, where people dress as the 'living dead' and wander around the streets of major cities. Some cities host annual gatherings where other events may simply be flashmobs. In 2001, a zombie parade was held in Sacramento, California, but the appellation 'zombie walk' was first used in Toronto in 2003. This first walk had six participants. In 2006, outside of Pittsburgh, 894 people gathered for such a walk, and in 2007, 1,100 people dressed up in Toronto. In Chile, 15,000 people took part in Santiago's annual zombie walk.

Anonymous, the international network of activists and 'hacktivists', has its members wearing the stylized Guy Fawkes mask as it was portrayed in the graphic novels by Alan Moore and David Lloyd in the 1980s, and later adapted to the big screen in the film, *V for Vendetta* (2006), directed by James McTeigue in 2006. They wear their masks to signify their belief that governments should fear their citizens rather than the situation being the other way around. They are very active online and oppose internet censorship and control.

Recently, according to Britain's Office for National Statistics (AFP 2014), 187 babies were given the name 'Arya'. This is the name of a character from the *Game of Thrones* stories, but we should be careful not to read too much into this as 'googling' the name 'Arya' reveals that it is not connected only to this fictional character. However, 50 babies in the UK were named 'Khaleesi', and the connection with the Pygmalion process is here direct and impossible to miss. In the US, Miller (2014) finds that, according to the Social Security Administration Records, 146 babies were given that name in 2012, and 20 baby boys were named 'Tyrion', after another main character from the series.

Another example is the RLSH (Iouchkov 2012; Mak 2010), which is the focus of this chapter. We will first explore this phenomenon in the light of recent fieldwork. We will then concentrate on the participants' understanding of religion and spiritual development to conclude that this movement could be understood as an implicit hyper-real religious group.

Real-life superheroes

The twenty-first century has seen an almost relentless surge in the popularity of superheroes. Cinemas see the release of numerous films based on superheroes or other comic books, as new television programmes such as *Gotham* (2014–present), *Marvel's Agents of S.H.I.E.L.D.* (2013–present) and *The Walking Dead* 2010–present) also enjoy success from their core basis in comic book literature. Video games such as *Batman: Arkham Asylum* 2009) and its sequel *Batman: Arkham City* (2011), which involve the player controlling the titular protagonist with a mixture of combative, stealthy and investigative interactive simulations have been received with critical acclaim from gamer communities, and have marked the dawning of franchised superhero-themed interactive entertainment that sees both critical and financial success.

The release of Mark Millar's comic series *Kick-Ass* (2008–2010, 2010–2012, 2013–present) and the consequent 2010 film adaptation follows the story of Dave Lizewski, a teenager who emulates the superheroes he reads about by directly intervening in neighbourhood crimes under the self-created *ad hoc* persona 'Kick-Ass'. Though conceived as pure entertainment, *Kick-Ass*'s grounding is on the conceptual tightrope hoisted above fiction and reality; our focus in this chapter is the latter, the 'real', the RLSH community.

The RLSH community is a worldwide group of individuals who engage in various forms of community action under self-created superhero-inspired identities. Their activities most commonly traverse neighbourhood watch-like community safety and crime prevention patrols, social/community outreach programmes (for example food drives, charity/fundraising and raising public awareness of known local offenders), and other general acts of goodwill; however, it is not uncommon for these to overlap in a RLSH's activities.

There is no official or legally binding registry for RLSHs, which makes their numbers difficult to ascertain, though as recorded by Flock (2011), 720 members were registered on the now-defunct RLSH forum www.reallifesuperheroes.org, with potentially 'hundreds' of RLSHs patrolling across American cities. As of 2015, however, 'Real-Life Superheroes – The Forum' appears to have replaced www.reallifesuperheroes.org and, at the time of writing, has 1,040 registered members,[1] the majority of whom are based in the United States but also active in Canada, throughout the United Kingdom and Europe, and in Australia. In academia, there is currently a small but growing body of research concerning RLSH (Iouchkov 2012; Iouchkov and Birch 2015; Mak 2010).

It is not difficult to draw parallels between RLSHs and those who participate in cosplay. As already noted, it is a subculture in which its participants recreationally dress as figures from popular culture, often superheroes. What separates RLSHs from cosplayers, however, is that cosplay is traditionally based on the *replication* of a pre-existing character for the purposes of novelty, entertainment and occasionally charity, all of which can intertwine. For example, a cosplayer with tailoring skills can create their very own home-made *Batman* outfit, modelled specifically and closely after any of its many incarnations from the character's first appearance in *Detective Comics #27* in May 1939 to the modern multimedia age. Furthermore, these are often reserved for special pop culture conventions, such as the famous *San Diego Comic-Con* in the United States, or Australia's own *Supernova*. When a cosplayer dons their outfit and attends such conventions, their claims of "I am Batman" are very likely to be accepted by others just as they are intended; as recreational, oftentimes humorous.

However, generally speaking, it is not within the tradition for cosplayers to build outfits which are entirely self-created and not modelled after any figures of popular culture. RLSHs, on the other hand, not only use identities which are entirely self-created (although clearly influenced by fictional heroic characters of popular culture), but they also introduce an element of social utility to these creations. Conclusively, the two things which separate RLSHs from cosplayers are: a) the former's social utilisation of their persona as opposed to the latter's recreational use of theirs, which are greatly subject to the former's creation of an original identity as opposed to the latter's complete replication; and, more importantly, b) the change.[2]

Methodology

The limited academic attention to RLSHs required this study to adopt an exploratory research design in order to successfully gather an unbiased understanding of any religious/spiritual processes of the community and its constituents. Utilising a purposive sample as defined by Bryman (2012), where participants are selected based on relevance to research, RLSHs were contacted online via social media and 'Real-Life Superheroes – The Forum' for participation in semi-structured interviews. In total, 45 interviews were conducted (44 online and 1 face-to-face). Three participants were aged 46 or over, whereas the remaining portion ($n = 42$) were split equally between the age groups 18–29 and 30–45. Of the participants, 37 were situated in the US, 3 in Canada, 2 in each Australia and the UK, and 1 English-speaking RLSH in Sweden. Only two participants were female.

The data was put through a thematic analysis to identify and examine participants' experiences prior, during and (where applicable) after their process/-es of becoming and being RLSHs. The data consisted of: participants' accounts of their life narratives; reason/s for becoming an RLSH; the meaning of and connection to their RLSH persona; the nature and method of their RLSH activity (e.g., outreach, crime patrols); their religious/spiritual proclivities, or lack thereof; the 'transformative' aspect/s of RLSH, and any experienced 'personality shifts'; personal and social benefits and drawbacks of being an RLSH; changes to their everyday life; pop culture fandom; and public/police reactions to their activities.

Our focus in this chapter is specifically on the experiences of RLSH in regards to: participant 'origin stories'; interpretations of their transformative experiences; the 'feeling' of transformation and being a RLSH; and the impact that being an RLSH has on their everyday lives. Before we proceed, we would like to open this stage of the chapter with evidence that inquiry into transformative experiences was warranted, by examining a brief online guide to superheroism that serves not only as a mission statement for select RLSH, but is also comparable to a spiritual guide.

'12 Steps to Superheroism'

In addition to no official registry for RLSH (as stated earlier), there is also no official guiding text on how one can 'become' an RLSH, and/or rules by which each active RLSH must abide; that said, however, the website 'Superheroes Anonymous' outlines the 'sacred 12 Steps to Superheroism – the path one must take to become a fully realized Real Life Superhero'. This 'guide' is as follows:

1 We made the conscious decision to change our perception of the world and our place in it.
2 Chose to be better people and to become a force for good.
3 Explored ourselves and discovered the source of our inner Superhero.
4 Recognizing ourselves, we began to develop our Superhero Self.
5 Recognized our innate strengths and sought to develop our potential ones.
6 Opened our eyes to our environment, without shying away from injustice and despair.
7 Understanding our strengths, and our environment, we recognized how to best serve the world.
8 Our Superhero was then given a name.
9 As our Superhero Self, we took Action.
10 Now exposed to the trials of Superheroism, we refined and improved our Superhero Self.
11 Continued our Superhero efforts, and made our Name known.
12 Continue to Live our Truth.[3]

Based on these 12 steps, one cannot ignore the palpable indications of the 'Superhero Self' as being the product of conscious self-exploration, self-realisation, self-development, awareness (of both self and surroundings) and (to directly quote the steps) 'Truth', and is referred to as either a developed version of the self, or a new self altogether. What these 12 steps suggest is not only personal transformation or conversion into a 'Superhero Self', but the utilisation of this transformation/conversion in addressing 'injustice and despair', thereby integrating one's religious or spiritual journey with social action. Though this, of course, does not provide sufficient evidence

278   *Adam Possamai and Vladislav Iouchkov*

or accounts for the specific experiences of those who participate in RLSH activity, it does provide evidence for the presence – latent or otherwise – of a religious and/or spiritual element permeating the community, its members and their activities, thus necessitating further inquiry of this nature.

Transformations

The research identified an abundance and amalgam of catalytic experiences and events which contribute to one's decision to become an RLSH: a desire for novel outlets of prior altruistic tendencies; personal trauma (personal loss, victimisation/bullying, health-related issues, near-death experiences, suicidal tendencies and so on) that served as an awakening for doing good, that is, channelling negative experiences into positive ones; self-rehabilitation from substance use/abuse; manifesting a childhood desire; previous experience as an intervening or non-intervening bystander/witness to a critical situation, which was associated with helpfulness or helplessness, respectfully; and a 'higher calling' of a religious/spiritual nature which often coincided with a desire to realise one's full (or at least greater) potential. It is complex to identify a sole reason for why individuals in these activities undertake them in the first place, and more research is necessary before explanations can be proposed. Nevertheless, these catalysts elucidated with a variety of experiences interpreted by RLSHs as explicitly transformative. These data are presented in Table 16.1, demonstrating the varying degrees of transformation undergone by individuals in the process of becoming an RLSH.

The participants' feelings of personal change from the initial decision to become an RLSH bear subtle yet significant differences, and thus for the study were made more elaborate through classifications: "transformation" (T), i.e. the individual simply felt like they became a new person; "not transformation" (NT), i.e. the individual felt no change whatsoever once they made – and acted upon – the decision to become an RLSH; "not transformation, but realisation" (NT-R), that is, the individual did not become a

Table 16.1 Was becoming an RLSH a 'transformative' experience? (n = 42).[4]

	N	% *(approx.)*
Transformation (T)	11	26.2
Not a transformation (NT)	8	19.0
Not transformation, but realisation (NT-R)	12	28.6
Not transformation, but personal improvement (NT-PI)	8	19.0
Other	1 ("Not transformation, but a return to past practices")	2.4
Not sure	2	4.8

Real-life superheroes 279

"new person", but had realised their "untapped potential" and experienced a manifestation of character traits and values they felt they possessed (or had the potential to possess) but were not utilised; and "not transformation, but personal improvement" (NT-PI), that is, the individual did not become a "new person", but experienced certain improvements (mostly personality-wise) upon becoming an RLSH.[5]

Participants of the study thus did not all collectively interpret their experiences as explicitly transformative, neither (with the exception of one participant) did they claim to possess superhuman or otherwise metaphysical powers. Whilst a significant proportion considered becoming an RLSH as a transformation (T), others attributed their experience as something *akin* to a transformation, be it simply a realisation of potential or being (NT-R), or as part-and-parcel of a process of personal improvement (NT-PI); likewise, some participants attributed no transformation, realisation or sense of personal improvement to becoming an RLSH (NT). Whilst each group warrants investigation in their own right, for the purpose of this chapter, we will direct our attention specifically to RLSHs that explicitly considered their becoming and being an RLSH as a transformative experience (T).

RLSH-38

RLSH-38 is based in Canada, engaging primarily in social outreach and welfare. Though RLSH-38 is not an avid fan of comic books, he acknowledged an admiration for Spider-Man:

> I'm not super into comics, I was too poor as a child to afford them, and I'm poor as an adult. Spiderman was always a childhood fave, and even still I think about his struggles, even as fiction . . .

> Spiderman's adage is, of course, "with great power comes great responsibility". Even as a child, I could see myriad ways in which the world is fucked. Spiderman had this great strength, but it also meant he could never sleep, had to distance himself emotionally from his family and lovers, and secretly carry a burden.

> I think in my case, I would rework the phrase to say "With health privilege comes community responsibility". I feel like there's a lot of work to be done still, and it has nothing to do with catching bank robbers (never forget, the bankers are the thieves).[6]

> It's the total opposite of a figure like Superman (or Christ); simultaneously powerful and impotent (Must strength always show itself as strength?) Okay I'll leave the Nietzsche here.

It is already evident that the participant has thought extensively about the mythological and philosophical intricacies of heroism and superpowers;

280   *Adam Possamai and Vladislav Iouchkov*

later in this chapter, this will play a crucial role in how he understands his transformation.

RLSH-38's 'origin story' involved him being a victim of a homophobia-charged hate crime, a near-death-experience (NDE) which had left him with a permanent neurological disability. Whilst undergoing recovery, RLSH-38 claimed to experience suicidal tendencies, and dreams and visions which would set the participant on his path to becoming an RLSH:

> I received a kind of "download" or intimate and immediate understanding of what work was left to be done, I guess. I received a vision of resistance and solidarity that in any other terms would be the proverbial "white light" of NDEs. Upon waking I realized I had a newfound conviction, but could no longer remember the clear path to the end goal of my vision. My life since then has been actively trying to uncover the steps I need to take to get there . . .

> I found the RLSH community when I was looking for a framework to understand and present the kind of work I wanted to do in my community. These weirdos seemed to be the best fit for what I was thinking about.

For RLSH-38, being a 'superhero' does not appear to be a lifelong desire, a specific calling in itself, or even the end goal of the vision endured from his NDE; instead, RLSH activity is his vehicle towards actively reconstructing and making sense of that vision. Given that the end goal within the vision is ambivalent, even for RLSH-38 himself, we certainly cannot speculate as to what that may be; that said, it is evident thus far that RLSH activity and the transformation (or transformations) constituting it appear to be a means rather than an end for RLSH-38, that is, the RLSH activity itself is the journey.

RLSH-38 was then asked about the 'closeness' between himself and his superhero persona, and how he interpreted (or interprets) his own transformation:

Interviewer: How closely tied in are you and ['RLSH-38']?
RLSH-38:   Well, I introduce myself as ['RLSH-38'] in all my street encounters. I 'am' ['RLSH-38'], but in order to become them (they/them/their when referring to ['RLSH-38']), I do have to undergo a kind of ego death.
               There is this kind of inner/outer play.
               ['RLSH-38'] is nimble enough to balance on that knife edge.

Furthermore, we have not even to risk the adventure alone; for the heroes of all time have gone before us, the labyrinth is fully known; we have only to follow the thread of the hero-path. And where we had

Real-life superheroes 281

thought to find an abomination, we shall find a god; where we had thought to slay another, we shall slay ourselves; where we had thought to travel outward, we shall be with all the world.[7]

Interviewer:	Since you have brought it up – do you feel that your own journey into becoming ['RLSH-38'] has been akin to The Hero's Journey (monomyth)?
RLSH-38:	Yes?

I am not quite sure I'm entirely out of the labyrinth (and the narrative of a queer, disabled vegan outreach worker doesn't exactly have a clear analogy).

But, in the context of even my dream visions, that structure is there.

I am trying to uncover more and more of what the dream meant.

(We see increased militarization of police on a global scale, a continued occupation of indigenous lands and the resources contained within, as well as massive movements protesting neoliberal austerity; the more this all plays out the more my dream returns to me. I have a vision of resistance, and it looks a little like ['RLSH-38']).

Tarot readings, meditation . . . reading Derek [sic] Jensen even . . . they are all painting a picture of something I didn't quite see.

but is forming . . .

I would say yes, my transformation has been a spiritual one, but I have always been spiritual. Maybe I have taken too much LSD, but I feel like I have come much closer to knowing myself, inside and out; to knowing and being connected to my soul. When I walk the streets, yes, I ask the universe, and the city what it needs, but I also ask my heart and soul.

RLSH-38 very clearly conceptualises his transformation through making explicit references to mythologist Joseph Campbell's *The Hero with a Thousand Faces* (2008 [1949]), which details 'The Hero's Journey'. 'The Hero's Journey', or 'monomyth', is the conceptual result of Campbell's extensive analysis of ancient to modern-day myths (preceding the book's first edition in 1949), in which Campbell argues that heroic myths generally follow the same underlying narrative, or structure: in sum, this structure commences with the Hero leaving the 'ordinary world' to battle forces – literal and/or metaphorical – in the 'extraordinary world', continues with the Hero experiencing a death, rebirth and transformation along the journey, and concludes with the Hero returning to the 'ordinary world' a changed individual. This structure continues to be applied in modern works of fiction and popular

282   *Adam Possamai and Vladislav Iouchkov*

culture, such as *Star Wars*, *Harry Potter* and *The Matrix* franchises; these franchises have each spawned their own hyper-real religious followings (see Possamai 2012), and monomyth itself has been recognised as a developmental metaphor in counselling (see Lawson 2005).

One phase of the Hero's transformation for Campbell is the 'ego death', to which RLSH-38 made direct reference despite not describing in greater, more specific detail his actual process of 'becoming RLSH-38'. The 'ego death' (or, in Jungian terms, 'death of the psyche') can be described as a transitional, transcendent or indeed a transformative spiritual experience in itself, in which the individual surrenders their present 'self' in favour of an improved, or enlightened self. For Campbell, the Hero's 'death' – again, literal and/or metaphorical – is succeeded by resurrection as a new and/or improved version of self that is capable of defeating the foe/s the Hero faces, yet again, literal and/or metaphorical. Even on the surface, we can see this in superheroes who surrender their former selves to become their 'superhero selves', such as Peter Parker into Spider-Man or Bruce Wayne into Batman.[8]

Stating that he *is* yet must also *become* 'RLSH-38' via an ego death indicates that the 'RLSH-38' persona is not merely an end-point for the participant, but rather an internalisation of a higher 'superhero' self which requires a process of 'tapping into', so to speak; his innate potential, used for RLSH activity, becomes accessible to him via his process of ego death. We see here a complex identity of RLSH-38, self-aware that he cannot perform at greater potential at any given moment, yet understands the employment of his ego death ritual in order to 'unlock' this potential for his activities.

RLSH-38 exhibits an admiration of and personal relatability to Spider-Man, yet instead of applying a superhero myth to conceptualising his transformation, he instead opts for personal mythbuilding via 'The Hero's Journey', as a framework for his transformation and RLSH activity. His transformative experience extends even further than a utility for RLSH activity – it is part of his responsive journey to his higher calling, a means to uncovering "more and more of what [his] dream meant" rather than an end in itself. Though ambivalent about whether this journey is complete ("I am not quite sure I'm entirely out of the labyrinth"), RLSH-38 nevertheless explicitly attributes the structure of monomyth as being instrumental in his RLSH experience. Whilst considering his transformation spiritual, it is not an awakening *into* spirituality, as he claims to have always been spiritual; RLSH-38's transformation, self-interpreted through mythbuilding via the structure of monomyth, has essentially become a commitment through RLSH activity.

RLSH-08

US-based RLSH-08 was more explicit about his superhero fandom, citing that he drew most inspiration from The Spectre and Jonah Hex (both of DC Comics), and Green Hornet. Asked about how they inspired his RLSH transformation:

Real-life superheroes 283

RLSH-08:	When I decided that it might be possible to become a Real-Life Superhero, I looked at the images and concepts . . . Which concepts would really work in the world?
	When you try to apply the amazing concept into real life, you need to think about representing the ideals. Being a Hero to those who you see at that moment in time, whether you suck at being a regular human being or not. You need to be the best person you're capable of being once you put on the suit.
Interviewer:	What were the concepts you looked at most that helped inspire you?
RLSH-08:	The concepts . . . The idea that there is hope for the common or downtrodden person. I've been on the lower strata and I know how it is. Despair is not unfamiliar to me. But inspiring hope is something we all need. Can I do that? Does a belief that heroes exist do that? I don't know. But I do know that the people I help never seem to question why I'm dressed so strangely. They just accept the assistance and smile.

Though these responses did not provide a great deal of specific insight into how those superheroes influenced his transformation and RLSH persona,[9] we glean from this a clear goal to apply the 'amazing' into real life; sociologically speaking, a conscious appropriation of the sacred into the profane.

Unlike RLSH-38, US-based RLSH-08 did not express that he had been a victim of crime, let alone having victimisation play a role in his transformation into an RLSH. Aside from mentioning that he is "familiar with despair" and "being on the lower strata of society", the specific details of RLSH-08's life narrative were secondary to describing the transformation itself in the interview. Not unlike RLSH-38, however, RLSH-08 too was drawn to pursuing RLSH activity by way of vision-induced spiritual experience:

> I was pretty much at a low point in my life. I was at a crossroads . . . I went on a VisionQuest in a Native American way. I needed to find a path, my route in life. I went into the wilderness of Colorado and spent four days alone without a tent. My vision arrived and it was that I'm "Taller" than I thought. I translated that to mean that I was more capable of doing what I was currently doing . . .

> My potential had not yet been realized. I sucked as a human being. Now I had to change that. Redemption was in order.

In this case, the RLSH explicitly states that the contributing trigger that led him to seek the vision – and, as a result, RLSH activity – was the non-realisation of his human potential, his dissatisfaction with self. Drawing on Native American spiritual praxes (perhaps in line with Jonah Hex's affiliation with Apache and Navajo tribes) that put him into a strictly natural

284 *Adam Possamai and Vladislav Iouchkov*

environment, RLSH-08 sought a spiritual experience, though not specifically a superhero one. When asked how the Vision translated itself into RLSH transformation, RLSH-08 responded:

> My Vision was that I was "Taller". That was very weird and it lasted for only about five minutes. I stepped on various areas that I had gathered firewood before. I wondered if I was on a dip or a rise within five feet. I tested each and it seemed that I was taller on each. Not a whole lot taller, just about six inches consistently on each. And yeah, that freaked me out. I'm not really a metaphysical guy. I'm more skeptic than anything.
>
> But I had this "Vision" and I thought about it over my campfire that night. I knew there was something more that I could do with my life that I wasn't realizing.
>
> That's what Colorado left me with. And then I encountered the formative RLSH movement and knew that was it.
>
> I took "Taller" to be a metaphor.

RLSH-08 presents the case of a self-admitted skeptic with a spiritual experience which he attempted to rationalise. His temporary vision of being 'taller' was not accepted at face value, and his skepticism led him to apply empirical testing; in attempting to uncover the seemingly sacred as profane, the sacred persisted for RLSH-08 and was taken as a rather straightforward metaphor for striving towards a greater human potential.

Although RLSH-08 self-identifies as a skeptic (and employed skepticism to rationalise the vision which would prove to be a spiritual experience in itself), he also interestingly identifies as a longtime believer in God. This, however, does not inform his views on how RLSH activity ought to be conducted within the community:

> I grew up with a foundation of moderate religion. I'm a believer, but get pissed off at fervent people who have recently "found" God. He was always there and I have disputes with those who weren't looking for so long. To me, being a Real-Life Superhero should have no part of religion. Nor politics. There can be nothing that is potentially divisive about it. Doing GOOD just simply needs to be about doing good.
>
> There should be no further agenda other than helping others.

Though RLSH-08 is a case of a one-man smörgåsbord of religion, spirituality and skepticism, his views on RLSH activity are clearly secular as he stresses that "Doing GOOD just simply needs to be about doing good". He thus does not attribute an explicitly religious or spiritual element to what he called "the 'ritual' of the costume":

As you put on the "Gear" you shed all of your own problems. You become not you. You are now (in my case) ['RLSH-08']. A Hero who is better than you.

It is a transformation. I have my own problems and troubles in real life. Once I become ['RLSH-08'], I have none of those. They are forgotten and not any part of my mission to help others.

. . .

The Hero is my full potential. I'm not saying that I'm a total jerk, but I have my failings as a human being as most of us do. I can be impolite and regret it later, I might not do the dishes when I should, I might be lazy or not clean the cat-box as often as I should. When I'm ['RLSH-08'], I greet people with a friendly voice and smile and never pass by someone in need as many of us do every day.

I look for people in need, as opposed to walking or driving by.

It actually does filter back into my normal life, but not enough.

For RLSH-08, a human potential ethic (Possamai 2007) is clearly the ultimate overriding factor of becoming and being a Real-Life Superhero, as it was not only what led him to the RLSH transformation in the first place (via vision quest) but informs and impacts his continued RLSH activity. Though his approach is different, he, like RLSH-38, undergoes a ritual to 'access' his higher potential, meaning that this higher potential is latent and not necessarily homeostatic. We must note that neither the transformation nor RLSH-08's sense of this higher potential involve any supernatural or superhuman element, rather taking on a secular form in that he is able to achieve his ideal personality traits as his superhero persona. Nevertheless, he explicitly attributes this to a transformation towards a commitment to his RLSH activity.

RLSH-20

Our final case is US-based RLSH-20, one of the few female members of the RLSH community. On the day of the interview, RLSH-20 had just been initiated into a local RLSH faction that adopt a mixed approach to their activities, in that they are involved in both safety patrols and social outreach initiatives. When asked about the inspiration behind her RLSH persona, she responded with not only its function, but its feeling:

It's definitely a creation of mine, and I take pride in it as an artist of various forms. By strict terms, it provides me anonymity, and therefore some measure of security. As far as what it means to me, it does get personal, but I don't mind sharing. The better part of my life I've struggled with social anxiety, everything caused fear, and I was in a constant state of distress. At a young age, I turned to Marvel comics and cartoons etc. as an escape. I remember admiring the strong female characters; Storm [of X-Men] particularly. I would fantasize that I was a superhero when I was a kid to escape the fact that I had no friends, no outlet for my feelings of rejection. Enter adult me; I'm still awkward, I have few actual friends, and I've discovered that [a local RLSH] has a syndicate close-by. I muddled with the thought of joining for months; I wanted it, but it was new, and new things are scary. I cannot tell you how happy I am to have joined, though. We are making the world a little better. And as long as we do that, we've fulfilled our duties as human beings.

For RLSH-20, becoming a superhero is at once the manifestation of a childhood desire and a civic duty. Her experience represents the individual and social facets of RLSH transformation and activity; this informed the questions that would follow.

Asked about why she admired the character of Storm and how the aspiration to 'become' her (via RLSH) had helped with RLSH-20's social anxiety:

Storm epitomizes what I yearned for at that age. If you look at her character from the nineties X-Men, Storm rarely has personal problems, aside from the obvious duties of her position in Xavier's school. She was perfect to me, and I wanted to be her because she had it together, and I didn't. I still don't sometimes, it's a daily struggle, but such is life.

RLSH-20 has a clear superhero admiration which she applies into everyday life. This admiration is not idealised or one-dimensional, as she acknowledges that the character of Storm is not flawless. In contrast to RLSH-38's relatability to Spider-Man, we see in RLSH-20 not relatability to her admired Storm, but a clear aspiration to embody the character's positive personality traits, specifically resilience; it is crucial to note here that what stood out to RLSH-20 were the human facets of a superhero which she strives to adopt, rather than the superhuman facets.

Finally, RLSH-20 was asked if and how these admired traits had actualised for her through becoming a RLSH, and the pragmatism of RLSH activity:

The difference is honestly night and day. When I wear a mask, nobody can know who I am, therefore they cannot judge my person . . . I can truly be myself when I wear that mask. And this is actually something I realized at today's recruitment, because I had no social anxiety. I didn't need to take my anxiety medication. And I would like to emphasize that this is a huge step for me. Social events used to be the single most terrifying thing I could endure. I was walking up to people based on whether I thought they would be interested, something I've never done before, and certainly not so freely and cheerily. [Participant's name] approaches people with her head down, hoping they will accept her (yet, finding wonderful people all the time); ['RLSH-20'] is not afraid.

RLSH-20's experience as an RLSH bears both similarities and differences to the cases of RLSH-08 and RLSH-38 in both her origins and her transformation; first, she does not attribute her 'origin story' to any instances of victimisation (as part of RLSH-38's case), or to her socioeconomic status (as part of RLSH-08's case); and, second, RLSH-20's transformation is not constituted by any clear religious or spiritual element and is rather a conscious means of addressing her social anxiety rather than responding to a higher calling. Though more subtle, RLSH-20 nevertheless also strives to achieve a greater potential via RLSH activity, even if that greater potential is the version of herself which is socially confident.

Of course, there are similarities between these three cases. First, each has expressed an admiration for comic book superheroes; though their fandom varies, there is a clear superhero influence on their origins and consequent transformations, and we see that the social realities that they have constructed for themselves have been done so via schemas of heroism in one form or another, whether it is through The Hero's Journey (RLSH-38), a grounded belief in everyday heroes (RLSH-08), or an aspiration to the character traits of fictional heroes (RLSH-20). Second, the strive for a greater human potential undercuts each of our cases, though once again to varying degrees. This human potential ethic can transpire and manifest itself through: dreams, visions or otherwise spiritual experiences (RLSH-08 and RLSH-38); intermittent 'ego deaths' (RLSH-38); 'rituals of the costume' (RLSH-08); or purely from the observation of a fictional character's personality traits (RLSH-20). Ultimately, whilst RLSHs have widespread origin stories and vast degrees of transformative experiences – let alone interpretations of these experiences – the participants are clearly bound by an implicit nexus of social missions of community welfare and personal missions of self-improvement (i.e. achieving greater potential).

Conclusion

As previously stated, transformative experiences are certainly not universal among RLSHs, however they took on numerous manifestations for the RLSHs that had experienced them, at the core of which was to strive for and achieve a greater human potential, whether for their everyday life or to 'become' RLSHs for their activities. For RLSH-08 and RLSH-20, transformation was geared towards a more sociable personality and shedding stresses of everyday life. For RLSH-38, transformation was both towards better RLSH activity and as part of a personal journey to uncover the meaning behind his profound NDE-induced vision.

288   *Adam Possamai and Vladislav Iouchkov*

Given the widespread, informal and implicit nature of the transformational experiences of RLSHs, there currently appears to be no consensus on the self-interpretation on the RLSH experience, both in regards to the transformation and the activity itself; this may indeed be due to the fact that RLSHs may come from myriad religious/spiritual persuasions (or lack thereof, based on other participants of our sample), and the absence of an official text by which RLSHs can abide. Nevertheless, we see that for a solid portion of the community, becoming and being an RLSH can at once be both a means of spiritual seeking and/or spiritual conversion, and a result of it.

We thus do not propose that RLSH is officially a religion or spirituality in itself, according to the 'traditional' traits of religions and certain spiritualities. Instead, we highlight its implications for its participants' spiritual identities via their transformative experiences and praxes. We also highlight that the RLSH phenomenon provides the same kinds of commitments and serves some functional religious equivalents such as social goodwill and individual enlightenment/fulfilment. Just as RLSHs provide a novel approach towards informal social control and bystander intervention (Iouchkov and Birch 2015), so too do they provide a novel approach to the lived experience of religion and spirituality (whether secular or explicitly religious/spiritual) in late modern society, and speak volumes of the role and impact of popular culture on this lived experience. In light of these findings, it is thus difficult to call this group a specific hyper-real religion, although it shares some strong familiarities. The RLSH is clearly part of the Pygmalion process, but taking into account that close to a third of the participants do not see anything religious in this process, there is a need for refinement in our discussion. The work of Bailey (2009, 2010) on implicit religion comes easily to the rescue to shed some light on this phenomenon. Stemming out from the field of research on civil religion which highlights that secular ideologies can have similar religious functional attributes, implicit religion is a type of secular faith which refers mainly to people's commitments, be it religious or secular, and allows us to extend our analysis to parts of this phenomenon which are not *senso strictu* religious. The notion of implicit religion allows us to look at religiously similar effects in everyday life, rather than in the political sphere as it is the case with civil religion.

Whilst only one person made a specific connection to religion in this fieldwork, the majority of the RLSHs had still nevertheless a religious and/or spiritual background and attached some implicit spiritual/religious meaning to their transformation or realisation. For the majority of these participants, this would clearly be an example of the hyper-real religious phenomenon. However, whilst some of these respondents were clearly demarcating themselves to a religious or spiritual discourse and were talking about improvement rather than transformation, the process was nevertheless akin to following a secular type of human potential ethic. In light of these findings, this group, as a whole, could thus be called an implicit hyper-real religious group.

Notes

1 Source: www.therlsh.7forum.biz/. Accessed 15 June 2015.
2 We do acknowledge, however, that the cultural consumption of anime and cosplay has implications for one's spiritual identity, as noted by Park (2005).
3 Source: superheroesanonymous.com/the-12-steps-to-superheroism/. Accessed 16 June 2015. It must also be noted that the authors of the post acknowledge that not all RLSH follow these steps in their given order, but nevertheless do incorporate them into their becoming and being an RLSH.
4 Due to unclear responses and time restrictions, the opportunity to inquire about transformations was hindered, hence $n = 42$.
5 The final two classifications bore close similarities, but were divided based on interviewees' premeditated goals, or lack thereof: for NT-R, becoming RLSH was part of a prior active desire to achieve more from themselves; for NT-PI, the improvements were residual effects of RLSH activity yet not driven by any strong desires to realise their full potential.
6 Acknowledging it later in the interview, here the participant made reference to Umberto Eco's seminal 1972 essay 'The Myth of Superman', in which Eco criticises the character for directing his super strength mostly towards street crimes rather than applying them to combatting greater social injustices.
7 This is a direct quotation from Joseph Campbell's *The Hero with a Thousand Faces* 2008 [1949]).
8 Jewett and Lawrence (1977) introduced 'The American Monomyth', a variation of Campbell's monomyth applied into contemporary Western society and directly using the superhero as an example of the Hero. Whilst 'The American Monomyth' stresses more the actions of the Hero rather than their transformation or quest of self-discovery, it is nevertheless important to note that attention has been given to the social – albeit hypothetical – pragmatism of superhero activity.
9 That said, the character of Jonah Hex, while without superpowers, is of peak physical abilities and conditioning, and is notably bound by a strong moral code; Green Hornet is also without superpowers. The Spectre, however, is a murdered detective whose spirit is rejected from the afterlife by 'The Voice', a god-like entity that instead sends the spirit back to Earth with superpowers to combat evil.

References

AFP. 2014. 'Game of Thrones Inspires Baby Names as Fantasy Reigns Supreme'. *The Sun Herald*, 17 August, p. 22.
Bailey, Edward. 2009. 'Implicit Religion'. In P. Clarke (ed.), *The Oxford Handbook of The Sociology of Religion*, 801–818. Oxford, UK: Oxford University Press.
Bailey, Edward. 2010. 'Implicit Religion'. *Religion* 40: 271–278.
Bryman, Alan. 2012. *Social Research Methods* (4th edition). New York: Oxford University Press.
Campbell, Joseph. 2008 [1949]. *The Hero with a Thousand Faces* (The Collected Works of Joseph Campbell), 3rd edition. Novato, CA: New World Library.
Flock, Elizabeth. 2011. October 19. Real-life superhero movement growing, but not getting warm reception from police. *The Washington Post*. At: www.washingtonpost.com.
Iouchkov, Vladislav. 2012. *Kickin' Ass and Taking Identities: Understanding the Phenomenon of the Real-Life Superhero Movement*. Honours thesis, University of Western Sydney.

Iouchkov, Vladislav and Philip Birch. 2015. '"Masked Crusader": A Case Study of "Crime-Fighting" Activities By a "Real-Life Superhero"'. *Journal of Criminological Research, Policy and Practice* 1(2): 65–75.

Jameson, Fredrick. 1991. *Postmodernism or the Cultural Logic of Late Capitalism.* Durham, NC: Duke University Press.

Jewett, Robert and John Shelton Lawrence. 1977. *The American Monomyth.* New York: Doubleday.

Lawson, Gerard. 2005. 'The Hero's Journey as a Developmental Metaphor in Counseling'. *Journal of Humanistic Counseling, Education and Development* 442: 134–144.

Mak, Heusen. 2010. *The Amazing Everyday Man: a Study on Real-Life Superheroes.* Unpublished Honours thesis, University of New South Wales.

Park, Jin Kyu. 2005. '"Creating My Own Cultural and Spiritual Bubble": Case of Cultural Consumption by Spiritual Seeker Anime Fans'. *Culture and Religion: An Interdisciplinary Journal* 6(3): 393–413.

Possamai, Adam. 2005. *Religion and Popular Culture: A Hyper-real Testament.* Brussels: Peter Lang.

Possamai, Adam (ed.). 2012. *Handbook of Hyper-real Religion.* Leiden, The Netherlands and Boston, MA: Brill.

Index

abduction scenarios 255–6
Abide Guide, The (Benjamin and Eutsey) 154
Abraham, Alton 245–6, 249, 253
Academy of Arcana 268
acceptance 88
Adams, Fred (Frederick McLaren) 263
Adamski, George 255
Adler, Margot 17, 194
Advent Children 69
African-American ufology 9–10, 254–7, 258
Afrofuturism 254–5
Aguilar, Gonzalo 170
Alder, Margot 182
Alderton, Zoe 45, 52
Ali, Noble Drew 9, 246, 251
Allen, Marshall 250
American Digital Millennium Copyright Act (1998) 220
American Graffiti 272–3
Ames, Roger 154
Amidi, Amid 81
Anima Mundi 25
anime: conclusions regarding 115–16; cosplay ritual 104–8; Haruhiism 111–15; overview of 5–6
anime conventions 50
anime pilgrimage 5, 102, 108–11
animistic thought 102–3
Anonymous 220, 222, 274
Ansaar Pure Sufi 253
Archetti, Eduardo P. 161, 162, 166
Arden: The World of Shakespeare 232
Arkestra 245, 246–50
Arnold, Kenneth 255
astral-plane travel 93
Astro Black Mythology 250–1, 253, 257

Atlan Foundation, The 262
Atlan Torch, The 262
Atlas Shrugged (Rand) 261
Authentic Fakes (Chidester) 195
authenticity 11
awakening experience 46–8, 49
Axial Age 149, 152

Bacon-Smith, Camille 68–9
Bagnall, Jessica 66, 67
Bailey, Edward 288
Bainbridge, Barbara Constance ("Connie"): background of 227–9; *Neverwinter Nights* and 229–32; sailing and 235
Bainbridge, William Carey 234
Bainbridge, William Sims 3, 9
Ball, Ashleigh 91
Barkun, Michael 204, 205
Baron, Farid 249
Baudelaire, Charles 172
Baudrillard, Jean 2
Bauscher, Lance 190, 191
Bavarian Illuminati conspiracy 186*fig*
Baym, Nancy K. 138
Belanger, Michelle 48
Benares, Camden (né John Overton) 188, 206
Benitez, Tati 170
Benjamin, Oliver 6–7
Berger, Peter 2
Bey, Hakim (né Peter Lamborn Wilson) 189
Big Lebowski, The 6, 148–9, 154; *see also* Dudeism
Bilal, Enki 273
'binocular mode' 17
Bisclavet 41–2
Black Cat, White Cat 172

292   Index

Blessed Circle Dance 24
Blessed Realm, journey to via the Moon 24–5
Blount, Herman Poole *see* Ra, Sun
Blutopia (Lock) 250
bOING bOING 189, 190
Bombón, el perro 170
Book, The (Watts) 129
Book of Margery Kempe, The 60, 61
Bronies for Good (BfG) 85
Brony Chronicles 81
Brony Community: anime and 50; conclusions regarding 94; description of 45; devotees of 91–4; fan statistics and activities for 83–5; motivations for 85–9; origins of 81–3; overview of 5, 79–80; troubles of 89–91
Brony flats 84
Brony Original Characters (OCs) 92–3
Brony Study (Research Project) 84, 89
Bruzzi, Stella 168
Bryman, Alan 276
Buddhism 93, 135, 149, 150, 152, 153, 155, 188, 206, 266
Buljan, Katharine 5–6
Burkart, Patrick 220
Burns, Jimmy 158, 160
Busse, Kristina 67–8
Bynum, Caroline Walker 61

Calantirniel 16, 19, 20, 27, 31
Camino de San Diego, El (*The Road to Saint Diego*) 7, 159, 169–71
Campbell, Colin 50
Campbell, Joseph 6, 120–1, 129, 135, 281–2
Carmilla (Le Fanu) 43
Carroll, Peter 191
Castro, Fidel 174
Castronova, Edward 6, 135, 232
Cat's Cradle (Vonnegut) 262
cave paintings 42
Celestia, Princess 83
Cerrini, Daniel 163
Chasing Eris project 8, 181, 193, 194–5; *see also* Eris
Cherny, Lynn 65
chess boxing 273
Chidester, David 195
Children of the Valar 29
Chinatown 272–3
Christianity: Brony Community and 93–4; challenge/opposition to 200, 203, 243, 250, 251; conception of Heaven in 74; decline of literature

of 43; Dudeism and 149, 150, 152, 153–4, 155; Fard Muhammad and 251; Haruhiism and 112; Jediism and 135; Maradona and 163–4, 173; in Middle Ages 5, 63; theophany and 59; Tolkien spirituality and 19, 20, 26–7, 32; *see also* Julian of Norwich; Kempe, Margery
Christie, Richard Lance 10, 199, 261–2, 269
Church of All Worlds (CAW): artistic and cultural contribution of 266–8; beliefs of 265–6; Christianity and 203; evolution of 264–5; founding of 199–200, 262–3; introduction to 261–2; key figures in 268–70; overview of 10; ritual and theology of 263–4; satire and 201
Church of Maradona 163, 173, 174
Church of Scientology 201
Church of the Flying Spaghetti Monster 200, 201
Church of the SubGenius (CoSG): conclusions regarding 208–10; 'The Conspiracy' and 203–8; conventions and 50; description of 201–3; Discordianism and 188; introduction to 198–9; overview of 8; societal critique of 222
Classen, Albrecht 41
Cloppers 91
Clutterbuck, Brenton ('Placid Dingo') 8, 193–5
Colbert, Stephen 82
Cold War period 203
Coleridge, Samuel Taylor 106
Collective Unconscious 34
comic book fandoms 66–7
Coney, John 256
'conspiracism' 204
'Conspiracy, The' 8, 198–9, 201, 202, 203–8, 210
'conspiracy beliefs' 204
Conspiracy Theories in American History (Davidoff) 205
conspiracy theory/conspiracy theory narratives 198, 203–7, 208–9
consumer capitalism 199
conventions, role of 49–50; *see also* cosplay ritual
Coppa, Francesca 67
Coppola, Guillermo 164
copyright law 8, 213, 214–15, 219, 220, 221
Corbin, Henry 25–6, 34

Index   293

corpses 42–3
cosplay ritual 5, 50, 102, 104–8, 274, 275–6
Crowley, Aleister 187
Cthulhu mythos 206
cultural commodities 165
Cultural Creatives 10
Cusack, Carole M. 2, 4, 50, 52, 103, 111–12, 199, 207, 209
cyberculture 189
cyberpunk 189

Dammers, Jerry 250
'Dancing Sorcerer' 42
Dao De Jing (Hall and Ames) 154
Dark Lords of the Sith 136
Davanzati, Giuseppe 42
David-Néel, Alexandra 59
Davidoff, Solomon 205
Davidsen, Markus Altena 2, 4, 34, 51–2, 208
De Botton, Alain 154
Debord, Guy 207
deceased family members, revival of 226–7, 229–37
Deep Ecology movement 264
Denial of Service attacks 220
Dennett, Peter 249
Dery, Mark 255
desacralised context and religion 101, 102, 111, 113–14, 116
Devivals 202–3
digital piracy *see* piracy
digital rights activism 213, 220–2
Discordian Archive 181, 192
Discordian Illuminati thesis 185–6
Discordianism: Chasing Eris project and 194–5; Christianity and 203; Church of the SubGenius (CoSG) and 206; conclusions regarding 195–6; conspiracy theory narratives in 204; copyright and 222; *Historia Discordia* and 192–3; history of 183–90; introduction to 181–2; Maybe Logic Academy and 190–1; overview of 7–8; parodic nature of 200–1
Dobbs, J. R. 'Bob' 201–2
doctrinal dimension 123
Dracula (Stoker) 43
DragonCon 50
Drawing Down the Moon (Adler) 194
Drescher, Denis 85
Drew, Timothy 251
Drummond, Philo 201, 203
Dudeism 6–7, 82, 148–56

Dungeons and Dragons 9, 46–7, 228, 232
DuQuette, Lon 191
Durkheim, Émile 115

ecospirituality 10
Educational, Psychological, and Behavioral Considerations in Niche Online Communities (Shane) 54
Effective Altruism movement 85
ego death 280, 282
Egypt 245–6, 250, 254
Eldalondë Society 29
Elf Queen's Daughters 4, 17–18, 44, 46
Eliade, Mircea 101–2, 104, 105–7, 109–11, 113–15, 116
Ellenar 19
Elwin, Nathan 15, 19, 20, 27, 31
Enderi ritual 16, 23
Engström, Christian 214–16
Eris 183, 195; *see also* Chasing Eris project
Erisian Liberation Front 184
Eru 17, 20, 26–9, 32
Eruannlass 15
ethical dimension 124
ethics clearances, online ethnography and 41
Evil Dead, The 233
evolutionary psychology 153
experiential dimension 125–6
extra-terrestrials 255–7
Eyovah 46–8
Ezekiel 252

Factsheet Five 188–9
'Faerie' 34
familiars 93
fanfiction 67, 68
Farley, Helen 6
Farmer, F. Randall 137
Farrakhan, Louis 252, 257
Faust, Lauren 82–3, 85, 87
Fellowship of the Ring, The (Tolkien) 28–9
female gamers 65–6
Feraferia 263
fiction, definition of 208
fiction-based religions: origin of term 2; versus parodic 199–201; *see also individual religions*
Field Guide to the Otherkin, A (Lupa) 40, 48–9
file sharing 217, 220, 221

294   *Index*

film/television 40, 43; *see also individual films and shows*
Final Fantasy 5, 45, 53, 59, 69
Finley, Stephen C. 257
Fiske, John 64
Fitzgerald, Jonathan D. 86
Flock 275
forgeries 4
foundational texts, characteristics of 27–9
frame narratives 28–9
Francis of Assisi, St 124, 127
Free, Marcus 7
freedom of information movement 221
freestyle football 166–7
Freud, Sigmund 102–3, 163, 173
Friedman, Erica 107
Froid Equateur (Bilal) 273
Frow, John 113
Full Monty, The 167
functionalist methodological approach 80
Furries 44–5
Fusées (Baudelaire) 172

Gaea Thesis 264, 267
Game of Thrones series 274
GamerGate scandal 65–6
Gardner, Gerald 199
Garrison, Jim 204
geek culture 64–9
Gerson, Isak 8, 213, 214, 217, 219, 221
Gil Núñez, Antonio Mamerto ("Gaucho Gil") 163, 170
Gilmore, John 253
Golden APA, The 187, 188
Good, the Bad and the Ugly, The 172
Goode, Luke 222
Gorightly, Adam 7, 192
Grass, Randall 249
Gray Jedi 141
'Great Time' 107
Green Egg 10, 46, 200, 263, 264, 267
Greer, J. Christian 7
Grey School of Wizardry 267–8
guerilla ontology 184, 206
Gunderloy, Mike 188
Guy Fawkes masks 215, 274

hacking 189
Hall, David 154
Harper, Ethel 244–5
Harrad Experiment, The (Rimmer) 262

Harry Potter series 27, 28, 45, 52, 53, 60, 273
Haruhiism 5, 101, 102, 111–15
Harvey, Graham 16, 47
Hawkins, Coleman 256
Heinlein, Robert A. 10, 199, 261–2, 266
Hellekson, Karen 67–8
Henderson, Bobby 200
Henderson, Fletcher 245, 256
Hero with a Thousand Faces, The (Campbell) 135, 281
'Hero's Journey, The' 281–2
heuristics 151–2
hierophany 110, 114
hikikomori 89
Hill, Greg 183–4, 192, 200
Hills, Matt 166
Historia Discordia 7, 192–3
Historias mínimas 170
History of Middle-earth (C. Tolkien) 18, 28
Hlavaty, Arthur 187, 188
Hoeller, Stephen 19, 25–6
Homo Ludens (Huizinga) 143
Huizinga, Johan 6, 135, 143
human-animal transformations 42
human ethics clearances 41
Human Potential Movement 10
Hume, Lynne 52
Hutton, Ronald 199
Huxley, Aldous 154
hyper-real religions: origin of term 2; *see also individual religions*

Icke, David 207, 208
Iglesia Maradoniana 7
Illuminati 185–6, 186*fig*
Illuminatus! (Wilson and Shea) 185–7, 189, 206
Illuminatus! Nut Cult 187–8
Ilsaluntë Valion (Silver Ship of the Valar) 4, 15, 18, 20, 21*t*, 23–5, 27, 30, 31, 34–6
Imaginal Realm 15, 19, 25–6, 34–5
implicit religion 288
In the Hands of the Gods 7, 159, 166–9, 175
Insider's Guide to Robert Anton Wilson, An (Wagner) 192
institutionalization: of Discordianism 190, 191; as term 181–2
internet: authoritarianism of 222; file sharing and 220; geek culture and 64–9; impact of 43, 44; Kopimism and 214, 216

intertextuality 272
invented religions: narrative religion
  and 50; origin of term 2; *see also
  individual religions*
Invented Religions (Cusack) 2
inward acculturation 20, 22
Iordanova, Dina 172
Iouchkov, Vladislav 10

Jackson, Peter 18, 29
Jameson, Frederick 272–3
Japanese folklore 42
Jarrett, Keith 249
Jaspers, Karl 152
'Jedi Census Phenomenon' 44, 132,
  135
Jedi Creed 127
Jedi Crusaders 141
Jediism: clergy of 131–2; demographics
  of 132; doctrinal dimension of 123;
  emergence of 44, 135–6; ethical
  dimension of 124; experiential
  dimension of 125–6; history of
  126–7; how to join 127; increase
  in popularity of 82; minors in 128;
  mythological dimension of 122–3;
  overview of 6, 119–20; ranks of
  128–9; religious authority and
  11; ritual dimension of 121–2;
  sacralisation of fiction and 60; satire
  and 211n1; in Second Life 134–44;
  sermons of 131–2; six dimensions of
  Smart and 120–6; social dimension
  of 124–5; training and degree
  scheme for 129–31
Jenkins, Henry 64
Jenkins, Jacqueline 61
Jesus 150, 152
Johnston, Jay 52
jokes 82
joy effect 87
Joyce, James 206
Julian of Norwich 5, 58–9, 60–3, 70,
  72, 74
Jung, Carl G. 25, 34, 255

Kappel, Matthew 136
Keeley, Brian 205
Kempe, Margery 5, 58–9, 60–3, 70, 71,
  72, 74
Kendall, Lori 65
Keyworth, David 42, 52
Kick-Ass (Millar) 275
Kirby, Danielle 5, 8, 40, 43, 45, 49, 50,
  52, 53

Kitchen, Michael 6
Klein, Melanie 168
Koch, Karl 189
Kopimism: conclusions regarding 223;
  description of 214–16; introduction
  to 213; legitimacy and 217–19;
  overview of 8; piracy and digital
  activism and 219–22
Kopimist Gospel, A (Engström) 214,
  215
Kopyacting 214–15, 216
Korethalia 263
Kosnáč, Pavol 5
Kreiss, Daniel 248
Krishnamurti, Jiddu 6, 124
Kusturica, Emir 7, 159, 171–4

Law of Fives 186*fig*
Laycock, Joseph 45–6, 50, 52
Le Fanu, Sheridan 43
Legendarium 4, 31
Legendarium Reconstructionism: brief
  history of 18–19; cosmology and
  theology of 25–7; emergence of
  19–20; persistence of 29–30; rituals
  of 20–5, 21*t*
legitimacy 11
Leigh, Morgan 138
Leone, Sergio 172
Lewis, C. S. 61
Lewis, James R. 3–4
LGBT community 91
Lieb, Charles 252
Lindë Elenlótë 22
Lloyd, David 274
Lock, Graham 243, 250, 256–7
Lomelindo 19
Lomion 19
loneliness 88–9; urban loneliness effect
  89
Lord of the Rings (Tolkien) 4, 16, 28,
  30, 44, 232
Lovecraft, H. P. 201, 206
LSD 186, 187
Luckmann, Thomas 2, 91
Lupa 40, 48, 52, 54
lycanthropy 41–2

machinima 140
Madman National Cosplay
  Championship 104
magic circle 6, 135, 143, 144
magical thinking 40
Mallwen, Llefyn 19, 27
Mann, Paul 207

296   *Index*

Manning, Chelsea 220
Maradona, Diego: career of 160; downfall of 162–5; films regarding 166–75; introduction to 158–60; masochism and 173–4; overview of 7; political statements of 160; World Cup goals by 160, 161, 162, 172
Maradona, la Mano de Dio 158, 165
Maradona by Kusturica (Kusturica) 7, 159, 163, 171–5
Marcus, Ivan 20
Markham, Annette N. 138
'Mary Sue' 68–9
masculine identity, media fandoms and 65–9
Maslow, Abraham 10, 262
masochism 173–4
massively multi-player online (MMOs) 226–7, 232–4
massively multi-player online role-playing games (MMORPGs) 9, 134, 137
Maybe Logic Academy 7–8, 181, 191, 192
Maybe Logic: The Lives and Ideas of Robert Anton Wilson 190–1
McCloud, Sean 2, 53, 58
McDougall, Joyce 164
McIntosh, Angus 233
McIntyre, Elisha 8
McKenna, Terence 189
McTeigue, James 274
meaning, religion and 101–4
media fandoms 64–9
Mediakin 5
medieval texts 41–2
Melancholy of Haruhi Suzumiya, The (MOHA) 5, 102, 111–15
Melion 41–2
Menem, Carlos 160, 174
Mermaiders 45
Middle-earth Paganism 18, 29–30
Middle Pillar exercise 22
Military Bronies 84
Millar, Mark 275
Miller, Benjamin-Alexandre 6
Miscavige, David 204
Missionary Church of Kopimism 214
Mohammed, Warith Deen 251
Mondo 2000 189
monomyth 281–2
MoonOak, Luke 10
Moore, Alan 274

Moorish Science Temple (MST) 9, 246, 251
moral regeneration 87
Moreno, Jacob L. 9, 226
Morningstar, Chip 137
Morricone, Ennio 172
Moyers, Bill 120–1, 129
Muhammad, Elijah 251, 252, 253, 257
Muhammad, Wallace Fard 9, 251, 252
multiverse cosmology 93
My Little Pony: Friendship is Magic (MLP:FIM) 5, 45, 80, 82–3, 86–8, 93–4; *see also* Brony Community
myth: Campbell and Moyers on 120–1; of eternal return 115; function of in ritual 102, 104, 105–7, 116; Jediism and 122–3
mythical precedents 105
'mytho-cosmological mode' 17
mytho-historic approach 35
mytho-historic approach/mode 17, 25, 26
mythological dimension 122–3

narrative religion 28, 29, 43, 50
Nation of Islam (NOI) 9, 243, 246, 248, 251–3, 257, 258
Nelson, Alondra 255
NeoPagan movement 10, 16, 200, 264; *see also* Paganism
Neruda, Pablo 164
Neverwinter 9, 227
Neverwinter Nights 227, 229–34
new religious movements (NRMs), field of 1–2
New Sincerity movement 85–6
Newman, Jim 256
Newport, Robert 192
Niennildi 19
Nipe, Gustav 221
'Normals' 202, 206
Not In Kansas Anymore (Wicker) 48
novel, rise of 43
Nuwaubian Nation of Moors (NNM) 9, 243, 246, 251, 253–4, 257, 258

Ohnuki-Tierney, Emiko 42
Old Testament 150
online ethnography 41
Operation Mindfuck (OM) 184–5, 189
Order Of The Dark Jedi (ODJ) 141
Orwell, George 82, 209
Oswald, Lee Harvey 204

Index 297

Otherkin: conclusions regarding 53–4; Elven movement and 18; historical sources for 41–3; online 46–50; overview of 4, 5; popular culture and 43–6; scholarly discourses and 50–2; scholarly interest in 40–1

Paden, William E. 143
Paganism 10, 16, 263–4, 266–7; *see also* NeoPagan movement
Page, Joanna 169–70
Palmer, Susan 253
panentheistic traditions 27
Pan-Pontification project 182
pantheism 265–6
parallelomania 53, 58
Paratheo-Anametamystikhood of Eris Esoteric 184
parodic religions, versus fiction-based 199–201
Pastafarianism 200
pastiche 272–3
pathological transitional object 164
Peace Prayer 124, 127
Pearly Gates of Cyberspace, The (Wertheim) 74
Peller, Lili 161
Petsche, Johanna J. M. 9–10
Phelan, John Henry 126
Picture Infinity: Marshall Allen & The Sun Ra Arkestra (Zerr) 249
Pinch, Trevor 247
'Pinks' 202, 205–6
piracy 8, 213, 214, 219–22
Piratbyrån 222
Pirate Party (Sweden) 214, 221
Pirates of the Burning Sea (POTBS) 9, 227, 235–7
Pirsig, Robert M. 214
'Placid Dingo' (b. Brenton Clutterbuck) 8, 193–5
Plate, S. 143
Plato 29
play: definition of 143; role of 161–2
Ponysonas 92–3
Poole, Elijah 251
popular culture, versus higher culture 103
popular culture-based religions: overview of 1–2; social scientific methods for study of 2–4; *see also individual religions*
Possamai, Adam 2, 10, 52, 58

Power of Myth, The (Campbell and Moyers) 129
Prankster and the Conspiracy, The (Gorightly) 192
Principia Discordia (Hill) 184, 186, 192, 193, 194, 195, 206
'project of the self' 2, 53, 54
protectiveness 89–90
Psychic Vampire Codex, The (Belanger) 48
psychodrama 9, 226–7
psychodynamic, as term 158
Pygmalion process 272–4

quidditch 273
Quinn, Zoe 65–6

Ra, Sun: Afrofuturism and 254–5; Arkestra and 246–8; Black Nationalist religio-spiritual movements and 250–1; conclusions regarding 257–8; early years of 244–5; Egypt and 245–6; introduction to 243; later years of 248–50; Nation of Islam (NOI) and 253; overview of 9–10; visionary experience of 255–7
Raging Bull 174
Rand, Ayn 199, 261
Ranft, Michael 42
'reality tunnels' 183
Real-Life Superheroes (RLSH) Movement: conclusions regarding 287–8; context for 274; description of 275–6; introduction to 272; methodology for study of 276–7; overview of 10; RLSH-08 282–5, 287; RLSH-20 285–7; RLSH-38 279–82, 287; transformations and 278–9, 278*fig*; 12 Steps to Superheroism and 277–8
Redden, M. H. 86
Religion and Popular Culture (Possamai) 2
Religion for Atheists (De Botton) 154
Religious Experience of Mankind, The (Smart) 121
religious forgery 3–4
religious sentiment 102
religious thought 102
renaming 246
Revelations of Divine Love or *Shewings* (Julian of Norwich) 60, 61

298 *Index*

revenants 42–3
revival in virtual worlds: conclusions regarding 237; introduction to 226–7; in *Neverwinter Nights* 229–34; in *Pirates of the Burning Sea* 234–7
Richards, Barry 162
Rimmer, Robert 262
Ring cycle (Wagner) 226
ritual dimension 121–2
Robert Anton Wilson Explains Everything 190
Robertson, David G. 8
Robertson, Venetia 5, 45, 46, 48, 50, 51, 93
role-playing 6, 134–44
Rollefson, J. Griffith 255
Romano, Aja 67
Romanticism 40
Rosedale, Philip 137
Royal, Cindy 65
Rushkoff, Douglas 190

sacred-profane dichotomy 101, 102, 104, 105–6, 116
sacred-profane space 101, 102, 104, 108, 109–11, 114, 116
Salazar-Sutil, Nicolás 160–1
Sandmel, Samuel 53
Sarkeesian, Anita 65–6
satire 82, 200, 208
Schofield Clark, Lynn 43
Schwarz Andersson 217, 220
scientific thought 102
Scientology 204–5
Scott, Knoell 249
Scott, Suzanne 67
Scribner, Orion 50
Second Life 6, 134–44
secularism 102–3, 113–14
security 88
seichi junrei 108
self-actualisation psychology 10, 262
Sephiroth 69–71
Sephiroth, Mrs 5, 45, 53, 59, 69–73
Sephirothslave 5, 45, 53, 59, 69–73
septagram ritual 22
sexism 65–7, 73
shamanism 40, 42, 93
Shane, Margaret 54
Shea, Robert 185, 187, 188
Silmarillion, The (Tolkien) 17–18, 28, 29, 30

Silver Elves 4, 18, 44, 48
Silver Flame (Martha C. Love) 18, 44
Silverstar, Zardoa (aka Zardoa Love, Michael J. Love) 18, 44
Singler, Beth 138
Sinker, Mark 244
Sirius, R. U. (né Ken Goffman) 189, 191
Sith 136, 141
Situationists 209
slashfic 68
Smart, Ninian 6, 119, 120–6
Smith, Paula 68
Smith of Wootton Major (Tolkien) 26
Smullyan, Raymond M. 154
Snapists (SnapeWives) 45, 52, 53, 60
Snowden, Edward 220
social constructivism 2
social dimension 124–5
social media 138
Sorín, Carlos 169–71, 175
Soulbonders 5, 44, 45, 53, 58–60, 69–73, 93
"Space is the Place" 256
Spangler, David 10
Spatial AKA Orchestra 250
sports fandom 7
Stang, Ivan 191, 201, 202, 203, 208, 209–10
Star Trek 44, 50, 67–8
Star Wars 28, 60, 135, 138, 141–3, 247–8; *see also* Jediism
Star Wars: Knights of the Old Republic 136, 138
Stark, Rodney 229
Stern, Howard 90
Stewart, Jon 82
Stoker, Bram 43
Stranger in a Strange Land (Heinlein) 10, 199, 261–2
Stuckey, Sterling 246
(sub-)creative approach 25, 35
SubGenius Pamphlet #1 201, 205
Sufism 114
Sun Ra Arkestra 9
Sunde, Peter 215
Supanova Pop Culture Expo 273–4
suspension of disbelief 106
Suzumiya, Haruhi 102, 105
Swedenborg, Emanuel 255
Szwed, John F. 245, 246–7, 256

Taira, Teemu 218–19
Taoism 149, 150, 154

Tao is Silent, The (Smullyan) 154
Tao of the Dude, The (Benjamin) 154
Tao Te Ching, The 149–50
Taoism: The Parting of the Way (Welch) 154
Taylor, Charles 86
'teen witch' phenomenon 44
Temple of the Jedi Order (TotJO) 6, 119, 121–6; *see also* Jediism
TheaGenesis writings 264
Theology of Time, The (Muhammad) 253
Theory of Religion, A (Stark and Bainbridge) 229
Therianthropy: Brony Community and 93; conclusions regarding 53–4; historical sources for 41–3; online 46–50; overview of 4; popular culture and 43–6; scholarly discourses and 50–2; scholarly interest in 40–1
therioside 51
Thompson, Danny Ray 249
Thornley, Kerry 183–5, 188, 192, 200, 204, 206, 263
Three-Fisted Tales of 'Bob' 206
Tië eldaliéva (Elven Path) 4, 15–16, 18–23, 21t, 27, 30–3
Tillich, Paul 102
Time of the Gypsies 172
Tobin, Jeffrey 160
Tolkien, Christopher 17, 18
Tolkien, J. R. R. 4, 18, 28–9, 232–3
Tolkien spirituality: brief history of 16–19; overview of 15–16; *see also* Ilsaluntë Valion (Silver Ship of the Valar); Tië eldaliéva (Elven Path)
total works of art 226
transitional object 162, 164, 165–6, 167, 170
Tribunal of the Sidhe 17, 18
Trocco, Frank 247
Trois-Frères, Les 42
Turner, Victor 107
Twilight Sparkle 83
Tyson, June 248

ufology 243, 254–7
UFOs 255–7, 258
UK Digital Economy Act (2010) 220
ultimate meaning, search for 101–2
undead corpses 42
Underground 172, 174

V for Vendetta 274
Valar 4, 15, 17–18, 20, 21t, 22–3, 24–30, 32
vampires 43, 52
Varma, Roli 65
virtual funerals 236–7
virtual worlds 137
visualisation sequence 22–3
Vonnegut, Kurt 262

Wagner, Eric 192
Wagner, Richard 226
War on Drugs 188
Watts, Alan 6, 129
Weise, Elizabeth Reba 65
Weishaupt, Adam 206
Welch, Holmes 154
Wertheim, Margaret 74
When Father was Away on Business 172
Wicca 199, 203
Wiccan Calling of the Quarters 22
Wiccan circle casting ritual 20, 21t, 22
Wicker, Christine 48
Wikileaks 220
Williams, Ash 6
Willis, Paul 165
Wilson, Robert Anton 8, 181, 184–5, 187–91, 198, 204, 206
Wind, Tundra (né Jim Wilson) 188
Winnicott, Donald 162, 166, 170
Wired magazine 65
Wired Women (Cherny and Weise) 65
Wojcik, Daniel 255
Woledge, Elizabeth 68
World Cosplay Summit 104
World of Warcraft (WoW) 226, 233–4
wu wei 149

Yap 234–5
York, Dwight 9, 243, 253–4, 257

Zell, Morning Glory (formerly Diana Moore) 49
Zell, Oberon (formerly Tim) 10, 46, 49–50, 199–200, 268
Zen 188
Zen and the Art of Motorcycle Maintenance (Pirsig) 214
Zerr, Sibylle 249
zine scene 188–9
zombie walks 274

Taylor & Francis eBooks

Helping you to choose the right eBooks for your Library

Add Routledge titles to your library's digital collection today. Taylor and Francis ebooks contains over 50,000 titles in the Humanities, Social Sciences, Behavioural Sciences, Built Environment and Law.

Choose from a range of subject packages or create your own!

Benefits for you
- Free MARC records
- COUNTER-compliant usage statistics
- Flexible purchase and pricing options
- All titles DRM-free.

REQUEST YOUR FREE INSTITUTIONAL TRIAL TODAY

Free Trials Available
We offer free trials to qualifying academic, corporate and government customers.

Benefits for your user
- Off-site, anytime access via Athens or referring URL
- Print or copy pages or chapters
- Full content search
- Bookmark, highlight and annotate text
- Access to thousands of pages of quality research at the click of a button.

eCollections – Choose from over 30 subject eCollections, including:

Archaeology	Language Learning
Architecture	Law
Asian Studies	Literature
Business & Management	Media & Communication
Classical Studies	Middle East Studies
Construction	Music
Creative & Media Arts	Philosophy
Criminology & Criminal Justice	Planning
Economics	Politics
Education	Psychology & Mental Health
Energy	Religion
Engineering	Security
English Language & Linguistics	Social Work
Environment & Sustainability	Sociology
Geography	Sport
Health Studies	Theatre & Performance
History	Tourism, Hospitality & Events

For more information, pricing enquiries or to order a free trial, please contact your local sales team:
www.tandfebooks.com/page/sales

The home of Routledge books

www.tandfebooks.com